TOURISM PUBLIC POLICY, AND THE STRATEGIC MANAGEMENT OF FAILURE

ADVANCES IN TOURISM RESEARCH

Series Editor: Professor Stephen Page
University of Stirling, U.K.
s.j.page@stir.ac.uk

Advances in Tourism Research series publishes monographs and edited volumes that comprise state-of-the-art research findings, written and edited by leading researchers working in the wider field of tourism studies. The series has been designed to provide a cutting edge focus for researchers interested in tourism, particularly the management issues now facing decision-makers, policy analysts and the public sector. The audience is much wider than just academics and each book seeks to make a significant contribution to the literature in the field of study by not only reviewing the state of knowledge relating to each topic but also questioning some of the prevailing assumptions and research paradigms which currently exist in tourism research. The series also aims to provide a platform for further studies in each area by highlighting key research agendas which will stimulate further debate and interest in the expanding area of tourism research. The series is always willing to consider new ideas for innovative and scholarly books, inquiries should be made directly to the Series Editor.

Published:

WILKS & PAGE
Managing Tourist Health and Safety in the New Millennium

BAUM & LUNDTORP
Seasonality in Tourism

ASHWORTH & TUNBRIDGE
The Tourist-Historic City: Retrospect and Prospect of Managing the Heritage City

RYAN & PAGE
Tourism Management: Towards the New Millennium

SONG & WITT
Tourism Demand Modelling and Forecasting: Modern Econometric Approaches

TEO, CHANG & HO
Interconnected Worlds: Tourism in Southeast Asia

Forthcoming titles include:

THOMAS
Small Firms in Tourism: International Perspectives

PAGE & LUMSDON
Progress in Tourism and Transport Research

Related Elsevier Journals - sample copies available on request

Annals of Tourism Research
Cornell Hotel and Restaurant Administration Quarterly
International Journal of Hospitality Management
International Journal of Intercultural Relations
Tourism Management
World Development

TOURISM PUBLIC POLICY, AND THE STRATEGIC MANAGEMENT OF FAILURE

BY

WILLIAM REVILL KERR

Alloway, U.K.

2003

Pergamon
An imprint of Elsevier Science

Amsterdam – Boston – Heidelberg – London – New York – Oxford
Paris – San Diego – San Francisco – Singapore – Sydney – Tokyo

ELSEVIER Ltd
The Boulevard, Langford Lane
Kidlington, Oxford OX5 1GB, UK

First edition 2003

Library of Congress Cataloging in Publication Data
A catalog record from the Library of Congress has been applied for.

British Library Cataloguing in Publication Data
A catalogue record from the British Library has been applied for.

ISBN: 0-08-044200-5

⊗ The paper used in this publication meets the requirements of ANSI/NISO Z39.48-1992 (Permanence of Paper).
Printed in The Netherlands.

Contents

List of Figures

List of Tables

Appendix Contents

Acknowledgements

I would like to thank my editor Professor Stephen Page of the University of Stirling for taking time out from a very busy schedule to work with me on this book, also for his encouragement and patience, and his recognition that my research into tourism in Scotland should be brought to a wider public.

Also, Professor Roy Wood, Principal and Managing Director IMI/ITIS International Hotel Management and Tourism Institutes in Switzerland without whose expertise, enthusiasm, professionalism and vision this work would not have come to fruition.

I am also indebted to Amanda Wyllie, Sheryl McCurdie, Libby Moffat, Michelle Wilson and Beverley Watson for their painstaking typing of the transcripts, and running off endless drafts, and to my former colleagues Joan Dunlop, Andrea Hutchison, and Evelyn McCann for their very valuable support over the duration of the research; and to my brother Gordon who blazed the trail.

And finally to Maria for her understanding, encouragement and forbearance.

Introduction

This book is concerned with the development of tourism, and tourism public policy, the growing value and potential of which in the 21st century it will argue, in comparison to other industries, is not held in high enough esteem by government and politicians, and for which the industry must share responsibility. That the tourism industry chooses to operate within such a convoluted institutional, group/network and elite framework that has a detrimental widespread impact on the manner in which it is valued, and which undermines its commercial potential is a fundamental weakness that besets few other industries, and which will be exposed as this book progresses.

Although the book's main focus is on the relevance of individual countries' public policy to their tourism industries, because the industry chooses to operate within a framework such as that described above it is also concerned with the application of such frameworks, approaches and theories to these policies. For example, in the opening chapters while dealing with tourism on a global basis it also focuses on the manner in which individual countries approach their tourism industry. Meanwhile, in the latter chapters the particular focus is on the strategic management of failure of tourism in Scotland, and its inability to challenge competitor destinations and realize in full its ultimate potential.

The particular salience of this book lies in the fact that it has been conducted during conceivably the most interesting (politically) and volatile (globally) period for the world's tourism industry. Increasing competition; economic; and environmental issues; combined with the continued threat of terrorism, necessitated governments assessing and redefining their approach towards tourism public policies. These approaches and those that they superseded are reflected in the initial chapters of the book.

The latter chapters focus on a small and arguably peripheral northern European country, Scotland, whose tourism public policy issues in the late 1990s were focused, concentrated, and mutated by globalization, political devolution, and the restoration of the Scottish Parliament in 1999. During the lifetime of the first Scottish parliament in almost three hundred years, Scottish tourism was confronted by significant challenges. Apart from the expectations the tourism industry had of its new parliament and its newly-elected politicians, it also had to contend with foot-and-mouth, the terrorist atrocities in the USA, the combination of which for a short but crucial period virtually decimated its North American tourism trade. Meanwhile, its trade was threatened further by unrelenting terrorism activity in Bali, Indonesia (October 2002), and Mombassa, Kenya (November 2002). This was compounded by a short recessionary period in Scotland in 2002, by continuing world unrest in terms of both the economic downturn, and furthermore war in Iraq and the Sars virus. How such crises were managed, or mismanaged, will be of particular interest, and will be pursued as this book progresses.

One contextual factor of importance in this respect is the emergent debate over the appropriate role of government in the development of the tourism industry and those organisations that participate in it. For example, following the 1969 *Development of Tourism Act* a groundswell of opinion favoured the establishment of a dedicated tourism ministry. However, an indication of the government's antipathy towards such bold step was demonstrated in 1972 when a Private member's Bill did not gain the government's support, and so was lost (U.K., House of Commons 1971/1972, col. 1454, from Elliott 1997: 65). Furthermore, the philosophy of the Thatcher era saw successive Conservative governments (1979–1997) retreat from active intervention in tourism policy, and the Blair government, which promised so much in opposition, reneging on such undertakings when it eventually came to power in 1997 (see Labour Party's Breaking New Ground: Labour's strategy for the tourism and hospitality industry 1996).

Meanwhile, across the Irish Sea, the Republic of Ireland government, buoyed by grants from the European Community, and a ready made North American market, and despite a war taking place on its border, pursued an interventionist tourism policy while investing successfully in its tourism product, infrastructure and marketing. Taking a similar interventionist stance, in India the government through the Indian Tourism Development Corporation invested heavily in tourism facilities such as ski resorts, and hotels, and in tourism services such as travel agencies, buses, car hire, and airlines. Many developing countries, too, have tended to play a supportive role in tourism development, by providing infrastructure, and a representative national tourism authority (NTA). Yet, arguably the most successful tourism destination of all has no travel agency the Regan government having abolished the United States Travel Service (USTS). Although it was later to re-emerge in a smaller form as the United States Travel and Tourism Agency (USTTA), the Clinton government, when it came to power, abolished it too. Therefore, there appears to be no definite pattern that reflects the role of government in the development of the tourism industry, a fact that this book will pursue particularly as the Republic of Ireland's interventionist and the USA's non-interventionist strategies appear both equally successful.

All of this is important because until devolution, tourism in Scotland, as with the tourism industry in many other parts of the world, generated little significant public concern or controversy regarding its longer-term potential. Following devolution, the Scottish Executive, in effect the Scottish government, initiated various strategies designed to reflect the changing nature of the consumer supplier relationship. For example, in the 21st century the basis of power was shifting away from traditional providers towards the consumer who wished to experience products and services in a highly personalised way. This meant the flexibility to combine a number of activities and experiences together with the basic needs of hospitality, food, accommodation, and transportation, and to change these plans effortlessly (Woods *et al.* 2000). Destinations that were compatible with these aspirations would be ascendant, the remainder would suffer accordingly, and these among other challenges which will be discussed as the book progresses, are among the fundamental global challenges facing the Scottish tourism industry in the 21st century.

Furthermore, other than the author's doctoral research *a study of the attitudes of tourism industry professionals towards the future of Scottish tourism* (2001) no such integrated contemporary account of Scottish tourism public policy existed. In a Scottish context, the best extant commentary up until then was represented by a volume of papers edited by MacLellan and Smith *Tourism in Scotland* (1998). However, it tended to the fragmented rather than holistic (Kerr 2001) and, having been published prior to devolution, takes no account of its impact, or that of the first Scottish parliament in 300 years on Scottish tourism. Nor does any similar account exist of the impact of devolution or, indeed, of the combination of devolved and residual reserved powers on tourism public policy. This research, and building on the aforementioned doctoral research, therefore, will stand uniquely as a study not only of tourism public policy and of countries such as Scotland's strategic management of failure of its tourism industry, but also of the impact of public policy on tourism brought on by devolution.

As will be elaborated upon in Chapter 2, because of the fact that the majority of tourism policy research is underdeveloped in terms of frameworks, approaches, and theories, to illustrate tourism policy accurately there is little option but to turn to alternative policy literature such as John's *Analysing Public Policy* (1999); Rhodes *Understanding Governance, Policy Networks, Governance Reflexivity and Accountability* (1999); Sabatier's *Theories of the Policy Process, Theoretical Lenses on Public Policy* (1999); and so on. That is not to claim that there have not been previous attempts to model the relationships between politics and public policy-making in tourism, of which Hall and Jenkins *Tourism and Public Policy* (1995); Hall's *Tourism and Politics, Policy, Power and Place* (1994); and Edgell Snr's *Tourism Policy: The Next Millennium* (1999) are some of the most recent and authoritative. A number of other more general attempts have also been made in sections of books such as Lickorish and Jenkins *An Introduction to Tourism* (1997); Elliott's *Tourism: politics and public sector management* (1997); Youell's *Tourism, an introduction* (1998); and Lockwood and Medlik's *Tourism and Hospitality in the 21st century* (2001). Although these serve as a guide towards specific ideals, such ideals cannot be realised without an understanding of what actually happens in the formulation and implementation of tourism policy, and it is upon these disciplines, combined with the failure of tourism to realise its commercial potential, that is the focus of this book.

To make sense of all of this, this book has adopted a heterogeneous approach, an approach that aligned the most appropriate characteristics of contemporary theories such a John's *Evolutionary Theory* (1999) and synchronized them with the environment in which Scottish tourism operated. This approach provided the ability to understand and explain the processes behind the dominant issues and controversies in Scottish tourism in both the lead up to and for the length of the first parliament, enabling us also to make sense of the complex environment in which the Scottish tourism industry operated at that time. It also brought an ability to the research to deal with a number of issues pertinent to Scottish tourism during an era of rapid and uncharted change. In particular, the tourism networks; the individuals involved in them in their pursuit of specific agenda (the power elite); and the interaction between the various private and public sector Scottish tourism organizations such as Scotland's prime public sector tourism organization, STB/VisitScotland; and economic development agencies Scottish Enterprise (SE) and Highlands and Islands Enterprise (HIE). Furthermore, adapting a heterogeneous approach enabled us to understand better the processes that contributed to making such a convoluted environment and also the mechanisms by which tourism public policy-making in Scotland was derived.

What might be determined as a bye-product of this book, and which because of its synergy with tourism has developed quite unconsciously as the book progressed, is an account of the evolution of Scottish economic development policy since the inception of the Highlands and Islands Development Board (HIDB) in 1965, and the Scottish Development Agency (SDA) a decade later. Both organizations have since been superseded with the establishment in 1991 of Highlands and Islands Enterprise (HIE), and Scottish Enterprise (SE): organizations which had a cataclysmic impact on the economic development of Scottish tourism. Along with the Scottish Tourist Board (STB), and its successor organization VisitScotland; HIDB, SDA, HIE, and SE have been the means by which first the Scottish Office (pre-devolution), and the Scottish Executive (post-devolution) have implemented a series of initiatives, consultations, reviews, and strategies they determine as Scottish tourism policy.

Regardless of these initiatives, consultations, reviews, and strategies sadly Scottish tourism is still failing to challenge competitor destinations or realise its ultimate potential, and although this book is not meant to be a panacea for the deficiencies of Scottish tourism it is intended that the reader will have a more informed understanding of why Scottish tourism is in its present predicament, and also that it will stimulate debate in the second parliament about the future direction of Scottish tourism, and that this will be followed by action rather than words.

Bill Kerr
Alloway
May 2003

Part I

Global Tourism

Chapter 1

Aspects of the Tourism Industry
in the 21st Century

Introduction

In the latter part of the 20th century, tourism emerged as the world's fastest growing industry, a position it looks set to sustain well into the 21st century, and beyond. Nevertheless, in order to maintain this momentum, to regulate the industry while still allowing it room to manoeuvre, and to plan for its future, it is evident that governments require to demonstrate greater recognition of this phenomenon and of the tourism industry's role in global and national economies than at present. To maintain this momentum necessitates the development of creative and dynamic strategic public policies that are integrated with other complementary policies, acknowledging the evolving problems the tourism industry will face in the 21st century as it continues to grow; combined with the environmental; cultural; and societal challenges further growth will cause.

Apart from archetypal issues such as congestion; transport infrastructure; international crises; seasonality; spatiality; and regionality, if it wishes to maintain its growth momentum and therefore reap the financial awards, government has little alternative but to address policies that encompass skills deficiencies; labour scarcity; increased labour wage demands; demographics; advances in information communications technology; price disparity; price transparency; planning and development; climate change; increased homogeneity; and so on. Furthermore, the development of such policies depends on their evolving from an inclusive process involving all stakeholders, all taking a non-partisan sustainable and long-term view. By this, I mean governments; economic development agencies; tourist boards and/or associations; local authorities; education; employment services; the business community; the workforce; and the wider community. Furthermore, such roles and relationship have to be clearly defined in common with national, regional, and local priorities.

That government should treat tourism as an equally significant industry in relative terms to other industries is, for the industry, a long-term goal. For example, there is an enduring tourism industry sensitivity manifested by frustration that those who devise and legislate on public policy that affects tourism directly or indirectly, accord less status to it than to other policies, thus either failing to integrate it successfully with contemporary policies and strategies, or denigrating it in comparison to them. This lack of status manifests in the media; the press; in academia; in education; in the general populace; and could be argued is self perpetuated by the industry as a defence mechanism against its many inadequacies. This results in tourism being undervalued, and recognised wrongly as a lesser career than other occupations and professions, and less of a subject to research to find the remedies needed to improve it. Furthermore, in terms of the importance of tourism to many country's economies, it would assist its case if it would aspire to a point whereby widespread recognition of it in terms of the significance of its impact on the economy; employment; local communities; the environment; congestion; transport; and so on, was fundamental to policy decision-making.

There should also be recognition of its potential in terms of its societal and cultural impacts, and its ability to embrace those with inadequate skills, transforming them into economically viable contributors to society e.g. as an industry there are endless opportunities for those that failed to aspire to the traditional professional disciplines. Furthermore, as will be demonstrated in later chapters, where the emphasis of this book turns to Scotland, should the Scottish Executive and the private sector so desire the future success of Scottish tourism in the next decade could be based successfully almost solely on aspects of its cultural and environmental aspirations, creating thousands of employment opportunities along the way.

Tourism's Potential

As opposed to say fifty years ago, tourism today is a potential activity of all nations, not just as it was back then the affluent ones. As will be demonstrated later, it is also an important contributor to economic well-being, and stability; to employment opportunity; under achievement; and a significant measure of a nation's quality and equality of life. However, to cultivate tourism's potential there is a need to develop in parallel tourism and other public policies designed to sustain and enhance peoples' economic and social welfare; their way of life; and their culture. This is without spoiling or defacing the landscape or environment in which they live; congesting their living space; grinding to a halt their transport systems; or skewing the patterns of demand of employment and skills' sets patterns of modern day life dictate.

Furthermore, although it would be ill-construed to make a case for according tourism public policy the status of policies on health, education, and law and order, governments and other significant institutions and individuals do need to recognise the tourism industry's potential growth, the positive and negative implications of this, and the resultant impact both on the economy and on society. For example, less well recognised is the every day contribution of tourism to the way we lead our lives or the experiences taken away by visitors and consumers of our counties, towns, cities, and villages. Such experiences contribute towards the formation of visitors' opinions of us as individuals or of our society, and these opinions, as is known to those of us who have brought back from abroad unfavourable impressions of countries we have visited, may be deep-rooted, long lasting, and on occasion misguided. For example, negative experiences may generate deep-seated prejudice that places little value on the way we lead our lives or our standing as a nation, resulting in visitors not only never wishing to return, but also influencing others' opinions of us. On the other hand, positive impressions create a predisposition towards us; according us status; an environment to which visitors are eager to return; a growing and eventual pride in ourselves and the nation of which we are a part. In essence, governments need to recognise the impact that more strategically driven, integrated, and inclusive tourism public policies could have on the fabric of nations (Edgell 2001), in a sense, and fundamentally, much of what this book is about.

The Tourism Phenomenon

In the near six decades since the end of the Second World War, after which the majority of the world's society's expectations and aspirations changed in their entirety as in no previous modern era, the tourism industry has become a major economic and social phenomenon. However, due to its inability to measure accurately or convincingly its performance, or raise significantly its status, it has not been possible with any degree of certainty to provide precise, valid, or reliable data about the extent of the impact of worldwide tourism participation, or its impact on society. This has made it problematical when endeavouring to ascertain the industry's actual economic impact, its creation of jobs, or its genuine effect e.g. social, physical, and financial.

In many cases, similar difficulties arise when attempts are made to measure the impact of domestic tourism, despite the fact that substantial investment and policy decisions are often made on such information. For example, Scotland's sudden inexplicable elevation from a $3.85/£2.5 billion industry (VisitScotland 2001) to one that according to Star U.K. (2002) is generating $7/£4.5 billion: the reasons, and methodology behind which are investigated in Chapter 7. In fact, endeavouring to calculate the impact of tourism on individual countries' economies, never mind the world's economy, is far from an exact science. Furthermore, the knock-on effect of tourism on economies makes the above all the more problematical.

Take for example, the comparators: the World Tourism Organisation (WTO), and the World Travel and Tourism Council (WTTC). One uses purely tourism statistics while the other utilises travel-related statistics, which inflates dramatically tourism's impact on the economy. On the one hand the WTTC (1998) believes that when measured by traditional means the contribution made to the world economy and employment statistics by the travel, tourism and hospitality industries is vastly underestimated. Such calculations based on direct spending ignore the unplanned or compound benefits of tourism and hospitality to the world economy. This includes the expenditure in restaurants and cafes or the contribution by tourists and travellers to retail sales, or to the arts or sport or even rural and country pursuits. If these had been taken into account, pre-Millennium travel and tourism output figures would have accounted for $3.600/£2.250 billion, or 11% of the world's gross domestic product (GDP), and more than 198 million jobs directly and indirectly; jobs that could grow to 248 million by 2010, an increase of 25% (WTTC 1999; WTTC 2002).

As described in Table 1.1, by 2002 the WTTC (2002) forecast travel and tourism income world wide could reach $4.211/£2737 billion and 10% GDP; and for 2012 $8.614/£5.599 billion and 10.6% GDP: growth of 4.5% per annum. The WTO (1998), on the other hand, according to Table 1.2, and extracting the knock-on effects, values annual tourism revenue to be approximately $462/£300 billion.

It also forecast that by 2020 tourism-related visits will triple, with 1.6 billion tourists visiting countries abroad annually. Other forecasts suggest that air traffic alone could increase by 168% by 2017. This means that in less than 15 years time, airlines could be carrying nearly three times as much traffic as at present, (Skapinker 1998), an observation

Table 1.1: WTTC Tourism Satellite Account (TSA) estimates and forecasts.

World	2002			2012		
	US$ bn	(%) of Tot	Growth*	US$ bn	(%) of Tot	Growth**
Personal Travel & Tourism	2,039.0	9.9	−0.9	3,875.2	10.6	3.8
Business travel	379.1	–	−3.5	738.1	–	4.1
Government expenditures	203.6	3.8	3.2	360.0	3.9	3.0
Capital investment	642.2	9.2	−0.4	1,264.8	9.5	4.2
Visitor exports	514.7	6.5	−4.9	1,302.6	6.6	6.5
Other exports	432.8	5.4	−0.3	1,073.2	5.4	6.3
Travel & Tourism demand	4,211.1	–	−1.3	8,613.8	–	4.5
T&T industry GDP	1,195.1	3.6	−1.6	2,271.4	3.8	3.8
T&T economy GDP	3,282.5	10.0	−1.1	6,351.9	10.6	4.0
T&T industry employment	71,709.5	2.8	−2.5	90,819.1	3.1	2.4
T&T Economy employment	198,098.0	7.8	−1.6	249,486.0	8.6	2.3

Source: WTTC 2002.

*2001 Real growth adjusted for inflation (percent).

**2002–2012 Annualized real growth adjusted for inflation (percent); Employment in thousands.

Table 1.2: WTO international tourism receipts by sub region.

	International tourism receipts (US$, billion)					Market share (%)		Growth rate (%)		Average annual growth (%)
	1990	1995	1999	2000	2001	1995	2001	00/99	01*/00	00*/95
World	**263.4**	**406.5**	**456.3**	**474.4**	**462.2**	**100**	**100**	**4.0**	**-2.6**	**3.1**
Africa	**5.3**	**8.1**	**10.6**	**10.9**	**11.7**	**2.0**	**2.5**	**2.9**	**8.1**	**6.0**
North Africa	2.3	2.7	3.5	3.7	4.2	0.7	0.9	3.6	15.6	5.9
West Africa	0.6	0.7	1.0	1.1	–	0.2		4.9		9.7
Central Africa	0.1	0.1	0.1	0.1	–	0.0		0.0		6.6
East Africa	1.1	1.9	2.6	2.6	2.7	0.5	0.6	-0.7	4.5	6.0
Southern Africa	1.2	2.6	3.2	3.4	–	0.6		4.6		5.0
Americas	**69.2**	**99.6**	**122.3**	**132.8**	**122.4**	**24.5**	**26.5**	**8.6**	**-7.8**	**5.9**
North America	54.8	77.5	92.1	101.0	91.3	19.1	19.8	9.7	-9.6	5.5
Caribbean	8.7	12.2	15.8	16.8	16.9	3.0	3.7	6.6	0.4	6.7
Central America	0.7	1.6	2.8	3.1	3.2	0.4	0.7	10.9	3.9	14.2
South America	4.9	8.4	11.6	11.8	11.0	2.1	2.4	2.2	-6.9	7.0
East Asia and the Pacific	**39.2**	**73.7**	**74.3**	**81.4**	**82.0**	**18.1**	**17.7**	**9.6**	**0.8**	**2.0**
North-East Asia	17.6	33.5	37.6	41.1	43.1	8.3	9.3	9.2	4.9	4.1
South-East Asia	14.5	27.9	23.8	26.5	25.6	6.9	5.5	11.3	-3.2	-1.1
Oceania	7.1	12.2	12.9	13.8	13.3	3.0	2.9	7.3	-3.5	2.5
Europe	**143.2**	**212.9**	**233.2**	**233.0**	**230.1**	**52.4**	**49.8**	**-0.1**	**-1.2**	**1.8**
Northern Europe	24.7	32.6	34.8	34.6	30.4	8.0	6.6	-0.8	-12.0	1.2
Western Europe	63.2	82.0	82.9	80.7	80.1	20.2	17.3	-2.6	-0.8	-0.3
Central/Eastern Europe	4.8	22.7	26.1	26.1	27.2	5.6	5.9	0.0	4.3	2.8
Southern Europe	44.6	65.8	79.3	78.2	79.3	16.2	17.2	-1.4	1.4	3.5
East Mediterranean Eu.	5.9	9.7	10.1	13.3	13.1	2.4	2.8	32.8	-2.0	6.6
Middle East	**4.4**	**8.7**	**11.5**	**11.5**	**11.2**	**2.1**	**2.4**	**0.7**	**-2.5**	**5.8**
South Asia	**2.0**	**3.5**	**4.6**	**4.9**	**4.7**	**0.9**	**1.0**	**7.5**	**-5.1**	**7.2**

Source: World Tourism Organization (WTO)© (Data as collected by WTO June 2002).
*2001 Real growth adjusted for inflation (percent).

that gives rise to concerns over environmental, safety and congestion issues. As might be imagined, such statistics are unremitting and on occasion paradoxical. However, for the sake of clarity and consistency, and without undermining the WTTC, this book will from this point on reflect the WTO methodology, therefore valuing world tourism in 2003 at approximately $500/£325 billion; approximately an eighth of the WTTC value.

International Tourism Receipts

For many countries, both developed and developing, tourism is a very important source of foreign currency earnings and employment. For example, internationally, as is demonstrated in Figure 1.1, in 2001 half of all receipts were earned by Europe ($231/£150 billion); 26% by the Americas ($120/£78 billion); 18% in East Asia and the Pacific ($83/£54 billion):

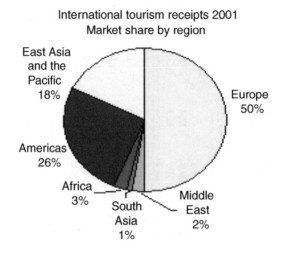

Figure 1.1: International tourism receipts/market share by region 2001. *Source:* World Tourism Organisation 2002.

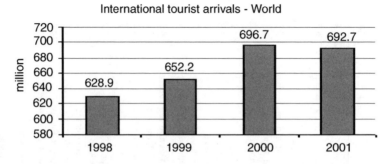

Figure 1.2: World international tourist arrivals 1998–2001. *Source:* World Tourism Organisation 2002.

2.5% in Africa ($11.6/£7.5 billion); 2.4% in the Middle East ($11.1/£7.2 billion); and 1% in South Asia ($5/£3 billion). The slight decrease in receipts in 2001 exceeded decrease in volume somewhat, both because of September 11 and the economic downturn. This was an example of consumers not only refraining from travelling but also by trading down. Furthermore, the trend towards closer-by destinations accessible by land transport after September 11 as demonstrated in Figure 1.2, appeared to depress further the number of international arrivals in 2001, and hence spending levels.

Tourism as a Commodity

As Tables 1.3 and 1.4 demonstrate, in 2002 France, Spain, the USA, Italy and China were the world's largest tourism earners. However, more than 80% of international tourists were derived from just 20 countries, unsurprisingly all from the developed world. The 20 consists of 17 in Europe, plus the U.S., Canada and Japan. Just five nations: the U.S.; Japan; Germany; France; and the U.K. account for almost half of all global tourism spending, with 70 countries receiving more than one million visitors a year (Cusick 2002). These figures are all the more remarkable when one considers that in 1950, a mere 25 million people

Table 1.3: World's top 15 tourism destinations.

Rank		International tourist arrivals (million)		Change (%) 2001*/2000	Market share 2001*
		2000	**2001***		
1	France	75.6	76.5	1.2	11.0
2	Spain	47.9	49.5	3.4	7.1
3	United States	50.9	45.5	−10.6	6.6
4	Italy	41.2	39.0	−5.3	5.6
5	China	31.2	33.2	−6.2	4.8
6	United Kingdom	25.2	23.4	−7.4	3.4
7	Russian Federation	21.2	–		
8	Mexico	20.6	19.8	−4.0	2.9
9	Canada	19.7	19.7	−0.1	2.8
10	Austria	18.0	18.2	1.1	2.6
11	Germany	19.0	17.9	−5.9	2.6
12	Hungary	15.6	15.3	−1.5	2.2
13	Poland	17.4	15.0	−13.8	2.2
14	Hong Kong(China)	13.1	13.7	5.1	2.0
15	Greece	13.1	–		

Source: World Tourism Organization (WTO) © (Data as collected by WTO June 2002).
*2001 Real growth adjusted for inflation (percent).

Table 1.4: World's top 15 tourism earners.

Rank		International tourism receipts (US$ billion)		Change (%) 2001*/2000	Market share 2001*
		2000	**2001***		
1	United States	82.0	72.3	−11.9	15.6
2	Spain	31.5	32.9	4.5	7.1
3	France	30.7	29.6	−3.7	6.4
4	Italy	27.5	25.9	−5.7	5.6
5	China	16.2	17.8	9.7	3.8
6	Germany	17.9	17.2	−3.7	3.7
7	United Kingdom	19.5	15.9	−18.8	3.4
8	Austria	10.0	12.0	19.7	2.6
9	Canada	10.7	−		
10	Greece	9.2	−		
11	Turkey	7.6	8.9	17.0	1.9
12	Mexico	8.3	8.4	1.3	1.8
13	Hong Kong (China)	7.9	8.2	4.5	1.8
14	Australia	8.0	7.6	−4.8	1.6
15	Switzerland	7.5	7.6	1.6	1.6

Source: World Tourism Organization (WTO) © (Data as collected by WTO June 2002).
*2001 Real growth adjusted for inflation (percent).

crossed international borders (Skapinker 1998), the majority of which were confined to Europe and North America, with 97% of all tourist trade focused then on just 15 countries (Cusick 2002).

For many countries, tourism is a vital activity that brings significant technological; social; cultural; environmental; and economic benefits to every facet of their inhabitants' modern-day life. In fact, McIntosh *et al.* (1995: 4) suggest that tourism has become the largest commodity in international trade for many world nations, and for a significant number of other countries it ranks second or third. For example, tourism is the major source of income for countries such as Bermuda; Greece; Italy; Spain; Switzerland; and most Caribbean countries (Theobald 1998: 5). In addition, Hawkins & Ritchie (1991: 72–73), suggest that the travel and tourism industry is the number one ranked employer in Australia; the Bahamas; Brazil; Canada; France, Germany; Hong Kong; Italy; Jamaica; Japan; Singapore; the U.K.; and the USA.

It is a growth industry of increasing power, influence, and importance, highly competitive in both a national and international sense. However, although tourism has a positive influence on local communities, it also has negative aspects such as environmental concerns; planning anomalies; litter; congestion; and gridlock; and recently exploitation through forms of sex tourism. Furthermore, uncontrolled and unplanned tourism has led to natural, cultural and social degeneration inside the so-called host nations (Cusick 2002). There is also speculation that the tourism industry does not provide real jobs. Yet, most countries have demonstrated that the tourism industry does produce worthwhile jobs along with income from taxes and foreign currency, which are vital to economic stability; social structures; and cultural heritage (Brent Ritchie & Goeldner 1994: xiii & 3).

Political Benefits of Tourism

In the aftermath of September 11 tourism generated significant public concerns and controversy regarding its national economic and political significance. In consequence its importance to world economies became all too clear. In addition, in Scotland, these issues were brought more to the fore by political devolution and the restoration of the Scottish Parliament in 1999; the impact of the Spring 2001 foot-and-mouth epidemic; and, of course the impact on tourism arrivals in 2002 by the affect of September 11 2001; and in 2003 by SARS and the war in Iraq.

Many world leaders and statesmen also began to recognise the benefits and attributes of tourism. Most recently, and notably, in countries not previously renowned for having encouraged overseas visitors. Russia, for instance, despite its ongoing but recently under-reported conflict with Chechnya, is becoming more dependent on the dollars generated by its fledgling tourist trade. China, too, after years of isolationism, has to a certain extent opened up its borders, transforming its economy by becoming one of the top five tourism earners in 2002. For example, Hong Kong, which returned to Chinese rule from the U.K. in 1996, is, in fact, still a great world tourist destination, and to China a high dollar earner, and perhaps a sign to their vast population of things to come. However, sadly the diplomatic impasse that exists between China and Taiwan has meant a lack of direct cooperation such as transport links between the two nations, a barrier to the growth of tourism in the region. Furthermore, the Chinese authorities very closely regulate and monitor tourism entrants to Tibet. This is in order to cast their occupation of the territory in a positive light to Western tourists and media (Hall & Page 2000).

There is also a dark side to tourism. For example, Cambodia's new openness, as with Thailand, attracts those who pursue sex tourism. Nevertheless, as with all else, sense normally prevails, as was witnessed in May 2002 when Aung San Suu Kyi, the Burmese pro-democracy leader was released after 18 months of house arrest, her release having an immediate impact on inbound tourism in Burma. Even Fidel Castro has once again welcomed tourists to Cuba, and significantly, countries such as those that belonged to the former Yugoslavia are using grant aid to position themselves in the tourism firmament once more.

Crises in Tourism

Since the end of the Second World War, a widely differing range of problems such as natural disasters; serious social conflicts; wars; economic crises; and terrorism has adversely affected tourism. During this time, the tourism industry has developed an extraordinary capacity to adapt and survive. Take, for example, the period following September 11 when

Figure 1.3: International arrivals % change. January to August/September to December. *Source:* World Tourism Organisation 2002.

it demonstrated its resiliency and stability as fear subsided, and business gradually returned to normal.

Recovery was most visible in intraregional travel, and in the regions of the Pacific; Europe; and Africa, while East Asia, pre-Bali, experienced a very positive growth influenced by the football World Cup. In consequence, and in comparison to the preliminary estimates of a massive downturn, the salient fact was as is revealed by Figures 1.3 and 1.4 that although there was a −9.2% reduction in international tourist arrivals between September and December 2002, the reduction in world tourism was much less than anticipated. This resulted in 693 million international tourist arrivals in 2001 compared with 697 million in 2000, a decrease of only 4 million or −0.6%. In any case 2000 tourism growth had been influenced by the activity surrounding celebrations of the new Millennium, and although 2001 was the first year since 1982 that had lacked tourism growth, despite September 11, it was understandable that this growth would not be maintained.

Furthermore 2001 also experienced deterioration in economic conditions affecting major North American, European and Asian economies, with worldwide economic growth reducing to 2.5% in 2001, down from 4.7% in 2000, with some economies even slipping into recession for part of the year. Although the terrorist attacks of 11 September severely aggravated the situation, not every destination was equally affected. While South Asia experienced a reduction of −24% in the period September-December 2001, the Americas −20% and Middle East −11%, in all three cases this followed an already weak January-August

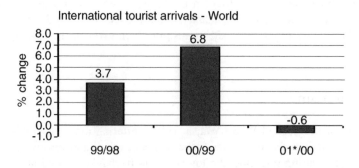

Figure 1.4: International arrivals (%) change. *Source:* World Tourism Organisation 2002.

period. On the other hand, the Americas and South Asia experienced a reduction of only −6%, the Middle East −3%, while East Asia and the Pacific increased arrivals +5% and Africa +4%. Meanwhile, Europe as a whole, and in the same year that it experienced foot-and-mouth disease, nevertheless recorded only a small decrease of −0.6% (WTO 2002). Of course for the U.K. there was an altogether different scenario, one that virtually decimated the tourism industry in many areas, particularly rural ones, much of which will be discussed as we progress.

Although there had been previous crises e.g. the 1973 energy crisis; the second oil crisis; martial law in Poland; the Falkland war; and the conflict between Israel and Lebanon in 1982; the USA attack on Libya in 1986; the 1991 Gulf War; the terrorist attacks on tourists in Luxor in 1997; the Asian financial crisis 1997–1998; the Kosovo conflict in 1999; tourism has always had the ability to resist and overcome crisis. However, an attack on the American mainland was a new form of terrorism to the USA, and one that an insular society such as the USA took time from which to recover, the outcomes of which the tourism industry which is so reliant on arrivals from the USA is still learning how to deal with. This is particularly true of those countries which saw a massive downturn such as Scotland which had no policy or crisis plan in place to deal with such eventualities; or indeed for subsequent events such as SARS or war in Iraq.

At this point it is worth stressing that not only is there no written down text of a discernable Scottish tourism policy, there is also no written down text of a U.K. tourism policy. Instead, the notion of tourism policy not only for the U.K., but also for Scotland, is derived implicitly from a series of strategy documents, such as those discussed in later chapters, which the industry, ministers and others understand to be tourism policy, and it is in this context that this book is researched and written.

The Impact of Devolution on Tourism

For the reader it is important to understand why this particular research is important to the understanding of tourism and tourism public policy. The answer is quite simply that pursuit of this research was motivated by a curiosity to understand and explain not only tourism public policy, but also the dominant issues and controversies in Scottish tourism both pre-and post-devolution, which came about in June 1999 after a referendum that took place in September 1997. For the Scottish people this meant a new parliament in Edinburgh with a devolved administration: the Scottish Executive. It became responsible for education; training and lifelong learning; planning; enterprise development (including the functions of Scottish Enterprise (SE), Highlands and Islands Enterprise (HIE)); some areas of agriculture; some aspects of transport (e.g. the road network; bus policy; ports and harbours); justice; rural affairs; housing; and health (Scottish Executive, FEDS 2000); and of course tourism and the Scottish Tourist Board (STB), now VisitScotland.

As much as devolution brought about a wide range of opportunities, it also brought with it uncertainty across a broad range of policy issues. For example, how the Scottish Executive would approach future tourism policy formulation and implementation in Scotland; the ministry tourism would be subsumed by (it was assumed that there would be no dedicated tourism ministry with a seat in cabinet); the potential difference in tourism policy relative to the rest of the U.K. (which since devolution means comparisons with other U.K. countries' policies, and which will be built upon in subsequent chapters); the likely influence of interest groups and individuals in the new political environment; the role of tourism in the wider economic development firmament; the shape of the tourism infrastructure (BTA, STB, ATBs); future tourism funding; and, importantly the overall administrative arrangements for the tourism sector in Scotland.

A Perception of Failure

Research for the author's doctorate *A Study of the Attitudes of Tourism Industry Professionals towards the Future of Scottish Tourism* (2001), revealed that in the late 1990s there were sensitivities to ambiguities in the beliefs, views, and actions of tourism professionals in Scotland. Put crudely, it was evident that at the tourism industry's grassroots there was deep dissatisfaction with Scotland's arrangements for the administration of tourism. It was equally clear that at both the grassroots and higher policy-making level, there was a plurality of views as to the importance of the tourism industry and how it might be administered to the future benefit of both the industry and the Scottish economy. It is the sources of this plurality at both levels, which generated the initial research questions for the above thesis and led to the formulation of the research embodied in this book. What was rapidly ascertained was that the history of the issues and controversies that have characterised Scottish tourism in the last decade or so is to a large degree the history of the behaviour of government and quasi-government organisations through their policy-making or non-policy-making activities (Kerr 2001).

For instance, Dye claims that public policy is whatever governments choose to do or not to do (1992: 2). Meanwhile, Hall (2000: 8) claims that this definition covers government action, inaction, decisions, and non-decisions as it implies a deliberate choice between alternatives. For a policy to be regarded as a public policy, at the very least it must have been processed even if only authorised or ratified, by public agencies (Hall & Jenkins 1995), which is why in regard to Scottish tourism the various strategies alluded to in this book are recognised widely by the industry as policies. This is an important caveat because it means that although the policy may not have been significantly developed within the framework of government (Hogwood & Gunn 1984: 23), because it has been developed by governments' associated agencies it is still recognised as such.

General Outline of the Book

To understand the policy specifics of tourism this book not only deals with tourism globally; its concept of public policy, and public policy as it evolved worldwide, but also with the development of Scottish tourism to this point in time. This is in terms of the evolution of institutions, organisations, and elites involved in Scottish tourism administration, up to and including the immediate post-devolution period, which encompasses the historic first term of the new Scottish parliament. In addition, it places the recent economic performance of the Scottish tourism industry in a wider international context. As we progress, contemporary policy issues both globally, and in a Scottish context are reviewed as are the arrangements of tourism, leading to an analysis of how recent policy initiatives have evolved and been perceived by members of the industry.

Part One

Turning to the structure of the book itself, following on from this chapter's introduction, which is intended to capture the general environment in which tourism is currently operating, its value and its relevance to individual countries, and to set the scene for the following chapters, Chapter 2 discusses tourism and public policy, analysing a set of political science approaches and theories as they might be applied to tourism, focussing upon alternative approaches and theories. On reflection, these perspectives lead to consideration of those most relevant to the book, and the adaptation of a homogeneous approach that seeks to capture those elements of theory most appropriate to examining the key issues of the research. Nevertheless, there is sufficient by way of conceptual and theoretical development in tourism policy to be of use in formulating an overarching framework for the prosecution of this particular research.

Chapter 3 addresses tourism and public policy approaches from the across the globe such as the different methodologies, and the variances between them e.g. why do some countries choose interventionist strategies while others choose non-interventionist strategies, or carve a fine line between both; how these differed from U.K. and Scottish approaches, or indeed influenced them. Meanwhile, Chapter 4 investigates tourism public policy in the U.K. from the 19th century to the 1960s; then from the 1960s when the *Development of Tourism Act* (HMSO 1969) came into being, to the present. It also reflects on tourism and devolution in Wales and Northern Ireland, plus the direction tourism in England after devolution is taking. There is also an appraisal of the relative success of the Republic of Ireland often held up as a prime example of a modern Western European tourism economy. In effect, the first part of this book reflects tourism in its wider sense, and creates a foundation to investigate tourism public policy as it has been applied in one small Northern European country.

Part Two

Part two of the book is devoted almost wholly to tourism in Scotland, both pre- and post-devolution. However, and this is worth stressing, although there is no intention to proposition a crude positivistic testing of hypotheses, investigative hypotheses, or propositions that were examined are considered important to framing the research. These are as has already been recorded, that in the late nineties there was deep industry dissatisfaction with Scotland's arrangements for the administration of tourism. There was also a plurality of views at grassroots and the higher policy-making level, both on Scottish tourism's institutions and structures, and on its importance to the economic well-being of the country.

To put this in context, Chapter 5 provides an account of the origins of Scottish tourism, the development of tourism policy and institutions with specific reference to the period 1990–2003, and the influences absorbed during that time. This is justified because apart from research for the author's doctorate (*A Study of the Attitudes of Tourism Industry Professionals towards the Future of Scottish Tourism* (2001)) not only is such an account currently unavailable in the public domain (indeed, constructing such an account is, because of a reliance on primary materials, a necessarily complex task); but it is also a necessary precondition to the exploratory component of the book. This part of the book, as with Chapters 6, 7, 8 and 9, incorporates large elements of original research defined in terms of the identification, location, and analysis of documents and related materials germane to the presentation of a contemporary historical account of Scottish tourism.

Following on, Chapter 6 explores the impact of devolution on Scottish tourism and the influence and potential conflicts of reserved powers on both tourism and devolution. This is important because it is evident that the devolved powers that Holyrood has had bestowed upon it are inadequate in terms of their impact upon the Scottish economy. Chapter 6 recognises, in fact, that the economic levers of the U.K. are geared more towards the South-East of England: the U.K.'s one real growth engine, while the remainder of the U.K. squabbles over who gets what share of the public proceeds of that growth (Young, The Herald, 22 November, 2002). This leads us to Chapter 7 which focuses on the strategic management of failure of successive governments responsible for Scottish tourism and their inability to work with the industry to realise fully its potential. In essence, it is a criticism of the obsolescent management of failure of Scottish tourism.

Chapter 8, building on Chapter 2's analysis of political science approaches and theories, investigates approaches to Scottish tourism public policy as they might be applied to Scottish tourism. It also explores interest groups as organisations relative to those of individual professionals working within the tourism industry in Scotland; and, examines their role in the tourism policy process. Furthermore, it investigates the roles of the elites; the majority of whom form the more strategic and well-connected interest groups, or are in a position of power both as operators and as chairs or directors of public sector or other bodies.

The penultimate chapter, Chapter 9, addresses the various reviews and strategies that evolved during the first term of the Scottish Parliament, a number of which are dealt with in wider economic development terms, while Chapter 10 in concluding the research speculates on the direction Scottish tourism should be taking in the second parliament and the remainder of this decade; the shape and structure of the industry; and the challenges it will have to face, and perhaps some solutions.

The Research Context of the Book

The study is, not, however, simply a loose history of the evolution of tourism policy both globally, and in Scotland, although such a narrative is critical to the work as explained earlier. The research is more concerned with the planning and development of public policy in tourism as it emerges within a political context. This subject has been largely ignored or neglected by tourism specialists, as has the political dimension of the allocation of tourism resources, the generation of tourism policy, and the politics of tourism development. Political science too has also all but ignored the role of tourism in modern society. For example, defence; housing; health; energy; environmental issues; and social policy have all been studied in depth by political scientists and policy analysts throughout the world, but tourism rarely concerns them (Hall 1994). Furthermore, according to Weiler (2002: 82–93) tourism researchers have moved themselves psychologically and physically from research consumers, e.g. industry. Her argument according to Lockwood and Medik (2002: 306) is that little tourism research is meeting industry needs; that there is too much low quality research published, and much of the output is written in a way that makes it difficult for industry to access and/or understand, resulting in distinct gaps in the body of knowledge. These charges are serious and have implications for the future of the industry since inadequate research is likely to lead to inappropriate or incorrect decisions about investment development, and operations. Furthermore, and as will be demonstrated in Chapter 3, the tourism and hospitality industries have poor reputations with respect to investing in research, compounding the problem (Butler & Jones from Lockwood & Medik 2002: 306).

This is compounded further, and perhaps to a certain extent explained by the fact that there appears to be little relevant research on the subject of tourism public policy in Scotland that can be brought to the attention of the Scottish Executive or the Westminster government. This is particularly true of the relationships between politics and public policy, which is one of the reasons that this particular book is not only necessary, but also timely. For example, almost thirty years ago Mathews wrote that the literature of tourism lacked political research (1975: 195–203). A quarter of a century later Hall (1994: 1) claimed that despite the vast amount of research currently being conducted elsewhere in the social sciences on tourism-related subjects, the politics of tourism was still the poor cousin of both tourism research, political science, and policy studies. Some authors have also pointed out the lack of overtly political analysis of tourism as compared with the related field of leisure (Hughes 1994). As Smith claims (1998: 45), this criticism is justified, and it is far from clear as yet how closely or otherwise the evolution of central or indeed local government strategies for tourism might relate to a bona fide tourism policy.

In addition, there appears to be reluctance on the part of many decision-makers both in government and in the private sector to acknowledge the political nature of tourism. There is also a lack of official political interest in conducting research into the politics of tourism. Nor, perhaps because of some of the problems described above, is tourism regarded as a serious scholarly subject (Hall 1994: 4). The methodological problems attendant on conducting political and administrative tourism studies compounds these facts further. Therefore, it is possible that the lack of research into the politics of tourism exists because tourism politics seldom generates sufficient controversy to become an issue on the political agenda and therefore attract the attention of politicians, political scientists or the media (Brent Ritchie 1984: 2–11). Similarly, unlike the politics of abortion; equal rights; the environment; energy; or education, tourism politics evokes few strong feelings among established groups or citizens (Mathews 1983: 303). The combination of the above may be as Hall claims (1994: 10) the result of the unwillingness of both governments and significant individuals within the policy-making process to be scrutinised and therefore to be held responsible for the decisions that they have made e.g. their inept handling of the recent onslaught of foot-and-mouth disease. Paradoxically, foot-and-mouth may have brought rural tourism to the forefront as a political (and economic) issue, particularly as in 2001, American tourism income to Scotland was reduced by 25%, much of this downturn blamed on the outbreak.

However, as will be discussed in subsequent chapters, although the Westminster parliament set up a Rural Taskforce to look into affects on tourism of foot-and-mouth, which covered issues such as access to the countryside and disposal of carcases and so on, there was no similar initiative in Scotland or immediate input to this taskforce from Scotland (Cotton, B. Personal Communication 2001).

Tourism Planning and Development

A responsible approach to tourism policy as described above would have facilitated community participation in the development, management, and protection of tourism during foot-and-mouth. As a consequence, appropriate, all-inclusive structures at national, provincial, and local levels need to be created to ensure future policy development and implementation deals with such crises. These should be linked to the highest decision-making structures. Hence the need for strategic planning of the tourism industry which is of the utmost importance in order to maximise tourism's impact on socio-economic development and to avoid potential pitfalls.

Poor tourism planning has also left some countries at the mercy of seasonal variations. In others the benefits of tourism have not always accrued to the host country, instead leaking out substantially to foreign consortiums and interests, therefore not generating the potential foreign exchange that is part of tourism's attractiveness. This has occurred through special concessions, franchise and package tour arrangements and other forms of transfer pricing. In essence, in some countries, tourism has not had a re-distributory effect, but has instead led to increased urban/rural polarisation as well as the concentration of wealth in the hands of owners of tourism plant at the expense of the population as a whole. Inappropriate tourism planning has also often led to the use of seasonal and contract labour at the expense of permanent employees. In the past, because of inequalities and abuse, tourism has also led to the exploitation of local cultures and community groups (Department of Environmental Affairs and Tourism, SA Tourism Green Paper 1995).

In most countries, tourism is also statistically invisible and usually only the most obvious sectors or those devoted exclusively to tourists are enumerated in official tourism data (Williams & Shaw 1988c: 1–11). Inevitably, this tends to be the accommodation sector, and perhaps cafes and restaurants. This has probably contributed to tourism not being taken seriously as a priority area for policy development. For example, government attention to tourism is focused more on promotion of inbound tourist businesses rather than on a more general approach that deals with reduction or removal of restrictions to tourism on a worldwide basis. Nor is tourism policy, implicitly or otherwise, integrated across government departments. For example, the fact that there was no apparent policy to deal with the impact of the aforementioned foot-and-mouth disease on tourism raises the question of why there is no apparent U.K. or Scottish tourism policy. Also, if there is an understanding that such a policy exists it should be explicit (written) as opposed to implicit (derived from politicians, pronouncements, and strategies). Such a policy, one would assume, would include a crisis management plan for most eventualities, e.g. how tourism would deal with the eventuality of the foot-and-mouth crisis, or the contingency of the fallout from the New York and Washington terrorist attacks; or SARS; or war in Iraq?

Government Approaches

As an activity characterised by goodwill, tourism can promote nation building and peace amongst the people of nations as well as internationally. Nevertheless, governments have not fully assessed the impact of tourism on their laws and regulations and policies concerning international relations. For example, as will be demonstrated in subsequent chapters political; economic; monetary; and financial considerations often conflict with and override tourism policy. Also, for the most part, the international organisations such as the WTO, the WTTC, and to a certain extent the national tourism organisations (NTOs), or authorities (NTAs) that address problems of tourism deal with them mainly in piecemeal fashion and not with tourism as an integral unit. Although there is some co-ordination among international organisations on tourism matters, there is also a lack of general, internationally accepted rules and principles for dealing with new problems as they arise, and of a mechanism for dispute settlement (Hall 1994: 63–64). Similarly, as has already been highlighted, they also treat statistics differently, or alter the methodology for measuring and valuing tourism (see Chapter 7).

Nevertheless, and despite the difficulties, for many countries, tourism is one industry fast superseding a disappearing manufacturing base. Yet, in countries such as Scotland, in comparison to other industries, tourism in the late nineties was less of a Government public policy priority than other sectors. This was due to the general approach of successive U.K. governments. Although they accepted there was a need for administrative and funding support for the tourism industry, they minimised and marginalised the formal development support roles. In this sense, as Smith (1998: 44) claims, the U.K. fits easily into the European context, lying somewhere close to the middle between the more dirigiste and the more laissez-faire approaches adopted by other governments.

Since *the Development of Tourism Act* came into existence in 1969 U.K. governments have chosen to pursue varying policy objectives in relation to tourism, shifting from balance of payments problems, and as will be discussed in subsequent chapters, to regional development concerns, to employment creation hopes (Goodall 1987: 109 & 123; Heeley 1989). This is a process that is being rectified (e.g. Hall 2000: 1), but it is not unreasonable to assert that studies of the relationships in tourism of the kind described above, between government, quasi-government and non-government organisations and individual professionals are in their relative infancy. For example, the political dimensions of tourism occur at a number of different levels: international; national; regional; community; business; and individual, all of which are discussed in this book, and provide for complexity in the manner in which tourism is dealt with.

Regardless of the level of analysis, the political process is dominated by the state which too is exceedingly complex in structure, and which eludes precise definition (Held 1989). The concept of the state is also broader than that of the government or bureaucracy, but for many tourism researchers the government is the state. This has meant that the analysis of state involvement in tourism has been somewhat restricted and has failed to appreciate the advantages of a broader conceptual category in the study of tourism policy and development (Hall 1994: 22). Nevertheless, it is of crucial importance in understanding the contours of public policy, because the state translates values, interests, and resources into objectives and policies (Davis *et al.* 1993: 19).

While the state is extremely difficult to define, in fact McCrone (1996: 16–33) argues that Scotland is a nation and not a state, it is broader in extent than the idea of the government or the bureaucracy. Therefore, an understanding of the relationship between tourism and the state is perhaps best achieved by identifying the main institutions that constitute the state. Taking Scotland as an example, by this, we mean central government (Scottish Executive (and previously Scottish Office)); administration departments; the courts and judiciary; enforcement agencies; and other levels of government. In relation to tourism we mean the national tourism organisation VisitScotland (renamed from the Scottish Tourist Board (STB) following the 2000 STB review); and to a certain extent economic development agencies such as Scottish Enterprise (SE) and Highlands and Islands Enterprise (HIE); their Local Enterprise Companies (LECs); and other tourism related agencies. An understanding of the development and activities of these organisations is critical to any comprehension of the circumstances of the tourism sector during the lead up to and post-devolution, as is an understanding of their predecessors: a theme that will be developed in later chapters. Of particular importance, as will be shown, is the interaction between these organisations in terms of remit, complementarity, and competition, and of the pursuit of specific agenda.

Interest Groups and Individuals

It is equally important to observe that such organisations do not exist in a state of grace, but are susceptible to external influences. Furthermore, organisations comprise people and, in the context of Scottish tourism, despite the many government, and non-government organisations that exist to promote some aspect(s) of tourism, the number of individual opinion formers is relatively small. Contact between these individuals is regular, and the intensity of such relationships, and their rivalries might be supposed to be a fruitful locus for investigation of the processes of policy formulation, provided these are properly contextualised within an organisational/institutional framework. At the same time, all organisations to a greater or lesser extent act as a focus for interest groups. Indeed, many organisations exist solely for this purpose, and this is no less true of the Scottish tourism industry than any other. In the context of governmental or quasi-governmental organisations and the policy-making process, the influence of such organisations is difficult to chart or quantify (Kerr 2001). Nevertheless, Chapter 8 investigates how interest groups, and individually those who comprise them, a number of whom are seen as an elite by the remainder of the industry, seek to contribute to the tourism policy-making process. In consequence, the major characteristic of this part of the research is that it offers an object case for understanding issues relating to influencing tourism policy, and of those who influence it primarily.

In a Scottish Context

Yet, as Brown *et al.* (1996: 93) claim, Scotland even pre-devolution always enjoyed a level of autonomy over aspects of domestic policy that has provided a specific role for the policy elite within Scottish society. However, they do recognise that there has been a growth in central state powers during the 1980s and 1990s, particularly since New Labour came to power. There has also been an attack on other sources of power held by local government and key policy-makers in Scotland, together with an increased role given to the then Scottish Office which took a top-down approach to implementing central government policies on Scottish society, much of which Scotland did not want e.g. the poll tax. Therefore, often claimed consensual decision-making processes and negotiated compromises that typified the outcome of policy formation in different areas of social and economic policy in the past have come under considerable strain.

The outcomes of all of the foregoing concern for global and Scottish tourism in the 21st century will be investigated fully in subsequent chapters. However, it is clear thus far that as change defines the nature of modern tourism policy either in its own context or in tandem with other extraneous factors, capturing the transformation that is taking place globally, and the impact this is having on Scottish tourism is one of the real challenges of the book, and one to which subsequent chapters will give considerable attention.

Summary

This chapter sets out the background to this book, its motivation, its rhythm, and its contribution to knowledge of the tourism industry in the 21st century. It outlines both the general form and focus in both a global and national context. For example, globally, it encapsulates the daunting issues facing the tourism industry in the 21st century, most of which will be investigated in subsequent chapters. Nationally, it investigates the problems associated with a small northern European country whose traditional tourism values have been eroded by globalisation; poor customer supplier relationships; inaccessibility; inferior product; quality and standards; and, years of misadministration.

It also captures the environment in which the tourism industry was operating at the time the book was written (2001–2003), demonstrating that it is a dynamic and exhilarating industry, and one that is able to quickly recover from crises and to adapt to circumstances, that at the time appeared insurmountable. In doing so, it also reveals future challenges for the industry such as the emphatic change in the consumer supplier relationship; the unstable world situation; and the dilemma for governments as to the tourism policies and approaches they adopt to meet these challenges, all of which will be discussed as we proceed.

Chapter 2

Tourism and Public Policy Approaches and Theories

Tourism Public Policy — Introduction

This chapter builds upon previous public policy research in particular John's *Analysing Public Policy* (1999); Hall's *Tourism and Politics, Policy, Power and Place* (1994); Hall and Jenkins *Tourism and Public Policy* (1995); Sabatier's *Theories of the Policy Process: Theoretical Lenses on Public Policy* (1999); Rhodes *Understanding Governance, Policy Networks* (1999); Edgell, Snr's *Tourism Policy: The Next Millennium* (1999); and a number of others which are identified in the Bibliography, and Further Reading sections.

In consequence, and as is demonstrated in Figure 2.1., this chapter sets out to consider the various tourism public policy approaches and theories applicable to tourism, and in particular Scottish tourism, which due to the dearth of tourism approaches and theories, instead analyses a set of political science approaches/theories that have been applied in the wider field of policy-making, and which are equally applicable and apposite to tourism.

It also addresses the question of whether or not there should be a tourism policy, and if so, who participates in policy-making; how it should proceed; the instruments used; and, the most applicable model of policy-making. These perspectives lead to consideration of the most relevant approaches and theories to the progress of the book, and the adaptation of an approach that seeks to capture those elements of theory most appropriate to examining the key issues in tourism public policy in the 21st century. These approaches enable subsequent chapters to consider why tourism policy so often fails to impact positively on the industry, or if because of the changing nature of politics and of politicians and their roles there is an almost perverse built-in obsolescence to many tourism policies.

Policy Analysis and Research

There are substantial conceptual problems entailed by policy analysis in tourism. In effect, empirically, the mainstream of tourism policy literature is developed insufficiently in terms of frameworks, approaches, and theories. This means, as has already been described above, that to illustrate tourism policy accurately there is little option but to turn to alternative policy literature such as John's *Analysing Public Policy* (1999). Furthermore, in instances where there is persuasive tourism policy literature, these invariably reflect a wide variety

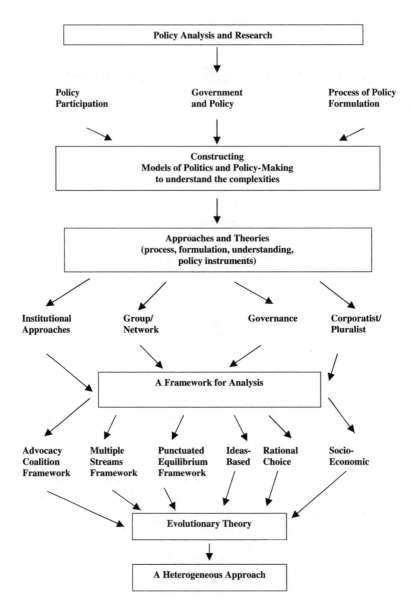

Figure 2.1: Constructing a public policy analysis for tourism: a guiding framework.

of frameworks, combined with conceptual and theoretical approaches to tourism that have yet to be examined thoroughly.

In a Scottish context, tourism researchers have worked (and continue to do so) either in relative isolation from their contemporaries or their work has been absorbed by a wider U.K. agenda. Although progress has been made this has been built on past work, particularly where there is clear evidence to suggest that there has been a failure to engage fully in mutually beneficial research, or in Scottish tourism specific research, instead researching more general topics, or topics more applicable to the U.K. However, with the advent of globalisation, and now devolution it has grown gradually more difficult for tourism researchers in Scotland to work in isolation from their contemporaries, or indeed from other disciplines, or to ignore Scotland altogether as has been the case in the past. Furthermore, the formation of research groups in Scottish tourism introduces a comparable set of partially contradictory goals. The more widespread research becomes, and the more accessible global communication becomes, particularly since the advent of the world-wide-web and e-mail, Scottish tourism researchers will have no alternative but to cooperate with their conceptual contemporaries and be rated accordingly (Hull 1988c). This, in turn, will benefit Scottish tourism as it will be project specific, concentrating on the eccentricity of Scottish tourism as opposed to the generalities of U.K. tourism.

All of this reinforces the fact that the relationship between tourism research on the one hand and that of public policy on the other is not generally regarded as optimal by the Scottish tourism industry, by Scottish academia, or by the Scottish Executive. In addition (and this does not only apply to Scotland), there is a universal perception that tourism research is not as highly valued as that of other disciplines, particularly where the benefits are not life-changing or even immediately compatible with the ever-changing needs of industry in general. Nor does this relationship contribute to theory building. Instead, there is a perception of a deficiency in tourism theory in a pioneering sense. For example, exploration of research issues in tourism tends to circumvent macro analysis on which to base tourism policy hypotheses. As will be demonstrated in subsequent chapters, this means that within many areas of tourism research, structures, institutions, and oligarchies become primary impediments to progress. This results in a dearth of incentives for problem-oriented interdisciplinary and applied research (TAB 1997), and hence manifests in a combination of the weaknesses described above, and ultimately industry and government indifference.

There are conflicting but legitimate views as to why this is the case. According to Sessa (1984: 283–286 from Hall 1994: 6), the deficiency in the understanding of the connection between tourism theory and policy formulation is undoubtedly connected with the weak state of tourism theory. Although Sessa made this connection almost twenty years ago because of the difficulty of defining tourism theories or separating them from economic development theories the situation remains. Moreover, Franklin & Crang (2001: 5–22) posit that the trouble with tourism studies, and also paradoxically one of its sources of interest, is that the growth of the research object e.g. tourism, has accelerated rapidly, while circumventing lateral definition. Furthermore, in comparison to other research communities, tourism research is relatively new and somewhat narrow, particularly in countries such as Scotland, which has a small but not unimportant tourism research community e.g. Baum, Jenkins, Lennon, Morrison, Page, Wood and so on. Indeed, at times, due to its relative infancy, and the resultant growing pains, it has been unclear which was growing more rapidly tourism or tourism research, much of it insignificant to the industry, or to our understanding of tourism policy-making. The most appropriate research to the tourism industry, therefore, in persuasive terms, must be research that is theoretically conversant with the nuances and tensions of the industry, bears simulation, has a pragmatic objective in the real world, and may be converted into an economic, environmental, social or cultural benefit (Weiler 2002: 93).

Indeed, one could go further and ask whether in a diverse and multi-sectoral activity such as tourism, is it possible to model anything other than the process of policy formulation, and if it is, who should input to policy-making? A related issue is what institutional structures are required to support the process and implementation of tourism policy, the networks, groups, and so on? Furthermore, what policy instruments require to be applied, subjects that are explored as this chapter progresses, with examples from the various continents demonstrated in Chapter 3, and from the U.K. and the Republic of Ireland, and Scotland, in Chapters 4 and 5.

Policy Participation

According to Holloway (1998: 69), a growing feature of the tourism industry is the extent of the alliance, voluntary or otherwise, that has recently taken place between businesses and/or public sector bodies. For example, the changing role of the public sector, the concepts of governance, and the increasing participation of local and/or regional authorities and enterprise companies in the design and implementation of tourism policies, is now a consistent structural and theoretical feature of the policy-making process. Furthermore, the development of partnerships with the private sector, aligned to the increasing integration of environmental, cultural, and societal concerns in the formulation of tourism policy, and the major role in determining policy direction played by the new macroeconomic indicators for tourism provides a significant and ongoing challenge that the tourism industry is having difficulty in overcoming.

The private sector, too, is aspiring to play a much more active role in defining policy and driving policy initiatives, and a continual challenge for government is how to increase its contribution equitably to policy-oriented activities aligned to these public private partnerships. For example, balancing the needs of sectoral, destination, or tourism associations that share similar interests or complement one another's interests in some way. These community, trade, or professional organisations, in many instances rely on the public sector to kick-start them or for longer-term resources, ensuring their sustainability. Nevertheless, as is all too common, the challenge for the public sector is not only to define an exit strategy, but also to enact it at the appropriate time, without propping up an edifice that has all too clearly become unsustainable, or attracting undue criticism for exiting, a situation with which Scottish tourism is all too familiar.

Governments and Policy

All of this is complicated further by a crucial and ironic principle. Though governments only occasionally enact legislation primarily aimed at tourism development, governments will also set through its more general policy decisions the general economic and regulatory parameters within which the tourism industry operates (Hall 1994: 6), invariably subordinating tourism policy activities in favour of other disciplines. All of this will, of course, be determined by the approach, the degree to which tourism is integrated with other policies, and the political scope of government intervention or influence. This might be in the form of the provision of infrastructure; planning; environmental grant aid; zoning regulation; skills and training support or initiatives; and so on. In the U.K.'s case, as we will discuss in subsequent chapters, Europe pre-determines much of the criteria. It will also be determined by the perceived sustainability; the current trends influencing the industry; the future skills sets required; the existing skills gaps; the prevailing legislation; party political dogma; fluctuating consumption patterns; the changing perceptions of customers; the effects on the environment; the proximity of an election; and on the equality of tourism of both globalization and of the new economy; and in Europe, the forthcoming enlargement. It will be affected further by the driving forces behind it e.g. socioeconomic changes such as the pattern of leisure time; levels of disposable income; increased awareness of sustainability measures; diminution of the government's role; changing demographics; the increasing influence of the private sector; and the ongoing reliance of the private sector for resources from the public sector (TAB 2002).

Although there is growing recognition that the market economy on its own will not produce sustainable tourism, and that some government intervention is necessary (Bramwell 1998: 361), what is of interest here is that the system of government is not the sole determinant of state intervention (Holloway 1998). Those governments that use interventionist strategies such as the Republic of Ireland, are more likely to be those whose countries are either highly dependent upon tourism's economic benefit or where tourism is growing into a significant economic factor, bringing with it all the attendant benefits, and in many instances problems. Those countries whose tourism industry is in its infancy or are mature will, in all probability operate within a general public policy framework that, as in the U.K. is reviewed infrequently, or materialises following the election of a new government, the manifestation of a new department to which tourism is allocated, or the appointment of a new minister. Furthermore, and this is an important fact, as Lickorish & Jenkins (1997: 207) argue, tourism because of its social, environmental and cultural impacts, is in any case too important for government to leave to market forces, to make its own way in the world, a corporatist view that will be discussed later in this chapter.

Process of Policy Formulation

In much of the literature on policy-making, there is in fact a tension between the desire to model policy and focus upon how policy is, if at all formulated i.e. the processes by which policies are made or broken, or as occurs in some instances compromised. What is not in dispute is that public policy is the focal point of government activity, and although it does not in itself elevate political parties into office, it is the maxim by which they are in the longer-term judged and evaluated in historical terms. Furthermore, its analysis seeks to understand how the machinery of the state; political participants; individuals; and groups and networks interact to produce public actions (John 1999: 1).

Governments are a salient fact in tourism in the modern world. Although there are occasions when they appear unsupportive; unimaginative; uncooperative; discouraging; or preoccupied with other disciplines, the industry could not survive justifiably without them. Governments, after all, have the necessary and legitimate power to provide the

ISSUES — structure, funding, marketing, ICT, skills, STB (VisitScotland), ATBs, Minister for Tourism, September 11, Sars, war in Iraq.
CHANNELS OF COMMUNICATION — industry, politicians, political parties, tourism fraternity, media.
SECONDARY FORCES OF OPINION — status, class, religion of those who influence tourism policy, and where they stand in the tourism hierarchy.
PROXIMATE FORCES — the politics of those involved in tourism and of those who influence policy.
POLITICAL ATTITUDES — the change in voting patterns that might be brought about with a Scottish as opposed to a Westminster election. Alternatively, if two opposing parties are in power in both parliaments.
BEHAVIOUR — the heart ruling the head. The Kailyard. I kent your father attitudes.

Figure 2.2: Structures and features of the political system. *Source:* www.sfu.edu/amerpol/lectures5.htm

political stability, social infrastructure, security, and the legal and financial framework to smooth the progress and development of tourism. For example, in negotiating and making agreements with other governments on issues such as immigration procedures, flying over, or landing on, or sailing into or from universally recognised airports and ports (Elliott 1997: 2). Nevertheless, how governments use such powers, how they devise and implement policy, and assess its impact, will depend upon many factors including their political culture; socio-economic issues; environmental outlook; the political and economic power holders/brokers; and, of course, their perception of the tourism industry on their economy or society. Furthermore, such policies will be influenced by the political philosophies and ideological preferences of the government of the day, and the minister in charge, combined with the wider political environment in which they find themselves. Public policy-making is also influenced by the economic; social; environmental; and cultural characteristics of society as well as by the formal and informal structures of government, and society, and other features of the political system such as are demonstrated in Scottish terms in Figure 2.2. For example, political parties compile manifestos. These affirmations of proposed political policy, once a party comes to power, are the subject of public scrutiny that results in informing public opinion, one of the outcomes of which is support for a particular party through votes, or in some instances abstention. Figure 2.3 reveals this process, again in a Scottish context, illuminating that tourism policy and the resultant decision-making process, is extremely complex.

Politics of Tourism

Apart from social and economic contexts in which to frame policy there is also a political context whose successful interrelation is crucial to the policy outcomes. Unfortunately, this means that political interventions may produce deformation of policy when widely held expectations are unrealized. This invariably results in failure because of fragmentation

SOURCES	EXAMPLES	VARIABLES
ISSUES	Election	Elites, interest groups, grassroots movements, (decision-making, group theory)
CHANNELS OF COMMUNICATION	Media, attentive publics, peer groups	Communication theory, agenda-setting function of media news gathering practices; economic pressures on media; or role of national and local press
SECONDARY FORCES OF OPINION	Race, region, social class, educational level, gender, age, religion	Political socialisation and sociological constraints on opinion development
PROXIMATE FORCES	Party identification, issues, and candidate orientation	Theories of political and social psychology
POLITICAL ATTITUDES	Preference for a particular candidate: Conservative, Liberal Democrat, Labour, SNP	Personality, belief and social-psychological theories
BEHAVIOUR	Vote: Conservative, Liberal Democrat, Labour, SNP etc. Non-voting	Political science theories of voting behaviour and change. Party change

Figure 2.3: Public opinion. *Source:* www.sfu.edu/amerpol/lectures5.htm

from the social and economic aspects of policy, a situation with which the Scottish tourism industry is all too familiar, and which will be explored in subsequent chapters. This may be due to a spatial diffusion of organizational forms over a period of time combined with the territorial expansion of individual organizations and the tensions caused by this. In essence, such organizations are unable to sustain performance in the political, social, cultural or economic climate, resulting in failure or indeed, due to the finite nature of the tenure of governments or ministers, built in obsolescence (see page 242), a subject we will return to in Chapter 7.

According to Archer & Cooper (1998: 69) political scientists have contributed relatively little to the analysis of tourism, and most of the work in this field has been concerned with the work in particular countries. Perhaps this is because there are substantial methodological problems in conducting political and administrative studies of tourism. For example, problems have arisen because of the multiplicity of potential frameworks for analysis and the implicitly political characteristics of the results of the research process (Gallie 1955–1956: 167–198). Therefore, the lack of a clearly articulated or agreed upon methodological or philosophical approach to politics, let alone the politics of tourism, may create an intellectual and perceptual minefield for anyone attempting to write and research a book such as this. This is particularly apt in the study of politics, where the value position of the researcher will have an enormous bearing on the results of any research e.g. his or her politics, occupation, gender and so on (Hall 1999: 6). This makes it all the more important to understand that in studying the politics of tourism, the researcher, the student or the analyst, is forced to recognise the questions of political theory and political values that underlie explicitly or implicitly, public policy decisions, or why many of these are doomed to failure, or become obsolescent (Stillman 1974: 49–50 from Hall 1999: 198).

From what has already been determined above, this is not easy to define, or understand, or even to explain. For example, according to Jenkins (1978: 20), different analytical tourism frameworks contain multifarious strengths and weaknesses, and a decision has to be taken as to the approaches chosen to attack the issues of tourism policy, while understanding their many relationship and attitudinal nuances, and tensions. This leads to the appropriateness of tourism public policy to a particular discipline, and the activity surrounding it, which is many and varied, and works on a number of different levels which no model of the tourism public policy process has as yet been able to wholly encapsulate: another reason why this book's approach (see later in this chapter) is timely.

This is made all the more difficult because public policy is an intentional course of action with an explicit end goal its objective, which as it strives to integrate with complementary policies is open to a number of different interpretations, and influences. Its success, therefore, is dependent upon the prevailing environment, the economy, and the cultural and social conditions in which it operates at the time of its conception and gestation. e.g. the political, economical and environmental circumstances at the time. Nevertheless, according to Theodoulou & Cann (1995), it is generally meant to reconcile conflicting claims on scarce resources; establish incentives for co-operation and collective action that would be irrational without government influence; prohibit morally unacceptable behaviour; protect the activity of a group or an individual, promoting activities that are essential or important to government; and, above all provide direct benefits to citizens.

What we are striving for here is a fundamental understanding of public policy, and how it affects the tourism industry. For example, Edgell (1990) claims that the highest purpose of tourism policy is to integrate the economic; political; cultural; intellectual; and environmental benefits of tourism cohesively with people; destinations; and, countries in order to improve the global quality of life and provide a foundation for peace and prosperity: in essence, a statement of governments' vision, goals, and objectives. Furthermore, when aligned with an overall strategy, such as the Scottish Executive's *Making it Work Together: a Programme for Government* (1999), government policies describe what it is trying to accomplish how it wants to achieve these, and where certain disciplines fit in. It is how industry influences, interprets, and interoperates such policy, and what leads all too often to its failure or obsolescence that is of interest here.

Models of Politics and Policy-making

For many, process is central, if not the central focus of policy to the extent that they argue that a conceptual understanding of the policy process is fundamental to an analysis of public policy (Jenkins 1978: 16). Developing this theme, Hall (1994: 49) claims that descriptive models of policy-making through their emphasis on the policy-making process represent a refutation of the rational, policy/administration dichotomy that characterises prescriptive approaches to policy analysis, and devises his own model. It reveals four components of the policy-making process relevant to specific tourism policy issues. An important facet of this study of public policy is that each particular policy development area should be set within the context of a policy arena. In this arena, interest groups, institutions, significant individuals, and institutional leadership (politicians and civil servants) interact and compete in determining tourism policy choices. An example being how wide-ranging tourism industry consultation contributions were made towards the new Scottish parliament's first attempt at a tourism policy *A New Strategy for Scottish Tourism* (2000), in effect a strategy, not a policy, which is discussed in subsequent chapters, but upon which, as with its predecessors, industry contributions had little real impact.

A danger of Hall's (1994) model, and which *A New Strategy for Scottish Tourism* (2000) exemplifies is, as with many models, that it seeks to generalise. Real world conditions may be different. Hall's model claims to recognise the existence of the broader environment within which policy-making occurs. This includes institutional arrangements, and, values and power arrangements, but neglects to highlight the rules of engagement, predictability, and so on, which often reflects the fragmented and fractious nature of diverse multi-sectoral activity, such as tourism. In addition, it fails to take into account the opposite extreme that in many developed countries there is no formal tourism planning mechanism and whatever planning is done is usually incorporated into regional rather than national plans (Lickorish & Jenkins 1997: 175). Nevertheless, it does bring into being the activity surrounding policy-making decisions; the policies and ideologies; the various choices affecting decision-making; the questions as to who makes the decisions; an individual, an elite or a coterie; the processes by which decisions are made, and how they are implemented and applied to the community (Jaensch 1992).

Should there be a Tourism Policy?

Hall (1994), in common with many tourism scholars, assumes that there should be a distinct tourism policy as opposed to one that might be captured in a wider economic development or other policy, apparently sharing this view with Wanhill (1987: 54), and Edgell (1999: 1–12). In addition, there is a widespread failure to consider the fact that a tourism policy may be subordinate to wider economic development policies, or indeed entirely unnecessary. Indeed, the lack of separate, independent tourism ministries is fundamental to this question in that tourism is too wide and diverse that it is impossible and impracticable to focus all of these disciplines under one ministry. In any case the fragmentation of the tourism industry and its lack of financial or political power militate against it and against governments' recognition of the need for a distinct tourism policy (Elliott 1997: 63).

Nevertheless, Wanhill (1987: 54) claims that the answer to the question as to why governments should involve themselves with tourism should not lie solely in economic reasons i.e. also for cultural, environmental, and societal reasons. Meanwhile, Edgell (1999: 79) claims well-conceived tourism policies will benefit the consumer, government, the private sector, and the world community at large, and will be a major factor in improving every aspect of the tourism product. Furthermore, Wanhill (1987) claims that every government must have a policy for tourism both at national and local level, and to adopt a laissez-faire philosophy and stand on the sidelines is to court confrontation between hosts and guests leading to poor attitudes, bad manners, and an anti-tourism lobby. Similarly, Williams & Shaw (1998b: 230) claim that the very nature of tourism with its heavy spatial and seasonal polarisation usually requires some form of government policy intervention whether it is for distributive or ameliorative purposes. Although not policies in themselves, examples of this at both national and local level in Scotland would be the STB's *Spring into Summer* and *Autumn Gold* campaigns designed to lengthen the tourism season, or a North Ayrshire Council (NAC) employment initiative, *Wintrain*, which was designed by the local authority to support out of season jobs. The objective being that not only would staff be kept on at the end of the season when in the past they would have been let go, but also the skills developed through a corresponding training scheme would impact on the business concerned the following season and in the longer term sustain both the jobs and the business. Yet, as will be demonstrated in the Scottish context in subsequent chapters, regardless of the fact that it might be more apposite, or that the Scottish Tourism ministry has since been aligned with Culture and Sport, tourism policy in terms of its appropriateness to economic development policy can clearly be dealt with in economic development frameworks or strategies.

Equally as important, are the relationships of the various organisations and individuals in countries involved in tourism policy formulation, whether this be strategies, initiatives or indeed factual policies, particularly where this is an inclusive process. Crozier (1964: 107), for example, is of the opinion that the behaviour and attitudes of people and groups within an organisation cannot be explained without reference to the power relationships existing among them. This makes modelling such relationships a specific rather than a general task (Lickorish & Jenkins 1997), a topic because of its relevance to Scottish tourism that will be addressed more fully in subsequent chapters. Of course, in other countries, such as the developing or third world, it is highly likely that a top-down model rather than an inclusive tourism policy formulation model prevails, and therefore the need for a clear, distinct tourism policy. Regardless, in most academic accounts of tourism, tourism policy or the strategies and initiatives purporting to be tourism policy is predictably and explicitly linked to tourism planning and development.

Nevertheless, in some political cultures, politicians and members of the tourism industry may regard planning as an unacceptable and dangerous government intervention into the affairs of the industry, seeing this as socialistic and in corporatist terms going against the free movement of the market. Those who support this position can follow a disjointed incremental or ad hoc policy approach to tourism development, the United States being the best example of this (Elliot 1997: 116), a path that Mrs Thatcher almost followed in the mid-eighties. Similarly, national tourism policies and plans are usually a deliberate tool of regional development strategies and/or broader trade policies, such as in Japan, where the government has invested substantial funds into the development of resorts for the domestic market (Hall 2001: 19). Furthermore, in countries such as Israel national tourism development plans have been drawn up in which government decides which sectors of the industry will be developed, the appropriate rate of growth, and the provision of capital required for expansion (Mill & Morrison 1985). Further examples will be discussed in Chapter 3.

It is debatable as to how such a policy could be implemented in Scotland. According to Lickorish & Jenkins (1997), planning at national level is usually a function of the size of the country, so it would be virtually impossible for government to plan for tourism development in the USA. This does not mean, of course that at sub national level tourism plans do not exist or that specific considerations of tourism have not been taken into account e.g. many U.S. states have distinctive tourism policies that include the ability to raise taxes on visitors. Furthermore, in stressing the importance of planning not taking the place of policy guidelines, for as a concept policies precede planning, and introduces the political aspects of planning. This concept indicates the primacy of policy over planning, suggesting that policies will provide the framework within which planning takes place, ensuring that market forces alone do not dictate tourism development, and that policy instruments be the vehicle by which policy is achieved (Lickorish & Jenkins 1997: 180–181).

Policy Instruments

Although there is little intention to dwell upon them here (see Chapter 3 for a fuller account), there are many policy instruments available for steering micro-economic factors in the direction desired in terms of consumption, production, and investment. For example, Tinbergen (1995) claims that there must be as many instruments as there are targets of policy. These policy instruments may be classified in several ways. One approach is to group the policy instruments along a continuum in terms of the degree of influence which the state seeks to exercise over micro-economic factors (Pantin 1995), whereby the various disciplines diversify according to the criterion in which they function. Some suggestive examples of the types of policy instruments which fall into these categories are legal; financial; organisational; and personal. For example, laws that compel people and organisations to do things; allocating funds to encourage or penalise organisations and people; the applying of bureaucratic power to solve problems; or, by persuading others to achieve goals (John 1999: 6). Nevertheless, as Pant (2002) cautions, unless we match policy instruments with policy goals, the disequilibrium in the economy will be further widened as happened in Argentina recently and in East Asia in 1997, subjects we will return to in Chapter 3.

Policy-Making Approaches and Theories

The Process, Formulation, and Understanding of Policy-making

Sabatier (1999: 3) claims that the process of public policy-making includes the manner in which problems are conceptualised and brought to government for solution. For example, in an ideal world, governments traditionally formulate alternatives and select policy solutions based on consultation; and those solutions are implemented, evaluated, and revised for as long as a government is in power, its successor makes changes, or until the minister responsible for it moves on. A complication here is that apart from there being a number of policy-making approaches or theories that may apply to the above, the same policy differs according to the different branches and levels of government where it is being decided, and also the importance which the government attaches to it (John 1999: 8–11).

Clearly, some understanding of current thinking on public policy in tourism is required here. However, as has already been ascertained, other than Hall, Hall and Jenkins, Elliott or Edgell Snr, there is little literature concerning tourism public policy that is of sufficient stature. Yet an exhaustive review of the wider theory of policy-making would be inappropriate for a book of this kind. The resolution of this problem is eased because there are a number of widely acknowledged and relatively discrete theories that seek to aid understanding of policy formulation and implementation that are relevant to tourism. Furthermore, as will be demonstrated as we proceed, there is a degree of maturity among writers in the field that concurs that no single perspective is likely to yield holistically adequate analyses. For example, Sabatier (1999: 6) claims that until recently, the most influential framework for understanding the policy process, has been the *Stages Heuristic* (Anderson 1975; Brewer & deLeon 1983; Jones 1970), termed by Nakamura (1987) the textbook approach, of which there is little evidence of its being applied to tourism policymaking and implementation. Perhaps this is because the *Stages Heuristic* does not function in the manner hypothesised (John 1999: 23), and that some more complex frameworks, a number of which will be discussed in tourism terms as we proceed, have superseded it.

At this point it is worth bearing in mind that studies of the political aspects of tourism should attempt to understand not only the politically imposed limitations on the scope of decision-making, but also the political framework within which the research itself takes place i.e. the broader environment. To achieve this, and as has already been described, will require acceptance of a far wider range of theoretical standpoints and academic traditions than that which has previously been the case in tourism research (Hall 1994: 14). This, in turn, will require a more thorough and deeper understanding of the relationships, nuances, and tensions between the various research disciplines.

In public policy as elsewhere, such model building is a routine, but not mundane aspect of scholarship in the field (John 1999; Sabatier 1999: 8–9), for it is much more than just repetitive. A similarly pragmatic approach is adopted here. The argument is simply that some perspectives on policy-making are of greater relevance to the material featured here than others. For example, although consideration was given to discussing alternative approaches to policy-making, among them the aforementioned *Stages* models, in this study, alternatives are chosen in order to facilitate an emphasis on the perception of politics and policy-making in tourism. Indeed, it is these elements that have been at the centre of debates about the gradual replacement of Government as a process by *Governance* (an issue that will be revisited later in the chapter), an emerging integrative approach to public policy making, and to which, along with *Institutional, Group* and *Network, Corporatist* and *Pluralist, Ideas-based, Rational choice, Socio-economic approaches* and some *Integrated* approaches (*Evolution Theory*) attention now turns.

Institutional Approaches

Hall & Jenkins (1995: 24–31) approach to institutional tourism public policy arrangements is that not only are they and the role of the state significant for the tourism industry such institutions must be understood as more than being just the state. Furthermore, by disaggregating the state, it might be possible to identify the impact of macro-structures, particularly as they are more prominent when the processes of tourism public policy can identify how the various sectors' policies vary from one another. Indeed, the importance of tourism's public policy role to the state may be determined by the exigencies of the peculiarities of each country to the point that many countries feet it necessary to centralise policy-making powers in order that it might create an environment in which tourism might prosper.

In developing this theme, Huntington (1993: 22–49) acknowledges that there are inherent tensions between political and economic developments Following large economic changes in society political change amplifies the adjustments that take place, as well as, encompassing new social developments such as the emergence of tourism as a social phenomenon. For example, the influence on early tourism development on policy, and on decision-making by the institutional approach, an approach that represented the way in which political scientists understood decision-making in the first half of the twentieth century; its advantage being that it corresponded with the formal arrangements of the then political systems as it did the progression of tourism development, and could be argued, conditioned and restrained tourism development.

Institutions, in effect, are the arena referred to by Hall (1994) earlier, within which policy-making takes place. They possess distinctive characteristics; their structures influence policy battles; and they succeed through incrementalism. They also have cultural rules giving collective meaning to particular entities and activities, integrating them into larger schemes, and include the political organisations, laws, and rules that are central to every political system. However, they also exclude political participants such as interest groups in public decision-making (Schattschneider 1960), a situation indicative of tourism in Scotland pre-devolution. Furthermore, and within a rigid structure, they constrain how decision-makers behave; apportion powers and responsibilities between the organisations of the state; confer rights on individuals and groups; and impose obligations on state officials to consult and deliberate; a scenario that is redolent of the manner in which the Scottish Executive under Jack McConnell operates.

The term institution refers to many different types of entities, including both organisations and the rules used to structure patterns of interaction within and across organisations (Sabatier 1999: 36). In consequence, institutional change is both a cause and effect of the development of tourism in that tourism has become reliant on the various forms of government, and government, as evidenced by Holyrood, and by its very nature is highly institutionalised.

Group and Network Approaches

Interest-Group and *Network* approaches are synonymous with *Corporatist* and *Pluralist* theories, but are also analogous to *Institutionalism* in that they generally explain policy stability better than policy change (John 1999). However, the most significant problem in examining the role of interest groups in the process of tourism policy-making is determining then maintaining the proper relationship between the interest group and the government or the government body with which the interest group is dealing e.g. instead of being consulted the interest group is influenced by the policy process; by its inclusion in the process excludes other interest groups; or the views or politics of those representing the interest group are not representative of the group as a whole (Hall & Jenkins 1995: 59).

Group Approaches

The commercial explosion of tourism in the 1950s saw group approaches to tourism materialize as a vital response to institutional approaches, stressing the importance of the nuances and interactions between the various component parts of the process of tourism policy-making. In essence, as was demonstrated clearly in the famous Hawthorne experiments at the Western Electric Company (Roethlisberger & Dickson 1939, from Mullins 1996), and is as equally applicable to tourism, group consciousness is necessary to gather all the facets involved in problems extending well beyond the abilities of single minds or disciplines (Cochrane 1997: 99).

The group approach to tourism encompasses the notion that associated relationships among the component parts influences and resolve policy. For example, it is not just the government as the legislature that makes decisions on tourism policy: policy should emerge because of informal patterns of association such as groups influencing the legislative processes and executive decisions. Although they can be demanding of and frustrate governments, governments need groups e.g. the Scottish Executive's need of the Scottish Tourism Forum (STF), the British Hospitality Association (BHA), and so on. They have come to realise that groups can be a resource, an iterative fund of ideas on policy, a provision of expertise and by accepting and implementing policy can legitimise it i.e. obtaining STF's endorsement of *A New Tourism Strategy for Scotland* (2000), as though it were one of the author's of the strategy.

Network Approaches

The network approach to tourism, which evolved along with the new techniques of management gurus such as Peters and Waterman (*In Search of Excellence* 1988) in the 1980s, continues the above themes. For example, to the detriment of the progress of tourism policy-making, institutionalists continue to reassert the importance of the state and the salience of routines in politics.

In the network approach the general notion is translated to mean that strategic actions are efforts by participants to influence, change, or preserve their positions in networks in which they are associated (Mullins 1996). In the tourism environment, these include associations and informal relationships, both within and outside political institutions that shape tourism and associated policy decisions and outcomes. The existence of a tourism policy network both influences, although it clearly does not determine, policy outcomes, and reflects the relative status, or even power, of the particular interests not only in tourism but also in a broader policy area (Rhodes 1999: 29). In effect, all tourism organisations function because of networks of interdependent activities (Mullins 1996: 607).

Although tourism networks have superseded tourism group perspectives in the study of tourism public policy, and although the network approach is used to describe and explain relationships between decision-makers as they operate in other policy sectors, the expression of groups as important entities is still salient. For example, diverse and fragmented tourism group representative associations, institutionalised bureaucrats, career politicians and other decision-making participants influence the diverse manner in which tourism policy is expressed by political systems.

Rhodes (1999: 56) claims that policy networks changed fundamentally after 1979, when Thatcher came to power in the U.K. They expanded to include more participants, most notably from the private and voluntary sectors. Thereafter, the challenge for government was to recognise the constraints on central action imposed by the shift to self-organising networks; and to search for new tools for managing such networks. The main criticisms of tourism policy networks, however, according to John (1999: 87), are that they do not have an account of institutions and the state e.g. networks invariably circumvent the more formal aspects of politics. It is possible; however, to acknowledge the role of institutions in the network approach (Peterson 1995), as institutional strategies are the basis of the relationship within networks.

In developing this theme, Marsh & Rhodes (1992a: 261) claim that tourism networks exist to routinise relationships. Networks with a dominant economic or professional interest are the most resistant to change, an example being reputedly the Civil Service. Meanwhile, a network will run its own affairs if the policies are of low salience to the government. In effect, change becomes incremental. The analysis of change, therefore, must explore the relationships between tourism networks and how they affect tourism policy outcomes. In addition, the source of the change may lie in a network and in its relations with sub-sectoral networks, depending on the extent to which it can set the policy parameters (Marsh 1996 cited in Rhodes 1999: 12), and its own fundamental relationships.

Although interest group and network approaches are similar to institutionalism in that they generally explain policy stability better than policy change, it is not clear from the way in which networks operate how change comes about (John 1999). Despite their obvious flaws, nevertheless, the strengths and weaknesses of these approaches can to a degree be overcome by considering a recent development of integrative theory as alluded to earlier, namely governance.

Governance

Tourism presents interesting variations in the outcome variable of governance. For example, some national governments are active in developing tourism policy, while others leave these efforts to local or regional authorities. Some efforts at international-level governance are also evident. At the same time, when we disaggregate the issue-area of tourism, we find substantial variation in the potential explanatory factors and through time some issues and regions exhibit notable economies of scale or externalities, while others do not. The complexity of the development of the tourism industry over time also presents variation in these variables (Martin 2001). Nevertheless, tourism networks evolve more expeditiously than tourism institutions. For example, while Mitchell (1995) claims that in the mid-nineties the Conservative view of Britain was of a unitary state while the view of Labour was that Britain was a union state (Mitchell 1996), Rhodes (1999: 4) claims that since 1945 Britain has changed from a unitary state to a differentiated polity. This means that policy networks of resource dependent organisations, such as those in the tourism firmament, are now a defining characteristic of the public policy-making process. One of the outcomes of such a scenario and which has been consolidated by devolution is that there has been a shift from a strong (Scottish Office) to a segmented executive (Scottish Executive), characterised by bargaining games within and between networks. This is a consequence of governance, as an unplanned, unheralded governing structure, as characteristic of government policy-making as the more vaunted markets and competition (Rhodes 1999: 45).

By governance, Rhodes refers to a change in the meaning of government, referring to a new process of governing (Rhodes 1999: 15). He does, however, point out the danger to government. In tourism terms, it has to recognise the constraints on central action imposed by the shift to self-organising networks, and the search for new tools for managing such networks. He also points out the dangers in that game playing; joint-action; mutual adjustment; and networking are the new management skills. They treat networks as a tool of government. This, he claims, becomes a challenge for democratic accountability.

Moreover, according to Marsh & Rhodes (1992a: 265), networks can destroy political responsibility by shutting out the public; and by creating privileged oligarchies; and being conservative in their impact, because, for example, the rules of the game and access favour established interests, a theme that will be pursued in Chapter 8. Rhodes (1999: 59) further claims that governments will have to learn to live with policy networks and that the challenge for governments is to understand these new networks, and devise ways of steering them and holding them to account (Rhodes 1999: 110). This means that the challenge for the Scottish tourism industry is to understand the Scottish Executive and the Westminster government, and devise ways of influencing them in the best interest of the industry as a whole.

According to Pyper & Robins (2000: 307), for the Thatcher governments, governance equalled the minimal state plus the new public management. Reform was largely limited to aspects of the economic and financial polity. Under the Blair government, despite tendencies towards a nanny state, it is possible to discern the emergence of a fuller, more comprehensive concept of governance. In Scotland, under successive First Ministers, first Dewar, then McLeish, and now McConnell, these principles are slowly evolving.

John (1999), as does Hall (1994) and Edgell (1999), however, somewhat incongruously, ignores governance, focusing instead on relationships, and applying labels to describe those relationships. In his view, the network approach does not account for how those relationships form and why they change, an essential tenet in the understanding of governance. Nevertheless, according to Pierre & Peters (2000: 19), one of the most familiar forms of contemporary governance is a policy network. Rhodes (1999: 15) acknowledges this, claiming governance refers to self-organising, interorganisational networks characterised by interdependence; resource exchange; rules of the game; and significant autonomy from the state: a facet of public policy theory apparently disregarded by John, Hall and Edgell.

Pierre & Peters (2000: 114–115) develop this theme describing the state as stepping back and allowing subnational and international institutions and participants to gain importance. They suggest that there is a conscious state strategy, which is much more than surrender to local and transnational pressures for greater control and autonomy. Such a strategy has significance for Scottish tourism. For example, due to devolution, for the first time since tourism was recognised as an industry opportune to Scotland, Scotland has the ability to decide its own tourism policy, or ultimately whether it even needs such a policy, and if it does what form it should take. This is due to the fact it represents a very different type of regional institutional reform compared to the Scottish Office previously existing in Whitehall and Edinburgh. Whether or not tourism policy networks rather than tourism institutions will influence such a policy (or the need for such a policy), or for that matter, interest groups, networks, or elite's is addressed as this book progresses.

This reform is significant in terms of governance. However, John cautions (1999: 40) that institutions embody cultures and past political decisions. For example, formal rules and structures agreed or introduced long ago influence how political participants exercise their current choices e.g. the Scottish Area Tourist Board (ATB) consultations. Moreover, the variety of traditions embodied in institutions explains the complexity of political behaviour and unlocks the intricacies of the policy process. Furthermore, whereas political movements, parties, and interest groups come and go with the cyclical fluctuation of issues, the institutional context that shapes policy agendas change much more slowly. Instead they bring together the institutions into a coherent whole, where each country has a state tradition that is an amalgam of cultures, ideas, and institutions (Dyson 1980).

Dyson (1980) expands on this theme claiming that recent developments in Britain (this theme is applicable to devolution) have turned out differently, owing mainly to the extraordinarily strong British *etatiste* tradition and the politicisation of regional autonomy, primarily with respect to Scotland. Pierre & Peters (2000: 208), however, have a salient warning; governance is not so cosy and consensual as it is sometimes made out to be. They claim, instead, it is to a significant degree about defining goals and making political priorities, as is evidenced by devolution, and there is little reason to expect those decisions to be any less controversial in a governance perspective than it was in the conventional view of government.

Corporatist and Pluralist Approaches

According to Rhodes (1999: 29), Schmitter (1979: 15) identified two models of interest group intermediation *Corporatism* and *Pluralism*. Corporatist theory developed as one approach to analysing the relationship between the state and organised interests in most western states in the post-war period, and is equally applicable to the tourism industry. In effect, there is also considerable debate about whether or not corporatism can in fact be distinguished from pluralism, which recognises that people operate not only as individuals but also within groups with specific interests (Brown *et al.* 1996: 98–100), such as tourism networks.

Corporatist

Pierre & Peters (2000: 34) claim that of the two conventional models of the relationships between government and society, the corporatist model provides the closer linkage, officially sanctioning interest groups such as STF as representatives of their sector. Nevertheless, although corporatism is a political system in which economic and social policy is made through agreements between government, business sector interest groups, and trade unions, one effect of this is to lessen the scope of the free market, therefore hindering economic growth.

All of the advanced capitalist societies display some corporatist features, but the degree of corporatism differs considerably, with countries such as Germany, Austria and Sweden clearly corporatist in function while countries such as France, the USA and U.K. are much less so. For example, in terms of the U.K., the political and economic policies of the Thatcher government in the 1980s included a reliance on the mechanisms of the free market which impacted greatly on the tourism industry. During her premiership there were reductions in public spending, changes to the tax system, and privatization/de-nationalization. More prominence was also given to enterprise, entrepreneurship, and individual accountability as opposed to the collectivism and corporatism of those governments she succeeded. Regardless of Thatcherism, Brown *et al.* (1996) claim that in drawing distinctions between policy developments in Scotland and England, Scotland despite devolution remains more corporatist in nature.

As Andreson (2000) claims, with the development of the European Union (EU), corporatism is now reaching a new stage, where the tripartite discussions on the EU level are playing an increasingly important role, and will play the leading role in the development of the class dictatorships in EU dominated Europe. Phelps (2000), however, claims that Europe has been less successful in economic terms that North America because the core of the typical European economy is still organised on the corporatist model.

Pluralism

Pluralism distinguishes itself from both monism, the view that one kind of thing exists, and dualism, the view that two kinds of things exist, because it represents any speculative or abstract theory that maintain that reality is composed of a diversity of well-defined, elementary entities. In essence, there are weak and strong forms of pluralism theories. The weak form holds that there are many distinct individual things, whereas the strong form holds that there are many distinct kinds of things (Honderich 1995).

Dahl (from Mayhew 1997) used this term to denote any situation in which no particular political, cultural, ethnic, or ideological group is dominant. For example, although there is often competition between rival groups such as those that comprise STF, or previously the Scottish Tourism Coordinating Group (STCG), the state or local authority may be seen as the arbitrator. It has been asserted that this is the way that cities are run, rather than by an elite, and may also be attributed to the manner in which some cities in Scotland operate their tourism function e.g. Glasgow. The theory thus relates to the nature of power, but may also be used to signify the cultural diversity of a plural society. It is, in effect, a condition in which power is diffused throughout society with no single group controlling all decisions.

A pluralist state, on the other hand, is one in which decision-making is divided among many independent groups: for example, government, the civil service, interest groups, and local authorities. In common with advocates of elitism, who believe that power is in the gift of an elite, advocates of pluralism recognize that, even in a democracy, a small minority makes decisions, but they maintain that no single group should dominate all decisions (a discussion on Scottish tourism elitism takes place in Chapter 8). They also believe that individuals should have an opportunity to become involved in making decisions, even if they often choose not to do so (Issacs *et al.* 1998).

Pluralism also encapsulates the existence of legal opposition parties or competing interest groups in a unitary state, where what is pluralized is not culture or religion but political opinions and conceptions of material interest e.g. in Scotland the tensions over membership and turf between the Chamber of Commerce and the Federation of Small Businesses (FSB). The ruling group, whatever its character, concedes that its ideas about how to govern are not the only legitimate ideas and that its understanding of the common good must incorporate some subset of more particular understandings (Honderich 1995).

A Framework for Analysis

There is no single theory to explain every relevant factor present in tourism. However, the application of a select number or combination of theoretical approaches, helps to establish a proper framework for analysis of tourism. Furthermore, despite all of the ground breaking research and theorizing being done on tourism, it still remains a phenomenon and although we succumbed to speculation in Chapter 1 as to its growth potential, its growth and impact cannot reliably be predicted.

Nevertheless, research on tourism's political impacts needs to connect the substance of policy i.e. the general focus on data with the process of policy-making including the relationship between power, structure, and ideology (Hall 1999: 14). For example, if this is neglected, and this is an important point, the capacity of the researcher to explain how Scottish tourism is threatened on the one hand by globalisation and on the other by outmoded institutions and structures is severely limited. As is his or her ability to define the opportunities presented by globalisation or by de-institutionalisation. For the researcher, this is compounded by the fact that the politics of Scottish tourism today involves many more complex networks of governance than in the past. This means that in terms of research, policy frameworks are required to cope with the multilevel nature of tourism policy change and variation, and encapsulate them in terms of reference to governance.

John (1999: 167–182) building upon research by Sabatier (1999: 9), but defined in more general terms, claims that three are of particular interest: *The Advocacy Coalition Framework*, *The Multiple-Streams Framework*, and *The Punctuated-Equilibrium Framework*. What is of interest here is to align these with tourism.

The Advocacy Coalition Framework

Where network participants join together to advocate for particular policies, it may be claimed that an advocacy coalition has formed (Sabatier 1987: 649–692). However, due to the need for a critical mass of participants to lead to action, and the increasing complexity of the tourism policy arena, the creation of tourism policy advocacy coalitions are becoming increasingly difficult (Hall & Jenkins 1995: 58). Nevertheless, one means by which the complexities of such coalitions may be understood is Sabatier and Jenkins-Smith's Advocacy Coalition Framework (1993: 147–156). It focuses on the interaction of advocacy coalitions that consists of constituents who share a set of policy beliefs e.g. STF as groups and networks, the BHA as individuals. It also regards policy-making as a continual service with no strict beginning and end, and from which participants learn over time. Yet, it also encompasses the fact that all have a role to play in the dissemination of ideas (John 1999).

The Multiple-Streams Framework

The Multiple-Streams Framework is based on the idea of continual interplay of problems, solutions and politics in a garbage-can model of policy choice (see Kingdon 1984. Cohen *et al.* 1972), which sees policy-making as an outcome of the essentially chaotic and unplanned manner in which organisations process decisions e.g. the former Scottish Tourist Board (STB). It views the policy process as made up of three streams of actors and processes: a problem stream consisting of data about various problems, and the proponents of solutions to policy problems; and a politics stream consisting of elections and elected officials. In Kingdon's view (1984), the streams normally work independently of one and other, except when a window of opportunity such as elections permits policy entrepreneurs to couple the various streams (Sabatier 1999: 9). However, although this approach is highly attractive, it also has a tendency to rely too much on change and fluidity of which Scottish tourism is not the best exemplar (John 1999).

The Punctuated-Equilibrium Framework

The Punctuated-Equilibrium Framework (Baumgartner & Jones 1993) argues that policy-making is characterised by long periods of incremental change punctuated by brief periods of policy change (Sabatier 1999: 9). It is a model of agenda setting, which seeks to describe how agendas and policies move from periods of being highly stable to times of rapid change and fluidity. In effect, this could describe the process with which Scottish tourism has been dealing with since devolution. However, although it neatly contrasts stability and instability in the account of policy-making over time, it is not entirely clear that it explains the transition between stability and change, and back again (John 1999). If, as we claim it describes the current situation for Scottish tourism, its weakness is its inability to describe the transitional processes. Also, if, as described above, there is a change of government either at Holyrood or Westminster, or both, or different parties are in power, this model is inadequate in its perception to reflect such changes, or not, as the case may be.

In terms of policy approaches, comparison of governance to the above three frameworks is complicated by their diversity. One maps changes in the coalitions that are often driven by external changes, another interacts with policy problems, policy solutions, and politics to produce policy change, while another explores agenda expansion and the potential for disequilibrium in policy-making systems (John 1999: 201). Although these can be related to the tenets of governance their capacity to embrace governance in its entirety are restricted by the fact that since their inception there has been a shift in perspective with regard to state-society relationship and dependencies, including tourism. An example of this would be STF's increasing prominence, as described in subsequent chapters. Also, although one could dispute Pierre & Peter's (2000) claim that government is no longer the obvious locus of political power and authority it could be argued that, in Scottish terms, the new devolutionary model given time will be a much more consultative and participative one than the previous Westminster model. This in particular, is because of its powerful committee system (The Enterprise and Lifelong Learning Committee figures prominently in subsequent chapters) and the electorate's expectations of it, combined with many Member of the Scottish Parliament's (MSP's) wishes to distance themselves from Westminster.

The approaches too, are rather partial and, as John observes (1999: 169), their insights need to be pushed further. Furthermore, as Pierre and Peters recognise (2000: 208), studying governance means essentially observing something that works. However, governance failure is difficult to observe because it can only be studied by observing its consequences, not the phenomenon itself, as is the case with the three aforementioned theories.

Ideas-based Approach

Apart from the above approaches John (1999: 144–166) also considers Ideas-based approaches, claiming that the policy process is permeated by ideas about what is the best course of action, and by beliefs about how to achieve goals. Because politics is defined by disputes about how to achieve things and the means to get there, participants in the policy process advocate contrary ideas and engage with others to try to influence them. In Scottish tourism, for example, there are many lobbyists for policy change, some arguing for radical positions such as compulsory (statutory) registration and a tourism tax, while others put forward conservative preferences such as continued membership of the British Tourist Authority (now VisitBritain) (BTA) or integration with the economic development network. These advocates may be bureaucrats, legislators, experts, and politicians as well as members of interest groups or networks, and the fact that each believes in their own case (John 1999: 145), means that there is a continual tension for prominence of ideas.

Rational Choice

Rational choice theory posits that individual choice is the foundation of political action and inaction. Its distinctiveness lies in the deductive method (Rhodes 1999: 174). Although it has been shown to generate paradoxes, and to create difficulties for inductivist theories its deployment has to be sharply constrained to prevent the problem that if all priori probabilities are equal, the possibility of learning from experience is excluded (Honderich 1995).

Socio-economic Approaches

Socio-economic approaches include, *Marxism*, *Regulationary*, *Developmental*, and *Globalisation* approaches, which according to Brown *et al.* (1996: 6), in terms of modernism and modernisation have been quite fundamental to sociology in that its founding fathers, notably the sociological trinity of Marx, Weber and Durkheim, had set out to explain how societies became modern, whether in industrial, capitalist or bureaucratic form. John (1999: 92), on the other hand, claims that these classic treatises be labelled as social determinist or a sociological approach to politics. What he means by this is that collective decision-making can be determined from the most powerful forces at work in the economy and society.

Evolutionary Theory

In devising an *Evolutionary Theory* (for a fuller discussion on this see John 1999: 182–188), John, in consequence, has heeded Sabatier's advice (1999: 270) that the use of integrated theories provides some guarantee against assuming a particular theory is the logical one. Different theories, too, may have the advantage in different environments, and being aware of other theories should make one much more sensitive to some of the implicit assumptions in one's preferred theory. Nevertheless, although John's *Evolutionary Theory* is a coalescence of synthesises of all of the aforementioned approaches, it does not wholly account for Governance or the tensions intrinsic to policy-decision-making in a newly devolved state. Nor is it in harmony with an amorphously diverse tourism sector where the needs and ambitions of one constituent part appear incompatible with the other, or does it deal with the fact that tourism in Scotland is policy driven from Edinburgh, yet and although there will be changes to the relationship from April 2003, is still integrated with a cross border authority through VisitBritain, formally BTA, and furthermore is subject to Westminster macro-economic policy, or indeed Europe.

It also does not take into account that Scottish tourism policy, in terms of strategy, appears to those it is endeavouring to serve to enhance the disconnect among disparate public sector organisations with contrary objectives, traditions, and cultures. The inherent weakness in the relationship between these bodies and the Scottish tourism industry's intensity of expectation of them appear in policy and decision-making terms contradictory, and raises the question of whether a policy for the tourism sector is realistic or indeed necessary, particularly when it could be integrated with economic development policy, as could be argued was the case prior to it being subsumed by Culture and Sport. Nevertheless, sound explorations of public policy in terms of both governance and of this research have to encapsulate the contrasts between stability and change, and to determine an appropriate theory or framework (John 1999).

John's theory's strength is that while synthesising some of the approaches already discussed, it also draws the best from the three aforementioned theories while seeking to incorporate the dynamic interplay between factors for change and adaptation and constraints on that action. However, even John (1999) claims that the synthesised approach does not imply beneficent progress or teleology. Instead, the rapid and contingent nature of change, the frequent obstacles to co-operation, and the limits to human capability mean that contingency and chance play an important role in explaining policy choices and in accounting for the salience of certain ideas. In consequence, although a case could be made for any one of the approaches favoured by John or Sabatier and Jenkins-Smith; Kingdon; or Baumgartner and Jones none is entirely satisfactory to tourism, but should not be discounted. For example, it is becoming clear that they can be further integrated in a possibly never-ending series of iterations and that it is possible to posit the characteristics that a satisfactory approach might have in respect of tourism in Scotland. For example, the most suitable theory, framework or approach it has to be advised, has to be one that can be synthesised, and can give a plausible explanation of policy formulation and implementation pertinent to this research, while taking into account the emergence of governance, the advent of devolution and the polarisation of expectations of the various sectors of the industry. In effect a heterogeneous approach.

A Heterogeneous Approach

The attraction of a heterogeneous approach is fundamentally its ability to understand and explain the process by which the dominant issues and controversies in Scottish tourism in both the lead up to and for the duration of the first parliament after devolution were resolved. It also takes into account the complex environment in which the Scottish tourism industry operated at that time; and the issues pertinent to Scottish tourism during an era of rapid and uncharted change. Of particular importance, would be the interaction between the various private and public sector Scottish tourism organisations and the individuals involved in them in their pursuit of specific agenda.

In consequence, as a framework, a heterogeneous one would be synchronous with the complex environment in which Scottish tourism operates that includes self-organised interest groups, institutions, elite's and policy networks. It would also address the processes of the concept and principles of governance combined with the tensions intrinsic to policy decision-making in a newly devolved state; to cross border authorities that create confusion in the policy process, and finally that of macro-economic Westminster dominated policies, or those of Europe. In essence, such an approach understands and explains how the issues of complexity of the elements to self-organised groups, institutions, elites and policy networks were processed for resolution as they strove continually to interact and adapt to an environment of constant change. For tourism this means the various disparate bodies associated with it, the constraints placed upon it, the external influences and so on, and recognizing the processes by which the participants habitually seek to influence decision-making and to interact with socio-economic processes such as demographics, fiscal policies, Europe etc., which are all also slowly changing and evolving over time (John 1999). Equally, its strength would come from not being a single perspective but one with an ability to move between many different complex and theoretical perspectives. A heterogeneous approach, therefore, would appear to be the most appropriate means by which tourism research can explain the nuances, complexities and vagaries of tourism policy, particularly in a Scottish context.

Summary

Despite the importance of tourism to the Scottish economy there has been no published study of Scottish tourism public policy, nor does any account exist of the impact of devolution or, indeed, of the combination of devolved and residual reserved powers on tourism public policy in Scotland. In tourism policy terms, devolved powers, which are reasonably extensive and far-reaching in some contexts, have to date failed to convince either the tourism industry or the consumer of their effectiveness, and despite numerous interventions, there is evidence to suggest that the Scottish Executive is replicating past policy failures by not treating the industry with the importance it desires, or by addressing the underlying problems.

In any case, as exemplified by this book, tourism policy can only be conceptually understood and substantively analysed once the philosophical guidelines and practical interests of tourism are investigated and described in a broad contextual framework (Edgell 1999: 11), Given that the process of policy-making is very complex involving many constituent parts, all with different objectives, perceptions, and policy preferences, this chapter considered the complex world of tourism research combined with a number of approaches relevant to the development of tourism theory. In simplifying them and, in order to understand their nuances, a conclusion was reached that that no single perspective was likely to yield holistically adequate analyses, instead synthesising them and applying to tourism, heterogenically, a fusion of approaches is the most suitable way forward.

Chapter 3

Tourism and Public Policy —
The Globalisation of Tourism

Introduction

This chapter is concerned with how public policy in tourism is applied globally, and builds upon the various approaches, frameworks and theories discussed in Chapter 2. Furthermore, it describes public policy's ability or inability to influence tourism directly or indirectly, and its impact on various countries' economies, culture and environment. In particular this chapter is influenced by the challenges brought on by the economic environments in which tourism operates in the 21st Century, as exemplified by mass globalization. This has been compounded further by SARS; war in Iraq; September 11; Bali, Mombassa; foot-and-mouth; and on-going zonal, regional, and religious conflicts as evidenced in: Israel and Palestine; North and Southern Ireland; Russia and Chechnya; India and Pakistan; the USA and Afghanistan, and the UN and Iraq.

Due to globalization the countries and destinations described below, and which are expanded upon as the chapter progresses, have had to alter their approach to tourism public policies dramatically. Among these were Russia where the burgeoning tourism trade in the former USSR was a totally different proposition from pre-1991 when its industrial economy was centrally planned, its society tightly controlled, and travel to and from Russia somewhat limited; Libya where the country's hard-line Arab socialist policies and antipathy to the west militates against any kind of tourism development; Saudi Arabia who as the largest producer and source of oil in the world, had little alternative but to develop tourism as part of a larger plan to diversify its economy; India where emphasis was given to harnessing tourism's direct and multiplier effects for employment and poverty eradication in an environmentally sustainable manner; the ASEAN nations, some of the richest and poorest in the world who joined together to stimulate economic growth; Australia whose visitors prior to the terrorism atrocities in Bali in October 2002 are expected to double in five years but where the capacity, the skills, and the infrastructure to accommodate this growth does not currently exist; Zimbabwe where issues of environmental sustainability and social equity needed to be specifically guarded; Belize which adopted a policy focused on responsible tourism, a form of governance, and the key guiding principle for sustainable tourism development; South Africa, post-apartheid, whose dependence on the long-haul markets of Germany, the U.K. and the USA was acute; Europe where the European Union was endeavouring not only to adjust the Euro, and the forthcoming enlargement, but also to transitional economies that within the next decade will enlarge it further; North America, the world's biggest tourism economy, in the wake of September 11; and, finally, Argentina's ability in relying on tourism as an important facet of its economy to emerge from its deepening economic crisis.

As will be demonstrated many governments are reacting to the changes brought on by the above events by adopting new promotional and financial strategies to lure back tourists, or are changing their approaches to policy-making. Others, in reviewing their policy arrangements, either foresee massive growth opportunities which their infrastructure is ill-equipped with which to deal with, or realise that by addressing internal problems these will impact significantly on their potential for growth. Furthermore, following September 11, countries and destinations that are highly dependent on U.S. outbound travel; those that are a long distance from their main generating markets; and, those of the Moslem world have seen their traditional markets contract (WTO 2002).

The Environment in which Tourism Operates in the 21st Century

Tourism Policy

In the modern world the control, supply, marketing, and consumption of tourism products and services, is dominated not by countries, but by large market driven transnational corporations (Ioannidis & Debbage 1998). Although such corporations' strategies are influenced ultimately by government tourism public policies and their ability to legitimate power to provide the political stability; social infrastructure; security; and legal and financial framework to smooth the progress of tourism (Elliott 1997: 2), in reality as much again of what these large corporations do is beyond the sphere of influence of governments. Furthermore, with the advent of globalization, and with little notice, such organizations can transfer their activities along with their profits to other countries. This makes it all the more surprising, as will be demonstrated later in this chapter, that a number of governments do not have a factual tourism policy that deals with such eventualities. Furthermore, and despite the fact we questioned the necessity of a dedicated tourism policy in Chapter 2, many governments' policies as in Scotland are either inferred in terms of strategies or initiatives, are non-existent, or are wholly inadequate to deal with tourism's increasing influence, impact, and sophistication.

Tourism Economy Leakage

Whether or not countries legislate for tourism policies, there are areas of tourism as described in Chapter 2 over which they have little influence. Additionally, any situation in which no particular political; cultural; ethnic; or ideological group is dominant, in itself causes problems in that it is used to signify the cultural diversity of a pluralist society. It is, in effect, a condition in which power is diffused throughout society with no single group controlling all decisions (Mayhew 1997).

For example, as large corporations' hotels, tour groups, and agencies often are not based in the destination country, only one third of the revenue from international tourism ever stays in the local economy (Knight 1999). Therefore, as the benefits of tourism have not always accrued to the host country, but substantially to foreign consortiums and interests, tourism fails to generate the potential foreign exchange for countries that is part of its attraction, and leaves behind only limited economic benefit with host communities (Preston 1996), instead taking advantage of their goodwill; their vulnerability; their naivety; their desperation; or their politicians' greed.

According to Cusick (2002), the World Bank estimates that 55% of all tourist income in undeveloped countries leaves host nations via foreign-owned airlines, hotels and tour operators, or for payment of imported food or drink, with leakage as high as 70% in countries such as Thailand, and 75% in the Caribbean. National laws, intended as economic barriers, are often pointless. In Costa Rica, it was illegal in the mid- and late 1990s for a foreign-owned company to own any coastal property. Nevertheless, 57% of all Costa Rican hotels and resorts were foreign owned. Furthermore, in Egypt one large hotel uses as much electricity as would 3,600 Egyptian families; the water used by a typical global tourist in a three and a half day stay in a city or resort would produce enough rice to feed a villager somewhere in Asia for a year; and in the Philippines an hotel guest uses as much water in 18 days as a rural Philippine family does in a year: all facets of an industry not wholly in control of its destiny, and evidence that the concept of responsible tourism is still in its infancy.

Polarization

In some countries, tourism has also not had the intended redistributory effect. In Scotland, for example, arguably a corporatist state, but one with pluralist tendencies, it has instead led to increased urban and rural polarization, which various tourism policy initiatives have endeavoured to address but failed miserably so to do (see Chapter 7).

In other parts of the world such as Africa or Asia the challenge for governments is that the concentration of wealth is in the gift of a small number of owners of tourism businesses at the expense of the population as a whole. One consequence of this is that the inherent inequalities and abuse built into their tourism industry's infrastructure has led to the exploitation of individuals, local cultures and community groups. Ultimately, such behaviours result in tourism being resisted by such communities who perceive tourism growth negatively because of past experiences.

There were also facets of tourism policies that revealed the negative aspects of tourism. For example, in Kenya, in the two decades to 2000, 1.5 million acres of land used by the Massi were lost to tourism and allied farming, and in Burma in the early nineties more than 5,000 villagers were evicted from their homes to make way for an international tourist development. In return, each villager was given the equivalent of £3 in compensation (Cusick 2002).

Weakening Tourism Economies

The advent of globalization means that business can now be contracted between two or more parties without the resulting revenue or profit having any positive influence or impact whatsoever on the destination where the final services are delivered. This results in further weakening economies, particularly in the developing countries, already undermined by the withdrawal of foreign short-term capital investments, bank loans and portfolio investments plus overvalued exchange rates and excessive credit expansion for speculation in land and real estate (Chamberlain 2002: 135).

Destabilization of such country's currencies combined with the resultant impact on their economic infrastructure reduces dramatically their tourism prices, offers, and margins. This results in a downward spiraling relative competitiveness, and as competition between such destinations is often on price alone, and as they are so reliant on tourism, not only are prices cut so fine that little profit manifests, but perversely it has become prudent economic policy for such destinations to devalue their currencies (Preston 1996). For example, between January 2001 and January 2002, against the U.S. dollar, the Namibian dollar (which was pegged to the rand) fell 70% in value, the Botswanan pula fell by 40% and the Mozambican metical fell by 33% (worldinformation.com 2002). Furthermore, as the vast majority of shareholders in tourism companies are from more prosperous developed nations, a major effect of this external investment is to enhance shareholder value in the developed world to the disadvantage of the developing world: in essence continuing to widen the gap between the richer and poorer nations of the world.

A Shift of Emphasis

The World Tourism Organization's (WTO) forecast of the change in the share of international tourism arrivals between developed and developing regions as illustrated in Table 3.1 shows a pattern of change over the next decade that may allay the above trends. Apart from revealing an underestimation of tourism in 2000 (there were in actual fact 697 million trips taken), the relevant fact is that the share of tourism volumes and related receipts, GDP, employment, and export earnings is expected to move away from the developed countries towards the less developed countries as a result of favourable economic; motivational; technological; and policy factors. The challenge for such governments is to devise an appropriate tourism

Table 3.1: Forecast change in the share of international tourism arrivals between developed and developing regions.

Regions	2000 arrivals in millions	Share%	2010 arrivals in millions	Share%	%AAG
Developed regions of the world	528	78.45%	730	69.79%	3.29%
Less developed regions of the world	145	21.55%	316	30.21%	8.10%
Total	673	100.00%	1046	100.00%	4.51%

Source: WTO Forecasts 2000 from WTO Tourism 2020 Vision (%AAG is average annual gain).

policy which has contributions from all interests; is aligned to other complementary policies i.e. economic development, education, and fiscal; is sustainable; places the environment above short-term gain; and embraces the principles of responsible tourism: a topic that will be discussed later; and which displays all the facets of governance. Equally, there is an indominatable challenge for those developed countries that as a result of the above trends will see a share of tourism volumes and related receipts; GDP; employment; and export earnings fall.

Homogenization

Another irony of modern tourism is that a visit to any world-renowned city reveals how information, economic pressures, and the tendency to imitate have left the world less different than it was a century, even decades, ago (McIntosh *et al.* 1995). This has led to a homogenization of products and services, and a growing demand from the more discerning consumer for specialized, time efficient, customized vacations and unique experiences, which results in tourism in its complexity, providing examples of both undifferentiated mass tourism, and specialist niche markets (Burns & Holden 1995). For some destinations this is difficult to reconcile, and this contradiction in terms is indicative of globalization's influence on and challenge to tourism.

While the above transnational corporation's manipulate the market-place using expensive sophisticated marketing intelligence (Middleton & Hawkins 1998: 109), opportunities to enter the global marketplace are open to all, from multi-national corporations employing hundreds of thousands of people to bed and breakfast establishments, a situation that would have seemed far-fetched a decade ago, and upon which tourism public policy has little influence, and is perhaps among the reasons why the ATB network is being reviewed (see Chapter 9).

Customers, in turn, are taking advantage of the fact that traditional competitive advantages in tourism have eroded. For example, restructuring and rationalisation combined with the proliferation of e-business has made it easier for developing countries to enter mature tourism markets and apply cost pressure to traditional leaders. This is compounded by the fact that despite SARS, war in Iraq, September 11, Bali and Mombassa, the growth in long haul international travel market will continue, as will more frequent holidays of shorter duration. In tandem with this, changing demographic profiles of tourists will produce new market opportunities, creating fundamental global challenges for the tourism industry (Douglas & SE 2000).

International Tourism and the Impact of September 11 and Other Crises

As was discussed in Chapter 1, and as is revealed in Figure 3.1, the percentage change in international arrivals in 2001 over 2000 was −1.3%. This was a combination of factors. For example the outbreak of foot-and-mouth disease in the U.K., Ireland and the Netherlands, resulted in a reduction to those countries of between −5 and −6% of international arrivals during the first eight months of 2001. This was compounded by the strength of the U.S. dollar,

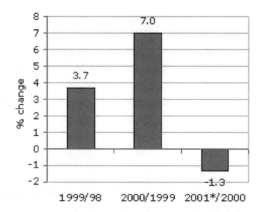

Figure 3.1: World international tourist arrivals (% change). *Source:* WTO 2002.

which contributed to a decline of −2.5% in arrivals to the United States for the first nine months of 2001; the on-going Israeli–Palestinian conflict that depressed travel throughout the Middle East; and, the economic crisis in Argentina, which reflected in tourism losses in neighbouring Southern American countries (WTO 2002).

As a result, and as is revealed in Figure 3.2 international tourist arrivals fell from 697 million in 2000 to 693 million in 2001. However, to take this out of context would be to distort the facts. Due to the Millennium celebrations which, in some cases, caused travellers to bring forward holidays that would have been taken in 2001; international arrivals worldwide were enhanced by 7% (WTO 2002).

Even before September 11 2001 arrivals to August worldwide grew by 3%, more than one point lower than the average annual gain of 4.3% in tourist arrivals over the previous ten years. Following September 11 there was a further drop of −9.2% in arrivals worldwide. In terms of the continents and regions this meant substantial decreases. This was the result of a change in travel habits, the majority of tourists choosing domestic

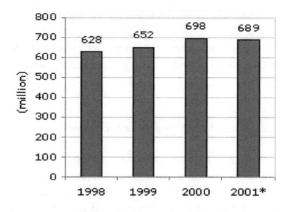

Figure 3.2: World international tourist arrivals (volume). *Source:* WTO 2002.

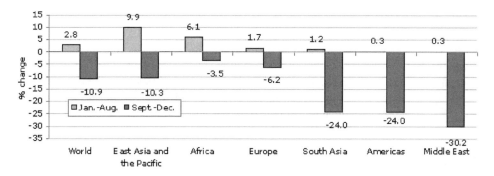

Figure 3.3: International tourist arrivals 2001 — regional trends. *Source:* WTO 2002.

trips over international travel, while large corporations placed a moratorium on their executives travelling, which saw a vast growth in world wide business video-conferencing. Holidaymakers also chose to travel by car or rail rather than by air, and consequently, visited familiar destinations that were closer to home, and perceived as being safer rather than long-haul destinations. Ultimately, these changes in travel patterns benefited rural tourism accommodation; ski resorts; camping grounds; and bed and breakfast establishments; and ironically destinations such as South Africa which were distant from the trouble spots (WTO 2002).

As is revealed in Figure 3.3, September 11 compounded an already troubled tourism economy which had been endeavouring to recover from other events that had a negative impact on the tourism industry in 2001. As this chapter progresses there will be a demonstration of how a number of countries dealt with such issues.

The Tourism Continents

Asia

Asia is the largest of the world's continents making up 33% of the earth's land area, with 60% of the world's population, and yet in comparative terms is the least visited, and therefore has the greatest potential; and perhaps because of the struggles associated with its internecine wars the greatest challenge.

This great land mass both physically and culturally falls into five broad sub-continents: North Asia; South Asia; the Far East; Middle South Asia; and Southeast Asia (Universal Dictionary 1994). Although the pre-September 11 growth rate was in the region of 8% its impact was such that international arrivals to Asia over all grew by only 4% in 2001.

Despite the above, and as much as Asia would appear to be the region where most of the world's major conflicts are taking place (Israel/Palestine, India/Pakistan, Russia/Chechnya, USA/Afghanistan, UN/Iraq) forecasts continue to reveal that it will continue to reap higher future tourism growth than any other destination. For example, although Hall (2001: 16) argues that the same factors that underpinned the extension of production networks which provided much of the region's economic growth in the early 1990s also left it vulnerable to the problems of the Asian financial crisis in the late 1990s, and that tourism suffered dramatically from the 1990 Gulf War; according to the WTO (2000) the Asian tourism economy will surface from these catastrophes to outstrip America to become second only to Europe in the number of visitor arrivals. For such a diverse region, this will present some significant socio-economic, cultural and environmental challenges.

North Asia

North Asia comprises most of the former USSR, and that part of it east of the Ural Mountains where tourism has yet to take much of a foothold (Philip's Illustrated Atlas of the World 1988). Post 1991 there has been a metamorphosis in the manner in which this area's fifteen former USSR, but now independent countries have dealt with tourism, and tourism public policy. For example, twelve are loosely linked within the Commonwealth of Independent States (CIS), an organization that prioritizes the benefits of tourism to its economies (www.cisstat.com/eng/cis.htm 2002). Meanwhile, the former reluctant USSR states of Lithuania; Estonia (a fuller account of Estonian tourism is described in the European section); and Latvia choose to remain outside the CIS, their tourism strategies in terms of promotion and development more closely aligned to their other Baltic near-neighbours: Finland (particularly Estonia); Sweden; Norway; and Denmark, taking advantage of their economies strength over their Russian neighbours.

Russia

Although it was not evident at the time, the former Soviet Union long recognized the political and foreign policy value of tourism. For example, the resolution of the 27th Congress of the Communist Party of the Soviet Union, held in 1986, and the Guidelines for the Economic and Social Development of the Soviet Union for 1986 and 1990 contained numerous provisions directly connected with developing international trade in tourism relations between the Soviet Union and other countries in the world. The political change that was brought about in 1989 when the USSR began to disintegrate opened up further opportunities for the tourism industry, and America, in particular, was not slow to take advantage, its large corporations investing heavily throughout the 1990s to meet the growing demand to travel to the East (Journal of the US–USSR Trade and Economic Council 1986: 5–6 from Edgell 1999: 27). However, this also meant that the Russian economy was subject to the market forces of Western capitalism as it moved from a Communist to a Corporatist/Pluralist state.

Evidence of this was the change that was brought about in 1997 in this region by the financial crisis that gripped Russia which coincided with the Asian financial crisis as a whole. This necessitated the government altering the structure of its tourism industry, which had been growing satisfactorily if not haphazardly since 1991. For example, in a throwback to the communist regime, it introduced policy instruments which decreased the number of Russian tourists traveling abroad and encouraged already hard-pressed tourist agencies to focus instead on increasing tourism within the country. This change of emphasis had a catastrophic impact on these agencies. They already existed in an environment of currency instability; an inability to complete even formerly routine financial transactions; client solvency; and a decrease in the number of clients. This combined with deficiencies in skills sets and infrastructure to meet government targets placed further pressure upon them. Furthermore, many in Russia's emerging middle class lost their jobs or had their salaries reduced by two to three times, while at the same time prices for previously inexpensive tours abroad increased dramatically due to the devaluation of the rouble. In consequence, travel agencies did not renew contracts with airlines, and both tourist agencies and airline companies suffered. This decreasing demand for tours abroad forced tourist firms to create new, inexpensive routes and pressurized airlines to lower airfares. In consequence, 40% of the 8,000 registered tourist agencies were forced to close down their businesses, the majority of the remainder posted significant losses with the turnover of tourist companies in September 1998 estimated at 50–70% of that in September 1997 (Vigdorchik 1998). Those that remained were focused on boosting efforts to attract tourists to the country, exploring new opportunities and creating new programs to entice foreigners.

Due to the devaluation of the rouble in 1998 and the rise in energy prices in 2000, an upturn in Russia's economic fortunes took place during 2000, which was to a great extent still recovering from decades of communist rule and the 1998 rouble crash (www.worldinformation.com 2002). However, in 2001, Russia's economic recovery underwent a setback brought on by the general global slowdown; falling energy prices; and a strong rouble against the U.S. dollar; lower external demand; and increased defence spending to finance the never-ending war in Chechnya.

Commonwealth of Independent States (CIS)

This slowdown also adversely affected CIS members other than Russia, and their hopes of significant economic development for the region. In consequence they either delayed or put to rest plans for significant tourism expansion. This was compounded by the unraveling of the long-standing special agreement (signed in the Kyrgyz capital, Bishkek 19 October 1992) which was meant to guarantee visa-free travel for CIS citizens within the commonwealth. For example, on 1 January 2000 following Turkmenistan's withdrawal from the accord in June 1999, Uzbekistan then suspended the Bishkek agreement. The Turkmen and Uzbek governments did not give precise explanations to their citizens for these sudden restrictions, offering only vague references to the need to protect national interests and to maintain stability and security. In retaliation, other regional governments introduced visa regimes for Uzbek and Turkmen citizens. This meant that while many Europeans could cross the borders of Tajikistan, Kyrgyzstan, or Kazakhstan freely, without visas, Uzbek or Turkmen passport holders/citizens wishing to travel to there were required to have entry visas to visit. Therefore, the envisaged free travel among the five states of Central Asia became a distant memory for the region's citizens. Furthermore, the closed-border policies came at a high economic cost, being one of the main obstacles that blocked regional development. For example, Turkmenistan's visa stance adversely affected the country's economy, and many observers believe that unless the Central Asian governments face reality and make regional integration a top priority, they will become further isolated, and the economic benefits of globalization will be lost (Eshanova 2002).

To overcome this those CIS countries such as Russia who have not followed Turkmenistan and Uzbekistan's path have endeavoured to formulate new CIS and regional policies on tourism to facilitate easier access and encourage more interplay between states (www.cisstat.com/eng/cis.htm 2002). However, despite this new policy initiative, the visa regime, the prices charged by airlines, hotels and other tourism companies for travel to the West, and to many parts of their own countries are still beyond the reach of those on average or below average incomes, and such travel is likely to remain the preserve of a relatively small and privileged group of individuals (Youell 1998: 62).

The East Asia Pacific Region

East Asia or the East Asia Pacific Region is made up of the temperate and sub-tropical parts in the east where most people are of the Mongoloid origin such as China, Japan, North and South Korea (Philip's Illustrated Atlas of the World 1988), all of which have differing tourism approaches, from the relatively closed state run China and North Korea to the more open although institutionalized Japan and pluralist South Korea. The latter two formerly enemies and recently remarkably co-hosts of the 2002 Football World Cup. In reality, the success to date of Asian tourism destinations has been based on the arrivals of Japanese, the resultant expenditure, and the confidence this gives to a region in which China, which is among the world's top five destinations in terms of arrivals and expenditure, remains relatively unaffected by outside pressures. For example, its economy is cushioned by substantial financial incentives from the government combined with high levels of domestic demand, making China's economy although one of the least developed by far the strongest in Asia, and a region of tremendous growth potential for tourism (www.worldinformation.com 2002).

Middle East

The hot, dry lands of the west, whose inhabitants are mostly of Semitic stock, many of whom are Muslims, comprise West Asia or the Middle East, the driest of the world's major regions (Universal Dictionary 1994), and an area where the oil states are using their vast wealth to diversify their economies into industries such as tourism against the day when the oil wells run dry. Although many of the Middle East states are highly institutionalised, there is little evidence of tourism structures that would be recognisable in the west, which is perhaps indicative of the strife pervading such countries, or economies that have been reliant on oil to the exclusion of all else for too long.

Saudi Arabia

Calls for change in the tourism sector in Saudi Arabia in the 1990s were particularly strong because tourism remained largely underdeveloped, and although the government appeared to be sympathetic, as with everything else it did, it moved excruciatingly slowly (Ady 1997; Ady & Wallwer 1989). However, minded that oil revenues in this decade will generally be lower than they were over the past two decades, Saudi Arabia is at long last intent on diversifying away from the energy sector, and reinvesting some of the country's wealth which is invested abroad e.g. an estimated $700 billion in the United States, in tourism (Martin 2002). For example, in September 1999 Saudi Arabia approved a plan to allow Muslims arriving for the umra pilgrimage to travel across the kingdom instead of being confined to the Muslim holy cities of Mecca and Medina, and in April 2000 the Supreme Commission for Tourism (SCT) was formed to develop programmes for tourism and remove any obstacles that might hamper tourism expansion (Simon 2002).

The SCT is an independent body reporting directly to the cabinet. Based in Riyadh, its main concern is with tourism within the Kingdom, enhancing the role of the tourist sector and removing obstacles facing it in its capacity as an important source of national income, and forging a general policy to promote the tourist sector. This includes evaluation of tourist-related infrastructure; establishment of programs necessary for its completion; removal of whatever obstacles might undermine tourist activity; the provision of facilities and incentives for investors, such as data centers and informational plans promoting tourism; a comprehensive survey of tourist locations in the Kingdom; encouragement of all efforts to boost tourism; preservation of tourist sites, and folklore items such as handicrafts, markets, and cottage industries; and coordination of efforts among concerned authorities, both government and private, and with other countries involved in tourism in the Kingdom. Meanwhile, tourist facilities for investment are undertaken by the private sector.

To demonstrate the seriousness with which Saudi Arabia now takes tourism to its economy the board of directors of SCT is chaired by the Second Deputy Prime Minister, who is also Minister of Defense and Aviation and Inspector-General, and is comprised of its Secretary-General, and other senior cabinet ministers such as the Ministers of Interior, Foreign Affairs, Planning, Commerce, Agriculture and Water, Education, Municipal and Rural Affairs, and Pilgrimage, plus the General President for Youth Welfare (saudiembassy.net 2000; Ain-Al-Yaqeen 2000).

The SCT has what might seem an impossible job: attracting tourists to visit an area where the temperature reaches 115 degrees; where it is virtually impossible to buy a beer; and where its two most famous cities (see Figure 3.4) are barred to non-Muslims. Nor is this a destination for backpackers e.g. no-one can enter the kingdom without a sponsor, and women cannot move easily from city to city unless accompanied by a husband or male relative. Furthermore, Saudi bureaucracy is a powerful disincentive to investment e.g. to obtain a license one has to deal with five different organizations which can take up to a year to finalise arrangements. Another impediment is the Saudi school schedule. Instead of vacationing in their own country, as soon as school ends each June, thousands immediately head to the United States and Europe, taking out of the country $15 billion. Furthermore of the 2 million outside visitors per annum, the vast majority are Muslims making the required pilgrimage to Mecca, birthplace of the Prophet Mohammed. Only Muslims are allowed there and in Medina, Islam's second-holiest city, while the annual number of non-Muslim visitors is approximately 6,000, most of them arriving in tour groups organized by Saudi Arabian Airlines (Martin 2002). Nevertheless, Prince Khalid

Figure 3.4: Saudi Arabia — Medina and Mecca. *Source:* ABC News.com 2000/Magellan
Geographix. www.i.abcnews.com/media/travel/images/map_saudi_arabia_000403_n.gif

Al-Faisal Emir of Asir province in Saudi Arabia, who believes tourism is the future of the
province, is leading by example, the area relying more and more on tourism to strengthen
its economy by attracting more than 1.5 million visitors in 2001, mainly from within the
kingdom and neighboring Gulf Arab states whose nationals do not need visas to travel to
Saudi Arabia (ABC News.com/Reuters/al-Eqtisadiah 2000). The Prince's region, situated
in the south west of Saudi Arabia, also made more than 2.2 million riyals ($290 million)
from tourism that same year. However, as with other Saudi regions most tourists to Asir
are Saudi citizens, although there were other visitors from the other Arab Gulf states
(Al Khoury 1999).

For Asir though, as with all Saudi provinces, the concern is that the government, in
granting infrastructural improvements and tourist concessions to local people, has to bargain
with tribal sheikhs in return for their people's commitment to conservation, effectively
buying them off. In addition, the government's philosophy for planning and managing
the countryside has to be based on the injunctions of the Koran and of Sharia law, and
the resultant restrictions. Additionally, it will be some time before habits of conservation;
internal tourism and environmental education are accepted by any large number of the
people. Furthermore, although local majority ownerships of business are mandatory on
a national scale, this is not the case on regional scales, causing further problems for the
advancement of tourism in the region (Child & Grainger 1990).

Middle South Asia

The generally humid tropical lands of Middle South Asia is largely the subcontinent of
India, including Pakistan, Bangladesh and Sri Lanka, where Dravidian and Indo-Aryan
people inhabit the world's most densely populated region of comparable size (Universal
Dictionary 1994; Philip's Illustrated Atlas of the World 1988), and where two of the largest
nations are threatening war over the ownership of Kashmir.

India

The evolution of tourism policy (since 1982)   India has a federal system of government where the 28 States and the 7 Union Territories have built up substantial tourism administrations, often with the division of powers between the various levels of state being designed formally through intergovernmental agreements (Richter 1989; Pearce 1992 from Hall 1994: 26).

Prior to the 1980s tourism policy and development in India was haphazard, fragmented and driven by vested interest. Recognising the advances made in other parts of the world, the Indian Congress Government introduced an era of liberalization which recognized the need to formulate a policy that highlighted the importance of the tourism sector (Tourism Policy of India: An Exploratory Study 2000). Consequently a *National Policy on Tourism* (1982) was presented in the Parliament in 1982. However, taking an institutional approach, the policy was formulated in an environment of a closed economy with rigid licensing procedures. Furthermore, it did not emphasize the role of private sector, and due to a lack of ambition and foresight foreign investment was not envisaged. Nor did it confer adequate emphasis on domestic tourism and the need for product development. Despite various other initiatives, this situation remained until the initiation of a structural adjustment programme in 1992, which included a *National Action Plan for Tourism* (Draft National Tourism Policy, India 2001). Between these two policy statements, various legislative and executive measures were brought about.

1986/1987   A National Committee on Tourism was set up in July 1986 by the Planning Commission to prepare a perspective plan for the sector, the *Seventh Plan*. By 1987, the Central Government declared more concessions for the sector which included tax exemption on foreign exchange earnings from tourism. For example, a 50% reduction on rupee earnings; a 100% reduction on earnings in dollars; a drastic reduction in tariff on import of capital goods; and concessional finance at the rate of 1–5% per annum. It also set up the Tourism Development Finance Corporation with a corpus fund. Until then, the sector was financed on commercial lines by the Industrial Development Bank of India, the Industrial Credit and Investment Corporation of India and other commercial banks (Draft National Tourism Policy, India 2001).

1988   In 1988 the National Committee on Tourism, submitted its aforementioned *Seventh Plan*, which provided the basic perspective framework for operational initiatives. Among its recommendations was to replace the existing Department of Tourism by a National Tourism Board, and a separate cadre of Indian Tourism Service to look after the functioning of the Board. It also submitted proposals for partial privatisation of the two airlines owned by the Union Government, and advocated vigorously that tourism be granted industry status. However, it took ten years to for most of the States to accord this status within their legislative framework (Draft National Tourism Policy, India 2001).

1992   At the beginning of the *Eighth Plan* (1992–1997), 15 of the 28 States and 3 of the 7 Union Territories had declared tourism as an industry, and four States hotels an industry.

The latter point being that the policy statement carried certain provisions in favour of the hotel industry i.e. that there should be provision for depreciation in the balance sheets of hotels. Also, being an export industry, hotels were to be given excise concessions.

The National Action Plan for Tourism, published in 1992, charted seven objectives as central concerns of the Ministry, among them socio-economic development of areas; and, increasing employment opportunities, all aimed at an increase in India's share in world tourism (from the then 0.4–1% during the following 5 years) (The National Action Plan for Tourism 1992, Draft National Tourism Policy, India 2001).

1993   In April 1993, the Government announced further measures aimed at export promotion. The existing Export Promotion of Capital Goods Scheme (EPCG) was extended to tourism and related services. Against the existing 35%, the tourism sector paid an excise duty of 15% only on capital goods import, subject to an export obligation of 4 times the cargo, insurance, and freight (CIF) value of imports. With an obligation period of five years, this came as a boon to the hotel industry. The cost of construction had also come down by 20%, and saw an explosion of hotel building (Draft National Tourism Policy, India 2001). However, the tourism sector's contribution to the national development priorities and strategies had so far been relatively limited, and this was India's biggest tourism challenge. For example, India's neighbours in South and South-East Asia have more effectively utilised tourism for economic growth and employment creation e.g. China's 8.6% tourism total of GDP; Sri Lanka's 8.6%; Indonesia's 9.2%; Malaysia's 12.9%; and Thailand's 13.9% far out weighs India's 5.3% (WTTC 2002).

2001   In 2001 recognising its tourism industry's inability to realise its potential the Indian Ministry of Tourism prepared a draft *National Tourism Development Policy* with the objective of positioning tourism as a major engine of economic growth. In addition, unlike the 1982 national policy, which followed an institutionalist model, it acknowledged the critical role of the private sector with government working as a pro-active facilitator and catalyst (National Tourism Development Policy Draft 2001; National Tourism Policy, India 2002).

2002   The National Tourism Policy (NTP) was published in summer 2002 and concentrated on the strong cooperation between private and public sector participation and development of domestic tourism. It also focused on infrastructure creation, destination development and the close cooperation with other service providers. Furthermore, in order to develop and expand tourism, development of domestic tourism is a new goal and the strategy for development is to ensure that its development is closely tied to the national development priorities of the country (Koul 2002).

The policy also highlights five key objectives: positioning tourism as national priority; enhancing India's competitiveness as a tourism product; improving and expanding product development; creation of world class infrastructure; and developing sustained, effective marketing plans and programmes (National Tourism Policy 2002). In effect, it aims to position tourism as a major engine of economic growth and to harness its multiplier effects for employment generation and economic development; also to position India as a global brand to take advantage of the burgeoning global travel and trade and the vast untapped potential of India as a destination. The policy also creates and develops integrated tourism circuits based on India's unique civilization, heritage, and culture in partnership with States, private sector and other agencies. It also ensures that the tourist to India gets physically invigorated, mentally rejuvenated, culturally enriched, spiritually elevated and feels India from within (Press Information Bureau 2002). However, the ongoing dispute with Pakistan over Kashmir militates against further expansion in the Northern areas, and Indian tourism looks towards the developed world for further expansion.

Southeast Asia

Southeast Asia, the remainder of the continent, has great ethnic and cultural diversity; many of its people derived from other parts of Asia in historic times. It includes Burma; Thailand; Laos; Kampuchea; Vietnam; Malaysia; Singapore; Brunei; Indonesia; and the Philippines (Universal Dictionary 1994). A number of these countries formed an alliance in 1967, the Association of Southeast Asian Nations (ASEAN), to stimulate economic growth, part of which is its facilitator the ASEAN Tourism Forum (ATF) (www.aseansec.org 2002; Teo *et al.* 2001).

It is a region of nearly 500 million people, ranging from some of the richest in the world, such as the Bruneians, to the poorest, including the Laotians and Myanmese, and boasts incongruously some of the world's finest hotels and the world's best airlines and airports. Since the economic crisis of 1997 combined with internal political and social problems Southeast Asia lost much of its competitive edge, and depending on their local economic environment, a number of Southeast Asian countries addressed the downturn in tourism arrivals by following different policies to promote tourism, create jobs, generate foreign exchange and attract investment (Asia Times 2001; www.aseansec.org 2002). However, tourism in those countries that were members of the ASEAN region followed a coordinated policy which resulted in their recovering significantly and more rapidly than the non-ASEAN countries from the 1997 crisis that gripped the economy. For example, and as is demonstrated in Figure 3.5, by 1999 ASEAN's international arrivals recorded a remarkable growth of 13.8% from 29.7 million in 1998 to 33.8 million, surpassing the 1997 record level of 31 million arrivals, with 2000s arrivals approaching the 38 million mark (www.asean-tourism.com 2002; www.aseansec.org 2002).

ASEAN

In 2001 ATF officially launched the Visit ASEAN Campaign (VAC), which was intended to build a stronger brand for ASEAN that would portray it as a single tourism destination in the new millennium. VAC was implemented in two-phases. The first phase was devoted to an intense promotion and marketing effort. In 2002 the second phase focused on promotion campaigns directed at end consumers, combined with ASEAN member countries embarking on their respective Visit ASEAN related programs (www.asean-tourism.com 2002).

Although much of this was aimed at external visitors the importance of intra-ASEAN travel (see Figures 3.6 and 3.7), and which makes up nearly 40% of ASEAN arrivals were

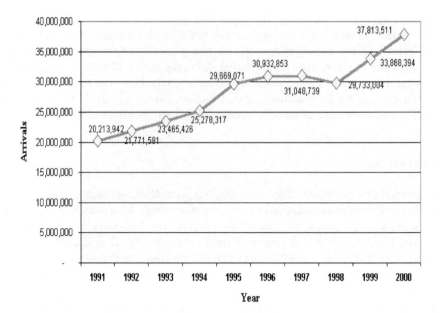

Figure 3.5: International visitors and arrival in ASEAN 1991–2000*. *Source:* www.asean-tourism.com 2002.

not ignored, particularly in countries such as Singapore (7 million), Malaysia (2.5 million), Indonesia (1.7 million) and Thailand (1.2 million) who have the largest ASEAN shares of tourism arrivals. Nor was intra-Asia travel flows ignored. They make up 30% of the ASEAN tourism industry. For example, in 1999, Japanese (3,344,800), Chinese (1,919,340), Taiwanese and Korean arrivals ranked as the first, second, fourth and sixth largest arrivals respectively in ASEAN. In consequence, the ASEAN NTOs gave priority to the facilitation of intra-ASEAN travel (asean-tourism.com 2002; aseansec.org 2002).

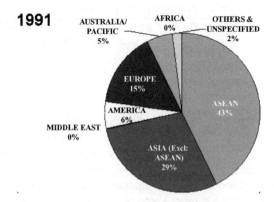

Figure 3.6: Origins of international visitor arrivals in ASEAN 1991. *Source:* www.asean-tourism.com 2002.

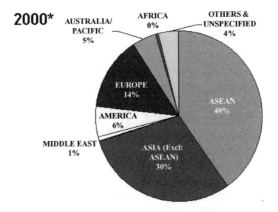

Figure 3.7: Origins of international visitor arrivals in ASEAN 2000. *Source:* www.asean-tourism.com 2002.

However, the bomb blast in Bali in Indonesia in October 2002 where an estimated 90% of all four and five-star hotels are foreign owned, and the SARS outbreak in Singapore has changed forever the pattern of tourism in the region, setting ASEAN tourism policy a challenge of Herculean proportions.

Greater Mekong Sub region

Four other Southeast Asian Greater Mekong Sub region (GMS) countries Cambodia; Laos; Myanmar; and Thailand have signed a tourism cooperation accord. The agreement envisages close cooperation among the four countries in various fields among them tourism multilateral cooperation. Thailand, for example, coordinated with its neighboring ASEAN countries and the Greater Mekong Sub region to promote regional tourist destinations. More products and services were also specially designed to attract specific market segments (Asia Times 2001). For example, tourism in Cambodia, which is one of the poorest countries, launched a new tourism strategy to position Cambodia as a leading culture and nature tourism destination. According to a study entitled The *Future of Tourism* (Muqbil 2001), over the last few years, the Cambodian government has created more favorable conditions for investors by enacting new laws to improve the competitiveness of service suppliers and liberalize trade in services (Asia Times 2001). Similarly Myanmar, one of the last two ASEAN countries still under a military government continues to face the stigma of being a dictatorship under economic sanctions from both the U.S. and Europe. Hence, while the country is known to be one of the region's most attractive destinations in terms of culture, nature and historic heritage, many visitors avoid going there as a political statement expressing their opposition to Myanmar government policies. To develop its tourism industry, Myanmar has signed tourism cooperation agreements with Cambodia, Laos, Thailand, Vietnam and China and has worked very closely, among others, with the Singapore Tourism Promotion Board (Asia Times 2001; Picard & Wood 1997).

Oceania

Oceania refers imprecisely to the lands of the Pacific Ocean such as Australia; New Zealand; the Malay Archipelago; Micronesia; Polynesia; Melanesia; New Guinea; and Papua New Guinea (Universal Dictionary 1994). Its tourism infrastructure is dominated by Australia and New Zealand whose economies, supported by lower interest rates, remain steadfast despite general weaknesses in the region (www.worldinformation.com 2002).

Australia

Australia has a prosperous Western-style capitalist economy, the equal of some of the dominant West European economies. However, while it has suffered from low growth and high unemployment characterizing the OECD countries in the early 1990s, and the recent financial problems in East Asia, since the mid-1990s the economy has nevertheless expanded at a solid 4% annual growth (OECD 2002).

Its tourism industry divides its responsibilities between the national and state governments established in the *Statement of Government Objectives and Responsibilities in Tourism* set out in the *Tourism Minister's Council Agreement* of 1976 (Australian Government Enquiry into Tourism 1987 from Hall 1994). While the national government tourism agencies have prime responsibility for the formulation and implementation of policies which operate at national level, and for the international dimensions of tourism, the states and territories have the responsibility for the promotion and marketing of state attractions and for the development of tourism facilities through such measures as land zoning, planning control and licensing (Hall 1994: 26).

Pro-rata Australia's tourism industry makes a larger contribution to the national economy than either the USA or the Canadian tourism industries. Furthermore, domestic visitors account for 80% of total tourism expenditure in Australia, with 50% of all tourism spend spent in regional Australia, reversing the trend whereby people, money and resources tend to flow from such areas into the cities. The almost 4.8 million overseas visitors is derived from just 19 countries (see Table 3.2), accounting for 1% in terms of its share of the present international tourism market (www.industry.gov.au/content/policy.cfm 2002).

Recognising the increasing power and impact of tourism to its economy, Australia established the Australian Tourist Commission (ATC) in 1987, and in 1991 appointed a senior minister responsible solely for tourism to the cabinet (Youell 1998: 219). In common with the U.K., but almost 20 years later, it had taken the decision to replace the existing private sector tourism organisation that had been subsidised heavily by government. Since then, tourism has been the responsibility of various different ministries which nevertheless have had a propensity to produce tourism strategies that were the result of extensive consultation, exemplifying its interest group and network credentials. However, in 1996, recognising that tourism includes such a wide and diverse range of functions, verging on the functions of so many other ministries the Department of Tourism was abolished and replaced with the Department of Industry, Science and Tourism (Elliott 1997: 63) which in itself was replaced in 2002 by the Department of Industry, Tourism and Resources.

Table 3.2: International tourism overseas visitor arrivals 2001/2002.

Source country	Number of visitors	Average annual growth 1999/2000 to 2001/2002	Market share
New Zealand	787,800	1.0%	16.5%
Japan	659,300	−3.3%	13.8%
United Kingdom	627,100	6.4%	13.2%
United States of America	424,300	−1.5%	8.9%
Singapore	295,800	3.3%	6.2%
Korea	181,100	14.0%	3.8%
China	172,300	28.0%	3.6%
Malaysia	154,300	2.5%	3.2%
Hong Kong (SAR of China)	148,700	−0.2%	3.1%
Germany	136,900	−3.5%	2.9%
Taiwan	99,100	−16.2%	2.1%
Indonesia	94,600	5.4%	2.0%
Canada	93,000	8.0%	2.0%
Thailand	80,100	8.5%	1.7%
South Africa	55,700	−1.7%	1.2%
Netherlands	54,500	−0.9%	1.1%
France	51,800	−1.7%	1.1%
Ireland	50,600	7.1%	1.1%
India	47,100	10.6%	1.0%
Total	4,768,300	1.2%	100.0%

Source: Overseas Arrivals and Departures Data, ABS, Cat No 3401.0.

Among the various departments' initiatives has been the 1988 discussion paper, *Directions for Tourism*. A further background paper was released in 1991, and the strategy *Tourism: Australia's Passport to Growth; A National Tourism Strategy* was released in 1992 (Elliott 1997: 76–104). Nevertheless, in November 1996, the Federal Government announced its commitment to develop a *National Tourism Plan* to provide a policy framework for the development of Australia's tourism industry to the year 2005 (Tourism Facts, Tourism Industry trends 1996). It was released in June 1998 as a National Action Plan for Tourism *Tourism — A Ticket to the 21st Century*, setting the direction for tourism policy development and industry planning into the new millennium. Meanwhile, a discussion paper released in 2002 *Australian Government 10 year strategic plan for tourism discussion paper 2002* (2002) recognised fundamentally that generally, the further a market is away from Australia, the greater the visitor expenditure, over a longer period of time, yielding a higher average expenditure per person; meaning that something that could be construed as a weakness was, if marketed properly, virtually a strength (Department of Industry, Tourism and Resources 2002).

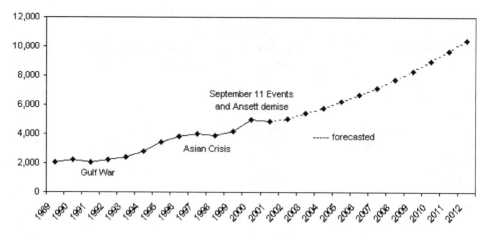

Figure 3.8: Projected international visitors (000s) 1989–2012. *Source:* Australian Tourism Forecasting Council (2002).

This partly accounts for Australia's capacity to capture a higher proportion of world tourism revenue, combined with an inordinately forecast future growth. For example, prior to Bali, ATC research (2002) revealed that the 2000 Olympic Games publicity increased the likelihood of people travelling to Australia with visitors expected to double in five years. Meanwhile, the Australian Tourism Forecasting Council (2002) expects around 10.4 million visitors per year to arrive in Australia by 2012 (see Figure 3.8), a figure it expects to double over the following decade. Furthermore, domestic tourism is also expected to grow by 20% over the same period.

Although the Bali impact has yet to take effect, and may mean even more Australians vacationing in their own country, the overall forecast growth in tourism has many implications for the industry, the wider business community and the government. For example, the capacity to accommodate the forecast growth does not currently exist. The impact of additional visitors to Australia, together with the growth in domestic tourism, will affect the whole tourism industry as well as regional communities dependent on tourism. It will also expose pressure points, in terms of both the adequacy of tourism infrastructure and the ability of particular destinations to cope sustainably with extra visitors and yet still offer a high quality tourism experience.

Africa

Africa is the second largest continent to Asia, consisting mostly of high, monotonous plateau, which drop dramatically to coastal plains, with a very short coastline for its area, few inlets and deep harbours (Philip's Illustrated Atlas of the World 1988). In the 20th century economic performance in Africa was mixed which was the result of the fact that more generalised economic development continued to be prevented by poor infrastructure, under-investment, political instability, and armed conflict. However, African governments answered these challenges with renewed commitment to regional integration, including the replacement of the Organisation of African Unity (OAU) with the African Union (AU). Nevertheless, political intransigence and economic protectionism remain significant obstacles in the path to African unity, as well as the mounting AIDS epidemic and high level of external debt (www.worldinformation.com 2002). However, perhaps the greatest barrier in any attempt towards attracting more visitors to Africa was the need for reduction in armed conflict within and, more importantly, between countries, combined with continuing famine in some countries. Zambia, for example, where the governments designated the 2002 food shortage a national disaster; Zimbabwe where invasions of white-owned land and plans to seize more farms for blacks caused a massive reduction in grain production which left six million Zimbabweans reliant on food aid; Mozambique where a combination of droughts and floods affected 100,000 households; Lesotho, where in April 2002 the government declared a state of famine; and, Swaziland whose 200,000 population were on the verge of starvation (Sunday Herald 16 June 2002). The November 2002 terrorist bombings in Mombassa, Kenya accentuated further the situation.

Zimbabwe

The institutionalised economic reform programme embarked on by the Zimbabwean Government from 1991 failed to yield the desired results in Zimbabwe because, in common with most developing countries, Zimbabwe concerned itself with the need to address national macroeconomic fundamentals at the expense of more holistic approaches. Although this policy resulted in substantial growth of the tourism sector, it failed to institute policies and strategies to address key issues of equity and sustainability. Furthermore, it neglected the fact that the involvement and full participation of local communities was an important element for the sustainability of the tourism sector (Dhlodlo 2002).

This was compounded by the crisis brought on by the Mugabe government's policy to usurp white owned farms which ultimately deterred potential tourists. Up until then, and despite failures to achieve the intended goals of economic reform, the tourism sector attained tremendous growth, and was until the late nineties the fastest growing sector in Zimbabwe ranking fourth after manufacturing, mining and agriculture. The sector was also the third largest foreign currency earner in Zimbabwe, and apart from South Africa, Zimbabwe was the only sub-Saharan country in the nineties to receive over a million tourists (www.worldtravelguide.net 2002).

The rapid growth of tourism in Zimbabwe was attributable to the attainment of peace after independence in 1980 and various measures introduced during the reform process. These measures included the devaluation of the local currency combined with trade, investment and financial liberalisation in general. It was quite evident, however, that while the reform programme identified the need for growth in the tourism sector, no specific measures were included to stimulate further development in a sustainable and equitable manner. For example, the tourism sector was largely dependent on wildlife and other natural resources whose shrinking habitat was basically shared with local communities. However, inequitable distribution of benefits to local communities, in this regard, and Zimbabwe's inability to create sector-specific policies and strategies for more equitable and

Table 3.3: International arrivals by mode of arrival.

Mode of arrival	1997	1998	1999	2000	2001
Cruise Ship	2,678	14,183	34,130	58,131	48,116
Sea	11,239	11,465	11,884	11,312	8,713
Air	98,208	108,568	115,089	131,634	133,775
Overland	243,632	192,211	154,463	168,800	53,467
TOTALS	349,277	304,562	288,098	326,642	195,955

Note: The table international arrivals includes all arrivals except Belizeans and less returning residents.
Source: Immigration Department, www.belizetourism.org/arrival.html

sustainable development, combined with the atrocities sanctioned by the Mugabwe regime, has seen tourism arrivals reduced dramatically (Dhlodlo 2002), and even the 2003 Cricket World Cup drawn into controversy over the English cricket team's refusal to play there.

Belize

The strength of tourism in Belize lies with the diversity of natural and cultural attractions, and although the statistics fail to correspond, Tables 3.3 and 3.4, and Figure 3.9, reveal sufficient information in regard to the scale of Belizean tourism, the stagnation of international arrivals, the decline in tourists traveling overland, and the impact of September 11.

Belize's tourism strategy (Strategic vision for Belize tourism in the new millennium 2002) was prepared with the expectation of stimulating economic growth, while protecting the country's environmental and heritage resources, and ensuring benefits to the local people. On this basis, Belize's Ministry of Tourism adopted a policy focused on responsible tourism. Responsible tourism, in common with governance, is an emerging integrative approach to public policy-making and is the key guiding principle for tourism development

Table 3.4: International arrivals by nationality.

Country of origin	1997	1998	1999	2000	2001
USA	106,420	113,786	136,569	104,717	106,292
Canada	13,426	12,278	11,681	9,205	9,492
United Kingdom	12,661	12,408	10,832	8,007	9,313
Europe	34,828	31,478	32,262	22,893	23,947
Other	137,227	118,148	135,298	50,944	46,911
TOTALS	304,562	288,098	326,642	195,766	195,955

Note: The table international arrivals includes all arrivals except Belizeans and less returning residents.
Source: Immigration Department, www.belizetourism.org/arrival.html

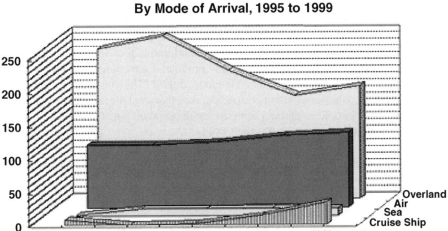

Figure 3.9: International arrivals by mode of arrival. *Source:* http://www.belizetourism. org/arrival.html

in the future, and despite its difficulties it was to its credit that Belize pursued such a policy.

Rather than attempting to define a type of tourism, responsible tourism refers to an ethos and a set of practices that chart a sensible course for all types of tourism, ranging from what may be called deep eco-tourism at one end of the scale to more conventional mass tourism at the other. In fact it may be defined as a way of carrying out tourism planning to ensure that benefits are optimally distributed among stakeholders and that tourism resources are managed to achieve optimum benefits for all.

The challenges, therefore, facing Belize's tourism industry included the need to develop strategically and upgrade its product; the need to maintain the pristine quality of its environment; the need to market effectively to high-potential, high-yield, niche markets; and the need to forge stronger linkages between the public and private sectors, non-governmental organizations and communities around the country (Strategic vision for Belize tourism in the new millennium 2002).

South Africa

The achievement of political democracy through the first democratic election in April 1994 signalled dramatic transformation of South African society, for during apartheid, South Africa used tourism to create favourable impressions for those countries which imposed trade sanctions (Pizam & Mansfield 1996 from Hall 2001: 22).

The improvement of life of all South Africans, and the quest to erase social inequalities particularly for the previously disadvantaged groups, became the stated priority of the new government. The process of formulating a tourism policy for South Africa occurred within this context. In consequence, the process of policy formulation and appropriate ways of governing the country was under constant scrutiny (Simmons 2002).

1994   In 1994, the Tourism Minister established the Interim Tourism Task Team (ITTT), consisting of representatives from national and provincial government; business; labour; and urban as well as rural communities. He charged the ITTT with the responsibility of initiating a working paper on a tourism vision, and with that went the principles under which a new tourism policy could be defined combined with proposed structures to carry out such a policy (SA ITTT Green Paper on Tourism 1995).

1996   Following the ITTT *Tourism Green Paper* in 1995, in 1996 a White Paper entitled *The Development and Promotion of Tourism in South Africa* was approved. The document proposed a total restructuring of the tourism industry including renaming the South African Tourism Board, creating a government tourism fund, and identifying presidential tourism projects for the provinces. It also suggested that standards and grading should be carried out by an independent body or the restructured Tourism Board (White Paper — The Development and Promotion of Tourism in South 1996), and which came into being in 2002.

The White Paper also identified that tourism had the potential to increase its then contribution of 4.7% of GDP to 8% of GDP by the year 2000, a figure that has as yet to materialize, and to 10% by 2005. It was estimated that should such growth be achieved, a million or more jobs could be created directly and indirectly, therefore improving quality of life for a substantial proportion of the electorate. It also recognized the constraints on growth such as inadequate resourcing and funding; lack of infrastructure; especially in the rural areas, as well as the growing levels of crime and violence which deterred potential tourists (White Paper: The Development and Promotion of Tourism in South 1996).

1999   In 1997 the Department had published *Tourism in Gear* and by 1999 South Africa launched a *Tourism Action Plan* (1999), the blueprint for the international marketing of South Africa as a highly desirable world tourism destination. The R180-million budget was the largest budget for international tourism marketing since Satour's (the international tourism marketing arm of government) inception in 1947. Furthermore, it forecast growth as revealed in Table 3.5 (Launch of Tourism Action Plan, Satour 1999).

The plan was the result of an historic co-operation agreement signed between government and business which led to the formation of the Tourism Forum. The Forum set up the Satour Marketing Partnership Committee (SMPC) to draw up a collaborative international marketing strategy aimed at boosting international tourism arrivals to South Africa.

2001   During 2001 guidelines were developed to provide a national framework for the tourism industry to exercise its commitment towards the principles of responsible tourism. These principles were embodied in the 1996 *White Paper on the Development and Promotion of Tourism in South Africa*. The White Paper concluded that tourism development in South Africa had previously largely been a missed opportunity, and that the earlier focus on a narrow market had reduced the potential of the industry to spawn entrepreneurship and to create new services.

Table 3.5: Projected South African tourism growth 1997–2002.

Projection 1998–2002	1997	1998	1999	2000	2001	2002
Tourists from Africa (+8% p.a.)	380,000	410,400	443,232	478,691	516,986	558,000
Tourists from Overseas (+12% p.a.)	120,000	134,400	150,528	168,591	188,822	212,000
TOTAL	500,000	544,800	593,760	647,282	705,808	770,000

Source: Satour 2002.

2002   In 2002 the Minister of Environmental Affairs and Tourism launched a number of initiatives among them a partnership with the private sector which formulated a strategy aimed at transforming the industry. The action plan of the strategy identified short, medium and long-term priorities that the Department intended to implement over a three-year period. This, combined with the new political democracy created commercial opportunities the tourism industry had been deprived of for a long time, and led to some improvement so much so that South Africa earned in excess of R7 billion from tourism in 2002. However, domestic tourism was still focused on the wealthier strata of South African society. For example, the majority of South Africans had not benefited from South Africa's vast tourist resources, nor have communities recognised fully the large untapped potential for tourism in the areas in which they live. Furthermore, although growing emerging tourism businesses from previously disadvantaged communities had been a high priority for government since 1994, it is only since the new Millennium that there had been visible evidence of increased transformation efforts by both government and the private sector. While there was evidence of an increased number of emerging small, medium and micro enterprises (SMMEs), transformation remains mainly at grassroots level. This meant that the new challenge for South Africa lay in elevating these businesses into sustainable, established enterprises that continued to grow and thrive in this highly competitive industry.

Morocco, Algeria, Tunisia, Libya

There are still examples of countries that have not fully grasped the importance of tourism to their economy. For example, while its near neighbours Morocco and Tunisia have embraced tourism, Libya's Colonel Gadaffi's antipathy to the west and the west's abhorrence of his regime has militated against any kind of tourism development in Libya.

Furthermore, since independence, Algeria's hard-line Arab socialist policies, currency restrictions and the difficulty of obtaining tourism visas have been further disincentives to tourism, as has been recent fundamentalist political violence targeting foreigners, particularly North Americans (Ady 1997). This has decimated what little tourism there might have been, and current Middle East tensions mean that for Algeria and Libya, in particular, tourism is likely to remain a negligible part of their economies for the foreseeable future.

Europe

Europe is the world's second smallest land area after Oceania, with 7% of the globe's landmass, 15% of the globe's population, and is the second most populous continent after Asia (Philip's Illustrated Atlas of the World 1988).

As the New Millennium dawned the European Union (EU) generally enjoyed increased prosperity, supported by strong economic growth, low inflation and falling unemployment. However, the economic slowdown that emerged in the U.S. in early 2001 soon had a negative effect on the rest of the world. The terrorist attacks on the U.S. on 11 September 2001, followed by a US-led military attack on Afghanistan in October 2001, produced further uncertainty in the global economic outlook. For example, according to the WTO (2002) international arrivals reduced by −0.7% in Europe in 2001, with the United Kingdom's fall of −6.6% compounded by foot-and-mouth. However, this was offset by gains in the Eastern Mediterranean and in Southern Europe countries all benefiting from their proximity to major generating markets. Destinations such as Spain; Greece; Austria; and France also benefited from their familiarity to most European holidaymakers, securing Spain, as indicated in Table 3.6, a firm place as the world's number two destination in 2001, despite a change in statistical methodology in 2000 that caused it to drop temporarily to third place behind the United States.

European Union

Now a conglomerate of states (and soon to expand further — for information on the accession states see Europarl www.eu/accesssion), the EU's governing body, the European Commission, in recognising the important role of tourism in the European economy, has been increasingly involved in tourism since the early 1980's. It does this in co-operation with the European Council (EC); the European Parliament; the Economic and Social Committee; the Committee of the Regions; and through the Tourism Unit DGXIII

Table 3.6: The world's top five destinations.

Rank	International tourist arrivals			
	2000 **(million)**	**Growth rate (%)** **2001*/2000**	**Est. 2001** **(million)**	**Market** **share (%)**
1. France	75.6	1.2	76.5	11.1
2. Spain	47.9	3.4	49.5	7.2
3. United States	50.9	−12.6	44.5	6.5
4. Italy	41.2	−5.0	39.1	5.7
5. China	31.2	6.2	33.2	4.8

Source: World Tourism Organization (WTO)© (Data as collected by WTO January 2002).

(Enterprise, Policy, Tourism and Social Economy). However, despite the fact that Europe has 53% of the world-wide tourism market, that it is the world's largest tourist region, that the industry accounts for 5.5% of the Union's GDP and 6% of its employment, the EC Treaty does not allow the Community to pursue a specific policy for tourism. Nevertheless Article 3(u) of the Treaty, which the *Maastricht Treaty* (1991) inserted, does authorise the Community to provide guidelines for the development of tourism as part of other policies. In this way the provisions on free movement apply equally to tourism as it does to persons; goods and services; small businesses; and regional policy. Indeed, perversely, the economic importance of tourism is such that the European institutions have justifiably focused attention on it despite the absence of a legal basis. For example, the first Council tourism resolution (10 April 1984), acknowledged the importance of tourism for European integration and invited the Commission to make proposals. A subsequent decision (Consultation procedure: CSA0278, 22 December 1986) established an advisory committee on tourism and required consultation by the Member States. In the same year a budget was established to fund a Community contribution to joint promotion efforts by Member States in markets outside the EC.

Although the aforementioned Tourism Unit DGXIII has fundamental responsibility for tourism in the European Union, as many as ten of the twenty-three Commission's Departments, the Directorates General, have some responsibility that impact upon Europe's tourism industry. Unfortunately, there is no system for coordinating tourism interests across the departments, and the countries of the EU are increasingly affected by its legislation across a number of disciplines. For example, the introduction of the Social Chapter, and changes in the labour market to meet the demands of an increasingly challenging business environment, which has necessitated government intervention e.g. financial incentives, assistance or grants.

The grants and aid tourism has received from the wider Structural Funds, especially EAGGF (European Agriculture Guidance and Guarantee Fund (guidance section)), and ERDF (European Regional Development Fund) reflect the importance of the contribution it makes to European regional development. ERDF, for example, offers financial assistance of up to 30% of the capital costs for tourism projects generated by public sector bodies within the Assisted Areas. This money can be used not only as pump priming for direct tourist attractions such as museums, but also for infrastructure development to support tourism such as airports or car parking facilities (Holloway 1998: 267). The EU also provides loans through the European Investment Bank (EIB) to small companies of less than 500 employees with interest rates lower in Assisted Areas within the EU.

For tourism in Europe, an important step forward was taken in 1986 with the establishment of the Tourism Advisory Committee (TAC), the role of which was to facilitate exchange of information, consultation and co-operation on tourism (Council Decision 86/664/EEC 22 December 1986; OJ No L 384, 31 December 1986: 52). Composed of representatives from the then 18 EEA countries the TAC provided information on the measures taken at national level in the area of tourism. Although this Committee meets several times a year, both its composition and raison d'etre will change dramatically when the accession states are admitted in 2004. Nevertheless the TAC was able to influence the Council of Ministers to declare the year 1990 The European Year of Tourism which was designed to emphasise the role of tourism and to develop a coherent policy approach (Council Decision 89/46/EEC of

21 December 1988; OJ No L 17, 21.1.1989, p. 53), along with the 1992 three year action plan (1993–1996) to assist tourism (Council Decision 92/421/EEC of 31 July 1992). Following this, in 1995/96 in order to stimulate a debate on the EU's role in tourism a Green Paper was written. However, it was not until November 2001 that the Commission presented ideas (Communication on working together for the future of European tourism 2001) on how best to exploit the European tourism sector's competitive potential, and to which we will return later.

The action plan was followed by Philoxenia (Proposal for a Council Decision on a First Multiannual Programme to Assist European Tourism 1997–2000, 30 April 1996). Philoxenia was designed to stimulate the quality and competitiveness of European tourism in order to boost growth and employment. A modified version was presented by the Commission in December 1996 taking into account amendments put forward by the European Parliament, as the Council of Ministers had not been able to reach a unanimous agreement on the proposed programme. Whereas the Commission's proposal received the favourable opinion of the other European institutions — the European Parliament; the Economic and Social Committee; and the Committee of the Regions, the Commission formally withdrew its proposal in April 2000. Instead, the Community activities representing tourism are now embedded in the Tourism and Employment process.

In the aforementioned document *Communication on working together for the future of European tourism* (2001), the Commission highlighted the need to enhance co-operation on and the consistency of tourism policies among the stakeholders involved in tourism. These included the European Commission; Member States; regional and local authorities; industry; tourism associations, and tourist destinations. The Commission aimed in particular to foster tourism's competitiveness and sustainability. This underlined tourism's contribution to sustainable development, with a special focus on environmental and cultural resources, which were high on the list of recommendations, and in accordance with Agenda 21 (a comprehensive plan of action taken globally, nationally and locally by organizations of the United Nations System, Governments, and Major Groups in every area in which humans impact on the environment) guidelines. Furthermore, and with a view to providing the tourism industry with a political platform and improving co-operation and co-ordination, an annual European Tourism Forum, a key interface with stakeholder groups, was proposed, and which first took place in December 2002. The event brought together leading representatives from the tourism industry, civil society, European Institutions, national and regional authorities dealing with tourism, and international organizations, and concentrated mainly on Agenda 21, and on contributing to the EU-wide debate and process, complementing their efforts to improve sustainable competitiveness in the European tourism sector. A further initiative, to understand the significance of tourism to the European economy particular attention was also devoted to the creation of a Community system of statistics in the sector. For example, Directive 95/57 (Consultation procedure: COS0257, 23 November 1995) set up a two-yearly programme to (unsuccessfully, as it turned out) harmonise national methods. In 2002 further consideration was given to a widespread adoption of Tourism Satellite Accounts (TSA) methodology, approved by the United Nations (UN), which allows governments to forecast the economic contribution to a national or regional economy (Mills, WTTC 2002).

Table 3.7: VAT, Deloitte Touche Study (in a BHA briefing document, hospitality and government in Scotland) (1999).

	European hotel accommodation VAT rates		
Country	**%**	**Country**	**%**
Austria	10	Ireland	13.5[a]
Belgium	6	Italy	10
Denmark	25	Luxembourg	3
Finland	6	Netherlands	6
France	5.5	Portugal	5
Germany	16	Scotland/U.K.	17.5
Greece	8	Spain	7
		Sweden	12

[a] Increased from 12.5 to 13.5% following November 2002 Budget. A further blow to the Irish tourism industry was a reduction in capital allowance relief for the sector (Garvey 2002).

The *Communication on Working together for the future of European tourism* (2001) was the final milestone of the tourism and employment process that was launched in 1998. It was the result of intensive work done since January 2000 with Member States, the industry and major civil society stakeholders, on five key issues: information; training; quality; sustainable development; and new technologies. In consequence, the Commission underlined the importance of exchanging more information and experience among interested parties, and began to prepare the implementation of the actions recommended in the communication (Communication on Working together for the future of European tourism 2001).

In essence, impacts of EU mainline policies on tourism are very considerable, in that for member countries it is by far the most important international organisation. However, the inception of the Single Market in 1993 has so far proved to be of little benefit to tourism, which was already largely a free international trade. Fiscal intervention has been unfavourable too, with VAT at high and varying rates (0–25%) in member countries (see Table 3.7), and extended to additional services such as transport. This distorts further trade and erodes Europe's competitive edge (Lickorish & Jenkins 1997: 196). In addition, intervention in labour, social and environmental regulation has burdened the industry with increased costs and the EU's emphasis on employment legislation is, for the tourism industry particularly hard to fathom. For instance, tourism became an essential part of the shift in the EU's development strategies because it was perceived as being highly labour intensive, and, according to the EU was generally agreed that it was particularly beneficial in times of difficult employment situations (Hall 1994). This was because it is a labour intensive industry, and its continuing expansion offers a valuable counterbalance to the unemployment which is devastating other sectors and the less favoured regions (Pearce 1988: 15). Also, major investment in the poorer regions and in transport through the structural and social funding programme assisted tourism developments, in some cases substantially (Lickorish & Jenkins 1997: 196).

Foot-and-mouth in Europe

A foot-and-mouth disease epidemic spread across the U.K. at the start of 2001, threatening the livelihoods of farmers, businesses and rural communities. The British government struggled to take control of the situation as over 3 million cattle were slaughtered, most burned on pyres scattered across the British countryside. The threat of foot-and-mouth spreading was taken seriously around Western Europe. For example, the EU placed a ban on U.K. livestock, meat, and diary exports; France received a temporary EU export ban following two cases of foot-and-mouth in April 2001; while the Netherlands launched an immediate vaccination programme and mass cull following a number of cases on Dutch farms (world-information.com 2002). The knock-on effect from the foot-and-mouth endemic combined with September 11 was responsible ultimately for the U.K.'s poor tourism performance in 2001, which will be addressed in Chapter 4.

Estonia

At the end of 2000 the administrative structure of tourism in Estonia was reorganised for the first time post its break from the Soviet Union. As with all else in Estonia and its neighbouring countries Latvia and Lithuania, this was in preparation for membership of the EU. As a result tourism functions were distributed between different institutions: the Ministry of Economic Affairs (strategy, tourism policy and economic analysis); Consumer Protection Board (supervision of enterprises); and, the Estonian Tourist Board (development, promotion and market research) (www.visitestonia.com/board 2002). The Ministry of Economic Affairs is also responsible for setting the policy framework of the tourism industry, while the Estonian Tourist Board (Eesti Turismiagentuur–ETB) is responsible for implementing national tourism policy. With this re-structuring ETB became one of the agencies of a business support foundation Enterprise Estonia (Estonian Entrepreneurship Development Foundation) (www.eas.ee/eng 2002).

The development of Estonia's tourism sector mirrored the development of the country following its independence from the USSR, and tourism played a significant role in the rapid transition from ineffective planning to full-scale competition. Furthermore, neither of Estonia's neighbours Latvia nor Lithuania enjoyed the luxury of having a relatively rich neighbour such as Finland, and Estonia reaped early benefits from alcohol tourism from Finland, which helped fuel the development of the country, develop the service and tourism sectors, and balance the deficit incurred from heavily unbalanced trade (Huang 2000). Its objective now is to progress from this phase of tourism to one that does not have as negative connotations as alcohol related tourism.

Spain

Benidorm's tourism industry is important to the Spanish economy in that it accounts for 1% of Spain's GDP. However, the Spanish admit that if they had to start from scratch they would do things differently, but while they promise environmental reform and regeneration they understandably do not want to do anything that will detract from the income generated by visitors from overseas to Benidorm (Cusick 2002), a situation that compounds the problem and is becoming more redolent of many tourism destinations in Costa del Sol and Costa Blanca.

Eastern Europe

In 2000, ten former Soviet bloc countries anxiously waited for the European Union (EU) member states to ratify the Treaty of Nice, which paved the way for EU enlargement in the period 2003–2005. These countries along with Malta, Cyprus and Turkey were desperately trying to meet the 31 economic, legal and social admission criteria. Since accession negotiations began in 1988–1989, EU regional aid had been vital to the development of these former Comecon states into free-market economies, with aid to grow their tourism economies among the most vital to them. By 2000, the ten transitional economies — Bulgaria, the Czech Republic, Estonia, Hungary, Latvia, Lithuania which had a lengthy Law on Tourism, Poland, Romania, Slovakia and Slovenia — had seen substantially increased GDP growth, lower inflation and unemployment and increased foreign investment, exports and international arrivals, a situation that would be boosted further by EU membership.

The Americas

The Americas' landmass and islands lie between the main bodies of the Atlantic and Pacific Oceans. With 28% of the world's land, the Americas approach Asia in size, but have only just over a quarter of its population, and are sub-divided into the highly prosperous North America and South America (Universal Dictionary 1994) where in the late 1990s, followed by the terrorist atrocities of September 11 2002, the economies caused massive problems for the region which it has yet to overcome.

North America

North America is the economies of Canada and the USA, the latter *the* superpower dominant world power and largest tourism economy. For example, in tourism terms the USA is undoubtedly not only among the world leaders in terms of international arrivals it is also among those countries that export more tourists to the remainder of the world. Furthermore, North America has been more successful in overall economic terms than Europe. Among other factors, this is because the core of the typical European economy is still organised on the corporatist model while the USA, in particular, is more pluralist.

USA

Pre-Tourism Policy

Until the advent of the Second World War the USA was less concerned with overseas economies than with those within its own boundaries, and with its own tourists than those from other continents. This was evidenced by the fact that in 1872 it had established national parks for its own citizens in areas of outstanding beauty (Elliott 1997: 25), that the vast country had more than enough attractions for its people without leaving their own shores, and by the Fair Labor Standards Act of 1938, which brought in the forty hour week for workers allowing them more leisure time (Elliott 1997: 26). However, following World War II Americans grew more prone to travelling abroad (only a small percentage of the American population are reputed to own a passport (10%)), and the wealth and cultural impact of those that did travel, had an immediate, liberating and financially beneficial effect on world economies.

Furthermore, until it acknowledged a large deficit in its tourism trade, the USA government encouraged its citizens to travel as part of its effort to stimulate the economies of Europe in the reconstruction period after the Second World War. For example, between 1949 and 1960 the U.S. travel deficit in terms of international visitors virtually tripled, from $360 million to $1.2 billion, a situation that could not be sustained (Edgell 1999).

The International Travel Act/ National Tourism Policy Act — USTTA

In 1961 the U.S. Travel Service was created in response to this growing travel deficit. Nevertheless, it was 1974 before a national tourism policy study that reflected concern for the deficit was approved through legislation that brought in the *International Travel Act* (USA Congress 1977, USA Congress 1978). It took a further seven years before the *National Tourism Policy Act* of 1981 was passed by Congress, and became law. This act created the United States Travel and Tourism Administration (USTTA), which replaced the United States Travel Service (USTS) as the nation's government tourism office. However, despite the new travel service's introduction, as more than 20 federal agencies possessed tourism programmes in addition to USTTA, of which 10 had significant responsibilities, the federal tourism promotion effort was fragmented (USA National Study on Trade and Services 1984; United States Council of State Governments, Tourism: State Structure, Organisations and Support 1979). Nevertheless, during this time travel and tourism evolved from an emerging sector to become an established leader in a modern services economy. For example, in terms of travel and tourism it grew from a $26 billion industry in 1986 to a $90 billion one in 1996, while its export contributions to the U.S. economy grew nearly 250% (Doggett 2000).

International Trade Administration (ITA)

In 1996 the U.S. Congress abolished USTTA, and placed the burden of governmental tourism policy in the hands of the individual states and the private sector (Edgell 1999: 9). The USA was not alone in coming to the conclusion that pressing social and economic needs took precedence over tourism, and countries such as Canada and Belgium took similar decisions in 1997 (Youell 1998: 3). Meanwhile, under the auspices of the Office of Travel and Tourism Industries (OTTI) the agency's critical tourism functions were transferred to the International Trade Administration (ITA), the structure of which is revealed in Figure 3.10 (ITA 2002).

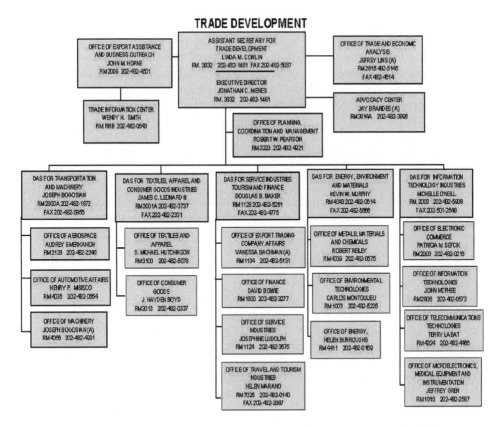

Figure 3.10: The U.S. Trade Development Department. *Source:* ITA 2002.

The Office of Travel and Tourism Industries (OTTI)

In 2001 a new post Deputy Assistant Secretary for Service Industries, Tourism and Finance was created, managing four separate offices, which develop trade policy and implement trade promotion activities for U.S. businesses in the service, tourism and finance industries. The Tourism Industries office was renamed the Office of Travel and Tourism Industries (OTTI) and merged with the offices of Service Industries and Finance, but very much retained the infrastructure described above (ITA 2002).

OTTI fosters tourism trade development and its Deputy Assistant Secretary represents the United States in tourism-related meetings with foreign government officials. It also serves as the principal point-of-contact for the U.S. tourism industry on policy and tourism trade development issues. It is also responsible for furthering the recommendations in the national tourism strategy from the White House Conference on Travel and Tourism (ITA 2002), and takes up research and technical assistance, although it does not market inbound international tourism: that role is instead assigned to new public/private sector partnerships.

According to its inaugural statement, OTTI was assigned three primary functions designed to increase the number of tourism exporters by providing research, and fostering economic development opportunities. It also provides research information; technical assistance and policy coordination primarily to state/local tourism offices and economic development entities, airport authorities and other government agencies.

Meanwhile, its responsibilities are divided among three groups. The Tourism Development Group became the official source for international travel data. The Tourism Policy Coordination Division represents the U.S. government in international trade negotiations and organizations and implemented bilateral agreements. It also houses the Tourism Policy Council, composed of the heads of 13 federal agencies and Amtrak which was designed to coordinate federal tourism policies. Meanwhile, the Office of the Deputy Assistant Secretary serves as the primary point of contact for the tourism industry of policy, international commercial diplomacy and tourism trade development issues.

The Tourism Development Group (TDG)

The TDG was responsible for economic policy and technical assistance for tourism development, for responding to thousands of requests from the public sector and private industry clients through an electronic customer inquiry system, the establishment of an electronic database of international statistics on the Internet, and to generate research report sales from the industry to help offset the actual cost of the research programs. It was the goal of the group to increase the number of businesses and communities exporting travel and tourism products by providing statistical research, policy coordination, advocacy, and technical assistance to companies and communities seeking to start or expand their tourism-related businesses abroad (WTO 2001).

The Tourism Policy Coordination Group (TPCG)

The TPCG serves as the secretariat and administrative arm of the TPC, and is composed of the Secretaries and heads of 13 federal agencies plus Amtrak. This group is also responsible for representing the U.S. government in trade and investment negotiations, and for representing it at conferences (Doggett 2000).

The Tourism Policy Council (TPC)

The Tourism Policy Council (TPC) is the interagency, policy coordinating committee composed of the leaders of nine Federal agencies and the president of the U.S. National Tourism Organization (USNTO), who serves as a non-voting member. The TPC members work cooperatively to ensure that the national interest in tourism is fully considered in federal decision-making affecting tourism development.

The TPC coordinates national policies and programs relating to international travel and tourism, recreation, and national heritage resources which involve federal agencies. The

Council seeks to work with the private sector and state and local governments on issues and problems that require Federal involvement. The TPC was created to coordinate federal tourism policies and to ensure that the national interest in tourism was fully considered in federal decisions that affected tourism development (Doggett 2000).

All of these agencies minds were concentrated by the events of 11 September 2001, which had a significant, negative effect on the global economy in general, and the U.S. economy in particular, as they are by SARS, and the fallout of war in Iraq. For example, according to the WTO (2002) international arrivals dropped by −7%, reflecting a trend that began well before September 11 due to economic problems in Brazil, Argentina and Japan, as well as decreasing levels of consumer confidence in the United States. Inbound and outbound tourism to the United States also suffered badly as a result of the attacks. For example, arrivals for 2001 fell by almost −13% and countries dependent on U.S. tourists also suffered, and much of what the above agencies are doing at present is to redress the situation, hopefully to the situation prior to September 11, when as Table 3.8 reveals the USA was aiming to realise its tourism potential. However, this is compounded further by the war in Iraq, SARS, and ongoing global uncertainty as to where terrorists will strike next.

Central America and the Caribbean

The Central American States are those countries of Latin America lying between Mexico and Columbia, bordered on one side by the Pacific and on the other by the Caribbean. Mexico, Central America and the Caribbean specialise in catering for U.S. visitors, where perhaps the greatest impact of the terrorist attacks of 11 September took effect. In the Caribbean, where the growth of the foreign-owned-all-inclusive resorts has denied locals access to public beaches (Cusick 2002), the tourism sector contracted by between 20 and 60% immediately after the disaster, with a significant decline in air travel. Furthermore, the hotel occupation rate for Jamaica was estimated at little over 10% in the fourth quarter of 2001, while a third of all hotel rooms in Cuba were closed. Nevertheless, although largely dependent on U.S. consumer behaviour, by the beginning of 2002, confidence returned to the sector. For example, visitor numbers from the EU remained buoyant due to promotion campaigns and many U.S. tourists chose to visit the Caribbean rather than resorts further afield, such as the Middle East (WTO 2002).

South America

South America is the land that straddles the North and South Atlantic to the East and South Pacific to the West stretching from Venezuela and Columbia in the north to Chile and Argentina in the south (Universal Dictionary 1994).

Argentina

Because of a military dictatorship that lasted almost 50 years, the war over the Falkland/Malvinas islands, subsequent economic crises and little investment in tourism

Table 3.8: Forecast of international travel to the United States.

Origin	2001e	% Change 01/00	2002p	% Change 02/01	2003p	% Change 03/02	2004p	% Change 04/03	2005p	% Change 05/04	% Change 05/01
Canada	13,518	−8%	13,711	1%	14,884	9%	15,869	7%	16,962	7%	25%
Mexico	9,558	−7%	10,175	6%	10,942	8%	11,891	9%	12,870	8%	35%
Overseas	22,425	−14%	22,448	0%	24,348	8%	26,179	8%	27,735	6%	24%
Europe	9,815	−15%	9,753	−1%	10,728	10%	11,514	7%	12,210	6%	24%
Asia	6,378	−16%	6,557	3%	7,026	7%	7,588	8%	8,017	6%	26%
South America	2,605	−11%	2,538	−3%	2,712	7%	2,934	8%	3,125	7%	20%
Caribbean	1,257	−6%	1,284	2%	1,368	7%	1,431	5%	1,480	3%	18%
Central America	807	−2%	822	2%	893	9%	955	7%	1,004	5%	24%
Oceania	622	−15%	642	3%	709	10%	768	8%	817	6%	31%
Middle East	652	−7%	551	−16%	588	7%	644	10%	718	11%	10%
Africa	290	−2%	300	3%	324	8%	346	7%	362	5%	25%
Grand Total	45,502	−11%	46,334	2%	50,174	8%	53,939	8%	57,568	7%	27%

Forecast of International Travel to the United States (estimates in thousands)

Source: OTTI 2001.

infrastructure, and although 70% of visitors only visit Buenos Aires, Argentina's tourism market has only begun to bear fruit over the last 10 years. However, in 2002, economic instability plagued Southern American countries with the debt crisis in Argentina and Brazil, investment flows drying up and a recession weakening the region's economies. As a whole, the region's GDP stagnated, and the decline of Latin America's third-largest economy triggered a massive devaluation of its currency, the peso, ending ten years of parity with the dollar, and caused a social crisis that has engulfed the country and brought down successive governments (www.worldinformation.com 2002). However, with the election of a new President, a new panorama for the country, in general, and tourism in particular being projected, and the new tourism minister working with the private sector in order to develop an exportation tourist consortium, integrated strategies between all the actors who participate in business are developing a true tourism state policy in order to create a National Tourism Plan which will bring to Argentina the necessary incomes to consolidate a economic sustainable model through the years (www.sector.gov.ar 2002).

Summary

In its simplest terms, tourism policy links the planning function and political goals for tourism into a concrete set of guidelines to give direction (Edgell 1999: x). In this chapter numerous such examples of policies, strategies, structures, and approaches have been revealed, analysed and explained. In doing so, it was important to build upon the various frameworks and theories discussed in Chapter 2, and which will inform subsequent chapters. To that end, this chapter aligns these with policy approaches as they apply to individual countries and destinations, as will Chapter 4 which relates specifically to U.K. and Irish tourism policy, and Chapter 5 which focuses on Scottish tourism policy. Nevertheless, it is evident that with a few exceptions countries and destinations worldwide recognise tourism as being a crucial and essential component part of their economic development policy, but due to the paramount importance of other issues such as education, social services, and health tourism per se has been relegated in most countries as unworthy of a seat in its own right at cabinet tables. Nevertheless, due to a combination of factors, such as the advent of globalisation; the expectations of an increasingly well-travelled, affluent and sophisticated clientele; fast-moving and unanticipated world events such as September 11; and, environmental disasters such as foot-and-mouth; all of which appear more than ever out of the control of individual governments, governments are being driven relentlessly to alter their approach to tourism public policy-making, and to integrate such policies with any number of complementary policies.

In local terms, the fact that there was no apparent policy to deal with the impact of foot-and-mouth disease on tourism in the U.K., or contingency for the fallout from terrorist attacks such as those in New York and Washington, Bali and Mombassa, or indeed SARS, speaks volumes about the U.K. government, as well as the Scottish parliament, and the Welsh and Northern Ireland Assemblies' unpreparedness for such events. It also highlights not only the complacency of the U.K. government that any number of policies and strategies were in place that could deal with the most serious of disasters (from nuclear attack to a meteorite hurtling to earth), but also that intra-governmental complimentary policies brought on by devolution were not of a cohesive nature. In essence, despite the lessons learned, the U.K. government, the Scottish Executive and the Welsh and Irish Assemblies have reacted to such events as opposed to pro-actively developing strategies and policies to deal with them. Instead policies are being driven, as irrevocably most governments policies are, by a short-term ideological focus that is intent in doing whatever is necessary to secure enough votes to remain in power.

Admittedly, as much as a network of terrorists' hell bent on destroying western civilisation or a lone farmer who covers up the existence of foot-and-mouth until it is too late and it becomes an epidemic is difficult for governments to deal with, the electorate's expectation is that among other things that is what governments and policies are for. Similarly, the electorate's expectations of governments' dealings with large market driven transnational corporations is that government policy as it reflects peoples' wishes takes precedence over all else. However, much of what such corporations do, and which is on behalf of their shareholders and not the electorate of the country in which they have invested, and which they take money out of, is also beyond the sphere of influence of governments. This results in a continual dilemma for governments in that they have in the first instance to attract such companies while extracting enough revenue without discouraging them, or forcing them to locate elsewhere where the economic environment is less draconian.

All of the above results in a multiplicity of approaches to tourism policy-making, a number of which sit uneasily within the formal models of politics and policy-making as identified in Chapter 2. Some were driven by the market, such as the USA and Sweden both of which disbanded their NTOs in the nineties, or were ideologically driven such as China, the former USSR, and Cuba, while others such as Germany, Switzerland and Austria were corporatist in nature, like Scotland of the opinion that because of its economic, environmental and social impacts, tourism was too vital to the economy to leave to market forces.

Meanwhile, for third world countries tourism is not only a vital element of their economy, it is also a vehicle for improving quality of life and erasing social inequalities, as is evidenced in South Africa where tourism policy pre and post-apartheid is recognisably and experientially very different. Zimbabwe's current tourism policy, however, seems almost regressive. Its inability to create sector-specific policies and strategies for more equitable and sustainable development, and the crisis brought on by the Mugabe government's policy to usurp white owned farms, have ultimately deterred potential tourists, seen tourism arrivals reduced, and produced an inequitable distribution of benefits to Zimbabwe's local communities.

In essence, although Chapter 2 constructed a public policy analysis for tourism which has been applied to this chapter, it is clear from the research above that there is no perfect policy for tourism. In effect, a country or destination's tourism policy reflects the environment in which it is operating both within and outwith its borders, much of the latter outwith its control, and which is changing constantly.

Chapter 4

The Development, Structure, and Public Policy of Tourism in England, Wales, Northern Ireland, and Republic of Ireland

Introduction

This chapter discusses the development, structure and public policy of tourism in the twentieth century in terms of how it is applied in England, Wales, Northern Ireland and the Republic of Ireland (the development of Scottish tourism and the ensuing tourism policy is discussed in Chapter 5). It is complicated by legislation enacted in 1999 which devolved certain powers to the Welsh and Northern Ireland Assemblies in Cardiff and Belfast respectively, and the Scottish Parliament in Edinburgh, while other powers such as Defence, Foreign policy, and Social Security were reserved to Westminster. However, in comparison to the Scottish Parliament and the Northern Ireland Assembly, the Welsh Assembly does not have legislative powers. Nevertheless, and although tourism in all three countries is a devolved matter, other policies with which tourism policy interfaces, and which influence it greatly such as Fiscal, Employment and certain aspects of Transport and the Environment are reserved. Furthermore, these responsibilities lie with other departments for whom tourism is, in many instances, a matter of lesser importance. This causes unnecessary tensions, and also unrealistic expectations of the Assemblies' and Parliament's ability to deliver particular, if not all, aspects of tourism policy successfully.

Moreover, because of the Republic of Ireland's proximity, its reputed success, its historical relationship, and its straightforward comparability with the U.K., and in order that the U.K. learns lessons from it, this chapter also addresses the Republic's development of tourism and tourism public policy. Although geographically part of the British Isles, the Republic is not only a very much different entity: both in terms of politics and culture from the countries that comprise the U.K., but also in terms of the manner in which it has developed its tourism industry. For example, in an interventionist way, and with a policy that is extremely pro-European, much of it with the support of European funding.

The Development of Tourism Policy

The Origin of Tourism

Although one could speculate on the definitive moment in the history of tourism that identifies specifically the exclusive basis for the development of tourism, the formulation of tourism policy, or indeed government intervention in tourism, there are too many people, companies and different countries involved in tourism and too many reference points to be explicitly accurate about this. In fact, it is difficult to ascertain the very early influences on tourism or the influence of tourism on society (Edgell 1999). Indeed, those that are compliant with the scriptures and the bible will recognise numerous scenarios and areas that are reminiscent of the opportunities and problems that face tourists that travel today. What we do know is that as far back as may be ascertained, apocryphally; tourism and all that it encapsulated had a suspect and dubious meaning. For example, for many it was descriptive of group travel which in itself because of the numbers and the difference in outlook between those that travelled and those that did not were threatening to the latter. For others it meant suspicious strangers, meaning that the communal antipathy exhibited towards outsiders, travellers, and foreigners was symptomatic of many distrustful and guarded communities who were inward-looking, ill-informed, and in many instances inbred. Furthermore, such communities also shunned those of an alternative religion, or from another geographical area of the same region or country, behaviours common to Wales, Ireland and Scotland well into the twentieth century, and perhaps beyond. Meanwhile, travellers from within communities, as distinct from groups, reflected the quality of their antecedents who not only held the community's respect, but also were associated with the more affluent; the educated; the aristocratic; the meritocracy; or recognised leaders of society (Lickorish & Jenkins 1997).

There was, of course, a clear distinction between those recognised as travellers and all that involved, and those who were acknowledged as tourists. For example, some had various easily determined and recognisable purposes such as being mercenaries, trading with other regions and nations, religious affirmations or educational affiliations; others were associated with leisure and recreation, recognized in those days as more frivolous and perhaps dilettante pursuits. It is quite ironic, therefore, that in the present day the word traveller is associated with itinerants e.g. gypsies, asylum seekers, tinkers, new age travellers etc., peoples reputed to live outwith the bounds of society, and to be an irritant to society, while a tourist is someone who although ephemeral to society. As much as they are valuable in terms of the economic benefit they bring, tourists may also be thought of as abhorrent in terms of the pollution they cause, ambivalent to the impression and perception they take away, conveying this experience to others, as they move on to other destinations.

The development of tourism had its modern origins in first the horse, the stagecoach, then the canal barge, followed by the rail and steamer network, the history of which is documented elsewhere (e.g. Bulleid 1963; Carter 1952; Hamilton Ellis 1953; Maggs 1999; Maxwell 1958; Siviter 1984; Tuplin 1963). However, the popularization of the motor car, the emergence of the aircraft, and legislation introduced in the thirties that awarded annual leave to employees all had the most fundamental and dramatic impact on the growth of tourism. Furthermore, a number of resorts, many of which were formerly fishing villages, began to establish themselves as tourist destinations that were supported and marketed by local tourist associations, councils, hoteliers, and travel companies. However, and despite local initiatives it was well into the twentieth century, and following the mass explosion of tourists who emerged after the Second World War before countries considered developing tourism policies that would regulate it, promote it and exploit it.

For example, post-war tourism became a high priority for the Organization for European Economic Co-operation (OEEC), which was formed to administer American and Canadian aid under the Marshall Plan for reconstruction of Europe after World War II. The OEEC valued highly tourism's potential in terms of dollar earnings and foreign exchange, and supported the European Travel Commission (ETC) with marketing campaigns to attract visitors from the USA. The OEEC's successor the Organisation for Economic Cooperation and Development (OECD), formed in 1961, adopted a tourism policy that became virtually the international model for tourism. Its annual report *Tourism Policy and International Tourism in OECD Member Countries* (OECD 1997), which has been published annually since the early eighties, describes the main features of what have come to be called the national tourism policies of the OECD members (Edgell 1999: 8–31), and a framework for the remainder. However, it was 1969 before the U.K. attempted to define tourism policy in terms of its relationship to its economy via *the Development of Tourism Act 1969* (which will be discussed below in terms of England, Wales and Northern Ireland, and in Chapter 5, in terms of Scotland), and 1981 before the USA published its first tourism policy (The National Tourism Policy Act of 1981), discussed in Chapter 3. Meanwhile, the Republic of Ireland's tourism policy as will be discussed later was developed over a number of years and, because of the frequency of elections and turnover of governments, was focused across a number of different departments. Nevertheless this did not detract from its success in growing an industry which during the nineties was the envy of its Celtic British competitor countries.

In that same decade the dissolution of the Soviet Union, the unification of Germany, and the rapid expansion of email and the World Wide Web had a dramatic impact on the way that the tourism industry conducted its business and also on the behaviour of tourists. However, although the industry had previously been beset by deep troughs resulting from the energy crises in 1973 and 1982; the Americans bombing Libya in 1986; the Gulf War in 1990; the war in former Yugoslavia in 1999; and foot-and-mouth in 2001; the downturn following September 11 2002 when Usama Bin Laden's Al Qaeda terrorists destroyed the twin towers of the World Trade Centre in New York, as described in Chapter 2, had a seismic and long-lasting impact on the industry the affects from which it is still endeavouring to recover. This is compounded by the uncertainty that now accompanies international travel, particularly after the October 2002 Bali bombing and the November 2002 Kenyan (Mombassa) bombing, massacring hundreds of people, and again the result of Al Qaeda terrorists. Further uncertainty for 2003 has been caused by the war in Iraq and SARS.

The United Kingdom

The Development of Tourism Structure and Policy

As will be described in the latter part of this chapter, tourism within the countries of the U.K. developed haphazardly and independently of one another well into the twentieth century, and it was not until the lead up to the Second World War that government began to recognise, albeit in a limited way, the importance of tourism to the economy. However, it was thirty years before this was formalised. Up until then, apart from the efforts of the British Travel Association (see below), tourism promotion, marketing and product development had been an uncoordinated effort with the various U.K. geographical areas following their own disparate strategies. This all changed in 1969 due to *the Development of Tourism Act* (1969) which created National Tourism Organisations (NTOs) e.g. the English Tourist Board (ETB), the Scottish Tourist Board (STB), the Wales Tourist Board (WTB), and the British Tourist Authority (BTA), (MacLellan & Smith 1998: 46), which replaced the British Travel Association.

Although the three NTOs, the Northern Ireland Tourist Board (NITB) and the BTA were funded by grants from central government, these grants fluctuated in accordance with the importance placed on tourism by the government of the day. Also, the Act itself and successive governments who have failed to amend it accordingly, have been criticised for the fact that no provision was made for a statutory regional public sector structure for tourism, or more contentiously to statutorily fund Regional (RTBs) or Area Tourist Boards (ATBs). In consequence, the ETB, STB and WTB created their own disparate regional tourism structures, which were beset continually with funding problems. Meanwhile the establishment of the BTA was to cause problems for Scottish tourism that are still unresolved (see Chapter 5).

The Development of Tourism Act 1969

The 1969 Act had three parts. Apart from providing a statutory basis for a British Tourist Authority (BTA) and national tourist boards for England, Wales and Scotland, until 1973, when Part Two of the Act expired, it also provided grants for hotel development and up-grading en-suite facilities. Of the additional 70,000 hotel bedrooms, and upgrading en-suite facilities completed, MacLellan (1998: 46) claims the majority of these were developed in London and the Southeast leading to temporary overcapacity, while Holloway (1998) claims that areas where hotel construction involved greater financial risk, such as Scotland and the North of England, did not benefit to anything like the extent needed. For example, in 1969 there were then only 900 en-suite hotel bedrooms in Edinburgh (the 2002 AA Guide lists 4002 en-suite hotel bedrooms), the capital city of Scotland (Lickorish & Jenkins 1997: 27). However, in 1989 these grants were withdrawn altogether in England but continued for Scotland and Wales, introducing an element of inequity as some regions in England were as deprived as those in Scotland and Wales. Furthermore, England also received less per capita for tourism than Scotland and Wales (Elliott 1997: 89) (refer to England section of this chapter).

The Act also provided for the compulsory display of prices, and a system of compulsory registration of tourist accommodation, a topic that will be discussed more fully in subsequent chapters. However, because the influential accommodation sector preferred a voluntary system of classification and grading inspection of tourism establishments, inspection remained voluntary, not compulsory, unlike the Republic of Ireland where an Hotel cannot operate outwith the system.

The Act, however, did not include Northern Ireland, which had a long-established tourist board, nor other U.K. areas operating independently outside the jurisdiction of the Act such as the States of Guernsey and Jersey Tourist Committees, and the Isle of Man Tourist Board, all of whom had their own island policies (Holloway 1998: 273).

The U.K. in the European Union

Although discussed more fully in Chapter 3, various other changes took place post-war that were ultimately significant to U.K. tourism. For example, the desire for international reconciliation after World War II was the impetus for the formation of the European Union whose predecessor the European Economic Community (EEC) came into being in 1958, and in 1967 assumed ever-wider policies. Despite being twice rebuffed in 1963 and 1967, in 1972 the U.K. was accepted by the EEC (as was the Republic of Ireland a year later) and signed the EEC Treaty which paved the way for significant investment in tourism than would have otherwise been the case had it stayed out of Europe.

The National Tourism Organisations (NTOs)

In the 1990s the U.K. and the Republic of Ireland tourism organisations were finding it difficult to stay abreast of the changes brought on by the phenomenon of globalisation, and in an environment of government inertia re-positioned themselves to be able to compete for their share of the global market. For example, both Northern and Southern Ireland's tourism bodies were set for major structural changes at the end of the decade, and the WTB, against much opposition from the more influential ETB, rather then align itself with the newly proposed English classification and grading system opted to emulate the Scottish system, which was quality based as opposed to quality and facility based. Meanwhile, Ireland delayed the creation of a single tourism scheme because politicians on both sides of the border could not agree how it should operate. Nevertheless, by September 1999 adverts promoting Ireland, as opposed to the Republic of Ireland or Northern Ireland were commonplace, frustrating Unionist politicians and cementing cross-border functions, and paving the way for a single all-Ireland tourism company (refer to their respective sections below).

The Euro

There was also the advent of the Euro, which meant that from 1st January 1999 businesses within the Euroland countries were able to make and receive payments in Euros as well as their national currencies. This was a significant new change. For instance, the Euro was the second largest currency in the world and one monetary policy applied across all eleven participating countries. Although the U.K. decided to opt out, it has not ruled out entry altogether setting itself various conditions for entry. For example, both the exchange rate and interest rates, which the government through the Bank of England's Monetary Policy

Committee (MPC) has been managing assiduously, must be in alignment, as must political as well as electoral will, which will mean a referendum at some point.

On 1st January 2002 Euro notes and coins were issued, and within a few months replaced the national currencies of eleven European countries, which ceased to be legal tender as from 1st July 2002, the majority of Continental European tourists using one currency, and the implications for the U.K. tourism industry clear, particularly the fact that the Euro made prices transparent. Furthermore, by July of that year the Euro achieved parity with the Dollar, an important fact in attracting tourists from North America.

Tourism U.K.

This followed closely the establishment of Tourism U.K. which was sponsored by the Chairmen of VisitScotland (the former STB), the English Tourism Council and the Wales Tourist Board (WTB), and will act as a platform for promoting the best interests of domestic tourism in the U.K. by providing a collective, coherent and strategic steer to governments on the common concerns, common purpose and common agenda of the tourism sector in the U.K.

The new tourism federation has pledged to raise awareness of the importance of the industry to the British economy, highlight its huge potential and communicate and advise on the need to guarantee sustainability to ensure future growth is targeted and relevant. Furthermore, it has outlined its determination to work together across national boundaries to provide the best possible service. It has also asked the government to acknowledge that there is now an impartial, intelligent voice, with no alternative agenda, which will advise, inform, and respond on behalf of domestic tourism in the U.K. It is also committed to delivering a ten-year vision for tourism through co-coordinated research and partnership, and has requested continued support of government at all levels in order to deliver this strategic plan (VisitScotland, Signpost November/December 2002).

England

The Development of Modern English Tourism

The development of modern English tourism owes much to the Bank Holiday Act of 1871 which created four public holidays per annum, and to the Education Act of 1870 which ensured a higher level of literacy and knowledge than previously. This, in turn, increased the demand for growth of the industry as tourists identified more attractive destinations and required more stimuli from their holidays such as visiting places of natural beauty and historical interest. This extra demand was one of the key factors that resulted in the development of the National Trust in 1895 as there was hardly any town or country planning legislation to control growth (Burkart & Medlik 1981: 21–22 from McKenna 1999). In the same era the invention of steam-power and the increase in the accessibility and popularity of seaside resorts rendered travel more widely available and was to have a far-reaching impact on the development of tourism (Youell 1998: 5).

With the advent of the twentieth century inexpensive and more widely available travel, paid holidays and packaged holidays brought affordable trips abroad to most sections of society. By 1916, during the First World War, a passport became a compulsory permanent requirement in Britain and for many a status symbol as were the number of entries on display. Later in the century the possession of a passport was akin to an affirmation that the possessor was a bona fide resident, and to own a British passport, was for many overseas people, particularly those from the British Commonwealth, a rite of passage. Furthermore, by the 1920s by which time the population had grown to 45 million (it had been 25 million in 1830 (Burkart *et al.* 1981: 11 from MacKenna 1999), 1.5 million workers were entitled to paid holidays, a figure that doubled by 1938 and which rose to almost 60% (11 million) of the 19 million workforce in 1939 when the British Amulree Report of 1938 meant *the Holiday with Pay Act* (1939) came into force.

The idea of a paid period away from work, once seen as a luxury for the few, came to be viewed as a right for the many (Gardiner & Wenborn 1995: 387), and as Holloway (1998: 31) claims, the entitlement to paid holidays became a key factor in changing attitudes towards balancing work and leisure time, and in generating mass holidays. Had it not been for the Second World War the acceleration of growth of the British tourism industry, and the government's participation in its promotion would have taken place much earlier. For example, due to the depression in the thirties the government had chosen for the first time to intervene in tourism, and undertook to support the British Travel Association (founded in 1929) in marketing Britain abroad, which effectively meant London. The association had previously been known as the Travel Association of Great Britain and Ireland, founded in 1922 as the Come to Britain movement, a forebear of the British Tourist Authority (BTA).

Within two years of the commencement of the war in 1939 the industry had contracted. For example, there were many fewer available hotel bedrooms in the U.K., than before the outbreak of war, and even less en-suite ones. In London alone there were 5,000 fewer. This situation deteriorated as the war progressed, and was mirrored throughout English cities and many rural areas where large hotels housed trainee pilots, or were converted to military hospitals. For the London hotels, this was the result of bomb damage combined with the Ministry of War requisitioning eight major hotels with between 100 and 400 bedrooms. Some, such as the Great Central and the Langham, were never to open again. This situation was compounded by the fact that it was 10 years after the war, in 1955 and six months after rationing ended when the first post-war hotel of any consequence, the Westbury in London opened (Bacon, personal communication, 24 May 2001), to cope with the growing American clientele.

Following the war, and the introduction of The August Bank holiday in 1945 there was more time for leisurely activities. This and the development in technology generated by the war proved to be one of the biggest influences on the new and developing tourism industry (Lavery 1996 from MacKenna 1999). Technological advances were to lead to the first viable commercial land-based commercial transatlantic flight between New York and Bournemouth, calling at Boston, Gander and Shannon (Holloway 1998: 32), as the government was concerned with increasing the number of foreign visitors, particularly Americans, in order to boost foreign exchange receipts. To this end the British Tourism and Holiday Board was established, and in 1947 the government's White Paper on Britain's *Four Year Plan* (1947) recognised the importance of tourism to the U.K.'s economy, as did the formation of the Interdepartmental Working Committee of the Civil Service which was designed to upgrade tourism reception facilities. In fact in 1953, while sweet rationing continued the government arranged for confectionary to be sold in the departure lounges of international airports, and by the time rationing ended in 1954 the U.K. had a tourism surplus balance of £2 million. However, by 1966 because of so many people travelling overseas, and the tourism balance moving into deficit, the government imposed a £60 travel limit on what people could spend overseas (Elliott 1997: 26–27). However, this did not deter tourists to foreign destinations, encouraging them to participate in package holidays as opposed to independent journeys (Holloway 1998: 32).

Although the world opened up dramatically after the war as people settled back into normal life, the period post-war saw the seaside holiday become firmly established as the traditional annual holiday destination for the mass of the mainland English public (Holloway 1998: 31). However, the war was to change the face of tourism forever, both for the domestic market which afterwards would expand overseas, and for the international market needed to attract foreign exchange. Furthermore, notwithstanding the fact that the travelling ambitions of troops that had been stationed abroad were no longer confined by the English and British borders and coastlines; the increase in the number of domestic telephones; the number of household televisions; increasing disposable wealth; and the extension of coloured screens to cinemas encouraged a growing number of people to experience more diverse and exotic cultures. This was facilitated by the advances made during the war by aircraft technology which in the late fifties saw the Boeing 707 jet replaced the ocean-going liners as the prime means by which to cross the Atlantic, not only opening up the routes by which more tourists could fly to and from England but also an increase in business travel, and by 1957 the number of passengers by air exceeded those by sea for the first time (Holloway 1998: 32).

In the late sixties, however, the charms of the seaside resorts and towns paled into insignificance in comparison to growing overseas competition. For instance, less expensive airfares, charter and package holidays were common-place, transporting holidaymakers to a variety of easily accessible and relatively inexpensive destinations. People also were in general better off, had more disposable income, and by 1970 the limit on taking monies abroad was relaxed. Combined with the liberalisation of air transport regulations, longer paid holidays, and the introduction of wide-bodied jets which could accommodate up to 400 passengers, this enabled them to take less expensive holidays more often mainly to the continent of Europe. Consequently, those who previously went to Blackpool, Scarborough, or Frinton now holidayed in resorts such as Majorca, Tenerife, and Rimini, while in the English resorts the clientele was redolent of the older generation or were families with much less disposable income, a combination which unconsciously devalued the resort, the consequence being a reduction in investment. Since then, whole new destinations have opened up such as Goa, Florida, and the Far East, attracting visitors from all over the world, and this is the dilemma for the English tourism industry and for its tourism policy, in terms of standards, skills, product development, and quality: what must it do to remain competitive in the twenty-first century?

English Tourism Policy and Structure

To claim that English tourism policy is indeed U.K. tourism policy, or vice-versa, would be to both underestimate devolution and to demean English tourism. However, for all of the twentieth century (arguably both pre and post-devolution) apart from six months of the final year, U.K. tourism policy was dominated by the influence of London both as a destination and as the place where policy was made. Although initiatives by the public sector organisations endeavoured to encourage tourists to parts of the U.K. other than London, and the nearby South-East, the fact that most of the tourist traffic from overseas flew into London, and that the capital was being promoted heavily by the private sector who had invested heavily both in its transport and infrastructure meant that London, despite devolution, as a destination, continued to dominate U.K. tourism. How this evolved is worthy of further exploration.

Since the late 1800s, the English boroughs and latterly local authorities invested heavily in the infrastructure upon which tourism grew and prospered, but had no real tourism policy, dealing with events in an ad hoc manner. Meanwhile, the private sector developed products on the back of the public sector through revenue-earning activities, admittedly enhancing the resorts and town's income while increasing rate receipts for the authorities, and tax receipts for the government (Wanhill 1998: 340). Furthermore, and despite the inherent tensions and the sometimes overbearing personalities of those involved, the public and private sectors appeared to have had an instinctive understanding of both the shared responsibilities and of the developmental and marketing aspects required of them. In consequence, English tourism evolved through a system of enterprise and benefaction, rather than strategy or policy-making, with the individual resorts competing for trade, and in certain instances by segmenting markets. Although the majority of these marketing initiatives were led by the private sector, while the public sector invested in amenities, festivals and special events (Lickorish & Jenkins 1998: 183–202), there were certain crossover functions that worked equally as well. Brighton, for example, formerly a small fishing village, with its proximity to London, clement weather, and pristine beaches, and which was patronised by royalty and minor nobility owed much of its success to this public private partnership, as did Bournemouth another former south coast fishing village. By this time, fuelled by the ambitions of enterprising speculators and never-ending possibilities as to the revenue potential and the votes to be derived from tourism, the boroughs and councils of England were in serious competition with one another, concocting evermore grandiose schemes e.g. the Blackpool Tower. Furthermore, stimulated by the growth of the railway network, the resultant establishment and growth of large resorts facilitated the development of local tourism administrations to carry out the responsibilities of the host destination, with some of these contracted to the private sector (Lickorish & Jenkins 1997: 201). Nevertheless, and despite the prominence given to tourism nationally, public sector intervention in tourism was until the early nineteen seventies, solely at the local level. The government's first clear intervention in tourism was when the Department of Overseas Trade supported the Come to Britain movement in 1928. The following year a grant of £5,000 designed to overcome the Depression enabled the British Travel Association (an amalgam of the various industry sectors such as the shipping companies, hotels, local government resorts, and the railways) to promote tourism to the U.K. from overseas. In the years that followed the British Travel Association lobbied successive governments to recognise the growing importance of the industry by assigning it to a government department and formulating a tourism policy. Nevertheless, it was forty years after the British Travel Association's formation before the aforementioned 1969 *Development of Tourism Act* came into being. As a result of the Act the BTA and the ETB became responsible to the Board of Trade (The STB and WTB as had their forerunners, became responsible to their respective Secretaries of State who delegated responsibility to the respective Minister for State). Following the 1969 Act, ETB set up 12 Regional Tourist Boards (RTBs). The RTBs were financially independent membership organisations that received 25% of their funding from the Exchequer, 50% from commercial activities, and the remainder from regional stakeholders including local authorities. However, by 1996 this number was reduced to ten due to a funding crisis which saw Thames and Chiltern Tourist Board collapse (1992), its area being allocated to the adjoining regions; and the amalgamation of the East Midlands, Lincolnshire and East Anglian Tourist Boards as the East of England Tourist Board. By 2003, this number will have reduced further to nine as Southern and South East Tourist Boards unify. Although this new structure improved greatly the planning and co-ordination of tourism in England, and was facilitated by an all-party Interdepartmental Tourism Co-ordinating Committee, the diverse nature of tourism, the dearth of proper funding; the tensions between the various interests; and its impact on so many different facets of English life made cohesive planning difficult while raising expectations that never could realistically be met (Holloway 1998: 276). All of this was influenced by the philosophy of the Thatcher era which from the 1980s saw a period of supposed retreat by central government from active intervention in tourism policy (Hall 2000: 17), and cultivated a debate on the appropriate role of the state in tourism. For example, in 1979 when Margaret Thatcher came to power tourism came under the umbrella of the newly formed Trade and Industry Ministry; formerly the Board of Trade. As much as the previous post-war Labour and Conservative administrations gave little direction on tourism policy, the Thatcher administration failed adjectively to give any clearer a direction, both in terms of its commitment to tourism, which appeared to be to leave it at the behest of market forces, and by later incongruously transferring responsibility for it to the Department of Employment. For example, by 1985, the Secretary of State for Trade and Industry, Lord Young, who was soon to become the Secretary of State for Employment, was asking why the government should involve itself directly in tourism which he thought was primarily a matter for private enterprise (HMSO 1995).

Young moved tourism with him reflecting that job creation was high on his agenda as the desired outcome of tourism development, a trend that was reflected in other countries' policies e.g. Ireland; Scotland; Wales; India; Australia: a strategy which was unsustainable in the longer term. Furthermore, Young believed that the best way to accomplish this and to assist tourism to flourish was for the government to provide a general economic framework which encouraged growth while at the same time removed unnecessary burdens or restrictions, as opposed to intervention (Wanhill 1987: 54–58). In fact, Smith (1998: 44) claims that in 1989 only after the intervention of the Tourism Society (1989: 5–6), an organisation which was established in 1977 to bring together professionals working in all sectors of the diverse travel and tourism industry and in fields related to it, did it manage to avert the high tide of Thatcherism sweeping away most of the U.K.'s tourism support edifice. Despite this, since then, at the national level, policies of deregulation, corporatisation, privatisation, free-trade, the elimination of tax incentives, combined with a move away from discretionary forms of macro-economic intervention, have been the hallmarks of the emphasis of smaller government and lower levels of central government intervention, an example that tourism is not immune from changes in political philosophy in its wider policy environment (Hall 2000: 17).

Following John Major's first electoral victory in 1992 (he became Prime Minister in 1990 when Margaret Thatcher was forced out of office), he created a new Ministry, the Department of National Heritage, where tourism operated awkwardly alongside sport; royal parks and palaces; the arts; libraries; broadcasting; heritage sites; and the press and media: its new Minister responsible for such diverse and unrelated disciplines as Film, Tourism and Broadcasting. Furthermore, when Labour came to power in 1997 there was disappointment that the new government reneged on promises made in opposition that it would increase the government's financial contribution to tourism when it came to power, particularly to the NTOs (see Labour Party, Breaking New Ground: Labour's strategy for the tourism and hospitality industry 1996). For example, in the decade to 1996, although the budget of the BTA was subject to incremental increases broadly in line with inflation, from 1992, when the Department of National Heritage became responsible for tourism, to 1996–1997, the grant-in-aid for the ETB declined from £16.2 to £10 million. This was compounded by the fact that in 1993 although Major's Government had been of the opinion that the case for supporting the ETB's work to promote tourism in the U.K. was less clear than the case for supporting the BTA, and that resources ought to instead be directed primarily through the RTBs, no tourism organisation benefited.

One consequence of this was that in 1996, the National Heritage Committee, one of whose parliamentary responsibilities was tourism, argued that the level of return on expenditure on the BTA in the form of increased expenditure in the U.K. (and thus increased VAT receipts) justified a large increase in the BTA's budget. The Committee recommended that the Government's financial support for the BTA should be quadrupled over five years to £100 million per year. However, it was not until 1999–2000 that the BTA's grant-in-aid was indeed increased, but only by £1 million. Furthermore, in the lead up to the outbreak of foot-and-mouth disease, the Government had planned to freeze the BTA's grant-in-aid in cash terms, thus reducing it in real terms. The grant-in-aid provided to the BTA in fact fell between 2000 and 2002 by £1.5 million to £35 million (£5 million less than the VisitScotland budget in 2002), a fact that the Department of Culture, Media and Sport (DCMS) claimed was wholly due to a change in an accounting convention, whereby funding for the London Tourist Board (LTB) was now channelled to that body through the newly created Greater London Authority (GLA) rather than through the BTA.

There was in fact an inequality in the manner in which the NTOs were funded pre and post-devolution. For example, in 1999–2000 STB was granted £19.4 million, WTB £15.4 million; and yet ETB received only £11.7 million. This meant that the grant-in-aid for the STB was the equivalent of £3.77 per head of population; and the grant-in-aid for the WTB the equivalent of £4.03 per head, while the corresponding Figure for English domestic tourism was 20 pence per head. Such figures, however, did not reflect the BTA expenditure which arguably targeted London as *the U.K.* destination above all the others. Nevertheless, the planned freeze of expenditure on the BTA was further evidence of sustained under-investment by the public sector in U.K. tourism that perversely, and despite the emphasis on London, disadvantaged English tourism in particular.

Furthermore, in 1998, there were also questions as to whether the fundamental economic importance of tourism was fully reflected in the priorities and objectives of the re-named Department for Culture, Media and Sport (DCMS), which also became responsible for Tourism. In response, the Department launched a new Tourism Strategy, *Tomorrow's*

Tourism (Department of Culture Media and Sport 1999), in which the Prime Minister gave solace to those who argued that English tourism policy is in fact U.K. tourism policy in another guise as, in the preface, he referred to Britain instead of England on whom the strategy was based, a tone that was evident throughout the document e.g. tourism statistics relating to the U.K. (Figure 4.1).

In consequence of this strategy, DCMS abolished the much maligned ETB and replaced it with the English Tourism Council (ETC) as a radical transformation of the existing NTO. The new NTO was established with the aim of being a leaner and more strategic body than its predecessor. This meant the new ETC being relieved of the direct marketing and promotional roles of its predecessor (ironically the prime objective of the other tourist boards); enabling it to concentrate more effectively on its research and policy formulation functions. In response, the Tourism Society expressed concern that the new body had been designed more by reference to the needs of the Government than with a focus on the customer. On the contrary, the Government argued that the ETC's new role was to support the business of tourism and to drive forward a long-term vision for a fragmented industry. Furthermore, it hoped to direct more government spending on tourism to the English regions

TOMORROW'S TOURISM
A growth industry
for the new Millennium
FOREWORD BY THE PRIME MINISTER

Britain is a wonderful country. Its people, landscapes, culture, character, history and traditions; its achievements, impact, successes, and standing; and its future, its vision, its potential. These are the things which make Britain great, and which make people - its own people, and people from across the world - want to see Britain, to know Britain and to understand Britain.

Tourism is central to how people from across the country and from abroad can begin to do that, and continue to do that. I want everyone, whether they're from different parts of the United Kingdom or from different countries around the world, to be able to enjoy the rich diversity of what Britain has to offer.

Of course, Britain has been a key tourist destination for many years - one of the most popular in the world. Currently, almost 26 million people arrive here every year to see what Britain is about. London is one of the world's favourite cities. All this will increase still further next year when our national Millennium celebrations place Britain at the centre of the world stage.

But the challenge facing us now is to create a competitive, world-class tourism industry in Britain which matches both the quality and the best of British business generally and the scale of tourism in Britain in particular. We must have a tourism industry which provides affordable quality, which is open to all and which makes the best use of Britain's resources. And a tourism industry which concentrates on our key resource - people.

I believe that the Government's new strategy for tourism - a strategy for England, but one which has clear implications for Scotland, Wales and Northern Ireland - will help towards this goal. It offers both vision and practical help. It is detailed and comprehensive. It is realistic and forward-looking. In partnership with all those working in tourism, I believe it is vital to our aim of making tourism throughout the UK as good as the best of British tourism already is - so that people can visit and enjoy the best of Britain.

TONY BLAIR

Figure 4.1: Tomorrow's Tourism. Foreword by Prime Minister, DCMS, 1999.

than to the centre, leaving ETC to support the domestic tourism industry in essential areas including conducting research and improving quality in hotels and seaside resorts. For example, in 2000, the regions received £6m against 1999's £3.8m (Caterer & Hotelkeeper 6 May 1999).

There were many differences between ETB and ETC, whose relationship with other organizations is explained in Figure 4.2, both in role and remit, and in ways of working, but perhaps the biggest change was that although the ETC retained a key role in supporting tourism marketing, the transition from the ETB to ETC marked the formal end of the direct consumer-marketing role of the England NTO. The role had been diminishing gradually over the previous years, as the majority of domestic marketing was being done by the industry, RTBs and local authorities, with overseas marketing undertaken by the BTA.

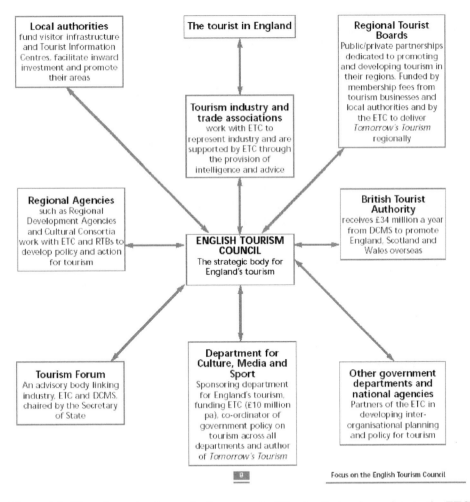

Figure 4.2: How the main players in the support of England's tourism relate to the ETC.
Source: Tomorrow's Tourism 1999.

Nevertheless, questions remained, and perhaps explained why the ETC's existence was to be short-lived. For example, the diminishing financial allocation to the ETC included all allocations to the RTBs from public funds, which in itself caused tensions. In fact, the transition from the ETB to the ETC was designed in part to release additional public funds for the regions, while a key component of the new strategy was to place greater reliance on the role of the RTBs. Nevertheless, although they received direct support from the ETC, that support was overwhelmingly in the form of funding for specified projects, and the RTBs did not have discretion over how the majority of ETC funding was spent. Moreover, RTBs were normally expressly prohibited from spending the money they received from central Government, through the ETC, on marketing or public relations. That prohibition limited the scale and scope of tourism promotion undertaken by the RTBs because such activity was funded only from funds generated by the RTBs themselves.

There was also concern that the ETC grant-in-aid was as previously described well below that for the WTB and the STB. Furthermore, that Scotland and Wales should be receiving grant-in-aid per capita some twenty times greater than that available to the ETC was clearly an anathema to the English tourism industry. Also, since England as a country had as much right to be promoted as a tourist destination as other countries of the U.K., a good deal of responsibility for promotion of England now resided with regional organisations as opposed to the ETC.

As a by-product of devolution, another significant change took place in 1998, with the advent of the Regional Development Agencies Act 1998 which established nine regional agencies (RDAs) in England with powers to further the economic development and regeneration of their areas (Area Regeneration Companies (ARCs) were also later established), while in London the GLA and London Assembly were established with a directly elected mayor whose responsibilities included promoting economic and social development, the environment and wealth creation. Through time these constitutional developments could very well act as a stimulus for the English regions to demand Assemblies similar to London or Wales. In fact, if they were to take this even further, and to demand legislative powers, the U.K. might indeed become a Federal state, redefining the role of the U.K. parliament (Cabinet Office 2002; McFadden & Lazarowicz 1999: 97–98), and which would have a dramatic impact on both English tourism development and policy.

Three years after establishing the ETC, on 31 October 2002, in an effort to address the £13 billion English tourism deficit (Walker 2002) and apparently without much consultation of her fellow U.K. tourism ministers (Settle 2002: 2), the Secretary of State for Culture, Media & Sport announced plans to abolish it and instead proposed to develop a single lead government body for inbound tourism to Britain and the marketing of England within Britain. The body would combine the resources and the strengths of the BTA and the ETC and as VisitBritain came into effect on 1 April 2003.

The new body which was not widely welcomed by the industry in Scotland and of which Peter Lederer, Chair of VisitScotland knew nothing before the November 2002 announcement (Settle 2002), will co-ordinate the marketing of England while continuing to promote the whole of Britain overseas under a new strategy that will reflect the different strengths and diversity of England, Scotland and Wales. The proposal was a result of a Government review of tourism and the BTA's own review of its strategy and support for British tourism from overseas. Furthermore, funding for overseas marketing will be ring-fenced and the re-organised VisitBritain will account separately for its overseas and English marketing activities, and will from April 2003 onwards report on its overseas activities to the Scottish Parliament and Welsh Assembly as well as to Westminster, further complicating the tourism infrastructure in the U.K.

Wales

The Development of Welsh Tourism

By the beginning of the twentieth century caravan sites had been established along the North West and southern coastal areas of Wales as workers from the industrial towns of England and South Wales, many of them arriving from England and Ireland began to take advantage of increased salaries, material expectations and leisure time. However, very few visitors were attracted to the more distant corners of Wales, particularly parts of the west which were still inaccessible: the roads, and accommodation/hospitality infrastructure being so inadequate. As a result, the number of visitors did not increase dramatically until the railway line from Euston was extended at the beginning of the twentieth century as far as Pwllheli (http://www.mikes.railhistory.railfan.net 2002). The rail line also increased tourism numbers in resorts close by Pwllheli such as Llanbedrog, Porthmadog, Cricieth, and Morfa Nefyn which aspired to attract reasonably affluent visitors from over the border. Of these visitors, a number purchased second homes. In the years following the end of the Second World War this became a serious problem since the economic recession and the depopulation that ensued, forced owners of large estates to sell large parts of their properties and land. Many of these were purchased by people from England among them people who had spent several holidays in the area and were attracted to the affordability of a second home combined with the slow meandering Welsh way of life (Phillips & Thomas 2001).

As the Depression dug deeper in the 1920s and 1930s, there was an enormous drop in the population of Wales as people traveled outside its borders to find employment, the majority of them never to return. This posed serious social, cultural, and economic problems, among them the threat to the continuance of the national language. Indeed, on several occasions since the 1970s the nationalist movement identified tourism as one of the principal causes of its deterioration. For example, in 1972 the Welsh Language Society was concerned that the growth of the tourist industry was destroying the age long lifestyle of Welsh villages, a fact that had no bearing on Gaelic in Ireland but also had an impact in Scotland (Phillips & Thomas 2001). Furthermore, through increased numbers of those from over the border purchasing holiday homes, combined with the general weakness of the rural economy, the social foundations of the most Welsh parts of Wales were being destroyed and anglicized (Webb 1972: 40 from Phillips & Thomas 2001). In fact, the reality was that the east coast of Wales was considerably anglicized by the end of the twentieth century. This was due to the popularity of the area among tourists from north-west England, particularly those who would later retire there, and who found it both less expensive and more scenic than their former bleak and industrial habitat. Their apparent relative wealth and ability to integrate, no matter the antipathy towards them, contributed further to reluctance, on behalf of many Welsh speakers, to embrace incomers and tourists. This was the result of a wide held belief that those from outside Wales i.e. the tourist industry, contributed to the deterioration of the language, the social fabric and the way of life. However, the effects of tourism on the Welsh language may be both contradictory and paradoxical. For example, the economic benefit brought to Welsh-speaking areas by tourists created employment, and actively promoted a national identity based on the native language and its unique culture, meaning that, contrary to what the Welsh Language Society claimed, tourism could be construed as highly beneficial to the continuity of the Welsh language (Phillips & Thomas 2001).

In essence, tourism was fast becoming an important element of the economic fabric of Wales that was growing to provide a key source of income and employment, particularly in the coastal and rural areas. It also offered an alternative source of income in areas which have been subject to major restructuring (Stationery Office, Cardiff 1999). Nevertheless, in common with other British tourism destinations, and as has been explained earlier in terms of neighbouring England, the popularity of resorts such as Llandudno, Colwyn Bay, Rhyl, Prestatyn, Bangor etc., had grown to its peak by the nineteen-sixties then declined dramatically in the nineteen-seventies in the main due to the availability of inexpensive holidays abroad, and the Welsh tourism industry's inability to keep pace. For the first time Welsh resorts faced serious competition from overseas resorts as opposed to among themselves, and from England. There is also evidence of a stereotypically outdated negative image of Wales and the Welsh held by its fellow Britons; a lack of awareness of it overseas; a dearth of top quality accommodation; a deficiency of nationally and internationally branded accommodation; the absence of a suitable range of coaching hotels and conference venues/hotels; and inconsistent standards of tourism outlets (National Assembly for Wales, Achieving our Potential — A Tourism Strategy for Wales 2002). Consequently, the downturn in income meant an inability to continue to upgrade; introduce new amenities; support the theatres; and refurbish the hotels; and the gap between what a consumer could expect abroad and that experienced at home grew wider. Furthermore, it was less expensive to go abroad than to stay at home. This changed forever the nature of resort tourism and indeed tourism in Wales, which led to the new strategies introduced in the eighties and nineties, such as the Framework Development Strategy (1988), Tourism 2000, A Strategy for Wales (1994), and building upon them, Achieving our Potential — A Tourism Strategy for Wales (2002), all of which are discussed below, and which are designed to improve dramatically both the standards, skills and product, but also the number of visitors to the country.

Development of Structure and Policy

The Government of Wales Act 1998 (Welsh Office 1998) established a directly-elected National Assembly for Wales which assumed most of the responsibilities of the Secretary of State for Wales (Cynulliad Cenedlaethol Cymru, National Assembly for Wales, http://www.cymru.gov.uk 2002). However, unlike the Scottish parliament, the Assembly does not have legislative powers: its powers are purely administrative. There is, however, a statutory duty placed on the Secretary of State for Wales to consult the Assembly on the government's legislative programme for Wales, including tourism. The Executive and the various subject committees also have the power to prepare secondary legislation for submission to the Assembly for debate and approval (McFadden & Lazarowicz 1999: 96–97).

The Assembly's predecessor, the Welsh Office had been set up in 1964 due to separatist and nationalist pressures and progressively assumed powers from a number of Whitehall Departments. During their tenures the Thatcher and Major governments enhanced the Welsh Office role by transferring administrative responsibility for areas such as Agriculture, Health and Education (McConnell 2000: 230). At this time, the Welsh Office was the responsibility of the Secretary of State and two junior ministers, one of whom was responsible for among other portfolios, tourism, which until 1988 and the launch of the first tourism strategy, *the Framework Development Strategy*, had little government priority (Cabinet Office 2002). Among his other responsibilities was the Welsh Development Agency (WDA) which sought to secure economic development and environmental improvements throughout Wales, and is now the responsibility of the Welsh Assembly. Although the Welsh Office and the WDA are perceived to have given Wales an advantage over the English regions their effects were sometimes counter-productive, from a networking standpoint, especially by disempowering their local partners (Morgan *et al.* 1999: 283), a situation that the Welsh Assembly's new tourism strategy, *Achieving our Potential, A Tourism Strategy for Wales* (2002), is supposed to address. Furthermore, although the Welsh Office did bring an element of administrative devolution including tourism it never attained the status, influence or responsibilities of its Scottish counterpart (McConnell 2000: 230). For example, while Scotland was able to undertake overseas marketing from 1984 (Tourism (Overseas Promotion) (Scotland) Act), it was 1992 before Wales followed suit (Holloway 1998: 273).

To date there have been two Welsh Office tourism strategies and, as has been described above, one Assembly strategy. The first, *the Framework Development Strategy* was launched in 1988, the second *Tourism 2000, A Strategy for Wales* in 1994, and the third more recently, *Achieving our Potential, A Tourism Strategy for Wales* (2002). The latter which has 49 action points was also an essential framework document for the preparation of the closely aligned *National Action Plan* (2002) for tourism, a key tool to ensure that EU Structural Funds are delivered in a coordinated and strategic manner (Bwrdd Croeso Cymru/Wales Tourist Board 2002).

The 1988 *Framework Development Strategy* followed a major review of tourism by the Westminster Secretary of State for Employment, and was closely aligned to strategies devised by both England and Scotland at that time, but still left the Welsh tourism industry fragmented and uncoordinated (Bwrdd Croeso Cymru/Wales Tourist Board 2002). Meanwhile, *Tourism 2000, A Strategy for Wales* (1994) included 142 policy statements, arranged both on a thematic and sectoral basis, grouped in five categories. Although the policy statements and objectives did not in themselves define strategic policies for tourism, they did set out targets, and a vision that *the Framework Development Strategy* had not properly articulated. Among the action points were the need to rationalize the range of promotional material to simplify the process of holiday choice for potential visitors to

Wales, and to set a target for jobs in the Welsh tourism industry (Achieving our Potential, A Tourism Strategy for Wales 2002), echoes of Lord Young's dictate that job creation was the desired outcome of tourism development.

In 1991 three Regional Tourism Companies (RTCs) were established in North, Mid- and South Wales as companies limited by guarantee i.e. not profit disbursing, replacing the previous Regional Tourism Councils (RTCs) and the Regional Offices of WTB that had been set up by the Wales Tourist Board following the 1969 *Development of Tourism Act* (http://www.cymru.gov.uk 2002). Alongside the RTCs, 22 county and county borough councils undertake integrated activities, and this parallel shift from a system of local government to local governance means that a wide array of services is now performed by a complex set of public and private organizations. This has led to a new governance system, which is largely composed of self-managed interorganisational networks (Rhodes 1991a, 1996), and which *Achieving our Potential, A Tourism Strategy for Wales* (2002) is endeavouring to address.

Rather than as a consequence of the 1988 *Framework Development Strategy* the current structure and division of responsibilities in tourism in Wales is the result of an evolutionary process over a 30-year period. However, despite *Tourism 2000, A Strategy for Wales*, which was meant to clarify roles and responsibilities, the industry, the public sector, sectoral organizations, politicians and government were still not clear who did what for tourism in Wales. This resulted in the then Chief Executive of Wales Tourist Board in July 1998, issuing a consultative paper, *Communication in the Tourism Industry in Wales — The Regional Challenge* (1998), which set out ideas for strengthening the relationship between WTB, the three Regional Tourism Councils, local tourism associations and the trade. This coincided with the launch of *Pathway to Prosperity* (1998), the new economic agenda for Wales launched in 1998 (Achieving our Potential, A Tourism Strategy for Wales (2002), wales-tourist-board.gov.uk (2002)). However, all of this was superseded by devolution when following the elections in June 1999, the Minister for Economic Development, who is also responsible for a number of other briefs, became Tourism Minster, with both the WDA and WTB reporting to him. In common with the other U.K. countries at that time tourism was not a dedicated cabinet post (http://www.cymru.gov.uk 2002).

The minister, in conjunction with the National Assembly for Wales (NAW) started immediately to work on a Quinquennial Review of the WTB. His aim was to strengthen the relationship between the WTB and the NAW and to provide opportunities for the NAW to identify ways in which the WTB could do its job more effectively. Interestingly, a common thread of both pre and post-devolution Wales is that of all the British tourist boards (although the Republic of Ireland also insists on all its hotels being members of its tourist board), the WTB whose Classification and Grading system is virtually identical with VisitScotland's, believes that providers of tourist accommodation in Wales should be legally obliged to register their existence and undergo inspection to ensure standards are met, in otherwords, statutory or compulsory registration. As will be seen in subsequent chapters an emotive subject, and one which has its roots in historically inconsistent standards of accommodation, service, hospitality, and quality (http://www.wales-tourist-board.gov.uk 2002).

As a consequence of the seriousness with which the Assembly is taking tourism's potential the minister managed to obtain an unprecedented £22.6m budget for the WTB designed to develop further the quality and standard of the tourism industry in Wales and boost visitor expenditure. The Board also received an extra £5.35m from the Assembly Government's Rural Recovery Plan in 2001 to help develop initiatives to encourage the industry's recovery from the impact of foot-and-mouth. There was also a significant increase in funding for tourism on a regional level with Regional Tourism Partnerships (RTP) receiving £2.5m in 2002 for a range of activities — more than double previously on offer (http://www.wales-tourist-board.gov.uk 2002). However, the problems facing the minister and Welsh tourism is all too clear. Apart from having to deal with the aftermath of foot-and-mouth and September 11, the Welsh tourism season has now contracted to the point that 60% of all tourism business transacted in Wales is done in three months — June, July and August. This is compounded by the fact that although Wales has 8% of all U.K. tourism spend, it only attracts 1.4% of the U.K. overseas spend. Furthermore, it is not conducive to the development of Welsh tourism that the average size of hotel/guest house in Wales is only 6 bed rooms, and only 6% of hotels had over forty bedrooms (Achieving our Potential, A Tourism Strategy for Wales 2002).

Ireland

That we are writing separately about tourism policy in both Northern and Southern Ireland speaks volumes for the political situation that has evolved there over the centuries. However, this is the reality, and although the majority of tourists care little about the border that runs from Londonderry to Dundalk, the tourism policies, and consequently the successes of this divided land are very different. This was evidenced by the fact that in the 15 years between 1985 and 2000, while the South tripled its visitor numbers, the North failed to even double them. For example, in 2000 there were 11 times as many tourists visiting the South as the North. Nevertheless, there was an increase of visitors by 65% in 1995 following the first ceasefires for which the market was quite unprepared and which produced an equally dramatic decline following the resumption of hostilities, demonstrating the potential of peace to contribute to growth in tourism (O'Maolin).

The Evolution of Tourism in Ireland

Decades of unrest which led to the War of Independence in 1916, followed in 1920 by the annexing of the six counties that became Northern Ireland, and in 1922 the formation of the Irish Free State (MacAnnaidh 2001), meant that tourism was not given the focus it had in other parts of the British Isles. Furthermore, by 1949, and the Second World War over, the twenty-six counties of Ireland, known since 1939 as Eire, had turned themselves into a Republic, claiming sovereignty over the other six (Kee 1980: 232), a claim which they relinquished in 1998 as part of the *Good Friday Agreement* (1998). By 1972, the British once more imposed direct rule on Northern Ireland, and it was another twenty-seven years before its politicians were again in control, this time due to devolution in 1999, but only until the winter of 2002 when the Assembly was suspended with direct rule returning to London. In all that time the North has been a battleground between those Northern Irish who wish to remain British and those who want the North to be subsumed by the South, not an environment one would have thought that would be conducive to tourism, or one in which tourism policy was a government priority.

During the various troubles, the railways suffered considerably, and consequently trade of those resorts at the end of the line. In the Easter Rising of 1916, stations in Dublin were taken over by the Irish Volunteers. Then the military authorities' restricted passenger traffic and used some of the stations as barracks. Certain areas were closed by the authorities and markets were stopped, so that the railways lost passenger and goods traffic. In addition, certain lines were closed altogether, further exacerbating trading difficulties for those resorts that relied upon them. Furthermore, during the Civil War in 1922 rails were torn up, bridges destroyed, and trains derailed or fired upon, and this had serious implications for both inward and domestic tourism, which Ireland while focusing on more life-threatening activities took a long time from which to recover.

Between the wars tourism continued to grow, albeit due to poor economic conditions and unemployment, slowly. However, the arrival of GIs in Dublin and Belfast during the war, and the benefits of the post-war upsurge of visitors from Britain were spread throughout the country. Nevertheless, in the fifties, as the island struggled to emerge from the shadow of economic stagnation, tourism remained a minor industry, and policy-makers of the day realised that there was little profit from attracting visitors to a country whose people were demoralised by unemployment and emigration (http://www.bftrade. travel.ie/downloads/FailteBusiness.doc).

In common with other destinations in the twentieth century the island's ability to attract and to export tourists was affected by first the emergence of the motor car, then the airplane. For the Republic its first *Programme for Economic Expansion* (Stationery Office 1958) also brought about a dramatic change in its economic philosophy, transforming decades of introverted protectionism into a new outward-looking, confident country in which investment was encouraged, exports promoted and barriers to trade dismantled. Furthermore, tourism was seen as an industry with considerable potential. Almost simultaneously, world tourism was growing too, thanks to new jet aircraft which were fast and economic and could transport large numbers of people over very long distances at affordable prices. Overnight, it seemed, for the Republic anyway, that it was a player in a world market; and that world market not only had an efficient means of travelling to Ireland but also a reason, many of them ancestors of those driven out of the country by the Great Famine (Bord Fáilte Business 2000; Guiney 2002).

The shift to air travel facilitated the development of airports such as Dublin, Cork and Shannon, and the establishment of Aer Lingus in Southern Ireland in 1936. As with the advent of the railways in the nineteenth century, the passengers required to be accommodated, fed and entertained. This resulted in numerous hotels, restaurants, and visitor attractions being built. In the main the visitors were people from Ireland who had themselves emigrated, or who were the children of emigrants. This influx of tourists was facilitated by the liberalization of the air transport industry in general which reduced substantially the cost of access to Ireland (Guiney 2002; 40). For example, transatlantic routes were commonplace by 1960, and in 1980 the first direct air service to a continental destination (Amsterdam) from Belfast opened (Wilson 1997: 150). The Republic's second air line Ryanair has since established itself as the market leader for inexpensive no frills flights. However, the impact of a century of conflict, the fact that the North and South marketed themselves separately until the eighties, and that the troubles have been mainly in the North since the nineteen-twenties has been more detrimental to it than the South, and has meant a much larger proportion of its population than in the South holidaying elsewhere. Also, while Belfast became more famous for conflict than tourism, indeed it was once renowned as the Beirut of Western Europe (McKenna 1999), Dublin established itself as a vibrant destination in its own right, competing with the world's renowned capital cities, in particular for short-break business, part of which it built on its almost unique literary heritage. Furthermore, while Northern Ireland's tourism policy was in the main at the behest of Westminster, the advantage taken by the Republic of a significant expansion in international access facilitated by adroit use of EU monies (Southern Ireland gained membership of the European Community in 1973) has enhanced its tourism industry's ability to out perform its Northern neighbour, both in growth and attracting visitors. For example, from 1986 to 1996, foreign earnings from tourism grew by 370% in the Republic, compared to between 95 and 191% in other EU countries (WTO 1999).

Meanwhile, Northern Ireland's income fell dramatically, particularly on every occasion a significant terrorism act was committed. For example, the outbreak of virtual civil war in Northern Ireland in the early seventies, and which resulted in direct British rule, reduced the number of visitors to Ireland dramatically, particularly British ones. A demoralized industry was encouraged by the politicians to appeal to the ties between Ireland and the Irish ethnic market, particularly in the U.K. and North America (Bord Failte Business 2002; Guiney 2002). However, Belfast was almost a no-go area for many people at this time, and although it has since invested heavily, particularly in its new waterfront area, and is endeavouring to market itself as a leading European destination, and that other more remote areas are experiencing a significant increase in visitors, the troubles are never far away. Its future success, therefore, is dependent on its divided population turning its back on its history of violence.

Northern Ireland

Development of Structure and Policy

In the same decade that saw Northern Ireland separated from the South, its small but determined tourism industry participated in the BTA's predecessor, the government sponsored Travel Association of Great Britain and Ireland, which was established in 1929. Between then and 1999 when the tourism industry had grown considerably and tourism became one of the powers devolved to the Northern Ireland Assembly, tourism policy in Northern Ireland was influenced heavily by U.K. tourism policy. Furthermore, those responsible for tourism kept a very watchful eye on developments in the South. Also, in common with Scotland and Wales, and with the advent of the *Development of Tourism Act* (1969) tourism became the responsibility of one of the Ministers of State. In this case the Minister of Economic Development, who reported to the Secretary of State, and to whom in turn the Northern Ireland Tourist Board (NITB) and the Tourism and Hospitality Training Council reported (CERT 1997).

However, under the *Development of Tourism Traffic Act (N Ireland)* (1948) Northern Ireland was the first of the home countries to frame tourism in legislation. It was also the first to establish its own tourist board, and to have a minister responsible for it. Its objective was to both develop the tourism product and to attract visitors from outside the Province, a difficult task when for the next fifty years it tore itself apart. Furthermore, in 1972, and coinciding with direct British rule, the Act was amended by the *Tourist Traffic (Northern Ireland) Order* that legislated for local authorities to provide or assist in the provision of tourist amenities (Holloway 1998: 273). This was done mainly through the Tourism Accommodation Grants Scheme, and the Tourist Amenity Grants Scheme (CERT 1997).

In 1985, concerned at the lack of direction of tourism in Northern Ireland, the NITB, influenced by the Republic of Ireland's tourism policy White Paper (see below), and by the debate led by Lord Young on the Westminster government's future role in tourism (HMSO 1985), sought responses to its own discussion paper on Northern Ireland tourism. This paper discussed its structure, its potential, and the difficulties facing the tourism industry in a war torn society. This was followed in 1989 by the Department of Economic Development's report on tourism, *Tourism in Northern Ireland — A View to the Future* (1989). It proposed a body outwith government taking control of Northern Ireland tourism in terms of both product development and marketing, but this took to 2002 to occur (see further on, Tourism Ireland Limited) (Wilson 1997: 153). Furthermore, because of the political climate at the time the report did not envisage this body even being an all-Ireland one.

The fact that this report was not acted upon was partly due to the Major government coming to power in 1990, and tourism in Westminster, to which Northern Ireland tourism policy was still in thrall, transferring responsibility in 1992 to the Department of National Heritage. Furthermore, the NITB, whose powers would have been curtailed by the new body, lobbied vigorously to ensure that it rather than any new body would oversee tourism in the Province. At the same time, further amendments were made to *the Development of Tourism Traffic Act (N. Ireland) 1948* when *the Tourism (Northern Ireland) Order* (1992) legislated to regulate tourism accommodation, extend the functions of district councils in relation to tourism, and incorporate the NITB, underpinning its survival.

By 1999, by which time the NITB had produced a further two initiatives: *A Sustainable Approach* (1993), and *A Development Strategy 1995 to 2000* (1995), *the Northern Ireland Act* (1998) had established a Northern Ireland Assembly, which has both legislative and administrative powers, and whose Department of Enterprise, Trade and Investment became responsible for tourism. With this went expectations of the Assembly's legislative competence. For example, due to the special political and religious circumstances of Northern Ireland, provisions have been made to ensure cross-community support for various measures. Among these are the appointments of the First Minister and Deputy First Minister (McFadden & Lazarowicz 1999: 97), and in a lesser sense that Ireland should be promoted openly abroad as a single product. This was a fact that had been evident since the 1980s when NITB, Aer Lingus, and Bord Fáilte (the Republic of Ireland Tourist Board) combined to promote all-Ireland holidays successfully in the USA, even if 80% of the Northern Ireland traffic derived from this initiative was generated from the South (Wilson 1997: 150).

Even before devolution both the names NITB and Bord Fáilte appeared in advertisements and promotions (CERT 1997), as opposed to the two component parts of the island marketing themselves separately. Although the NITB was an enthusiastic participant in the above relationship, during the troubles Bord Fáilte was uncomfortable about its identification with the troubled North. Its concerns have since changed. For example, the reduction in conflict in the North has made the whole island more attractive to the international holiday market, benefiting both north and south. Nevertheless, there are conflicting views of the peace dividend in terms of tourism. For the South, the relative peace in the North could have a negative impact at least in the early years, in that the more attractive the North becomes as a holiday destination the more shorter stays in the Southern market will be combined with trips to the North. Furthemore, as the troubles subside visitors previously attracted to the Republic may now visit the North instead, threatening the South's tourism income (Wilson 1997: 150). Nevertheless, to benefit both parts of the island needs a dramatic increase in overall visitor numbers, and/or in spend per visitor. The latter issue is particularly problematic in that spend per visitor is not increasing at the same rate as raw numbers; evidence that the vast marketing effort over the past 15 years has generated volume rather than value. Furthermore, the Republic's border region has not benefited proportionately from the tourism boom of the past decades, much of which was attributable to growth in Dublin city breaks. This has also had an impact on the border areas which have a much shorter holiday season, and this is also a severely limiting factor in Northern Ireland (O'Maolin 2000). However, with the current ceasefire the 5 Regional Tourism Organisations (RTO) (North West, incorporating Derry visitor and convention bureau, Belfast visitor and convention business, North East, South East, and South West), offer a unique opportunity to ensure that the marketing and development of their areas are closely focused to the management of the product in terms of both the natural and built environment (McKenna 1999). They do this in conjunction with the 26 district councils all of which are involved in marketing their own area and running tourist information centres, leisure facilities and visitor attractions. However, their role and that of NITB and Bord Fáilte is changing as a result of an agreement to form the aforementioned Tourism Ireland Limited, the first all-Ireland tourism body, which was incorporated formally in December 2000 by the North South Ministerial Council. It has taken over responsibility for the international marketing of the island of Ireland as a tourist destination with effect from the 2002 season and is undertaking a number of functions previously carried out by NITB and Bord Fáilte. These include ownership and management of Tourism Brand Ireland (founded in 1996), strategic all-island destination marketing in all markets outside the island of Ireland, and responsibility for the entire overseas office network. The new company is also responsible for the international delivery of product/regional marketing programmes on behalf of NITB and Bord Fáilte. However, the underlying products will continue to be developed by NITB and Bord Fáilte (Tourism Promotion — Tourism Ireland Ltd, News Release, Department of Tourism, Sport and Recreation 2002).

Concurrent with this radical initiative, tourism in Northern Ireland which unlike Wales and Scotland did not review its tourism policy following devolution, is only now in the process of carrying out a fundamental review of its international and regional tourism policy. The objective is to examine tourism policies over the last five years and to establish rural tourism communities which have up until now been marginalized by the troubles. Until this is complete tourism policy in Northern Ireland is effectively the *NITB Draft Corporate Plan 2002–2005*, aligned to various marketing plans and initiatives. However, by 2003, the Northern Irish Executive has undertaken to implement a new tourism development strategy by which time, and much to many hard-liners disdain, Tourism Ireland Limited will become a dominant and influential force in all-Ireland tourism, and a beacon of hope for eventual peace.

Republic of Ireland

Development of Structure and Policy

The Republic of Ireland government intervened directly in the tourism industry for the first time in 1924 when the then Minister for Industry and Commerce was supportive of the establishment of an Irish Tourist Association (ITA). Its main purpose was to elevate an industry riven by civil war from the mundane of everyday life, and for whose services there was an increasing, albeit class-driven demand. In a different form, the ITA had been established in 1893 when after failing to convince his employers to invest in the promotion of Ireland overseas the manager of the Thomas Cook office in Dublin resigned, and set up the ITA. In 1924, with the encouragement of the Minister for Industry and Commerce, two other Irish organisations the Tourist Organisation Society, and the West of Ireland Tourist Development Association, both formed in the early twenties, merged with the original ITA to form the new Irish Tourist Association. Furthermore, in 1926, the ITA undertook the first concerted campaign, supported by the government, to promote Ireland as a destination. However, it soon became obvious that the ITA could not effectively promote Ireland as a destination without substantial state support, and lobbied successive Governments for state intervention. However, this did not occur until 1939 when the *Tourist Traffic (Development) Act* (1931) was amended. This act was framed by a government intent that its economy recover quickly from the previous decade's civil war. Its intention was to make better provision for the encouragement and development of tourist traffic in saorstát eireann, and to enable local authorities to expend resources for that purpose (Tourism Traffic (Development) Act 1931). However, the development of tourism as specified by the Act was complicated by the economic war with the U.K., which Ireland suffered between 1932 to 1938 (Kee 1980; MacAnnaidh 2001). During this time, there was also a growing dominance of Catholic social values underpinned by the emergence of the struggle to resist profligate overseas Protestant influences, and this had a moral impact on what those involved in tourism could and could not do (Heuston 1997: 23). Furthermore, in 1939 the role of the ITA was changed to concentrate on local tourism promotion and the provision of information through local Tourist Offices, not unlike the service provided by Regional Tourism Authorities (RTAs) today, its role of promoting tourism abroad taken over by Bord Cuartaíochta nah Éireann (The Irish Tourist Board) which was established by the Government in that same year. The ITA was given a seat on the newly established Irish Tourist Board, and it also received an annual grant from the state body. The Act also obliged all hotels to register with the Irish Tourist Board. Those who did not comply had to remove from their premises any sign bearing the word Hotel. Unfortunately, war broke out in Europe soon afterwards and the momentum that was beginning to build up over tourism development was abandoned (Bord Fáilte Business 2002).

After the end of the Second World War, in which Ireland remained neutral, visitors returned and significant growth was recorded; both in incoming visitors and in domestic tourism. Unfortunately, this increase in visitors was unaccompanied by a relaxation in the attitudes towards the behaviour of visitors whose moral codes were much less strict than the Irish, and were perceived as a corrupting influence. Furthermore, the extension of opportunity for overseas travel meant that the Irish became more exposed to ways of life that were unfathomable to earlier Irish generations. This caused tensions between what the Republic as a tourism destination should offer, and what it could offer, without offending a large majority of its population, and worse still the Catholic Church within whose grip Irish tourism, and to a certain extent the government, was in thrall.

In 1952, the ITA had outlived its usefulness, and An Bord Fáilte was established to develop the Irish tourism product, while Fogra Fáilte was formed to promote and market the industry. In the spirit of institutionalism, endeavouring to reflect the disciplines of corporatism, they were amalgamated in 1955 to form Bord Fáilte Eireann, and then in an era of networking restructured again in 1994 as Bord Fáilte, to concentrate on three important areas: promotion and selling; developing products and markets; and, supplying market information (CERT 1997).

The publication of the aforementioned first *Programme for Economic Expansion* in 1958 was a watershed for the Republic. Within a few years it had embraced free trade, the development of exports and the attraction of industry from overseas, and changed forever the perception of a closed, protectionist economy and society. As a result, the work of Bord Fáilte became an integral part of Irish life. For example, it participated in this new, confident society by further developing tourism and taking initiatives in many areas of Irish life such as designing new signposts and co-operating with Local Authorities in a major re-signposting of the entire country (Bord Fáilte Business 2002).

The catalyst for Irish tourism was when Ireland joined the European Union in 1973 as a peripheral and relatively poor state with average per capita incomes at 62% of the EU average. Ireland's disadvantaged position was recognised in 1988 when all of Ireland was designated as an Objective One region, which meant that average incomes were at or below 75% of the EU average. In addition, since 1992 Ireland was one of four Member States to receive Cohesion Fund monies. Ireland has thus enjoyed priority status in the EU for the purposes of regional transfers. For example, since 1988, Ireland has prepared two *National Development Plans*, the first from 1988 to 1993 and the second from 1994 to the end of 1999. The latter plan and the accompanying *Community Support Framework* (CSF) (1993) identified four priority areas for expenditure in Ireland: support for productive investment; infrastructure; the development of human resources; and, harnessing the potential of local initiatives. These priorities were implemented as Operational Programmes covering such diverse areas as industrial development, tourism, transport, rural development and environmental services (EU Ireland 2002).

As tourism numbers grew and the realization dawned that there were not enough people with the skills to deal with consumers, in 1963 CERT was established to recruit and train workers for the hotel sector, its remit later extended to include all tourism employment (CERT 1997). Despite the increase in tourism traffic, it took until 1977 for tourism in the Republic of Ireland to be given greater emphasis by being included in a government department in its own right, and furthermore with a seat in cabinet. As a result of Jack

Lynch's Fianna Fail party regaining power the Department of Tourism and Transport was established, which evolved into the Department of Tourism, Sport and Recreation (Mac Annaidh 2001), and in 2002 the Department of Arts, Sport and Tourism. For the first time, Irish tourism had full ministry status with a Cabinet Minister and a Minister of State. The Department became responsible for the formulation of national policies connected with tourism, charging the state-sponsored bodies and executive agencies under the aegis of the Department with the implementation of these policies, while responsibilities in regard to tourism services were related to the Department's policy-making, funding and supervisory roles (Bord Fáilte Business 2002). Since then, and due to the nine occasions that the Republican government changed in 25 years, tourism has been the responsibility of numerous and varied ministries, some of them incongruous (for further information see Irish Government tourism web site). Furthermore, the role of successive governments has largely been in policy formulation, with more detailed and specific responsibilities divided among state and semi-state bodies (CERT 1997: 19–21; Guiney 2002).

In 1985 because of the disappointing statistics of the previous fifteen years, the Department of Tourism and Transport published a White Paper on *Tourism Policy*. This was the government's first official attempt to clarify thinking on tourism in a focused manner, and to clarify the broad objectives of policy (Wilson 1997: 117). Nevertheless the White Paper in common with most other European countries, placed job creation high on the agenda as the desired outcome of tourism development in Ireland, the antithesis of the present. Its policy objectives were further stressed in its 1987 *Programme for National Recovery*, and 1989 *National Development Plan* 1989–1993. The latter generated the first *Operational Programme for Tourism*, which ran from 1989 to 1993. Furthermore, the concept of partnership, which had existed within the industry for decades, was given a new impetus in the second *Operational Programme for Tourism* (1994–1999) which followed on. This saw an acceleration of development of the modern Republican tourism sector. For example, based on the outcome of the White Paper on *Tourism Policy* (1985), the Irish Government, with the assistance of large financial incentives from the EU, began to invest heavily in the potential of the industry. This coincided with the unsurpassed growth of the Republic's economy, which earned it the sobriquet the Celtic Tiger.

During this time the government commissioned consultants A. D. Little (1995) to report on the role and structure of Bord Fáilte. This report, published in 1995, recommended that Bord Fáilte should concentrate its resources on its marketing role and should divest itself of some of its traditional activities. Nevertheless, it retained overall responsibility for the registration and grading of accommodation, but did commission contractors to carry out the day-to-day operations of this responsibility.

With the undoubted economic success of the tourism industry have come new challenges such as the integration of the government departments other than the Department of Arts, Sport and Tourism that are currently involved in tourism — the Department of Community, Rural and Gaeltacht Affairs; the Department of Agriculture and Food; the Department of Tanaiste, Enterprise, Trade and Employment; and the Department of Transport. The combined challenges for these departments include not only the pressures on the environment in highly popular areas, but also the infrastructural deficits where development in supporting facilities has not kept pace with the expansion of tourism product. Furthermore, there is a risk to the warmth of the traditional Irish welcome as staff shortages arise in a tightening labour market, combined with a general increase in the pace of life leading to difficulty in differentiating the unique nature of the Irish tourism product. Of course, there is also the price competitiveness of Irish tourism being threatened by inflationary pressures, and exchange rate fluctuations.

Such growth has also led to a change of Government policy. For example, as we have already highlighted, the 1985 White Paper placed job creation as the key to the desired outcome of tourism development in Ireland. Now the emphasis is on sustainable and spatially balanced development. For example, the new developing strategy will be one that reflects a desire to ensure that the fruits of economic prosperity are shared throughout the country and the negative effects of development on the environment are minimized. However, this will put further pressure on Bord Fáilte and the six Regional Tourism Authorities (RTAs).

Set up in 1964 as Regional Tourism Organizations, and restructured in 1989/1990 so that geographically they corresponded with EU regional planning areas, the enhanced collaboration North and South of the border arising from *the Good Friday Agreement* (1998) has particular implications for the RTAs. For example, the government's express intention of exploiting the potential for joint marketing of the whole island of Ireland, combined with the review of Bord Fáilte and CERT, means that their role is set to alter again. An initiative by the then Department of Tourism, Sport and Recreation undertook a review of tourism policy in line with the *Irish Government's National Development Plan 2000–2006*, published in 1999, and which lays out the foundation for Ireland's continuing economic and social development into the 21st century, was again taken up in November 2002 by the newly formed Department of Art, Sport and Tourism.

One outcome of the initiatives described above, is as we have already described, the formation of the aforementioned Tourism Ireland Limited, which has superseded Board Fáilte, and NITB. Tourism Ireland was established under the framework of the Belfast agreement of Good Friday 1998 to promote increased tourism to the entire island of Ireland. The board of directors of Tourism Ireland is made up of twelve individuals representing leading tourism industry interests north and south, Bord Fáilte and the (NITB). A company limited by guarantee, Tourism Ireland is jointly funded by the two governments with the marketing based on a 2:1 ratio South/North. The role of Tourism Ireland is; to carry out strategic all-Ireland destination marketing in all markets outside the island of Ireland; to undertake regional/product marketing and promotional activities on behalf of Borde Failte Eireann (BFE) and the NITB overseas; to own and manage Tourism Brand Ireland and its associated communications materials.

Meanwhile, a successor organization to Bord Fáilte and CERT, Fáilte Ireland, will bring together in 2003 the functions they currently carry out, with an Interim Board and Chair already appointed (Department of Arts, Sport and Tourism News Release 25 November 2002; Fáilte Ireland Bill 19th November 2002; McDaid 2002). The National Tourism Development Authority Act 2003, which provides a statutory basis for the new National Tourism Development Authority (to be known as Fáilte Ireland) was signed into law by the President on 13th April 2003. Following this, arrangements were being put in place to establish it on a formal basis by the end of April 2003. The remit of the new Authority will be to promote tourism within and to the State and the development of tourism facilities and services, including the promotion of training, human resource and marketing skills development in the tourism sector. With responsibility for international tourism marketing now resting with the new all island body, Tourism Ireland Ltd., the intention is that Fáilte Ireland will work closely with the tourism industry, supporting the further sustainable development of the sector in Ireland. When the new Authority is established, Bord Fáilte Éireann and CERT will be dissolved and their functions transferred to the Authority (Department of Arts, Sport and Tourism News Release 6 November 2002).

Meanwhile, the then Minister for Arts, Sport and Tourism, Mr. John O'Donoghue, T. D., announced a major review of tourism policy (Press Release 6 November 2002). The review will be led by the Department of Arts, Sport and Tourism, in close consultation with the tourism industry that has recently, through the Irish Tourist Industry Confederation (ITIC), produced their own assessment of the challenges which currently face Irish tourism. The review will also include an assessment of the potential of the sector and identify the key determinants of both an industry and Government led strategy for the future sustainable development of tourism in Ireland.

Summary

It would be easy to claim that tourism policy in Wales and Northern Ireland (and Scotland) prior to devolution was at the behest of Westminster, and that no original thinking came out of Cardiff or Belfast, or that tourism in Northern Ireland while being dominated by Westminster thinking was influenced equally by what was happening in the Republic of Ireland. However, what is clear is that tourism policy in each of these countries has evolved haphazardly, and that in effect there is no real tourism policy, replaced instead by strategies and initiatives that imply explicitly that these are policies i.e. *NITB's Draft Corporate Plan 2002–2005*, which in the absence of anything better is along with various marketing plans effectively the present Northern Ireland tourism policy. Equally, and although it has a number of other priorities, is it not strange that unlike Wales and Scotland, Northern Ireland has not addressed tourism policy since devolution?

In any case, as Elliott (1997: 86) claims, formulating policy is made all the more difficult because tourism is highly fragmented. Think of the number of organisations, government departments, companies and individuals mentioned above, and this is only a small percentage of those involved in tourism. Furthermore, up until 1997, government and the political ideology of the time appeared to be that the public interest was best served by creating a very broad economic development framework, and allowing the industry and those involved in it to formulate their own policy, while pursuing their own interests. The existing Westminster government of the late nineteen-nineties and early two thousands appears to have done little to assuage the feeling that the above still stands. Nor have the individual countries' Assemblies or Parliament, and it is likely that it will be a very long time before tourism in any of them will receive the recognition its industry craves. What this means to English tourism, particularly in relation to the development of policy may be dependent on the present Labour administration's plans to devolve more power to the English regions, which would see tourism decision-making revert to the local level.

Part II

Scottish Tourism

Chapter 5

The Development, Structure, and Public Policy of Tourism in Scotland

Introduction

This chapter discusses tourism development, structure, and public policy in the 20th and 21st centuries in Scotland, and also the impact of devolution on Scottish tourism, an important outcome of which has been the elevation of tourism to cabinet status (the only such status in its own right in the U.K., albeit aligned to two other ministries: Culture and Sport, and since May 2003 somewhat downgraded in terms of ministerial status). However, although this was the uppermost pre-devolution wish of the industry it has not made it any less fragmented, disparate, or backward looking. There is also a continuing polarisation of opinions of those who view the industry as vital to Scotland's economic growth, those whose expectations of it are in terms of lifestyle businesses, and those whose opinions lie somewhere in-between. Since devolution the various strategies, initiatives and announcements that purport to be Scottish tourism public policy have endeavoured to address the tension between these views. Furthermore, despite continual reviews of tourism in Scotland there is still no distinct tourism policy, or evident means by which such a policy could be integrated with other relevant policies. In fact, it could be argued that the integration of tourism with culture and sport in November 2001, as opposed to its previous ministry (Enterprise & Lifelong Learning 1999–2001), where it was mainstream of economic development, has been to the detriment of Scottish tourism, a topic which will be more fully discussed in Chapter 7. In the meantime, how Scottish tourism arrived at this point in its evolution is of interest here.

The Development of Scottish Tourism

The Beginning of the Twentieth Century

By the turn of the century, railways in Scotland were commonplace as were steamer connections, and although certain parts of Scotland still remained inaccessible to all but the most determined walkers, climbers, and sailors, less active travellers took the opportunity to explore parts of Scotland that had previously been ordinarily unexplored. By this time the rail and bus companies made it easier to plan a holiday in Scotland by combining them with steamer trips to both the inner and distant isles, in effect the establishment of a composite transport system that reduced journeys and journey time significantly. Furthermore, it made the transport of goods and livestock much more efficient, created opportunities for employment, and opened up many communities to a different way of life. However, there was no co-ordinated strategy for marketing the product, for improving quality, or for training staff. In consequence, Scotland developed inconsistently, haphazardly and erratically as a tourist destination (MacLennan & Smith 1998). For example, towards the end of the previous century the railway companies built large luxurious hotels situated in the main railway cities and rural resorts. They were grand institutions with Swiss and French trained Chefs and Waiters, banqueting rooms, liveried staff, and obsequious managers, but the remainder of the industry left a lot to be desired, and for many years the gaps in standards and service between the dispirit parts of the industry grew alarmingly. This was accentuated by the First World War, and then the depression of the class-ridden late twenties and early thirties.

The War Years

Scotland, as it developed as a tourism destination, was promoted through private sector rather than public sector initiatives as is evident now. The early promotions were by railways, coach and ferry companies, regional trade associations, and Chambers of Commerce. However, by 1938 the STB's forerunner, the Scottish Tourist Development Association (STDA) had been formed, with the Treasury contributing £250 towards promoting Scotland overseas. Furthermore, with the introduction in that same year of *the Holiday with Pay Act* (1938), Scots descended in their droves to the seaside resorts, and Scotland became a holiday destination for its own people.

However, although the Second World War put an end to the momentum that had grown between the wars, the creation of an Act in 1943 brought forward to Westminster by the then Secretary of State, Tom Johnston, which legislated for the provision of hydro-electricity in Scotland had a vast impact on tourism in Scotland, particularly the Highlands and Islands. For example, bringing a domestic electrical supply to the most northern parts of Britain was, according to Devine (1999), the necessary pre-condition for the development of a mass tourist industry and the ubiquitous bed-and-breakfast establishment of modern times. Meanwhile, in 1945 under pressure from Johnston, the STDA became known as the Scottish Tourist Board, which according to Aitken (1992: 256) was autonomous from London, but still resolutely amateur in character. By this time local councils, mainly in the Highlands and Islands and on the west coast, led public sector tourism initiatives while other local tourist associations evolved haphazardly throughout the rest of Scotland, the most active perhaps being the British Hotels and Restaurants Association (BHRA), a forerunner of the British Hospitality Association (BHA) (Bacon, personal communication, May 2001).

The years following the war were grim for the Scottish tourism industry, and up until the late 1950s the seaside resorts, which had changed little since the 1940s and yet gave some respite from the year round toil of hard industrial or agricultural work, cornered the Scottish market, along with the now accessible north west of England. However, by the 1960s, less expensive airfares were common-place, as were easily accessible and more desirable destinations. Furthermore, new towns were being built, housing improved, and people also were in general better off, which led to greater expectations. Consequently, those who previously went doon the watter for the fair, followed the sun and now holidayed in foreign resorts, a pattern that has continued to grow ever since. This has changed the face of Scottish tourism from dependence on a product that was finding it increasingly hard to compete with the growing variety of destinations to be found abroad, with the warmer climate, and with the way of life to be found there, to one that is increasingly much more reflective of the history, culture, hospitality, food, environment, and geography of the country.

In effect, modern tourism development in Scotland started in the 1960s with the creation in 1965 of the Highlands and Islands Development Board (HIDB), and the passing in 1969 of the aforementioned *Development of Tourism Act* (see Chapter 4 for further information). However, from the late sixties onwards the history of the structure of tourism in Scotland from a public and private partnership perspective, particularly the way tourism developed and was marketed, changed dramatically. It is this important period that is explored in the next section of this chapter, and is chronologically encapsulated, and explained in terms of organisations and initiatives in the Appendix (Tables 1 and 2).

1965–1969

The Scottish tourism infrastructure of the sixties was one that was dominated in the Lowlands by eight regional councils and a voluntary association in Dumfries and Galloway, while in the Highlands and Islands the fifteen area tourist boards were co-ordinated through the newly-formed HIDB: a body that was designed to reverse the region's economic decline.

From Gladstone's Crofters Act of 1886, which gave security of tenure and the right to compensation for improvements made by the crofters (Scottish Crofting Foundation 1999), to the establishment of HIDB in 1965, there have been many efforts to reverse the decline in the Highlands and Islands economy. The establishment of HIDB was in fact a recognition that something had to be done not only to prevent economic decline, but also cultural and social decline (Linklater & Denniston 1992: 316). Furthermore, HIDB had, according to Devine (1999: 580), for 25 years executive authority over Highlands and Islands industry, transport, and tourism. In effect, it was also responsible for marketing tourism outwith Scotland. How the outside world perceived the area was, therefore, another of its priorities (Devine 1999: 607).

Apart from the decline in both cultural tradition and economic performance, the population of the Highlands and Islands too was decreasing rapidly. This had been in process for generations and was mostly caused by both the lack of previous government activity to stimulate the economy and the young, disillusioned at the lack of opportunity, leaving to find work elsewhere. Therefore, HIDB also took the lead role in not only stimulating the Highlands and Islands economy as a whole, but also in instigating a sense of community, and bringing back long-held but declining traditions. Nevertheless, despite huge grants to industry, the Fraser of Allander Institute's *Economic Commentary* (1991) noted that over the years of HIDB's existence, although it arrested the decline, the economic well being of the area had barely changed (Crichton 1992: 219), a situation, it could be argued, was a triumph in itself.

By the time of its demise in 1991 (see below, for further discussion on this point) the population of HIDB's 3.5 million-hectare area — almost a sixth of Britain's land mass and nearly half of Scotland's — had stabilised at around 370,000, some 7% of the Scottish total and back to the level of the years between the wars. As Aitken claims (1992: 316), the HIDB could not and did not claim sole credit for that, but few would deny it had a significant effect.

1969–1984

As has already been explained earlier in this chapter, government had begun to recognise, albeit in a limited way, the importance of tourism to the economy just prior to the Second World War. However, it was thirty years before this was formalised. Up until then tourism promotion, marketing and product development had been an uncoordinated effort with the various U.K. geographical areas following their own disparate strategies. This all changed in 1969 due to the aforementioned *Development of Tourism Act*; and, the creation of the Scottish Tourist Board (STB) as a result of the Act (similar name to the aforementioned Board, which had been independent of the government, set up in 1945 by Johnston, but resolutely different in character).

Even now, after devolution, Scotland is still part of the United Kingdom's National Tourist Organisational (NTO) structure, the legislative basis of which is the above Act, modified in 1984 in order that the STB could market Scottish tourism overseas, an action that was politically motivated by a government that was growing deeply unpopular in Scotland.

From the outset, STB was disadvantaged in that the Act that created it failed to articulate a clear policy for tourism, while omitting to set out clearly its roles and responsibilities (Lickorish 1988: 270–278). Friel (1995), for example, argues that to establish the Area Tourist Boards (ATBs) as statutory organisations, yet failing to provide statutorily for their funding was highly unusual and that that anomaly has since been exposed as Local Authorities, who in many instances are the prime ATB funders, faced more and more government budget cuts, and in some instances, capping. This meant that it was likely that there could only be one outcome if councillors had to choose between saving Local Authority jobs and services or giving discretionary funds to tourism. This is complicated further by the fact that the ATB network spent more time negotiating with the funding agencies than getting on with its prime function of attracting tourists. Also, prior to *A New Strategy for Scottish Tourism* (2000) (more on this later) many funding decisions were made too late anyway to allow the ATBs to plan properly for the following financial year. For example, and despite the above strategy, Greater Glasgow and Clyde Valley Tourist Board (GGCVTB), has to deal with seven local authorities, four Local Enterprise Companies (LECs), four Local Economic Forums (LEFs), and a vast membership.

In effect, the government had opted for NTOs in Britain purporting to operate at arms length from government which, in effect, they never did. For example, despite government's apparent lack of interest in them, they were never able to make strategic decisions without first ministerial consultation or approval, a situation that has been accentuated by devolution, recently almost to a point of inertia: a prime example being Wendy Alexander's handling in 2001 of the appointment of the new STB Chief Executive.

The Act also omitted any mention of local structures. Nor did it make provision for the involvement of Local Authorities or tourism associations in national policy making (Smith 1998). Relationships, too, between the ATBs became conflictive because of duplication, rivalry and overlap, a situation that the establishment of LEFs' business services review of 2001 (see later) was supposed to address. There was also difficulty in articulating links with other agencies responsible for related activities such as leisure, recreation and heritage (Heeley 1989). This was compounded by HIDB's extensive tourism activities particularly in relation to marketing, visitor services and development support.

Following the 1969 Act the STB (now VisitScotland), had responsibility for U.K. marketing of Scotland, grants, and a system of compulsory registration (through classification and grading), which was eventually established on a voluntary basis in 1975 when, in common with the other NTOs STB was left to devise its own scheme, confusing further the tourist in the U.K. It was also a focus for tourism as an industry, bringing to the public's attention the fact that this was an industry that, in comparison to other hard-pressed and in some cases declining industries had huge potential for growth. However, as will be discussed throughout this chapter there were a number of anomalies associated with its creation such as its inability until 1984 to market Scotland abroad or, as to the present, fund its network statutorily. The implications of both, particularly the latter, have had a long-lasting detrimental effect on the success or otherwise of Scottish tourism.

Various other changes took place during this period that were ultimately significant to U.K. tourism. These included in 1971 the introduction of decimalisation which had a significant impact on prices, and in 1972 the U.K. signing the EEC Treaty which paved the way for significant investment in tourism than would have otherwise been the case had the U.K. stayed out of Europe. In that same year a review of Scottish Local Authorities took place. The result of this was that in 1974 two-tiered local (53) and regional (9) councils were established including the massive Strathclyde Regional Council (SRC). In tandem, the three island groupings of Orkney, Shetland, and the Western Isles, became single-tier, multi-purpose authorities. This meant the demise of the old County Councils, many of which, particularly in the Highlands and Islands, had supported local tourist associations. These associations had been haphazard and uncoordinated enterprises, dependent on both the largesse of their council and of those operators locally who participated actively in promoting their area's product. Many councils had underwritten the local tourist associations, which, although capricious and unstructured, had assisted the councils by participating actively in establishing and promoting tourism in their areas. However, in 1982, following *the Local Government (Scotland) Act*, lower tier District Councils were given a discretionary tourism function that led to the setting up with STB of ATBs in Lowland Scotland (MacLellan & Smith 1998: 61). The new boards were based on the Highlands and Islands model and were established as a co-partnership between STB, the relevant district council(s), and the tourism industry, all of which contributed to the funding through grants or membership fees. In total, Scotland overnight had a network of 32 ATBs. However, six districts were sceptical about the scheme and neglected to participate, and a further four district councils chose to retain their autonomy over tourism matters in their area (Holloway 1998: 274–275).

In 1975, soon after the restructuring of the local authorities, Willie Ross, the then Secretary of State for Scotland, fuelled by a desire to emulate HIDB in Lowland Scotland, established the Scottish Development Agency (SDA). With a budget of £200 million and a remit which innovatively combined economic and environmental development, it absorbed three existing bodies: the Scottish Industrial Estates Corporation which administered a portfolio of land prescribed for factory space, believed to be 25 million square metres; the Small

Industries Council for the Rural Areas of Scotland, which was the regional policy unit for smaller outlying towns; and, a section of the Scottish Development Department, responsible for derelict land clearance (Aitken 1992: 317). It also took over the Scottish Council Development Industry's (SCDI) lead role in inward investment. To these were added some newly prescribed functions: industrial investment, particularly though equity and longer-term risk capital; business advice and consultancy; and, urban renewal (Aitken 1992: 317).

The SDA was, from the outset, charged with securing the maximum private sector input to what it did and, at its best, achieved leverage ratios of 7:1. However, Aitken (1992: 317) claims that level of leverage was usually possible only in times of relative prosperity, when investment optimism was high. He also argues that SE and HIE, SDA and HIDB's successors have inherited the paradox common to many remedial agencies. This is that the need for their work is highest when the resources to underpin it are at their lowest.

As it matured, the SDA focused increasingly on a small group of potential growth sectors such as electronics, biotechnology, advanced engineering and, assistance for academics to market their innovations. Tourism was not among these. In fact, although tourism was high on the list of priorities for HIDB, SDA never really grasped the potential of the industry and appeared content to leave the sector to the various councils, and STB who until 1993 were responsible for tourism grants.

During its 16-year existence, the SDA underwent various changes, including one change of political master, which almost saw its demise. When the Conservatives came to power in 1979 they considered scrapping it, but George Younger, the then Secretary of State was aware of the furore this would cause, particularly as his was fast becoming an extremely unpopular government in Scotland. Still wishing to see SDA operate more along commercial lines, he devised a strategy to reduce its employment-protection role, become a facilitator as opposed to an investor while being a catalyst for the forces of the market rather than a defence against them (Linklater & Denniston 1992: 318). SDA was also very active worldwide in endeavouring to attract inward investment, but despite its undoubted success in this field, the inward investment function was passed on to a joint SDA-Scottish Office bureau, Locate in Scotland (LiS), of which during the early nineties, the present SE CEO Dr. Robert Crawford was CEO. In addition, by 1985 plans had been made to dispose of its property portfolio and its investment portfolio. A devolved structure of seven regional offices was also introduced. It was hoped this would bring it closer to outlying businesses, but regardless of its efforts, politically it was under constant review and, as Aitken (1992: 318) claims, it was persistently saddled with the burden of having to justify itself constantly and to adapt to the nomadic whims of politicians, a situation with which the Scottish Enterprise network (SEn) and HIE are all too familiar, and perhaps even more so because of devolution.

SDA's eventual demise was of little surprise to anyone. The Thatcherites had been suspicious of it for all of Margaret Thatcher's time as Prime Minister, as it had, after all, been a creation of the Labour administration. Also, undiplomatically, it had made little attempt to ingratiate itself with the Scottish Office when the Conservatives took power, and valued its capacity to operate at arms length, and for Malcolm Rifkind, the then Secretary of State for Scotland, the SDA became a serious embarrassment. Despite the millions of pounds of public money being invested in Glasgow by the government through the SDA, the government received no credit and, worse still, no votes, and Rifkind, Kemp (1993: 188–190) alleges, found himself being treated with increasing distance by Mrs Thatcher. That it took so long for the Conservatives to deal with the SDA said much about its resilience, and even more about the Conservative's lack of real authority in Scotland in the eighties.

1984–1991

That it was fully 15 years before any significant alterations were made to the 1969 *Development of Tourism Act* reflects successive government's priorities in relation to tourism. For instance, the anomaly of the British Tourist Authority (BTA) being empowered to promote U.K. tourism overseas while STB was forbidden from doing so had long been a cause of dissatisfaction to the Scottish tourism industry. Until the modification to the Act in 1984, which at last permitted the STB to market Scotland abroad, this had meant, somewhat perversely, that while a regional council or the HIDB could promote tourism overseas, the national agency, the STB could not (Linklater & Denniston 1992: 256).

Three years later in 1987 and emulating the Westminster all-party Interdepartmental Tourism Co-ordinating Committee, the Scottish Tourism Co-ordinating Committee (STCG) was set up by the then Conservative administration in Scotland as a means by which the government could both interface with the tourism industry, and co-ordinate tourism across governmental departments. One of the Tourism Minister's responsibilities was to chair the STCG but although the Scottish Confederation of Tourism (SCOT) was a member, it was not until the mid-nineties following the formation of the Scottish Tourism Forum (STF) in 1994 that the industry felt that it had direct representation on the STCG. Nevertheless, it was very much top-down in terms of delivery and strategy, and failed to integrate policy across other government departments.

Until its demise in 2000 the STCG met three times a year and was, until the new parliament, chaired by the Scottish Office Industry Minister who was also Minister for Tourism, the last under the Westminster parliament being Lord Macdonald of Tradeston (formerly Gus Macdonald, Chairman of Scottish Media Group), who had other ministerial responsibilities, among them tourism which, it could be argued forcibly, was never high on his list of priorities.

Also in 1987 the STB (seen by some as the driving force behind the initiative), ETB and WTB agreed to a common classification and grading scheme which graded hotels into six categories using a criteria of one to five crowns, or a listed category for the most basic of establishments. By 1989 the three Boards improved the scheme further by awarding symbols from Approved, through Commended, and Highly Commended to Deluxe, but the English scheme continued to differ from the Scottish and Welsh one by emphasising facilities as opposed to quality.

1991–1993

Scotland's development agencies SE and HIE who superseded SDA and HIDB, also have a crucial role to play in present-day Scottish tourism. According to Aitken (1992: 272), Scottish Enterprise was the brainchild of Bill Hughes the then Chairman of the CBI Scotland, who was close to the Conservatives, and who convinced the Secretary of State, Malcolm

Rifkind, of the merits of an Enterprise Network. The consequence of Hughes action was that a White Paper, *Scottish Enterprise: a New Approach to Training and Enterprise Creation* (1988), was published, with the Secretary of State for Scotland publishing his response to submissions in July 1989 (Brown *et al.* 1996: 113). As a result, two agencies were created in 1991 under the terms of *the Enterprise and New Towns (Scotland) Act* of 1990 by merging SDA and HIE with the Training Agency (TA).

Both SE and HIE are now agencies of the Scottish Executive, with Boards comprised of the public, private and voluntary sectors, the latter now becoming more commonly known as the third sector. Their combined annual budget is circa £500 million, which is under constant threat (the SNP economic policy for the 2003 elections was to reduce the SE network from 12 LECs to 6 regional LECs, reducing the budget accordingly, an initiative that will put more pressure on the Scottish Executive, and may well also have repercussions for the Local Economic Forums and the ATBs). SE operates from Dumfries and Galloway to Aberdeenshire. HIE covers the remainder of Scotland including Orkney and Shetland, Argyll and the Isles and the Western Isles. Both exist to assist the people of Scotland generate and sustain jobs, prosper and create a high quality of life. They deploy a wide range of powers, resources and skills in pursuit of their mission — financial instruments; advisory services; marketing; training; property; new ideas; and networks. These resources are used as flexibly as possible to support customers and partners and to meet the needs of particular opportunities and challenges. Alongside local capability, SE and HIE has nation-wide planning and operational capability. This allows plans to be made and action taken to support key Scottish industries and to address issues that have a Scotland-wide dimension. Until winter 2001, SE also operated internationally on Scotland's behalf, through the aforementioned Locate in Scotland (LiS), for example in attracting inward investment and promoting Scottish products and services overseas (Connolly 1999). Under the banner of Global Connections, one of the Smart, Successful Scotland organising themes (2001) (see later in chapter), this function changed in 2001, when it became the responsibility of Scottish Development International (SDI), and reflects SE's change of emphasis on inward investment e.g. instead of inward investment in and exports out, Global Connections stresses knowledge in and knowledge out: a seismic shift in inward investment strategy.

In tourism terms, SE and HIE's roles (and despite *the Scottish Tourist Board Management Review and Recommendations* (2000)), are very much strategic. They have devised and supported initiatives in conjunction with the 22 Local Enterprise Companies (LECs), which although not created by statute became the means by which SE and HIE contracted their local delivery services in each area of Scotland. In fact, Tourism Training Scotland (TTS), which will also be discussed later in this chapter, would in all probability not have emerged as it did in 1992 but for SEn/HIE, which were anxious to improve and develop the industry's skills. TTS was seen as the perfect vehicle to drive such new initiatives, but was superseded in 2000 by the new Skills Group (Tourism People).

1993–1996

In 1993, as part of a further review of the Local Authority structure, it became obvious to government that the global market instead of a vast opportunity for Scottish tourism was fast becoming a new vibrant and very real threat. The review led to the publication of Lord James Douglas-Hamilton, the Scottish Office minister responsible for tourism's *Scottish Tourism, Strategic Plan* (STCG 1994), which revealed Scotland was failing to realise its full potential; the skills base was sadly shallow; and the perception of the industry was that it was low on skills, short on pay and long on hours. Furthermore, an analysis of its performance exposed Scotland's relatively poor tourism performance, particularly the domestic market.

A review of STB also took place. Ordered by the then Secretary of State for Scotland, Ian Lang, it was a by-product of a sweeping re-organisation of Scottish local government, which as will be recalled, was at that time two tiered; local and regional councils replacing the original single tiered authorities in 1974, the new model being 32 unitary authorities. This review produced some reallocation of responsibilities among the various public bodies involved in Scottish tourism. The most severe blow to STB was that the development powers set out in Section Four of the 1969 Act were transferred to the SE and HIE network (MacLellan & Smith 1998: 216). The implications for the tourism industry were clear. It was becoming mainstream of economic development, with the ability to learn from the experiences of other industries, not as it had been up until then, operating in isolation.

At the same time, perhaps as a form of compensation for the loss of its development powers, STB became accountable for the HIDB's successor HIE's responsibility for marketing and co-ordinating the Highland ATB's activities. This meant STB took on essentially a marketing role within Scottish tourism. However, during the review, SEn/HIE conspired unsuccessfully to take over the full responsibilities of the STB. This combined with losing their developmental powers has had a long-lasting impression on their inter-organisational relationships (Kerr & Wood 1999). This was compounded by the fact that the industry was under-represented at a national strategic level. Despite the increasing influence of the Scottish Division of the British Hospitality Association (BHA) whose membership comprised most of the prestigious hotels in Scotland, at this time there were a number of disparate organisations representing their own views, but no one organisation representing the views of the private sector in Scotland. Therefore, in 1994 the STF was formed. An amalgam of members who represented the broad spectrum of tourism business in Scotland; its remit was to influence national policy in tourism, participate in the STCG, to lobby for the industry, and to reflect the view of the private sector.

In 1993 another review *Taking Stock* (HMSO 1993) took place. This was of Scotland's place in the union, with one of the outcomes being the transfer of control of training from the Employment Department to the Scottish Office thus reinforcing the distinctiveness of policy in Scotland, ensuring that when Lang issued the Scottish Office's first consultative document on the future of training policy, he was able to claim he had formal responsibility for the Government's policy and resources for training (Brown *et al.* 1996: 114). Nevertheless, from then to the present Scotland has had to follow Westminster's line e.g. SkillSeekers, Modern Apprentices, Individual Learning Accounts and so on.

SE and HIE through the LECs were also instrumental in ensuring that the aforementioned TTS, a public and private sector initiative set up in 1993, under the Chairmanship of Peter Lederer, to promote training and staff development within the industry, met its objectives. Among these were to improve the market intelligence and research data available on Scotland's key competitors and new destinations; to enable businesses to achieve the highest standards in terms of facilities and services; to improve the skills of managers;

maximise the development potential of businesses across every industry sector; to ensure businesses recognise the importance of being ready to access growing opportunities and benefits from the advancement of IT; to improve links between education and industry; and to position tourism as a first choice career which would attract the right calibre of people to drive the industry forward into the next century (Tourism Training Scotland 1998).

It was always intended that TTS would not be a long-term initiative and at various stages in 1999, its future was open to discussion. At one stage, it was even suggested that TTS be subsumed by STF. Following this, at a meeting at Gleneagles in December 1999, facilitated by STB, SE and HIE and chaired by Peter Lederer to discuss new arrangements for address-ing skills issues in tourism in Scotland, it was decided to recommend to Henry McLeish, the Minister for Enterprise and Lifelong Learning, that building on the achievements of TTS, a new grouping of industry, SE, HIE, Springboard and the NTOs be put in place. As will be seen from the strategy document and as has already been discussed, the outcome of this meeting was the recommendation that a new skills development group be formed, replacing TTS, which led to the establishment of Tourism People.

1996–1998

By 1996, SE had published a *Tourism Action Plan* (SE 1996) that outlined various initiatives designed to deliver tourism strategies over the next three years. This plan concentrated on strategy development, projects, assisting industry associations and network development and support. HIE's equivalent, its *Network Tourism Action Framework* (HIE 1996), which also included issues such as seasonality and full-time equivalent jobs, was intended to be a bridge between the HIE strategy and the earlier strategy, *the Scottish Tourism Strategic Plan* (STCG 1994), which was reviewed in 1997 — *Scottish Tourism Strategic Plan, Progress Report* (STCG 1997). *The Tourism Action Plan* (SEn 1996) was seen by the industry as a demonstration of the more integrated approach that the public sector agencies would take towards future tourism support activities. It also laid down a number of targets for the industry for the year 2000. Fifteen working groups were set up to implement the strategy and regional applications of the plan were to be elaborated with SEn/HIE, ATBs and Local Authorities (McLellan & Smith 1998: 50–51). In effect this had little impact on the industry, and caused further frustration at the inability of politicians to make fundamental changes e.g. funding, structure, STB, the relationship with BTA, and ATBs.

The year 1996 was also a watershed in another sense. Due to the then Secretary of State Ian Lang's 1993 review, not only did the Local Authorities revert to single-tiered authorities, meaning the demise of the vast SRC, but also due to statute the ATBs were reduced from 32 to 14, the former oddly enough being the number of the newly-formed Local Authorities. Unfortunately, statutory powers did not extend to funding the ATB network, and although debatable, for many operators this has been at the root of the network's financial problems.

Another SEn/HIE/TTS initiative during 1996 was to provide funds to the LECs of up to 50% of salaries for the LECs to employ Tourism Training Associates (TTAs). The TTA's remit was to work closely with the industry locally on initiatives, encourage ownership of major issues, and to forge strategic partnerships with the industry, with local government and with education. The TTA's had limited success. This was in the main due to their two-year fixed contracts. This condition caused many difficulties, particularly in recruiting appropriately experienced personnel or when halfway through a contract, a TTA left to take up another opportunity and a one-year, or in some instances, a nine-month contract was advertised. With no assurances of another role at the end of the contract, few people were enticed to become TTAs. Therefore, in 1998 due to the contracts ending and no further funding being available, many LECs either let their TTAs go while others found roles that were much more cross-functional, a situation that left tourism for some time with less LEC focus than previously, particularly during the many LEC restructures that took place that year and in 1999.

Meanwhile, in 1997, the Chair of STF, Paul Murray-Smith of Scottish Highland Hotels (SHH) became increasingly frustrated that STF consisted of too many vested interests, and that too much time was taken up with the minutiae (Murray-Smith, personal communication 1998). For example, as 80% of Scottish tourism businesses represented on STF in 1998 were small businesses, those larger STF members that had greater impact on economic wealth and the creation of jobs felt disenchanted and held back by what they described as their less imaginative colleagues. However, after a period of reflection in 1998, and with a weather eye on devolution, STF decided to re-structure in order to become the prime influencing body on the STCG, and began to make changes by appointing a much reduced membership body — a council — to oversee the future of its activities including funding. At the same time, it made plans to recruit a Chief Executive. The immediate effect of this re-structure was that the Scottish Office began to take it more seriously seeing it as the perfect private industry vehicle by which it could drive forward its strategies. The Scottish Executive cemented this relationship.

The most compelling event of this time, however, was the positive outcome of a referendum (see Appendix — Tables 7 and 8) on Scottish devolution held in September 1997, which followed a Labour victory over the Conservatives in the 1997 election that ended 18 years of Tory rule. Although many in the industry were unsupportive of devolution (Kerr 2001) this set high hopes for the Scottish tourism industry that tourism would now be taken more seriously by politicians who would be more visible and accountable.

1999–2002

Since *the Development of Tourism Act* (1969), the Scottish tourism industry has undergone significant change, with which great swathes of it were unable to keep pace; one of many reasons behind the industry's failure to challenge competitor destinations and realise its potential. Others, of which there are many, are explained as we progress. For example, although tourism in Scotland grew by 43% in real terms between the inception of the Act and the accession of the new Scottish parliament, this growth brought with it significant change in the markets in which it operated, and in particular a fundamental change to the customer supplier relationship that appeared to pass by much of the Scottish tourism industry.

This change may be explained in terms of the anomalies of such growth. For example, in 1970 overseas tourists to Scotland took 620,000 trips; stayed for 8.5 million nights; and spent £26 million (£230 million in 1998 prices, or £445 million under the new United Kingdom's Tourism Survey (UKTS) methodology — see Chapter 7). Thirty years later this had grown to 1.6 million trips (a 158% increase); 15 million nights (a 77% increase); and £679 million (£1.3 billion under the UKTS methodology, a 192% increase). However, U.K. residents' visits to Scotland reveal an altogether different scenario which in its complexity reveals much more about Scottish tourism's predicament. While in 1970 such visitors took 12.3 million trips; stayed for 65 million nights; and spent £175 million (£1.5 billion in 1998 prices, and approximately £3 billion under the UKTS methodology), in 1998 they took 9.8 million trips (a reduction of 20%); stayed 44 million nights (a reduction of 32%); and spent little less in real terms than in 1970 (£1,540 million or again around the £3 billion mark). The deterioration continued into the new Millennium. For example, in 2001, U.K. visitors to Scotland took 8.8 million trips (a further decrease on the 1998 figures of 10%); stayed 37 million nights (a reduction on 1998 of 16%); and spent £2,252 million (£748 million less than 1998, a further reduction of 25%) (A New Strategy for Scottish Tourism 2000; Tourism in Scotland 2001; VisitScotland 2001).

It is clear from these figures that although the U.K. accounts for 92% of all tourism trips to Scotland, and that U.K. residents are spending more year on year, there is nevertheless a dramatic reduction in the number of nights U.K. residents spend in Scotland. In effect, as is identified in *A New Strategy for Scottish Tourism* (2000), this reflects the virtual disappearance of the mainstream holiday market of U.K. residents in Scotland, replaced instead by the market for short breaks. Furthermore, over the long term, apart from the role of hotels and catering as a producer service e.g. meeting demand from other industries, and the demands of the indigenous population (Bull & Church 1994: 248–269, see Chapter 9), the growth in tourism in Scotland up until foot-and-mouth and September 11 has come primarily from overseas markets, which because of the environment created around these events, and as is evidenced by the above figures, has in itself reduced dramatically (A New Strategy for Scottish Tourism 2000; Tourism in Scotland 2001; VisitScotland 2001). Furthermore, war in Iraq, and the ongoing terrorist threats to U.K. cities this could bring combined with SARS could have severe consequences for Scottish tourism, nullifying projected growth of the main markets.

The Main Markets

Overseas tourists spending on average £45 per night, stay in Scotland an average of 9.4 nights in any one trip, which accounts for 8% of tourism trips to Scotland, with the USA being the largest overseas market accounting for 27% of overseas trips (VisitScotland 2001). It is important, however, that Scottish tourism does not dwell overlong on the impact of USA tourists to its shores. For example, and despite the importance of the USA to Scottish tourism, over the past thirty years the number of visitors from other countries to Scotland has increased more dramatically than those from the USA. Visitors from France, for example, have increased from 36,000 in 1972 to 133,000 in 2001, an increase of 270%; visitors from Germany increased from 43,000 to 210,000, an increase of 388%; while USA visitors increased from 158,000 to 470,000, an increase of 197%. What these figures reflect is the growing importance of European tourism to Scotland which thirty years ago accounted for only a third of all overseas tourism trips but by 1998 had risen to almost 50% (A New Strategy for Scottish Tourism 2000).

USA

Regardless of the vast European marketplace on its doorstep, without doubt, for the present, the USA is Scotland's prime overseas market, particularly for those who visit Scotland from the North East, or from Florida, California, Illinois, and Texas: areas which have excellent air connections with the U.K., and above average tourism discretionary spends. Nevertheless, the dearth of immediate direct access to Scotland by air means that the majority of visitors from the USA to Scotland do so as part of an itinerary which commences in London, then visits other parts of the U.K. This means that time spent in Scotland, in many instances, although a necessary part of their itinerary, is an adjunct.

Germany

Germany is vital to the European growth of inbound Scottish tourism. For example, in comparison to those visitors from the USA who invariably progress to Scotland from London, German tourists view Scotland as a destination in its own right, spending their whole holiday there rather than visiting Scotland as just one part of a wider itinerary (A New Strategy for Scottish Tourism 2000).

France

France is important to Scottish tourism not only because of its historical relationship, but also because of its geographical proximity, and Scotland's accessibility. For example, there has been a dramatic increase in the number of direct flights per day into Scottish airports, and also access through the Channel Tunnel, and by sea and rail which means a potential to increase the number of visitors and to increase the proportion of Scotland-only visitors (A New Strategy for Scottish Tourism 2000).

Other Overseas Countries

Other nations such as the Republic of Ireland which generates 6% of overseas expenditure; Netherlands 4%; Canada 7%; Australia 8%; and Italy 3% are also vital and potential growth markets. Furthermore, as inexpensive carriers such as Ryanair open up more routes, and fly into airports such as Glasgow Prestwick International the above percentages are bound to increase, particularly from mainland Europe.

Tourism from Within the UK

One of the fundamental problems that Scottish tourism has been unable to deal with has been the demise of the traditional seaside holiday, and from which a number of resorts have been unable to recover market share. The fact that since the 1970s the trend in the

U.K. market has been progressively towards short breaks appears to have passed many of them by, the irony being that attractions that used to hold people in such destinations for a fortnight, no longer even have a two or three night appeal. For example, by the 1960s, one week and two week holidays were by and large spent abroad, or if they were spent in U.K. resorts were in the main by those who could not afford to go abroad.

By the 1970s, the average length of stay by U.K. visitors to Scotland had decreased dramatically from the normal annual holiday to the point that by the 1980s, it was 5.4 nights reducing to 4.5 nights in the 1990s, to 4.1 nights in 2001. Furthermore, in 2001 English visitors to Scotland who spent on average 4.2 nights at £60 per night, spent over £2 billion, while Scots who averaged 3 nights and spent £44 per night, spent £1,160 million in their homeland making the U.K. market Scotland's largest (A New Strategy for Scottish Tourism 2000).

Nevertheless, Scottish residents remain an important market for Scotland. While in 1998 they accounted for 43% of all holiday tourism trips from within the U.K. to Scotland, and 25% of spending, by 2001 this had risen to almost 50% and 34% of spend. However, there has been a long-term decline of the more than one week market largely as a result of increased affordability and desirability and affordability of overseas summer sun holidays. But this has been balanced to an extent by growth in one to four night trips. This is due to the fact that the market is volatile and expenditure fluctuates widely from year to year (A New Strategy for Scottish Tourism 2000).

Business Tourism

Under the new methodology, discretionary business tourism to Scotland is worth £880 million per annum. It is particularly important because of its high yield, out of season potential, and links with wider economic development. Key segments are: International Association Meetings; European Corporate Meetings and Incentive Travel; U.S. Corporate Meetings and Incentive Travel; U.K. Association Meetings; U.K. Corporate Meetings and Events; Scottish Internal Association and Corporate meetings and events (A New Strategy for Scottish Tourism 2000).

A New Strategy for Scottish Tourism

Although Lord Macdonald, in the 1999 *Scottish Tourism Strategic Plan Interim Review* (STCG/SE/HIE/STB 1999) claimed the industry, through STF would be fully involved in the review, there were genuine concerns that an industry funded across all disciplines by up to a reputed £85 million per annum, was finding it extremely difficult to fund STF in a proper sense. For instance, STF claimed early in 1999 to have secured 100% Year 1 funding, 75% of which was to be from the public sector, and that part-funding on a sliding-scale to Spring 2000 was already secured (Scottish Tourism Forum Strategy Document 4 August 1999). But the actual funding, at the time of the interviews that took place to appoint its first-ever Chief Executive was possibly only a third of what was required, not only to pay the CEO's salary but operating costs. This meant that the

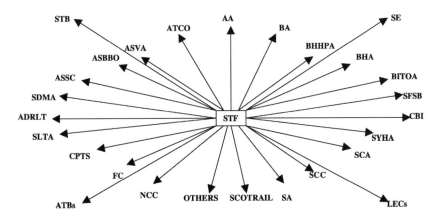

Figure 5.1: STF and the Scottish tourism environment. *Note:* Explanations of these acronyms may be found in the various tables relating to STCG, STF are in the Appendix — Table 9.

new Chief Executive, in common with his or her counterparts in the ATBs, and in other bodies such as Springboard U.K. (the government-funded initiative to make tourism and hospitality a first choice career), rather than champion the cause of the Scottish tourism and hospitality industry, spent much of their time endeavouring to raise funds to secure their future. Even Lord Macdonald, when he became the Scottish Office Minister responsible for tourism, was surprised to find that an industry generating £2.55 billion (pre UKTS figures — see Chapter 7), and employing 180,000 people, had at that time no one industry-based organisation with a full-time professional and administrational back-up to deal with the numerous facets of Scottish tourism. Since then, as is revealed in Figure 5.1, STF has become the prime industry-based tourism body with which the Scottish Executive will do business.

In March 1999, despite the fact that as of June the Scottish Parliament would be responsible for tourism and that the STCG was in reality a Westminster mechanism the aforementioned *Scottish Tourism Strategic Plan Interim Review* (STCG/SE/HIE/STB 1999) reported on progress to date on the 1996 plans and promised that the STCG would publish a revised strategy later in the year. Although this encompassed all aspects of Scottish tourism, it recognised that different parts of Scotland had different needs. For instance, the priorities for HIE is on community developments reflecting the economic fragility and unique cultural and social traditions of the region. Although relevant this plan was superseded by devolution, and a new strategy.

In 1999 SEn/HIE also introduced new strategies such as those surrounding the emergence of the knowledge economy, lifelong learning, clusters, and the rural agenda. They had also, of course, to deal with the outcome of their reviews by both the Parliament and the Executive — *Interim Conclusions of the Scottish Enterprise Network Review* (Scottish Parliament, Enterprise and Lifelong Learning Committee 2000), and *Modernising the Enterprise Networks, the Interim Conclusions of the Enterprise Networks Review* (Scottish Executive 2000), both of which led to a complete business transformation of SEn (originally known as the Knowledge Web, then as Business Transformation (BT)), and which affected its strategic responsibility for tourism, and left HIE virtually alone.

However, after the Scottish elections, there was widespread condemnation of the Government by members of STF, BHA and the ATBs when on 18 May 1999; the 22 strong Scottish Executive ministerial team was announced. They were disappointed that no-one appeared to have been given responsibility for tourism. The Scotsman (19 May 1999) of the following day led on the story in its business section and following enquiries made by its reporters, civil servants revealed that tourism was to be part of Henry McLeish's Enterprise and Lifelong Learning Ministry remit. As with Lord Macdonald's appointment to the Scottish Office, the previous year, when again tourism had not been mentioned as part of his responsibilities, the industry felt that despite the promise of devolution it had been sleighted in that it appeared to be less significant to the government than other industries.

Interestingly enough, when the new Scottish parliament eventually appointed the new Minister for Tourism, he was a former BBC journalist, 31 year-old Alasdair Morrison, a Western Isles MSP whose overall title was Deputy Minister for Highlands and Islands and Gaelic. In effect, Morrison's main responsibility was Deputy to the Minister for Enterprise and Lifelong Learning, Henry McLeish MSP. From that point on, however, McLeish appeared to take the lead role in tourism, as did his successor Wendy Alexander MSP, who was very different in her approach from her predecessor. However, the ambivalence of the industry over the integration of tourism with Enterprise and Lifelong Learning in a larger Ministry was clear. In consequence, it was put to the Minister that he should demonstrate his commitment to the industry through chairing the STCG (personal communication, August 1999). In response, McLeish highlighted both his enthusiasm for the industry and the advantage of integrating tourism within the Enterprise and Lifelong Learning portfolio, together with other key industries — oil and gas, electronics, for instance — as it also provided access to all the Enterprise and Higher and Further Education functions and funding (STF, August 1999).

Within a few months of his appointment McLeish, who had been influenced by the highly-influential Enterprise and Lifelong Learning Committee (ELLC) chaired by John Swinney MSP (soon to be the Scottish National Party (SNP) leader, replacing Alex Salmond), and by criticism of Scottish tourism by the *Scottish Affairs Committee Report on Scottish Tourism* (Scottish Affairs Committee 1999), launched a consultation, *A New Strategy for Scottish Tourism*, Edinburgh (ELLD & SE 1999), which raised hopes of some fundamental change.

Further change was envisaged when speeches by McLeish during the week beginning 6th December 1999, about improving the efficiency of SEn, revealed that any changes may even be part of a more strategic change to the whole economic delivery mechanism in Scotland. In the same week, a decade after putting forward the idea of SEn/HIE, its creator, Bill Hughes was among the first to call for its demise. In the *Herald* (6 December 1999: 1), Hughes demanded an overhaul of SEn to reflect the need for more enterprise initiatives and investment in order that the Scottish economy could compete globally. Furthermore, he wanted local organisations to remain but to be more orientated towards risk, through both government and private sector grants, with capital of upwards of £100m. That same week McLeish (*The Herald*, 9 December 1999) appeared to add credibility to Hughes stance, when he declared that there would be a full review of the workings of SEn/HIE. There was

Table 5.1: Objectives for Scottish Tourism.

AIM	To maximise the benefits for tourism for the Scottish people by developing a competitive industry that is economically, socially and environmentally sustainable
Objective 1	Scotland is a first choice destination for our target markets
Objective 2	Products and infrastructure that meets the needs of our visitors
Objective 3	All of Scotland benefits from tourism throughout the year
Objective 4	A skilled and enterprising industry
Objective 5	Effective collaboration among businesses, industry groups and the public sector

Source: Draft, A New Strategy for Scottish Tourism (1999).

even some suggestion that tourism might be subsumed by whatever it was that would replace them. Then, in the *Scotland on Sunday* (12 December 1999) Hughes set out his vision. This added to the speculation over Henry McLeish's tourism consultation that perhaps following all the doubts there might after all be a radical shift to the delivery of tourism in Scotland.

The response to the tourism consultation was *a draft of A New Strategy for Scottish Tourism* (Scottish Executive, November 1999). In common with its predecessors it did not address major issues particularly funding, structure and the imbalanced influence of sectors of the industry not creating wealth or jobs with which the industry was concerned. As Table 5.1 demonstrates, there was one overall aim and sub-categories of five objectives. It appeared that there was little that had not been discussed previously, and even acted upon, and that rather than an aspirational approach, what was really needed was a more fundamental one.

Although the eventual outcome was far from radical the actual strategy when published in February 2000 (A New Strategy for Scottish Tourism, Scottish Executive 2000) bore little resemblance to the draft. However, as will be evidenced by Table 5.2, the structures that underpinned the industry remained unchanged, and furthermore, as with the draft, as Reid claims (2001) it was more aspirational in tone than anything else.

At this point McLeish also took the opportunity of disbanding the STCG. The Minister claimed that in order to drive the implementation of the new tourism strategy a smaller group, the Strategy Implementation Group, meeting more frequently was required. He also undertook to chair it, and to ensure it comprised STF, ATB, STB, SE, HIE representatives and the chair of the new training group Tourism People. However, incongruously there appeared to be little activity or communication to the industry from the Strategy Implementation Group that replaced the STCG, or evidence that it ever met, or that McLeish or his successor Wendy Alexander actively promoted it. In fact, when he became Tourism Minister, Mike Watson, appeared to disregard it altogether instead opting for a Steering Group chaired by the minister and comprised of people such as Peter Lederer, Chairman VisitScotland; Andrew Mathieson, Scottish Tourism Forum; and Laurence Young and Peter Taylor, of the British Hospitality Association. The group's aim was to produce an Annual Report to Parliament in March 2003, setting out progress made against the actions listed in the *Tourism Framework for Action 2002: 2006* (Scottish Executive Education Department 2002).

Table 5.2: Highlights from A New Strategy for Scottish Tourism.

The establishment of a direct e-commerce booking system with a target of 30% of all accommodation businesses to be trading by e-commerce by 2002 and 90% by 2005
E-commerce expected to generate up to £360 million in revenue and create up to 2,600 jobs in the Scottish tourism industry
Tourism information and booking to be available through a single international telephone number for the 2001 season
A new multi-lingual call centre for tourist information and bookings
A new marketing campaign to increase the number of Scots holidaying in Scotland
A new strategy to target niche markets focussing initially on golf, culture, genealogy and activity holidays
Doubling the number of quality advisers to improve standards and encourage managers to take advantage of training opportunities
The creation of a National Transport Timetable by the end of 2000 to be incorporated in Scottish Tourist Board's website so that customers can plan visits using all modes of public transport
Set up, by April 2000, a major new industry-led Tourism Skills body to focus on meeting the needs of visitors through investing in the people who provide the service

---

Source: Scottish Executive (A New Strategy for Scottish Tourism 2000).

However, this was by no means the end of the activity surrounding tourism in 2000. Through his various wider economic initiatives e.g. *Framework for Economic Development Scotland* (FEDS), and reviews e.g. the review of SEn/HIE combined with the Enterprise and Lifelong Learning Committee's review of local economic delivery services, McLeish sought to bring tourism out of the periphery of the Scottish economy. In doing so he gave tourism a much higher role in the economic development firmament, particularly through ATB membership of the LEFs. LEFs had been one of the outcomes of FEDS, and were designed to get all local partners around the one table to sort out the confusion and duplication of economic development and business services, and other local economic problems. Yet, disappointingly, and although the STB also underwent a review (Scottish Tourist Board Management Review, Report and Recommendations, STB/PriceWaterhouseCoopers 2000), neither he nor his successor, Wendy Alexander MSP, the former Communities Minister who replaced McLeish, when McLeish succeeded Donald Dewar as First Minister in 2000, did anything to alter the structural or funding problems, or the relationship with BTA.

Alexander's appointment coincided with the publication of the outcomes of the STB Review — *Scottish Tourist Board Management Review, Report and Recommendations*, (STB/PriceWaterhouseCoopers 2000) which had been one of the outcomes of the new strategy. Within hours of its release, the STB CEO, Tom Buncle, stepped down. A week later, the STB Chairman Lord Gordon signalled his intention to leave his post at the end of his term, and within days of this the Gleneagles MD Peter Lederer was appointed Vice-Chairman, and through time became Chairman. In the resulting turmoil, it was clear that Alexander, as opposed to her predecessor who was more reactionary than proactive, was going to challenge the industry. However, in 2001 she was criticised somewhat by the manner in which she handled the appointment of Buncle's successor. Since Buncle's departure Peter McKinlay, the former Scottish Prison's supremo temporarily filled the role, resigning when Rod Lynch, an aircraft industry executive was appointed. Hailed as a world class appointment Lynch lasted four days until it was found out that he still had a strategic responsibility for an airline. After a protracted legal wrangle which resulted in large financial compensation for Lynch (£43k including legal fees), much industry criticism of Alexander and embarrassment for Lederer, and his new Vice-Chairman Mike Cantlay, Philip Riddle, an ex-Shell executive was appointed the new Chief Executive.

A Smart Successful Scotland

One of the challenges for tourism of *Smart, Successful Scotland* (2001) was the relationship between VisitScotland/SEn/HIE, and its understanding of the tensions that existed between the organisations in terms of the very fine line between organisational responsibilities for certain functions in relation to tourism in each of the organisations and in the wider Scottish tourism networks. For example, during 1999/2000 there was continuing speculation as to whether SEn would subsume STB or whether *all* tourism functions would become the responsibility of STB. The outcome of various reviews, one being STB's own review (the STB Management Review, Report and Recommendations 2000), clarified this to a certain extent, decreeing that the status quo would remain, with no question of tourism being subsumed by either organisation. Yet, the functions of SEn/HIE in relation to tourism, as per the recommendations of the review, were rather ambiguous. For example, the review recommended that the STB should request that the Enterprise and Lifelong Learning Department clarify that responsibility for tourism strategy and policy lay with STB, and reallocate the existing costs incurred in SEn/HIE to STB. Somewhat contradictorily, it also recommended that the STB should adopt a more sophisticated approach to its conduct of external relations built on the distinctive roles of the parties with whom relations were conducted. It also stressed that along with the bodies, with which it interacts, the STB should develop precise, unambiguous protocols that will guide and strengthen the relationships between the parties. The implications of this would be a change in the various public sector responsibilities, relationships and funding, but the question remains to what extent, issues that are addressed in later chapters.

Perhaps the biggest challenge to SEn/HIE was its own future. It had been set up under a Conservative administration and in late December 1999, as has already been referred to in the previous section; there were calls for the network to undergo a review. As a result, McLeish as Minister of Enterprise and Lifelong Learning, began a structural review of SE/HIE, while the ELLC, under the stewardship of Swinney, began to review the Local Delivery Organisation (LDO) network. The LDOs contracted with SE/HIE through the LECs to deliver the Small Business Gateway (SBG), and also the Local Authorities for whom many of them delivered other services such as inclusion based activities. Meantime, SE's Chief Executive, Crawford Beveridge resigned, his post being taken by the former LiS Director, Dr. Robert Crawford. Crawford's appointment coincided with SEn's own review that produced a strategy that would make it a more cohesive unit. Consequently, not only did SEn undergo a business transformation process, it also reduced its workforce by 25%; recruited new skills; introduced shared services; part of the LDO's operations were branded Gateways; and the LECs' area of operation was pre-fixed with the word Scottish. The latter change meant that from 1 April 2000, the SE LECs apart from Moray, Baddenoch and Strathspey Enterprise Company, who also had a Highland remit, and which would become a subsidiary of HIE, would be known as Scottish Enterprise companies. For example, Lanarkshire Development Agency (LDA), Glasgow Development Agency (GDA), and Lothian and Edinburgh Enterprise Ltd (LEEL) were to be known as Scottish Enterprise Lanarkshire (SEL), Scottish Enterprise Glasgow (SEG) and Scottish Enterprise Edinburgh and Lothians (SEEL) respectively. They also became subsidiaries of SE, and were to become major participants in the newly proposed LEFs. However, for many this meant centralisation, and through time there would be less discretionary spend on tourism.

The eventual outcomes of the above reviews informed *A Smart, Successful Scotland. Ambitions for the Enterprise Networks* (ELLD & SE 2001), the strategy for enterprise which proposed three key organising themes for the activities of the Enterprise Networks replacing the four existing ones of:

• Innovative and Far-Sighted Organisations;
• Competitive Place;
• Inclusion; and
• Positive Attitudes to Learning and Enterprise.

with

• Growing Businesses;
• Global Connections; and
• Learning and Skills.

Alexander's vision was a Scotland where creating, learning and connecting faster was the basis for sustained productivity growth, competitiveness, and prosperity (ELLD 2001), and the Enterprise Networks were to be key partners in delivering her vision. This led to the establishment of the aforementioned LEFs. There were numerous examples of such Fora throughout Scotland. Ayrshire, for example, had had one since the early nineties among whose achievements was the forthcoming extension to the M77, the survival of Prestwick Airport and the investment of £5 million pounds in its job strategy. McLeish, Swinney, and the ELLC were impressed by the achievements of not only Ayrshire's Forum, but also its sister Fora such as Grampian, Fife and the Borders. His network review set in motion a consultation on guidelines for such Fora throughout Scotland, coterminous with LEC boundaries, to include tourism and eradicate duplication of business services. This was followed by devising strategies for these areas that would be the economic development component of community planning.

The Tourism Framework for Action 2002:2006

In March 2002 a working blueprint *The Tourism Framework for Action*, a multi-partner initiative which drives forward and develops the actions contained in *A New Strategy for*

Scottish Tourism (2000), and was designed to reinvigorate the tourism industry, to out-class competitors and make Scotland a must-visit destination was launched. It developed and took forward the actions contained in *A New Strategy for Scottish Tourism* (2000), focussing on a partnership with all those involved in the tourism sector, and identifies three priorities for the development of tourism in Scotland. These are:

(1) Market Position — development of a better and stronger position with clearly defined brands and products to appeal to and meet customer needs
(2) Consumer Focus — to drive quality standards, develop new and enhanced products and services, improve customer research and skills in the industry
(3) Enhanced Status of Tourism — to ensure the importance of tourism to the Scottish economy is recognised.

The framework also acknowledged that since the publication of *A New Strategy for Scottish Tourism* (2000) developments have included the provision of expert advice on improving businesses through Scotexchange.net; new marketing campaigns by VisitScotland and ATBs; the launch of the Scottish "roots" tourism website; ancestralscotland.com which was now being heavily promoted overseas; and the delivery of 1000 Modern Apprenticeships (MAs) in the industry through SEn/HIE.

Furthermore, Mike Watson, who became Minister for Tourism, Culture and Sport in November 2001, chaired the aforementioned Steering Group to oversee the framework's progress, while promising an Implementation Group to monitor, engage and advise, undertakings his predecessors failed to keep.

Area Tourist Board Review

Just before Watson succeeded her, and she became Minister for Enterprise, Transport and Lifelong Learning, Alexander detailed the initial outcomes of the review of the Scottish Executive's tourism strategy, and announced the start of consultation on improving the role of ATBs in transforming the industry both nationally and at a local level. However, this consultation was barely underway when due to McLeish's resignation and Jack McConnell's ascension; Tourism was hived off from Enterprise and Lifelong Learning, and became the first Tourism Ministry in the U.K. to obtain named cabinet status in the Ministry of Tourism, Culture and Sport. As much as this was an important step for the industry it dislocated it from the mainstream of economic development the model preferred by McLeish and Alexander.

In May 2002 a further review of the ATB network was launched focussed on delivery of the most effective service to tourists and tourism operators in Scotland. Furthermore, it was meant to ensure that the boards could deliver the key objectives in the Scottish Executive's *Tourism Framework for Action 2002: 2006*, launched in March 2002. However, to help direct the debate, Watson highlighted issues raised by the industry over recent months. These included questions over the future role of the Boards and how should they relate with VisitScotland; special arrangements for cities as gateways for tourism; the present structure of the 14 Boards; the role the local authorities should play in ATBs; the relationship the ATBs should have with LECs; the best way for ATBs to engage with businesses; and, how ATBs could more effectively distribute information to visitors? The consultation period lasted for longer than the originally agreed three months, and the ATB network, under its own volition, set up a co-ordinating group to help facilitate the review. However, in March 2003, the election looming, and no clear consensus, Watson was minded to leave implementation of any outcomes of the review until after the election.

Other initiatives coincided with the review such as Support for Tourism: An International Comparison (2002), the Enterprise and Lifelong Learning Committee Inquiry into Tourism (2002), and Final Report on Lifelong Learning (2002), all of which are discussed more fully in Chapter 9.

Summary

The particular significance of this chapter to the book is that having reviewed all of this material and the development of the Scottish tourism infrastructure it sets out the environment in which the various tourism organisations had to operate, particularly since the 1969 *Development of Tourism Act*, the establishment of HIDB in 1965, SDA in 1975 and SEn/HIE in 1991, combined with the constraints placed on such organisations by politicians in terms of particular policies, structures and funding. Furthermore, this is significant in that such information, particularly in regard to pre and post-devolution has previously gone unrecorded.

It also clarifies the fact that change in the industry invariably came about not because of the industry's demand for change, but because successive Ministers, first in the Scottish Office and then in the Scottish Executive instigated change: change that would never satisfy an industry that is so polarized, it can never know what it actually wants of government other than loads of resource thrown at it. Nevertheless, anyone looking back on the history of tourism in Scotland from this point a hundred years from now will, it is hoped, see a less fragmented industry and one where every player is marked out by the quality of their product and service delivery, and where there is world renown for the distinctive qualities that we bring to the industry and consequently attract visitors here. This is all the more important in that the outcomes of devolution, and perhaps eventual fiscal autonomy or independence, may mean that the Scottish economy, due to the decline in manufacturing, will be all the more reliant on the wealth created by the tourism and hospitality industry and the jobs resulting from the anticipated growth of the industry.

Chapter 6

The Impact on Devolution and Scottish Tourism of Reserved Powers

Introduction

The question of the impact of reserved powers on devolution is an intriguing one, and one which due to the fledgling nature of the Scottish Parliament, and the current polarisation of views of all sides of the political spectrum, may be too early to address conclusively. However, its importance must not be underestimated, particularly the impact of such powers on the Scottish economy in relation to Scottish tourism policy e.g. interest and exchange rates, employment legislation, fiscal policy. It is equally important to understand how devolution evolved, why certain powers that are vital to the Scottish economy were reserved, leaving devolved ones undesignated, how these were decided, the tensions this engendered, and what it meant in the longer-term to Scottish tourism.

What we do know is that fundamentally, devolution did not create a separate Scottish Parliament but one embedded in U.K. and EU governance structures (Lynch 2001: 3). For example, according to the devolution settlement, it was immediately apparent that although the new Scottish Parliament had extensive powers to influence the business environment in Scotland (Scott 2001) (see Table 6.1); it had no macroeconomic powers with which to stimulate its economy. For example, apart from the fact that it can raise taxes by 3p, rates of taxation including corporation tax, excise duty (whisky), VAT, and the value of sterling are set outwith the jurisdiction of Holyrood. Meanwhile, and without reference to it, or Scottish representation, the Bank of England sets interest rates which affect the entire U.K. fiscal policy, and are more often than not determined by the economy of the south-east and the midlands, than peripheral areas such as Scotland. Furthermore, instruments with which the Scottish Executive can stimulate its economy are still bound heavily by U.K. and European guidelines. For example, while grants have been very often a decisive policy instrument in attracting inward investment to Scotland, the amount of financial assistance Scotland can offer is determined by Westminster. Furthermore, despite devolution, such grants require to be negotiated with the Department of Trade and Industry, and approved by the Treasury. Therefore, until such times as Scotland has fiscal autonomy, a model that is already successful in Spain, Switzerland and Belgium (even the Faroe Isles and Crimea enjoy significant financial freedom from Denmark and Ukraine respectively (Nicolson 2002: 7)), ways in which U.K. macroeconomic and Scottish microeconomic policies interrelate are crucial to the dynamics, stability and growth of the Scottish economy. Ironically, it could

Table 6.1: Business-influencing devolved powers.

Scottish devolved powers to influence the business environment in Scotland

---

Planning
Local taxation
Business rates
Economic development
Enterprise
Transport
Education
Training
Lifelong learning
The private finance initiative (pfi)
Environmental protection
Civil and criminal law
Licensing
Tourism

Source: Scottish Parliament Public Information Service 2001, 2nd edition.

be argued that it is the sensitivities, peculiarities and dynamics of this very mechanism that renders the Scottish economy moribund, unable to anywhere near achieve the GDP or growth of its southern neighbours. In essence, unless future change devolves additional powers to Scotland, or until political power changes hands, the Scottish Executive's ability to influence its economy, and hence tourism, is limited. There is, of course, *Smart, Successful Scotland* (2001) its strategy for enterprise, or as in the case of tourism, *A New Strategy for Scottish Tourism* (2000), or *the Tourism Framework for Action 2002: 2006* (see Chapters 5 and 9), all of which are important to the future of the economy and hence tourism, but none of which have an overriding ability to influence the economic levers that really matter. How this environment evolved is of interest.

Short-term Horizons

In the lead up to the setting up by the newly elected Labour government of a Scottish Parliament in the late nineties, the impact on the longer-term economic performance of Scotland of reserved powers following devolution was relegated in favour of other more pressing short-term matters e.g. the parties' selection processes; getting elected; MSPs' remuneration and allowances; what it would mean to MPs in terms of both their responsibilities and boundary changes; the location of the parliament, and so on. Prior to that, and due to Conservative government policies of the eighties and nineties, devolution of any shape, colour or size would have been preferable to the then unitary system of government to a large tract of the Scottish electorate, and also to Labour MPs who had spent eighteen years in opposition, some fighting their own party as much as the Conservative government.

Although Labour was the dominant party in Scotland during that time, the equally dominant southern Conservative vote and larger majority of MPs in England meant that Labour was unable to do anything about policies to which it was diametrically opposed, and which it argued in the main took more account of southern England's needs than the diverse needs of Scotland. However, in the process, debate on the inability of limited devolved powers to deal with wider Scottish economic events in both the short and longer-term was neglected. This has not only contributed to poor planning, flawed strategies, and inadequate policies it has also led to sustaining Scotland's historically poor social and economic performance, and hence Scottish tourism's inability to realise its full commercial potential. In effect, it has been a contributory factor in the continuing failure of Scottish tourism; its structure, its strategies, and its mind set still wedded to the institutionalism of the 1969 *Development of Tourism Act*. Furthermore, would a country whose reliance on oil is well documented, and which had the ability to take its own decisions, squeeze the oil industry further as Gordon Brown, the Chancellor of the Exchequer did in early 2002? Brown's long-term aim is to deliver a tax regime that delivers sustainable investment while giving a fair return to all of the British people. Nevertheless, to the detriment of the oil industry on which Scotland is reliant, his 2002 *Finance Bill* (U.K. Parliament 23 April 2002) legislated to raise tax revenues through a supplementary charge of 10% on North Sea oil profits, and it is this kind of macroeconomic decision that appears to take no account of Scotland.

The Scottish Constitutional Convention

The Scottish Constitutional Convention (SCC) (1989–1995) was the catalyst for present day devolution. In the early 1990s the SCC debated its possibility, and the form in which it would be acceptable to both the Scottish electorate and Westminster. It also suggested powers that should be reserved, and those that should be devolved, and the electoral system: the latter eventually adopted by the U.K. government. Based on the proportional representation electoral system known as the Additional Member System in use in Germany in the years following the end of the Second World War, it allowed voters two votes: one for a constituency member and a second for a regional list member (Paterson *et al.* 2001: 67). However, the SCC first had to gain consent for its scheme from a range of Scottish organisations (Lynch 2001: 11–23), among them the tourism industry which was overwhelmingly unionist in spirit (Kerr 2001: 241–269), and of course Westminster.

While negotiating these political, personal, and organisational tensions, and driven to achieve devolution at almost any cost, it too lost sight of the real impact certain reserved powers could have on Scotland's economic and tourism performance, particularly if the policies were biased towards the exigencies of the economy south of the border, and in tourism's case to the British Tourist Board's (BTA) strategy of attracting visitors primarily to London. In consequence, and in reality with little alternative, the SCC conceded that foreign affairs; defence; social security; nationality; immigration; and economic and fiscal responsibilities; should be reserved matters, the latter in particular of crucial long-term importance to the Scottish economy and to Scottish tourism.

Apart from the Conservatives who wanted to preserve the Union and the nationalists whose desire was independence, the SCC's proposed reserved powers appeared acceptable

Table 6.2: Devolved powers.

Scottish devolved powers

Health
Education and training
Local government
Social work
Housing
Planning
Tourism
Economic development
Financial assistance to industry
Some aspects of transport, including the Scottish road network, bus policy and ports and harbours
Law and home affairs, including most aspects of criminal and civil law, the prosecution system and the courts
The Police and Fire services
The environment
Natural and built heritage
Agriculture, forestry and fishing
Sport and the arts
Statistics, public registers and records

Source: Scottish Parliament Public Information Service 2001, 2nd edition.

and sensible to the various interests that comprised the SCC, and the majority of those with whom it consulted (there is no documentary evidence that it consulted with the tourism industry in depth, an indication of both how undervalued the industry was, and also of the industry's inability to influence at that level). Furthermore, it assumed that if these were satisfactory to the Scottish politicians and parties then these would also be acceptable to Westminster. However, when the Scotland Act finally transpired broadcasting; abortion; equality; transport safety; the constitution; employment legislation; and regulation were among others that had been added by the government (McFadden & Lazarowicz 1999) (for full lists see Tables 6.2 and 6.3), while fiscal responsibility remained in London, and on which there was to be no compromise. This resulted in tensions arising from the eventual decision on which powers would be reserved. Nevertheless, although the fact that broadcasting was eventually reserved caused controversy, as did abortion, reserving macro-economic policies or indeed immigration or powers over customs and excise raised few eyebrows, as did the continued existence of cross border authorities such as the BTA. These factors, among others over which it has no control or indeed influence, and which have both long and short-term implications for the Scottish economy, including tourism, continue to create tensions, confusion and disappointment in the devolution outcomes.

Table 6.3: Reserved powers.

Westminster reserved powers
Constitutional matters
UK foreign policy
UK defence and national security
Fiscal, economic and monetary system
Immigration and nationality
Energy: electricity, coal, gas and nuclear energy
Common markets
Trade and industry, including competition and customer protection
Some aspects of transport, including railways, and transport safety
Employment legislation and social security
Gambling and the National Lottery
Data protection
Abortion, human fertilisation and embryology, genetics, xenotransplantation and vivisection
Equal opportunities
Regulation
Broadcasting

Source: Scottish Parliament Public Information Service 2001, 2nd edition.

The Impact of the Scotland Act on the Political Composition of MPs

The new proposed reserved settlement as it appeared in *the Scotland Act* (Stationery Office 1998) was designed to appease Labour MPs who following eighteen uninterrupted years of Conservative rule, and their party's internecine strife for most of the eighties, were now in power. In consequence, they were less supportive and passionate about devolution than they had been in opposition, which was indicative of the wider Labour Party apathy towards devolution (Mitchell 1996). It meant a dilution of their responsibilities, and an erosion of their powers. Furthermore, they were conscious that devolution exposed the fact that Scotland was overrepresented in terms of Westminster MPs. This necessitated a review of the electoral boundaries designed to reduce Scottish representation at Westminster from 73 to 59 MPs by 2005 (Scotland Act 1998: s.86), a situation that if it comes to pass will see some cabinet rank ministers constituencies disappear altogether, and perhaps necessitate a further review by 2007 (when the third parliament will be elected) of Holyrood electoral boundaries (the Secretary of State for Scotland decided in December 2002 that the planned change to reduce MSPs from 129 to just over a hundred would not now take place but this is still open to question). Furthermore, exclusion from discussion of purely English matters, a situation that may through time increase the influence of opposition parties in England, is also a not unreasonable expectation of Scottish, Welsh and Northern Ireland MPs by MPs representing English constituencies.

Due to the nature of the Holyrood voting system which elected both first past the post (FPTP) MSPs (73) and regional list members (RLM) (56), devolution also allowed opposition parties through their RLMs, who had no direct responsibility or allegiance to a particular constituency, the opportunity of building power bases in Labour MSPs and MP's constituencies that will be of use in future elections. This situation manifested in unforeseen tensions between them that has continued, and has to a certain extent undermined relations between the two levels of MSPs and the two parliaments' politicians.

Overlap, Disputes and Duplication

In any case, there is already much scope for friction between Scotland and the Westminster parliament where reserved and devolved powers overlap, among them tourism; its anomalies being the continued existence of the BTA (subsumed by VisitBritain in April 2003), and the establishment of Tourism U.K. (subjects covered in this and subsequent chapters). Should this occur there are complicated procedures in place to ensure that Acts of the Scottish Parliament do not encroach into reserved matters and thus open themselves up to challenge as *ultra vires*. For example, in Scotland, it is up to Presiding Officer of the Scottish Parliament to be satisfied that any Bill or legislative proposal to be introduced is within its powers. If there is any dispute, it is referred to the five Law Lords that comprise the Judicial Committee of the Privy Council. Presumably, Westminster could legislate contrary to any decision. But it is not likely to be practical politically for Parliament to act in this way, and so it becomes very significant that it is the Judicial Committee, acting in reality like a final constitutional court, which is the arbiter and not the legislature (UK Law Line 2002).

The Sewel Convention, too, allows for the Westminster Parliament to lead and initiate legislation in devolved areas, a motion that was used 38 times during the first three years of devolution, some affecting tourism (Electronic Communications Bill, Enterprise Bill, Food Standards Bill, Learning and Skills Bill) while the Scottish Parliament passed 44 bills. However, one act passed by Westminster was not subject to any Sewel motion, and therefore trespassed into devolved issues. This sets dangerous precedents as a future Conservative government at Westminster could legislate for Scotland, without recourse to Sewel, citing past precedent (Hassan 2002).

There are also mechanisms to resolve disputes between the different levels of government such as the Joint Ministerial Committees (JMC). A product of the concordats over which there had been a veil of secrecy until 1999 (see Lynch 2001 for further information), the JMCs were designed to facilitate intergovernmental relations and dialogue, and meet in plenary form once a year, chaired by the Prime Minister; and in functional formats as meetings of the various ministers (Hazell 2000: 187). For example, in the case of tourism JMCs take place between the Westminster Tourism Minister from the Department for Culture, Media and Sport, the Minister for Economic Development in Wales, the Minister for Enterprise, Trade and Investment in Northern Ireland, and the Minister for Tourism Culture and Sport in Scotland. Apart from an exchange of information subjects such as harmonising their respective Classification and Grading schemes, but without compromising their existing ones, are discussed. Nevertheless, the worth of the tourism JMC to the Scottish tourism industry is not immediately apparent, particularly when the Scottish minister is not a regular attendee.

The Evolution of Devolution

Scotland's wider aspirations are reflective of the fact that ever since the Union of the Parliaments in 1707, there has been a growing desire for some measure of Home Rule, particularly since the 19th century when the movement gained momentum. For example, in the 1920s the Scottish Home Rule Association (SHRA) campaigned and failed to establish a parliament, as did the National Party for Scotland; the Scottish Covenant Association; the Campaign for a Scottish Assembly; and, of course, the SNP, plus, and depending on whether or not they were in or out of power, certain Labour and Conservative factions (see Thatcher 1995 for a fuller discussion). Meanwhile, during this time Scottish tourism was building cross border relationships with the precursor of the British Hospitality Association (BHA) the Incorporated Association of Hotels and Restaurants, which by 1929 embraced two regional divisions in Scotland, or in the post war years the British Travel Association, later to become the BTA (Bacon, Personal Communication, 24 May 2001).

It was not until 1968 that one of the major parties openly declared support for devolution. Ted Heath, the leader of Conservatives, much against the will of his party which was then in opposition, with the *Declaration of Perth*, committed the Conservatives to a Scottish Assembly. This along with growing nationalist support, particularly following the SNP's by-election victory in Hamilton in 1967, provoked Harold Wilson's Labour government in 1968 into establishing a Royal Commission on the Constitution of the U.K. (Lynch 2001: 10), but without doing much to bring devolution to statute. However, by 1970 Heath's Conservatives regained power, and by 1973 the Kilbrandon Commission recommended legislative devolution for Scotland. Nevertheless, although Labour had set up the Commission, that the Conservatives had included devolution in their 1970 manifesto, and that the Commission's position was one with which the major parties openly concurred (Thatcher 1995: 322) both disregarded the Commission's advice (McFadden & Lazarowicz 1999: 3), for which Labour would later pay a hefty price.

Despite the fact that Labour MPs, who were now back in power, and for reasons already explained, were wholly opposed to devolution, and that the Conservative were reduced to third place in terms of the Scottish popular vote, nationalist and other pressures for reform of the existing system grew. In consequence, the minority Labour government, which was eventually propped up by the Liberal party, was forced later that year to make concessions and to put forward legislation to establish a Scottish Assembly. That, it took a further four years for an Act, *the Scotland Bill*, to receive Royal Assent, and five years for a referendum to be held says much about the tensions surrounding devolution at the time, and the fact that the minority Labour administration was more concerned with staying in power than with apparent peripheral issues such as devolution.

The negative outcome of the 1979 referendum, followed acrimonious dissent by both Labour MPs and its membership: the MPs fearing an erosion of their powers; the membership fearful of the break-up of the U.K. In consequence, during the passage of *the Scotland Bill* various amendments by the disgruntled MPs necessitated a post-legislative referendum, the crucial amendment ironically by an émigré MP. It was damning in that it required that 40% of the Scottish electorate support devolution as opposed to a majority of those who actually voted. That 51.6% of those that voted were transposed to only 32.8% of the electorate, led to a defeat for devolution, an act that designated Scotland to virtually see out the twentieth century without self-government. This, ultimately, led to a vote of no confidence in the Government and its defeat in the subsequent general election. Concerned that devolution would lead to fragmentation of the U.K., and despite the 1968 *Declaration of Perth*, the new Conservative government failed to support devolution as proposed in the 1978 Act, and this situation remained for the following 18 years.

During the four Conservative government terms that followed (1979–1997) support for constitutional reform in Scotland grew. This evolved from an inherent dislike of Thatcherism by the majority of Scots, and mistrust with the policies being followed by the U.K. Government e.g. the poll tax; the miners' strike; the decline in manufacturing; and subsequently the sleaze with which the Conservatives were associated. This led to in 1997 to no Conservative MP being elected north of the border (the 2001 election increased this figure to one). Wary that there was an emerging sense of a distinct Scottish cultural identity that could lead to nationalism this led to the Labour Government holding a referendum on the issue in September 1997. Despite the fact that many Scottish Labour MPs were opposed to it, who had originally been supportive of it, the outcome of the referendum was clear majorities for the two questions relating to the creation of a Scottish Parliament, and its ability to raise tax (see Appendix — Tables 7 and 8). It also led to the passing of *the Scotland Act* (1998), the founding statute of the new Parliament, and to the normally conservative Scottish tourism industry questioning what this might mean to it, and to the future of the BTA.

In contrast to the scheme of devolution and the Assembly proposed by the Labour Government in the 1970s, which was more limited than the present, and the Conservative proposals to finance devolution by North Sea oil revenue (McKillop 2003; Thatcher 1995), the 1997 referendum was held prior to the legislation. The resulting Scotland Act 1998 established that the Scottish Parliament should deal with all aspects of life in Scotland apart from those matters deemed reserved. However, it did not specify devolved powers, only reserved powers, allowing the Scottish Parliament to exercise government functions (for devolved powers — see Table 6.2) outside of these reserved areas (Lynch 2001: 15). Furthermore, the Westminster Parliament continues to be the sovereign parliament of the United Kingdom.

The first elections to the Scottish Parliament about which the Scottish tourism industry was less than enthusiastic (Kerr 2001: 241–269) took place on 6 May 1999, and with echoes of the late seventies Lib-Lab pact, resulted in a Labour Liberal coalition government, its cabinet responsible for powers other than those that were reserved, and which appeared undecided about which minister was responsible for tourism (see Chapter 5). Nonetheless, there is the possibility for future adjustments of reserved/non-reserved issues if agreed to by both Parliaments, the most pressing being those that have the ability to influence the economy e.g. fiscal autonomy. For the present, according to Schedule 5 of *the Scotland Act* (1998), a number of very important powers remain for the present reserved to the U.K. Parliament (Table 6.3) (Scottish Parliament Public Information Service 2001 2nd edition), and which impact greatly on the performance of the Scottish economy.

Table 6.4: Reserved tourism powers.

Reserved matters of importance to tourism
Constitutional matters
Fiscal, economic and monetary system,
Immigration and nationality
Energy, electricity, coal, gas and nuclear energy
Common markets
Trade and industry, including competition and customer protection
Some aspects of transport
Employment legislation
Social security
Customs and excise e.g. duty on whisky
Gambling
Data protection
Equal opportunities

Source: Scottish Parliament Public Information Service 2001, 2nd edition.

While a number of these reserved matters have little or no relevance to tourism the remainder such as listed in Table 6.4 have, and it is their impact on Scottish tourism public policy that will be discussed as this chapter develops.

Devolution in Practice

The Scottish Parliament operates as a self-contained and fully functioning Parliament in its own right, and it can approve legislation without adherence to the Westminster Parliament, including the functions of tourism. Furthermore, and as we have seen above, although the U.K. Parliament at Westminster retains power to legislate on any matter, the doctrine of devolution is based on the fact that the U.K. Parliament will not normally legislate on devolved matters without the endorsement of the Scottish Parliament, a situation that has also been discussed above (the Sewel Convention), and which could lead to tensions should a party other than that in power in Holyrood sit in Westminster.

Devolution has different connotations to the countries of the U.K., and has been designed to meet both the individual countries' needs and the settled will of their peoples. For example, Scotland differs from the experience of devolution in Northern Ireland and in Wales. In Scotland the Parliament is seen as an expression of the political will of the people whereas in Northern Ireland it is seen as a mechanism by which political will can be redefined in new ways so that conflict can be resolved, in future, by peaceful means. Meanwhile, in Wales the Welsh Assembly has executive powers, not legislative powers, much as was proposed for Scotland in 1979, the Welsh desire for devolution, as witnessed by both the turnout and vote in the 1979 and 1997 referendums, much less strong than Scotland (50.3% for, 49.7% opposed (Duff *et al.*), although it must be noted that of the 2.25 million eligible to vote, over half a million had been born outside Wales, and felt no particular affection for their adopted country (even less for its culture and language) (Brittania.com 2003).

Furthermore, there is another category which remains with the U.K. Parliament. For example, in the case of Northern Ireland, Westminster has held on to some powers (Retained Powers). Among these are understandably policing and the criminal justice system. Nevertheless, these could be transferred through time to the Assembly if the security situation and the success of the Assembly allowed it.

Unlike the Welsh and Northern Ireland Assemblies, the Scottish Parliament also has the power to raise or lower the basic rate of income tax by up to three pence in the pound (meaning approximately £200 to £600 million per annum). Such monies as raised in exercise of this power would be in addition to sums granted by the Scottish block grant (currently £20 billion rising to £25 billion by 2007) and as long as the Barnet Formula (for further information see Lynch 2001: 23–24) would have no effect on it. However, other means by which these monies could be escalated are few and far between. For example, although the Scottish Parliament could raise or lower business rates (Scottish business rates are inexplicably consistently 9% higher than in England (Rafferty & McSherry 2002). Council tax, too, is higher in most areas of Scotland and across most tax bands than in England), corporation tax remains a reserved matter and, accordingly, is not open to alteration by the Scottish Parliament (Weir 2002). This means that should the Scottish Parliament support a proposal to reduce corporate taxation as a policy instrument to stimulate the economy, which has been in a factor in the success of economies such as the Republic of Ireland, it is powerless to do so. Equally, it is powerless to intervene in other areas vital to tourism such as interest rates, customs and excise and exchange rates: the latter in particular consistently disadvantageous to Scotland over the nineties and now in the 21st century making Scotland a comparatively expensive destination. Nor would Scotland, if the decision was left to it, pitch the duty so excruciatingly high on Scotland's most identifiable export whisky, or on petrol derived from its North Sea fields. This is compounded further by the Westminster government's deliberation on joining the Euro, the negative aspects of which — the cost of exchanging currency, the perceived expense of Scotland as a destination — are barriers to access, and are again a contributory factor in Scotland's poor tourism performance, and which by joining as will be demonstrated later in this chapter would be more advantageous to inward investment than the present monetary system.

The Political, Social, Cultural and Economic Development of Scotland

The modern political, social, cultural and economic development of Scotland has evolved unequivocally from its relationship with other parts of the British Isles, in particular England. Further influence has been derived from the continent of Europe, and latterly from the USA primarily through the mediums of film, television, literature, music and the arts and drama. However, prior to devolution due to England's dominance of Westminster, there was an imbalance of influence on both the development of tourism, and economic development policy, and of wider public policies in Scotland. Furthermore, social and political tensions between Scotland and England, particularly during 1979–1997 when the party in power in the U.K. was unrepresentative of Scottish parliamentary seats in

Westminster, was complicated further by Scotland's long-standing, historical relationship with the continent of Europe, and with the success of various models of devolved powers, an environment apparently closed to Scotland by the present government, perversely many of them Scots.

In previous centuries Europe influenced greatly Scotland's public policy and social aspirations, and continues to do so only now through EU legislation, the adoption of the 1998 *Human Rights Act* (EU 1998), and easier accessibility both to and from it, and to its markets. These, rather than its constitutional ties reflect the fact that as it evolves, the Scottish Parliament will be judged more in terms of whether it helps to create a new Scottish democracy, rather than as a legislature in terms of making laws, and holding the Scottish Executive to account (Lynch 2001; 5). Furthermore, as has already been explained in terms of the Sewel Convention and contraventions to such a convention, it will also be judged in terms of its relationship with Westminster, and will be put severely to the test when opposing political parties are in power on either side of the border. Although this might be far off it is a future distinct possibility, and the tensions this will cause could very well have a momentous impact on the structure of the U.K. In British politics up until now, no single political party has stayed in power indefinitely. This latter point means that Scotland could one day elect a government that will pursue nationalist or federal policies. However, it would need to canvas the electorate through a referendum on whether it should seek an alternative home to the London centric U.K. e.g. the EU. Unless this was for outright independence from both Westminster and Europe, a positive result would see a number of the present powers reserved to Westminster, instead reserved to Brussels. A negative result might see Scotland implode. Alternatively, Scotland could seek another route already successful in a number of European countries — economic independence/fiscal autonomy. This would see Scotland raise all its own taxes and duties from which it would meet its wider U.K. responsibilities such as defence, the foreign office, the national debt, and social security. An alternative system, as has already been mentioned, would be federalism, the long-term objective of the Liberal Democrats.

Cross Border Authorities

Devolution is complicated further by the fact that as we have seen in Chapter 4, and to which we have already referred, some reserved/devolved areas are administered on a joint basis. For example, Northern Ireland with the government of the Republic of Ireland through the North/South Ministerial Council and the establishment of the new institutions such as Tourism Ireland Limited, also discussed in Chapter 4.

Scotland, too, shares cross border authorities with England, and with Wales e.g. the Forestry Commission, energy, and of course for tourism, despite the recent changes, the BTA (now VisitBritain, see Chapter 4). And yet, under *the Scotland Act* (1998), tourism is wholly devolved to the Edinburgh Parliament. Therefore, although as a matter of constitutional law, all the statutory links between the Department of Culture, Media and Sport (DCMS) and the then STB (now VisitScotland) have been repealed and tourism politically is totally the responsibility of Edinburgh (Holyrood from 2004), under section 88 of *the Scotland Act* (1998), the BTA has become a cross border authority a mechanism Lord

Thurso (personal communication 1999) claims was invented for things like the Forestry Commission (FC).

A further cross border mechanism for tourism is the newly formed Tourism U.K. which is addressed in Chapter 4 and whose intention is to act as a platform for promoting the best interests of domestic tourism in the U.K. by providing a collective, coherent and strategic steer to governments on the common concerns, common purpose and common agenda of the tourism sector in the U.K.

Where Does All of This Leave the Scotland Office?

According to Lynch (2001: 42) prior to devolution the Scottish Office existed for many years as a federal administration. Following devolution it was renamed the Scotland Office, and its former civil servants although continuing to be members of the Home Civil Service, accountable ultimately to Westminster, transferred their roles and expertise to the Scottish Executive. Nevertheless, and somewhat incongruously, the Prime Minister, as opposed to the First Minister, continued to appoint the head of the Scottish Civil Service, evidence of the nature of the power of control of Westminster despite devolution: control the civil servants and one would ultimately control the politicians.

Although it has been difficult at times for the Secretary of State for Scotland to recognise who the de facto head of Scotland is ultimately, the Secretary of State's role has been changed dramatically. For example, although continuing in the role of Westminster cabinet minister which gives him or her capacity for participation in central government that is not available to the First Minister, the Scottish Executive or Parliament (Lynch 2001: 134), one could question the value of the new role of the Scottish Secretary (In June 2003 it became a part-time post, combined with the Secretary of State for Transport); whether it is sustainable in the longer term; and whether indeed the next U.K. elections will deliver a Secretary of State for the devolved countries; amalgamating the Irish, Welsh and Scots posts.

From virtually ruling Scotland, the Secretary of State is now a liaison between Scottish and U.K. governments and Parliaments, representing Scotland's view to the U.K. government on reserved issues. He or she also ensures mutual understanding between relevant Scottish and U.K. Departments and the Scottish Executive and the Scotland Office, is responsible for the payment of the Westminster block grant to Scotland, and along with the Presiding Officer of the Scottish Parliament ensures that Acts of the Scottish Parliament do not impinge on Westminster's reserved powers, nor are incompatible with the U.K.'s international obligations (Scottish Office News Release 27 February 1998).

In effect, and even though they are rooted in the same political party, all of the above has created a tension between the offices of the Secretary of State for Scotland and the office of the First Minister, as has devolution for MPs and MSPs, the former now with much less responsibility. For example, they are only able to legislate on reserved matters, and are under pressure from their English colleagues not to participate in debates on English matters such as education and health. The true test of the relationship between the Scottish Secretary, if such a post remains, and the First Minister, and indeed of the union, will be when they are from opposing political parties, or when unlike now Scots do not hold such positions within the U.K. cabinet and are relegated to minor roles: both scenarios which may yet come to pass.

Another interesting aspect of this post is that up to the present the Secretary of State for Scotland is a Scot, and always has been, whereas in both Wales and Northern Ireland the Secretaries of State have been and are as this book is being written other than the nationalities of those countries. The fact that this scenario has never arisen in Scotland reveals the sensitivities that both the Labour and Conservative governments have about the power of Scottish nationalism.

Post Devolution

Although Scotland was technically in recession by the end of 1999 (Macwhirter Sunday Herald 11 August 2002), but was not widely recognised as being so, by the summer of 2002 the newly appointed Minister for Enterprise, Transport and Lifelong Learning, Iain Gray, accepted that Scotland was officially in recession, the first recession in twenty years.

Despite criticism of its policies, and its economic development agencies, Scottish Enterprise (SE) and Highlands and Island Enterprise (HIE), and that the Scottish Executive and the Parliament had its priorities wrong e.g. Section 28–2b; the ban on fox hunting; the abolition of feudal tenure, land reform, funding elderly care; Gray, without any alternative, instead pointed to the opportunities for the economy envisaged by the Scottish Executive's longer-term strategy *Smart, Successful Scotland* (2001), Wendy Alexander's strategy for enterprise. Powerless to intervene with financial or policy instruments as the Scottish Executive had no control over economic and fiscal matters, the real economic levers of power remained in Westminster, *Smart, Successful Scotland* was the only game in town, and as with the A New Strategy for Scottish Tourism (2000), was more aspirational in tone than anything else.

Although Scotland was to recover from recession in late 2002, the fact that the Scottish economy is still being out performed by the remainder of the U.K.; that its business birth-rate continues to be only a fraction of that of England; and that Scottish tourism figures are still dismally disappointing in comparison to rival destinations leads us to ask some fundamental questions. For example, would the Scottish economy and indeed Scottish tourism as is the evidence of the Basque region in Spain, perform better if the Scottish Parliament had fiscal freedom? Would it attract and sustain more businesses and consequently jobs, and also more visitors if it had the ability to change the immigration policy; raise its own taxes and duties (and reduce these); and use instruments and mechanisms such as corporation tax; or even the ability to adjust interest rates; the exchange rate; devalue the pound; or join the Euro? Indeed raise a tourist tax, which could be invested in the tourism industry (for further information see Barron *et al.* 2000)?

What we do know is that during the first four years of the parliament fiscal autonomy grew to be an increasingly important topic, and was grist to the mill of those who had argued in the lead up to devolution that it was the slippery slope to independence — the more Westminster gave the more Edinburgh (Holyrood eventually) would want! Furthermore, it is a question that is not going to go away, and in the process is bound to cause tensions not only between political parties and politicians, but also the business community and those organisations that represent businesses and employees. In addition, if two opposing parties are in power in Westminster and Holyrood (post-2007), which is highly likely at some point no matter how distant, given the history of U.K. politics it would appear inevitable that the tensions between the two administrations could be untenable and would lead to the break up of the U.K.

Scottish MPs

It would be remiss of me not to address the situation in regard to Scottish politicians' relationship with Westminster. It is also very timely that this subject be aired, for apart form their being a disproportionate number of Scottish MPs at present, there is also a disproportionate number of Scots in political positions of power and influence in Westminster, a situation that is unsustainable, and may indeed as less and less Scottish politicians gain prominence or promotion in Westminster, have repercussions for the devolved settlement in particular if it is seen to be that Scotland has less influence on U.K. policy-making. In fact, it could be argued that having gained recognition on a bigger stage, and still determined to control Scottish affairs, such politicians appear more interested in their own positions and influence than in the wellbeing and future of their own home country. Of course they will argue that it is better being within the umbrella of the U.K. and all that goes with it, and that by being in such positions of power they are in fact protecting Scotland's interests within the union, but it could also be argued that for them their future prosperity and their guid conceit of themselves is guaranteed by being on the world stage than assisting with the transformation of the country in which one was born and bred. It is one thing that an island twenty miles off the mainland may eventually become an integrated Ireland governing itself without reference to Westminster, but a cross border adjunct never: which reveals much about the personal ambitions of Scottish politicians in power in Westminster down through the years, and never more so than now, a situation that is bound to change dramatically within the next decade as the influence of such politicians wane.

The First Parliament's Final Throes

Scotland was in the final throes of its first parliamentary term in over three hundred years, as this book was being completed, a time during which it alone among U.K. countries gave cabinet status to tourism, which led to expectations that have as yet to be realised. Whether this is the responsibility of the individual charged with the portfolio or the fact that tourism has been divorced from the mainstream of economic development policy remains to be seen. Moreover, the outcomes of devolution have been relatively disappointing, and the country seems disillusioned with the parliament and the politicians that it is no further forward than it was four years ago, so much so that at the 1st May elections the numbers of those elected from smaller parties grew significantly. Furthermore, despite the levels of activity the tourism industry is disillusioned with strategies such as *A New Strategy for Scottish Tourism* (2000), *A Framework for Scottish Tourism* (2002), and ATB consultations (2001/2002 and 2002/2003), which although well intentioned does not address the fundamental problems facing Scottish tourism businesses. Nor are any of these in actual fact policy. In fact it could be argued that the economy and ergo tourism is in a worse state than four years ago, particularly with the massive downturn in inward investment; the movement of many previous inward investment businesses and jobs to Eastern European countries; and the dearth of visitors post foot-and-mouth and September 11, and probably post Iraq and SARS.

Furthermore, there is a growing realisation that there is no quick fix. For example, it is unlikely that there will be future massive inward investments creating thousands of jobs, and with Scottish tourism competing in a global market place it is unlikely that unless it changes its focus, it will in the short-term be no more than a minor player. Nor will Scotland be able to address its skills gaps by altering immigration policy, which in particular would assist greatly Scottish tourism, or in transport where government transport policy is exposed in that not only is petrol more expensive than anywhere else in the U.K., it appears to render Scotland inaccessible to key international markets by air. That the new Secretary of State is also the Westminster Secretary of State for transport is also a recipe for conflict. Nevertheless, until Scotland is responsible for its own economy, it has no alternative but to pursue the Scottish Executive's economic development strategy *Smart, Successful Scotland* (2001), which reveals a vision of a Scotland, where creating, learning and connecting faster will be the basis for sustained productivity growth, competitiveness, and prosperity. However, this is a long-term strategy, the realisable benefits too far out to be of any benefit to the current crop of politicians who in any case were too intent on their own survival in the frenzied lead up to elections to the second Scottish Parliament; the impact of reserved powers on devolution not among their priorities, a situation for which the Scottish economy and hence tourism has paid the price.

Summary

Since 1997 when Labour came to power Scottish tourism saw an autonomy that was previously alien to it. Devolution brought further autonomy in that the Scottish Executive was able to devise tourism strategies such as *A New Strategy for Scottish Tourism* (2000) and to integrate these with economic development strategies such as *Smart, Successful Scotland* (2001), and *The Way Forward — Framework for Economic Development in Scotland* (2001). However, these are justifiably long-term strategies that will take at least a generation to have any real and sustainable impact. Meanwhile Scottish tourism's performance, as revealed in research commissioned by the Scottish Parliament (Stevens; Scottish Tourism Research Unit 2002) continues to deteriorate (Briggs 2002).

Furthermore, the Scottish Parliament's inability to assist Scottish tourism achieve its potential is not only hindered by its own lack of vision and foresight to radically change the dated practices of the industry, it is hindered by its lack of powers in areas such as those that govern fiscal and economic, immigration, and transport policies, and by those Scots who in holding sway in Westminster politics and government subjugate Scotland to their own ambitions. A truly dynamic and sustainable economy would have the ability to administer these functions without continued reference, or a backwards glance over its shoulder. That this is not the case in Scotland leads us to the conclusion that Scottish tourism is suffering endemically from institutional failure, to which it and its politicians have contributed greatly, and unless the second parliament treats it with vastly more importance than the first, will continue to do so.

Chapter 7

The Strategic Management of Failure of Scottish Tourism

Introduction

This chapter deals principally with the recent failure of Scottish tourism to realize its commercial potential. For example, the declining tourism income year on year in Scotland since 1997 is evidenced by VisitScotland's own statistics (see Table 7.1), and by the need in 2000 to review Scotland's National Tourism Organisation (NTO) VisitScotland's predecessor the Scottish Tourist Board (STB) (see Scottish Tourist Board Management Review, Report and Recommendations (2000)), following which the organisation underwent radical change. In consequence, it replaced its Chairman, Chief Executive and six senior divisional managers with new personnel and a new leaner, flatter structure, and which coincided with a considerable budget increase. At the same time, the Scottish Enterprise network (SEn) commenced on a business transformation which had a fundamental impact on its approach to tourism, particularly towards grants and support to the industry. This was compounded in November 2002 when tourism was removed from the Scottish Executive's Enterprise and Lifelong Learning Department (ELLD), instead merging with Culture and Sport, and functioning from within the Education Department (see below).

Ascertaining failure also means reviewing government involvement, and the relationship between the public and private sectors' and their individual responsibilities for tourism. For example, a much different model of influence and power to that currently evidenced in Scotland is emerging between the private and public sectors in other successful competitor tourism destinations such as Denmark where the private sector is very much to the fore (Stevens 2002). However, in Scotland, where the public sector is dominant, strategies and initiatives have been set rigidly within the boundaries established by whichever political party has been in power, and whose overriding concerns have been for tight control of the industry. Combined with the structure and composition of the industry, this has resulted in a culture that has been almost wholly dependent on the public sector, and echoes Scotland's wider social, cultural and economic dependency ethos as a whole.

To make a cohesive sense of all of this, this chapter also refers to the phenomenon of failure in tourism in a wider sense, referring where applicable to other areas where there may be similar problems or failings, or where something different has been done to overcome such problems. For example, unlike Scotland other countries have learned to

Table 7.1: Volume and value of tourism in Scotland 1997–2001.

	Trips (m)	Nights (m)	Expenditure (£m)*
U.K. tourists in Scotland			
1997	21.2	77.9	4,134
1998	18.9	70.4	3,734
1999	18.5	69.4	3,780
2000	19.0	70.4	3,810
2001	17.5	63.2	3,412
Overseas tourists in Scotland			
1997	2.1	19.4	958
1998	2.1	19.9	1,011
1999	1.9	15.9	858
2000	1.7	14.4	813
2001	1.6	15.0	679
All tourists in Scotland			
1997	23.3	97.3	5,092
1998	21.0	90.3	4,745
1999	20.4	85.3	4,638
2000	20.7	84.8	4,623
2001	19.1	78.2	4,091

Source: Tourism in Scotland 2001, VisitScotland 2002.
* Expenditure in 2001 prices.

address negative social attitudes to tourism by improving public and political understanding of the role of tourism in their economies (Stevens 2002), and from which Scottish tourism and politicians could learn. Furthermore, and in an effort to map the wider economic impact of tourism activities, in 2000 the methodology which measures domestic tourism, the United Kingdom's Tourism Survey (UKTS) was revised, and it is these newly revised figures against which Scottish tourism's sense of failure and its potential is now being measured, and to which we now turn.

Measuring Failure

Scottish tourism's failure during the 1990s to realize its commercial potential or to challenge competitor destinations resulted in a fiscal gap between current income and potential income of 20%, or £1 billion per annum. The importance of this potential income and Scottish tourism's failure to realise it in terms of its contribution to the Scottish economy should not be underestimated. Theoretically, this is a sum that would create thousands of jobs, reducing dramatically the current Scottish unemployment claimants, yield a considerable sum in taxes, and revitalise the Scottish economy. However, there appears little recognition of this or of measures that could be taken to realise this situation. This is because economically, politically and in sections of the media tourism has historically had a low and at times unflattering profile. For example, the fact that it is not recognized by U.K. National Accounts as a sector distinct from alternative economic activities as is the manufacturing industry speaks volumes about the government's value of it. Instead elements of tourism sub-sectors such as hotels; restaurants; bars; cafes; museums; sport; and other recreation activities have been grouped together with elements of the transport and travel trade to produce an estimation of the value of tourism (Department of Culture Media and Sport 2001).

In the seventies, following the 1969 *Development of Tourism Act*, and despite the fact that the measurement was less than scientific, individual U.K. country tourism revenues were published for the first time, and as these and the jobs created were becoming increasingly significant to the economy it meant that the English (ETB), Welsh (WTB), Northern Irish (NITB) tourist boards, along with the STB became the focus of their tourism industry's performance and aspirations. Although these tourism headline figures are determined in terms of overall revenue, underneath these are layers of statistics that measure domestic visitors; visitors from the rest of the U.K.; overseas visitors; visitors from individual countries; their individual spend; their length of stay; their age profile; tourism employment and so on, and which are compared year on year. Furthermore, individual Regional Tourist Boards (RTBs), Regional Tourism Councils (RTCs), and Area Tourist Boards (ATBs) produce and compare similar statistics, and act accordingly. However, the value of this information and its interpretation has been complicated further by a recent change in the way in which tourism is measured, and which will confuse future researchers unless explained properly, particularly as it has a bearing on targets as set out by *A New Strategy for Tourism in Scotland* (2002), which the Scottish Executive undertook to measure progress against.

In an attempt to map the wider economic impact of tourism activities, in 2000 the methodology which measures domestic tourism, the UKTS was revised. Up until then tourism in Scotland was recognised universally as a £2.5 billion industry. Indeed one of *A New Strategy for Scottish Tourism's* (2000) objectives was to increase this spend by 24% to £3.1 billion by 2005; the equivalent of £6 billion under the revised methodology. Conveniently, neither figure nor progress against them is to be found in *the Tourism Framework for Action 2002: 2005* (2002). Perhaps this is because overnight tourism in Scotland first became a £5 billion industry (converted under the new methodology from 1997's £2.635 billion), or more recently because of the downturn since 1997 a £4 billion industry (converted from 2001's £2.127 billion). This means that to achieve the 2002 Strategy target of £6 billion (£3.1 billion under the previous methodology), Scottish tourism will have to improve its financial performance, and the component parts, by almost 47%.

Not only will this take a substantial increase in performance, it is worthy of further explanation. For example, Scotland's tourism income in 2001 under the new methodology was recorded as £4.091 billion as opposed to the previously recorded high (under the old methodology) of £2.635 billion in 1997 (TIPS 2002), and yet there was clear evidence that there were less visitors and spend. This inflated figure was the result of a new research methodology based on telephone interviews using the introduction of random digit dialing, which revised Scotland's 1997 performance at £5,092 billion; under both methodologies its highest ever recorded performance, which also reveals Scottish tourism's true potential.

Table 7.2: Scottish tourism revenue 1997–2001 under both the old and new UKTS system.*

Year	Old system £billion	New system £billion
1997	2635	5092
1998	2476	4745
1999	2412	4638
2000	2404	4623
2001	2127	4091

Source: Tourism in Scotland 2001, VisitScotland 2002/UKTS 2001. In 2001 prices.

While the key principles of the survey remained unaltered, there were some changes which affected the level of tourism volume and value reported by the survey. For example, the new methodology permitted a longer time period for interviewing, which enhanced the potential to make contact with those respondents who were difficult to trace because of absence from home and other reasons — including those away from home on tourism trips. This change has resulted in higher estimates of the volume and value of tourism than in previous UKTS methodology (Evans 2002), and as is demonstrated in Table 7.2, revealed a considerable difference in revenue than was previously thought. Indeed, there may even be a further change as the EU is considering a widespread adoption of Tourism Satellite Accounts (TSA) methodology, approved by the United Nations, which allows governments to forecast the economic contribution to a national or regional economy in not only traditional areas like Gross Domestic Product and employment, but also capital investment, visitor exports and government expenditure (Mills & WTTC 2002).

Nevertheless, regardless of whatever statistics are published or claimed by public sector agencies or UKTS, the headline figure for Scottish tourism revenue has declined considerably since 1997 (−£1 billion under the new methodology or −£508 million under the previous methodology), clear evidence that despite numerous initiatives, consultations, reviews, and strategies that evolved during the first Scottish Parliament (1999–2003), and which are addressed in Chapter 9, the industry is failing to realise its commercial potential or challenge competitor destinations. For example, since 1997 Scottish tourism income, according to both the old and new methodologies has fallen by 20% (VisitScotland 2002). In fact, if during the late nineties visitor growth to Scotland equated with visitor growth in the Republic of Ireland, Scottish tourism income would instead have increased by £1 billion per annum (Briggs 2002), twice the figure needed to be achieved between 2003 and 2005 to meet the *A New Strategy for Scottish Tourism's* (2002) target.

One effect of this declining competitive position is a tourism trade deficit. In essence, the overriding fact is that Scottish tourists are spending more abroad than is spent by visitors from the whole of the rest of the world in this country. Furthermore, expenditure by Scottish tourists in Scotland is not increasing as fast as their expenditure abroad, and not all attributable to foot-and-mouth and to September 11, but perhaps also to the strength of sterling particularly against the Euro, which made the U.K. a relatively expensive destination; and the escalation in fuel prices, particularly in rural areas (Department of Culture,

Media and Sport 2002): areas outside the jurisdiction of tourism, instead the responsibility of government.

A Reason for Government Involvement in Tourism

The U.K. government became directly involved in tourism in 1969 when, due to its need to increase the amount of foreign currency coming into Britain, and to redress the balance of payments position, it accepted that tourism was becoming an increasingly important part of the economy (Elliott 1997: 84). In recognising this it reluctantly became answerable through its newly formed tourism bodies, created by *the Development of Tourism Act* (1969) (as indicated in Chapter 4, Northern Ireland had its own tourist board since 1948), not only for the performance of tourism in the U.K., but also for its development. Furthermore, it recognised as a particular priority the support of overseas marketing and promotion for tourism. This was in recognition that a private sector dominated by so many small businesses could not be expected to promote its business overseas alone. On this basis, the BTA was established to encourage people living overseas to visit the U.K. This led to expectations and aspirations that became increasingly difficult to fulfill. It also led to tensions among the NTOs who claimed that BTA promoted London at the expense of all other U.K. destinations.

Although tourism in the nineteen eighties was one industry fast superseding a disappearing manufacturing base, and despite the 1969 act, it soon became apparent that it was less of a public policy priority than other sectors. This was due in part to the general approach of successive governments; both Labour and Conservative. Although Ministers responsible for tourism recognised the tourism industry had a case for administrative and funding support, rather than being fortified by the fact that it was part of a wider department, as opposed to a dedicated ministry, they were disadvantaged by the fact that they had other remits, sometimes unconnected or in conflict with one another. Furthermore, government ministers do what ministers do best: nothing that will endanger their advancement, or bring them into controversy. In a Scottish sense pre-devolution, this very much meant keeping abreast of Westminster's policy on tourism even though it was London centric. In consequence, the formal development support roles were minimised, marginalized, under resourced and fragmented. When Scottish statistics were compared with other parts of the world's tourism statistics they revealed that Scottish tourism was failing to challenge competitor destinations or realize its commercial potential. This failure and the causes of this failure are deep-rooted, and it is clear that despite the 2000 tourism strategy, *A New Strategy for Scottish Tourism* (2000), and the 2002 *Tourism Framework for Action 2002:2005* (2002), to galvanise the industry Scottish tourism would benefit from a clear and focused Scottish tourism policy devised by the private sector as opposed to continual reviews influenced by civil servants in Edinburgh, and at a distance, by their colleagues in London.

The reasons as to why this has not come about are manifest, but among these is the fact that unlike the politics of transport, health, the environment, crime, energy or education, tourism evokes few strong feelings among established groups or citizens outside the tourism industry. In consequence, tourism seldom generates sufficient controversy to become a consistent issue on the political agenda, the result being the unwillingness of both Edinburgh and

Westminster and significant individuals within the policy-making process to be scrutinised and therefore to be held responsible for the decisions that they have made (Hall 2001). For example, according to Stevens *et al.* (2002) for decades not only have politicians derogated responsibility for a clear Scottish organisational structure that reduces ambiguities in policy making; and that brings clarity of roles and responsibilities; they have also been unable to engender strong private sector involvement at all levels flexible enough to meet the needs of a dynamic industry.

Government's Role

One contextual factor of importance is the emergent debate over the appropriate role of government in the development of the tourism industry and those organisations that partici-pate in it. In a nascent economy governments historically have been heavily involved in the provision of infrastructure and resources to support a fledgling tourism industry. Whereas, for developed economies such as Switzerland or Thailand that depended previously almost exclusively on tourism, although still important to both, it is no longer the mainstay of either nation's economy (Shenoy 1997). However, this does not mean that the level of government involvement will reflect tourism's position on its economic continuum. The true level of government involvement is dependent on a number of factors. For example, a culture has evolved in Scotland where because of the special characteristics of tourism and its revenue-generating potential specific public sector support has been welcomed by the industry to the point that it has become over dependent. Ultimate responsibility for such support has been in the gift of a succession of U.K. government departments, including the Board of Trade (from 1929 to 1979), the Department of Trade and Industry (from 1979 to 1985), the Department of Employment (from 1985 to 1992), the Department of National Heritage (from 1992 to 1997) and the Department for Culture, Media and Sport (DCMS) (since 1997). Meanwhile the Welsh (WTB), Northern Irish (NITB) and Scottish (STB, now VisitScotland) tourist boards as had their predecessors, became responsible to their respective Secretaries of State who delegated responsibility to a junior Minister for State. Since devolution this has become the responsibility in Wales of the Department for Economic Development, in Northern Ireland the Department for Enterprise, Trade and Investment, and in Scotland the Department for Enterprise and Lifelong Learning (from June 1999 to November 2001), then the Department for Tourism, Culture and Sport (from November 2001), the latter the only outright Tourism Minister of cabinet status in the U.K. However, despite devolution DCMS is still all pervasive. Through its connections and relationships with other Whitehall departments, particularly those with reserved powers, and its responsibility for BTA (now VisitBritain), it is able to subtly influence tourism strategies and initiatives U.K. wide, and the recent formation of Tourism U.K. whose role in U.K. tourism has still to be made more explicit, and the fact that VisitScotland knew little about its formation (Settle 2002) gives emphasis to this. The fact that Scottish tourism is overridingly unionist in view (Kerr 2001) gives no rise to the dangers inherent in the establishment of another pan-British tourism organization alongside the BTA (VisitBritain), whose role has changed recently but still remains a cross-border function, and which nevertheless because it is perceived to favour London has many Scottish detractors.

What is clear is that centrally planned economies that exercised virtually complete control from policy-making and planning, to the building and operating of tourist facilities are now in the minority. Since the demise of the Eastern bloc, most other nations involved in tourism have developed diverse economies in which public and private sectors coexist, and collaborate in the development of tourism within their borders. Depending on the political will, dogma, or the concurrent tensions, the balance of public vs. private involvement varies (Holloway 1998: 262), as does the extent of leverage, monies and resources. However, and although there is a case for more private sector involvement in tourism in Scotland, due to the complex nature of tourism it is improbable that the private sector on its own can satisfy completely government policy objectives or cultivate equitably a balance between host and guest benefits (Wanhill 1998: 337–340).

In the U.K., the philosophy of the Thatcher era saw successive Conservative governments retreat from active intervention in tourism policy, and public sector support for the industry. This resulted in some instances in a steady decline in tourism revenue and in others failure to realise potential culminating in an inability to deal with the effects of foot-and-mouth and September 11 all of which exposed systemic weaknesses in the tourist industry. This decline was brought about by the failure of governments to radically overhaul the tax system in relation to the tourism industry (VAT, business rates, corporation tax); invest in the promotion of tourism appropriate to the structure of the industry; and to the revenue benefits to the public purse from expenditure generated by tourism. For example, although tourist bodies such as BTA, ETC, WTB, NITB, and STB were funded by grant-in-aid from central government, these grants fluctuated in accordance with the importance placed on tourism by the government of the day. This was the result of the fact that there was no provision made for a statutory regional public sector structure for tourism, or to statutorily fund any regional or area tourist boards, a matter that is currently being reviewed by the Scottish Parliament's Enterprise and Lifelong Learning Committee (ELLC) (for further information see the Stevens *et al.* report 2002), and is also subject to a Tourism, Culture and Sport Ministry consultation.

The Concept of Public Sector Intervention

The rationale for the involvement of government or the public sector in Scottish tourism is an extremely convoluted concept. To claim that the allocation of public sector support should be based solely on the prevailing market over simplifies the heterogeneous nature of tourism as discussed in earlier chapters. Indeed, this is a continuing quandary for governments, and for those agencies such as VisitScotland, and Scottish Enterprise (SE), Highland and Islands Enterprise (HIE), and their Local Enterprise Companies (LECs) whose limited resources, and pressure to use them elsewhere, cannot meet the demands made of them of Scottish tourism businesses. Furthermore, a large proportion of Scottish tourism businesses are founded on a lifestyle basis, and although they cannot match the larger businesses in terms of numbers of employees and impact on the economy, because of their dispropor-tionate numbers they have an inequitable influence at a local level e.g. dominating voting at ATB AGMs, lobbying, political pressure. This applies in particular to those businesses in rural and remote areas, many of which are a community lifeline, complementary to other businesses or activities in the area, or a link in a tourist chain or route that leads visitors from one town or village to another and so on. Nevertheless, and despite their importance to their communities, although they have a concept of market failure, there is still an endemic expectation of public sector intervention, whether or not there is a viable market for their service or product.

Meanwhile, across the Irish Sea, the Republic of Ireland tourism industry, despite the fact that it still lacks the matching road infrastructure, and public transport systems (Coleman & Fraser 2002), has been buoyed by grants from the European Community, and a ready made North American market with Irish ties. Its government despite being on the periphery of terrorism pursued an interventionist tourism policy which invested successfully in its tourism product, infrastructure and marketing. Furthermore, it facilitated access to Ireland through inexpensive flights from a wide range of European destinations. Taking a similar interventionist stance, in India the government through the Indian Tourism Development Corporation invested heavily in tourism facilities such as ski resorts, and hotels, and in tourism services such as travel agencies, buses, car hire, and airlines (see Chapter 3).

Many developing countries, too, have tended to play a supportive role in tourism development, by providing infrastructure, and a representative national tourism authority. Yet, arguably the most successful tourism destination of all has no travel agency the Regan government having abolished the United States Travel Service (USTS). Although it was later to re-emerge in a smaller form as the United States Travel and Tourism Agency (USTTA), the Clinton government, when it came to power, abolished it, leaving the promotion and marketing of tourism in the USA to private businesses and the individual states (see Chapter 3).

In essence, there appears to be no definite pattern that reflects the role of government in the development of the tourism industry. However, overall, research is clearly showing a changing relationship between the public and private sectors of the tourist industry. The public sector in many countries is becoming less important than was previously the case. At the same time there is increasing emphasis upon encouraging private sector leadership innovations and a greater appreciation of the influence of the market (Stevens *et al.* 2002), something with which Scottish tourism is out of kilter.

Political Discomfiture

What is clear is that government intervention does not mitigate failure, and can lead at times to political discomfiture. For example, in September (the month prior to the Bali terrorist bomb that killed almost three hundred people, most of them Australian) 2002 Australia's tourism industry was in decline, with the Federal Government concerned that the industry hailed as its economic saviour during the previous decade was sliding into crisis because of its failure to face reality. The industry faced a $2 billion deficit — much of it centred on Sydney. This sum, the equivalent of more than 12,000 jobs, represented the annual foreign exchange loss to Australia caused by the failure to redress the tourism slump after September 11, Ansett's collapse (an Australian airline) and the Olympics. To compound matters the $71 billion industry appeared to believe that the downturn was cyclical and easily arrested, ignoring the fact that the industry, now rivaling the minerals sector as an export earner, faced massive structural problems and that basic needs such as the roads, environmental and transport infrastructure were being ignored (Millet 2002).

In common with Scotland, the Australian tourism industry placed itself in this position because ultimately there was an imbalance in the relationship and responsibilities between the public and private sectors, which resulted in it responding too slowly to demographic and other social changes and to the fierce competition for international tourists. Furthermore, despite being Australia's fourth-biggest export earner and biggest services export, the industry had spent only $5 million on research and development in 2001/2002 or 0.7% of its annual income.

In Scotland total research and development on tourism is difficult to determine, particularly as this involves not only VisitScotland, but also Universities, Colleges, Local Authorities, Enterprise Companies, Chambers of Commerce, the Federation of Small Business and the private sector. What is certain however, is that in 2001 VisitScotland invested 1.5% of its income in research, futures and strategy, down from 2.1% in 2000 (VisitScotland 2002), or 0.016% of Scottish tourism income, and that between now and 2006 Scottish business needs to invest £750 million on research and development just to reach the average spend of the Oganisation for Economic Co-operation and Development (OECD) countries. Scotland at present spends 0.53% of GDP as opposed to the 1.54% for OECD countries. Scotland, too, fared badly in terms of comparative productivity. For example, while the U.K. was 92% of OECD average, Scotland was 84% (Kemp 2002).

For the U.K. government there was also the failure to manage media images of pyres of burning carcasses during foot-and-mouth. This was compounded by images of Tony Blair in a protective yellow suit on a visit to a mass burial pit at Birkshaw Forest in Scotland. While he had to be seen to be in control of events, such images were conveyed world wide discouraging hundreds of thousands of people from visiting the U.K. Embarrassing for government too was that Local Authorities refused to open footpaths to tourists — undermining Government attempts to bolster the ailing tourist industry. Furthermore, foot-and-mouth free counties kept their land out of bounds to tourists. Although the decision set them on a direct collision course with the government, they feared opening up the countryside would have increased the risk of spreading foot-and-mouth to their counties (Department of Culture, Media and Sport 2002).

Furthermore, in England, prior to the foot-and-mouth outbreak, only six out of the ten English Regional Tourist Boards (RTBs) provided web sites. Tourist Information Centres (TICs) were also hampered in their role as gatherers and disseminators of information by the relatively low proportion of such centres that were equipped with information technology. In that same period North West Tourist Board (NWTB) TIC's level of information and communication technology infrastructure was varied and thus made comprehensive data provision very difficult. Furthermore, only 60% of East of England Tourist Board (EETB) TIC's had e-mail facilities which made information gathering and dissemination quite cumbersome, fragmented and labour-intensive, all of which the government appeared oblivious to. Yet, there was a consensus in evidence that one of the few redeeming features of this period is that it has served to bring to wider public and political attention the crucial importance of the tourist industry to the British economy and to the rural economy in particular (Department of Culture, Media and Sport 2002).

In a Scottish sense, there was the failure to recognise tourism when Labour came to power in Scotland in 1997; when Lord Macdonald took responsibility for tourism in 1998; and in 1999 when the new Scottish Parliament announced ministerial portfolios; and failed to mention who would have the responsibility for tourism. Furthermore, the manner in which Wendy Alexander, the Enterprise and Lifelong Learning Minister, among whose responsibilities was tourism, mishandled the appointment of the new VisitScotland Chief Executive, Rod Lynch in 2001; and, her successor Mike Watson, the architect of the ban on fox-hunting, whose credibility was damaged by his compromising his position in regard to cabinet responsibility in 2001, when his constituency duties made him take a stance that he later voted against in Parliament, all of which has had a detrimental impact on Scottish tourism, contributing to its ongoing sense of failure.

Furthermore, in common with England, the low level of information technology provision in the Scottish tourism industry has been a hindrance to information collection and analysis, as has been Scottish computer destination marketing and reservations systems initiatives such as Integra, Ossian, and now eTourism Ltd. For example, in Scotland in 1998 Project Ossian, cost upwards of £4 million to develop. Ossian superseded Integra on which £900,000 was spent, and was now being superseded itself for much the same reasons its predecessor fell by the wayside — it would not meet the more demanding needs of the twenty-first century. Ossian was intended to support and promote tourism in Scotland by changing the way in which Scotland was marketed and the way in which information and services were provided to visitors (Scottish Tourist Board 1998). STB's intention was to provide an on-line booking system for accommodation and events and also serve as a source of management information. However, without being implemented it was replaced by eTourism Ltd a £6 million public private partnership (PPP) of which SchlumbergerSema, a global IT services company with headquarters in New York, took a 60% share with an option to buy out its public sector partners at the end of a ten year period. The brouhaha that followed split Scottish tourism — Western Isles (WITB) and Glasgow and Clyde Valley (GGCVTB) tourist boards refused to participate, relinquishing their VisitScotland funding in the process, and perhaps accelerating the demise of the ATB network in its present form. Indeed the brouhaha has continued with a number of Scottish tourism operators threatening to set up their own service in opposition to it, because of its failure to market their premises properly.

Further back, following the Scotland United conference (see Chapter 9 for further information) in November 2001, disquiet was spread by an article in the *Herald* (Wilson 21 November 2001) which claimed that Alexander, who had been widely expected to announce a shake up of the ATBs at the conference, had delayed her decision because Glasgow (GGCVTB) refused to become merely a branch office of VisitScotland in Edinburgh. Wilson claimed that GGCVTB believed that such change should not be implemented properly until completion of a Scottish parliament review of the position and prospects of Scotland's four largest cities. Furthermore concern was expressed, by Glasgow City Council that any change to the ATB network would lead to fewer tourist boards covering larger regions destroying Glasgow's growing reputation as a tourism centre. All of this opprobrium followed an article in the Glasgow Chamber of Commerce's publication, The Journal (November 2001), in which GGCVTB Chief Executive, Eddie Friel, claimed that devolution had resulted in an Edinburgh-centric world, that there was a reluctance to accept the principle of competitive cities, and furthermore, that the proposals for the re-organisation of ATBs would remove Glasgow's ability to market itself.

The Underlying Causes of Failure

The underlying causes of Scottish tourism failure that impinge on Scotland's ability to realise its commercial tourism potential are not difficult to identify. Indeed to its credit, the Scottish Executive has endeavoured to address these. However, the eternal reviews of Scottish tourism appear, as Friel (personal communication 2001) observes, to create an unenviable status of paralysis by analysis. Although this pattern of reviews and initiatives have purported to be Scottish tourism policy, previous chapters have argued that Scotland does not have a factual tourism policy, and that there has indeed been ambiguity over whether or not reviews and initiatives are de facto tourism policy. Furthermore, there has been little evidence of integration of such policies/reviews/initiatives with other policies/reviews/initiatives such as economic development; transport; culture; and education, and which has contributed to the failure of Scottish tourism to realise its potential, and confusion as to the various responsibilities of those involved in Scottish tourism. For example, with organisations such as VisitScotland; the ATBs; SE; HIE; the LECs; the Local Authorities, and many more public sector bodies involved in Scottish tourism, and vying for position and influence, it is little wonder that there is confusion and a lack of clarity of public sector roles and responsibilities of tourism in Scotland.

Such bodies' dominance of Scottish tourism has also led to an over-reliance on them, a dependency culture, leading to expectations they are unable to deliver or sustain. Furthermore, although the tourism industry welcomed the fact that tourism was awarded a cabinet brief in 2001, realigning it with Culture and Sport, it is clear that the unless there is policy integration the price paid in the longer-term will be a dislocation of tourism from economic development, and the inability to grasp the resultant opportunities.

An example of Scotland's failure to both capitalise on opportunities and to integrate policies is according to Stevens *et al.* (2002) the failure of Scottish tourism to take advantage of cabotage and air liberalisation, particularly low cost airlines which are targeting a range of non-traditional city destinations, providing new opportunities which Scotland appears slow to take advantage of. For example, it would appear that Scotland has yet to fully grasp the fact that low-cost air travel has led to a new geography, changing the map of tourism in central and Western Europe. The new inexpensive air services have been the catalyst for the acceleration of growth in tourism in a new sub regional destination encompassing Croatia, Italy, Austria and Slovenia as well as stimulating short break tourism to their cities. Meanwhile the recent incidence of Ryanair being unable to convince Highlands and Islands Airports Limited (HIAL), a company wholly owned by the Scottish Executive, of the necessity of the need to support flights from Stansted and Prestwick to its airports in Inverness and Lewis is a case in point, the £15 per passenger landing demanded by HIAL pricing Scotland out of the market (Naysmith 2002). In consequence, by providing locations for city breaks and short holidays that are accessible and inexpensive in comparison with many Scottish destinations, emerging countries and smaller regional destinations such as those described earlier appear more amenable and accessible to international travellers than Scotland.

This is compounded by the fact that in relation to other industries Scottish tourism is a comparatively weak industry in terms of its fragmentation, spatiality, and seasonality. Furthermore, the dominance of the central belt, particularly the area around Glasgow, Stirling, and Edinburgh inhibits dispersal of tourists to the remainder of Scotland. This, in turn, has implications for investment strategies as well as internal transport and accessibility (Stevens *et al.* 2002). For example, patterns of demand surrounding urban and rural tourism have historically different seasonal fluctuations. Although the central belt towns and cities year round business is becoming more evenly spread, for many businesses outwith this area the common pattern is to derive profit from the high season that will enable them to survive the shoulder months. Such patterns of business have profound implications for rates of business survival, for quality standards, and also for staff retention. For example, disappointing spring and autumnal figures in the early 1990s and recognition of the need to expand the tourism season led to the creation of the STB's Spring into Summer and Autumn Gold campaigns. However, although these campaigns were ultimately successful in expanding the tourism season on either side of the summer months for Scottish cities such as Edinburgh, Stirling and Glasgow, they failed to impact on businesses outwith the central belt in any meaningful way.

This is compounded further by the fact that Scotland has also failed to build upon its distinct culture, heritage and history, a scenario that reverts back to the lack of policy cohesion, and that decision-making on various aspects relating to the above such as broadcasting, regulation and some aspects of transport, including railways are reserved powers, the result being one of the most disappointing aspects of devolution. Apart from its landscape, environment and coast, few countries have such a distinct set of cultural disciplines on which to build and which over the years have been marginalised, or distilled into a wider British culture. For example, tourism in Scotland could be the key to a cultural renaissance by creating an awareness of the variety of activities as well as a pride in its theatre, music, cinema, dance, art, literature and its traditional inheritance of heritage and history, eventually attracting people of different communities to participate in economic activity.

Also, unlike other professions or industries, there is no barrier to entry to tourism as it is widely accepted that this would be difficult to police, and would be politically unacceptable particularly in rural areas. However, this situation has engendered a dearth of professionalism and a lack of appreciation of the appropriate skills of those who work in, or whose activities support, tourism in Scotland. Indeed the predicted future skills gap (see Boyle 2002 for further information) is already inhibiting expansion in the tourism industry, and poses deep questions as to how the industry would in any case meet the demands of future growth in terms of filling vacancies with those with the appropriate skills.

It is also accepted that in the wider sense Scottish tourism is but one thread in the tapestry that makes up the infrastructure of everyday Scottish life, and that in fact things could be simplified if there were fewer councils, economic development organisations, tourist boards and so on, and that any alteration of the Scottish tourism structure should indeed be part of a larger overall structural change. However, as has been evidenced by successive governments, and as will undoubtedly occur over the next decade, although there will undoubtedly be a reorganisation of all of these bodies during this time, unfortunately these will take place at different times, apparently with little reference to one another, remain inconterminous, and be subject to the vested interest of a small number of influencers. In the midst of such change, if the past is anything to go by, responsibility for Scottish tourism will shift from pillar to post consigning it to never realise its ultimate commercial potential, or challenge its competitor destinations.

Summary

Adherence to the principles of the 1969 *Development of Tourism Act* has led to a Scottish tourist industry that is institutionalised, fragmented, and devoid of vision. Above all the industry has a palpable sense of its own failure that is all too readily accepted as is the convoluted and complicated organisational environment in which it operates and in which despite the numerous initiatives and best wills of successive ministers (three in the first parliament alone) it continues to operate.

That it has failed to realise its commercial potential and challenge competitor destinations is due to a variety of issues such as those described above, that the industry has recognised and endeavoured to address. However, due to the systematic weakness of the industry in terms of fragmentation and the complicated relationships of the organisations and individuals involved in Scottish tourism, the material complexity of such issues appear irresolvable. For example, Scottish tourism appears fundamentally unable to organise itself effectively; or to regulate itself in terms of professional qualifications; or to insist on the implementation of rigid and arguably compulsory (statutory) standards and regulations that would address the divergence of quality standards. Furthermore, although Scottish tourism is unable to influence the macro economy e.g. exchange rates; interest rates; corporation tax; and duty, it should be able to operate within a fiscal environment which enhances it through the provision of an integrated transport infrastructure combined with means of easier access to Scotland, the latter along with the provision of skills emerging more and more as *the* vital issues for the future of tourism in Scotland. For example, regardless of the reviews and initiatives designed to improve the quality of tourism in Scotland, if tourists cannot gain easier access to Scotland, and if the industry continues to fail to recruit staff and then to provide them with the appropriate skills to service them tourists will instead continue to visit other more accessible destinations and the current decline with accelerate. Sadly, failure of the various sorts described above is endemic, and long-standing, and has many root causes which this chapter has attempted to address, and which the reminder of the book will now build upon.

Chapter 8

Approaches to Scottish Tourism Public Policy

Introduction

Building upon the heterogeneous approach to Scottish tourism advocated in Chapter 2 and used thereafter, this chapter instead adopts a policy network approach which explores the relative manner in which institutions; networks; interest groups, coteries; and elites endeavour to influence Scottish tourism public policy. It also compares their relative power, their relationships, and the contribution they make to Scottish tourism, and the wider field of economic development.

The rationale for adopting a policy network approach as opposed to alternative theories is that it focuses more on institutions and the links between them, both internally and externally in terms of the needs of the participants, and the resultant relationships. It also takes into account the transition from government to governance, where institutional and sectoral processes become contingent on each other and on their contexts (John & Cole 2002), which is particularly apt to Scottish tourism. This enables description of the processes by which Scottish tourism manages, organises and develops these complex relationships. Furthermore, a network approach allows analysis of the link between micro-levels and macro-levels of decision making: one dealing with the role of interests and government, in particular with policy decisions, the other which focuses on the broader questions about the distribution of power (Rhodes 1999: 29). It is, therefore, an ideal model on which to focus the tensions surrounding devolved and reserved powers on the Scottish economy, and on Scottish tourism's inability to influence those powers that are reserved and which in turn influence it: a symptom of devolution.

Although it clearly does not determine policy outcomes, the existence of a policy network both influences the affects upon policy and reflects the relative status, or even power, of the particular interests in a broad policy area (Rhodes 1999: 29). In consequence, Scottish tourism contains a pattern of policy networks in which the value and culture of decision-making elites and coteries sustain a distinct set of institutions and relationships (Moore & Boothe 1989, cited in Brown *et al.* 1996). Within these networks are found a number of individuals who affect to influence tourism policy-making in Scotland, and which are of interest here. Having, therefore, explored earlier the role of institutions, groups and networks in Scottish tourism; and theories, approaches and frameworks applicable to Scottish tourism policy such as advocacy coalitions, policy streams, governance and elites (see Chapter 2); we now explore the part they have to play in policy-making.

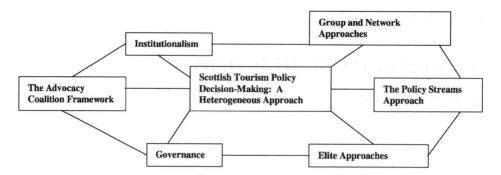

Figure 8.1: A model of the component parts to a heterogeneous approach to Scottish tourism policy-making decisions.

Approaches to Scottish Tourism Public Policy

To develop this theme, the proposal that an integrated approach to Scottish tourism, a heterogeneous one, has evolved from John's Evolutionary Approach (1999) and is demonstrated in Figure 8.1.

This model has the ability to move among many different, complex and theoretical perspectives that recognise that the constituent parts of Scottish tourism policy systems are irrevocably interrelated with wider policy systems, and within which elites and coteries participate at various different incoterminous levels.

In adopting a heterogeneous approach to Scottish tourism we have sought to substantiate its applicability to our understanding better the mechanisms by which tourism public policy-making in Scotland is derived. However, it is also important to substantiate how relevant this approach is to our understanding of the way in which tourism policy decisions are implemented in Scotland; the processes by which they are implemented; the relative power of any given tourism institution, group, network, coterie or elite to other tourism institutions, groups, networks, coterie or elites; and, simultaneously, to determine how much power they wield, and the strengths or weaknesses of their relationship, where there is one. Furthermore, it is necessary to determine within a given type of decision what contribution they make to that decision, given that the parochiality of many in the tourism industry in Scotland means that their contribution is mainly confined to the area (both geographical and subject matter) in which they have a vested interest. In consequence, they may become most formidable in their specialised area (Hoppe 1992) to the detriment of other areas, which are of little material interest to them. For example, the participation of elites and coteries in the policy process is based on the premise that although they may ultimately accept the group or network position, willingly, coercively or otherwise, it is only natural that they may also continue to seek to gain the best advantage for their own position, business or organisation.

An Institutionalist Approach to Scottish Tourism Public Policy

There is a divergence of opinion over the continued existence of the institutions of the state particularly since the acceleration of globalization and governance. One argument is that institutions are the bedrock of society, the other that policy-making systems need to respond to international economic pressures therefore rendering institutions less influential than previously (John & Cole 2002). In Scotland, although rapid institutional reforms and policy change has affected tourism policy decision-making, it is evident that inherent institutionalism is one of the contributory factors that renders Scottish tourism too slow to change to the demands placed upon it by the modern day visitor, and the pressures from competitor destinations. In essence, issues that concern Scottish tourism today and which contribute to its failure are not too dissimilar to those of forty to fifty years ago: evidence of long-term institutional failure (Kerr 2001).

On this basis, in institutional terms, it is important to ascertain who is influencing events, and to what end. For example, Hoppe (1992) claims that when events emerge from the impersonal facade of an institution, it is often answered by matching individuals of known power to their presence in those institutions. Alternatively, awareness of the behavior of the group means not having to estimate the behavior of the individuals in it separately, even though such individuals will put forward views that are at variance with one another. What is clear, however, is that an institutional approach is better at explaining policy stability than change, through the way in which choice is constrained. For example, if there is not enough push for change, institutions can keep a political system stable by limiting the impact of new interest groups and ideas (John 1999). An example of this was the relationship between the Scottish tourism industry and the Scottish Office pre-devolution, where membership of the then Scottish Tourism Co-ordinating Group (STCG) was ultimately in the gift of the minister for tourism, as was (and still is) appointments to the STB/VisitScotland Board and Scottish Enterprise (SE) and Highlands and Islands Enterprise (HIE) Boards, and the new Steering Group that evolved from the *Tourism Framework for Action 2002: 2005* (2002). However, the outcome of such a process and other processes where appointments are undemocratic is that aspirant participants' feel excluded from the policy process, an inner circle is created of the privileged few, and few progressive policy initiatives evolve: the likely reason as to why issues relevant a century ago still remain unresolved e.g. funding, skills, quality, access, structure.

Such institutions confer power on individuals. This includes their personal power and magnetism, their abilities, their energies, their relationships and their connections. Furthermore, institutional power and status is attained by virtue of an individual's institutional position such as the kudos of being a member of the newly formed tourism Steering Group (see Chapter 5), the Scottish Tourism Forum (STF), the British Hospitality Association (BHA) or the VisitScotland or SE/HIE/LEC boards. However, such individuals are often consumed by such institutions or alternatively often masquerade behind them, and it is sometimes difficult to ascertain their contribution, the status from being a member of the group the extent of some participants' activity. In this event, the penetration of the institutional curtain is necessary to ascertain the activity and the power of individuals (Hoppe 1992). It is whether they are willing to challenge and push against the institutional boundaries, or whether the institution consumes them that is of interest here. For example, the Steering Group established by the tourism minister in October 2002 is bound by the *Tourism Framework for Action 2002: 2005* (2002) the contents of which appear pedestrian in comparison to the recommendations contained within the Stevens and Scottish Tourism Research Unit Report (Support for Tourism: An International Comparison (2002)) commissioned by the Enterprise and Lifelong Learning Committee. Clearly, institutionally, the framework will take precedence, but if the Stevens Report findings are excluded from the policy process the eventual outcomes of the framework and its ability to influence positively Scottish tourism may very well be devalued.

Further back, it is also difficult to uncover any fundamental Scottish tourism policy-making decision made between 1997 when the Labour government came to power and the formation of the new Scottish parliament. For example, the Labour government, as with its fiscal policy, following its 1997 electoral victory, made no effort to alter the previous Conservative government's policy on tourism, instead pursing an identical route. The consequences for STB, SE, HIE and the LECs were far-reaching. Following the Labour victory they were apprehensive of the new administration, particularly SE/HIE and the LECs which were creations of the previous government, of what their future roles would be, and as to what devolution in the longer term would mean to their future survival. To compound matters further, anticipating (wrongly as it turned out) that a new government would bring its own positive change there was little real pressure put upon the politicians by interest groups such as the Scottish Tourism Forum (STF), which in 1998 was consumed by its own future (see Kerr 2001). Nor was there any pressure put upon politicians by those that comprised the then tourism elite whose political (with a small p) nous, had been blunted by years of Tory apathy towards the industry (see Chapter 5). As a result, and coinciding with Scottish tourism's dismal performance in 1998 and 1999 (see Table 7.1), Scottish tourism policy between 1997 and 1999 continued to be influenced heavily by Westminster policy on tourism, which in itself was a sedentary and London centric one.

Tourism, Politicians, and the Institutional Approach

Another interesting aspect of the institutional approach to tourism is that it is not particularly good at explaining the differences in policy-making across the various U.K. parliaments which influence tourism (Westminster, Cardiff, Belfast, and Edinburgh). Nor does it explain the approach of such politicians who because of their ability to influence reserved powers, as opposed to devolved powers, display disparaging tendencies about devolution that do themselves, the Scottish parliament and the Scottish people a disservice, as does the attitude of some MSPs towards their fellow MPs and Westminster: scenarios that have created tensions between them and the parliaments that will take a long and tortuous time to resolve, and because of which Scottish tourism as does other disciplines continues to suffer.

This is despite the fact most political systems have similar frameworks for making policy in each area of activity. Although there are some differences such as the level of government charged with responsibility for providing services (John 1999), the levels to which governance applies, the impact of globalisation, and of course the values of individual politicians (particularly those such as the aforementioned who gain reasonably high U.K. office), despite devolution U.K. ministers still set out to institutionalise and give precedent to U.K. policy as opposed to Scottish policy even where it has been devolved.

Take Scottish tourism, and the current and ongoing state of its affairs. Despite devolution it continues to support an infrastructure that appears to epitomize the approach of the wider well-tried U.K. institutions, which as has already been discussed elsewhere (see

Chapters 4 and 5), are wholly inappropriate in the modern environment. For example, the tourism sectors e.g. hospitality; visitor attractions; inward tourism operators; guest houses; museums; bed and breakfast establishments; and so on: their diversity, attitude and the polarisation of their economic and strategic contribution to tourism have created endemic tensions that have beset and held back the industry.

Furthermore, until it became part of the new Tourism, Culture and Sport Department in 2001, tourism was always primarily subject to and subjugated by wider economic development policy; itself subjugated by its inability to overcome the restrictions of reserved powers. Although the industry welcomed the opportunity of Cabinet status, there was growing disillusionment with the fact that the minister was consumed with other responsibilities such as the Scottish bid for the 2008 European Football Championships, with his controversial constituency stand on NHS proposals for the re-organisation of hospitals in Glasgow, and with the controversy sparked by Hamish Glenn's resignation from Dundee Repertory Company; a portent that the Minister did not value the arts as highly as the arts thought he should. That he was also the MSP responsible for the Private Members' Bill which resulted in a ban on fox-hunting in Scotland meant that he also alienated himself from many rural tourism businesses. There is also little evidence that the new office is one to which the noun progression might be prescribed, other than to that of individuals (politicians and civil servants) who have higher office in mind, and in order to smooth their own advancement avoid any radical policy or structural shift.

Since devolution, tourism policy decision-making has also exposed the differences between the U.K. countries' national tourism systems. For example, these differ in terms of structures; quality assurance; funding; marketing; and strategy. Nevertheless, they still come together uneasily under the auspices VisitBritain (formerly the British Tourist Authority, BTA), which despite the changes made in April 2003, is still incongruously a cross-border authority though tourism policy is devolved to the Scottish parliament; a situation with which the Tourism Minister to the chagrin of sections of the industry appears unperturbed. This give further vent to the impression that regardless of devolution, Westminster is still extremely influential on tourism in Scotland due to the dependence of reserved powers which impact upon the industry in terms of exchange rates; fuel duty; and employment law; and so on. This has been complicated further by the establishment of Tourism U.K. (see Chapter 4), whose presence particularly if allotted institutional powers could relegate further Scottish tourism's overall influence.

Nevertheless, John (1999: 65) argues that, in effect, it is comparatively easy to over-estimate the role of institutions as they tend to neglect the political and social context that affects how formal rules and norms operate. It would appear that he is perhaps making a distinction in wider terms than in Scotland. For example, in Scotland although the coteries and elites that have grown around the institutions have little influence over tourism policy, since the inception of devolution they have had some influence over the tourism agenda, certainly much more than the wider tourism industry. However, this small number of individuals, in the lead up to devolution, and it could be argued since has become analogous to an institution in itself, the perception given that its very existence, its innate conservatism, its guid conceit of itself, is in itself suppressing change. The influence of these individuals is investigated later in the chapter, but it is clear that between 1997 and 2002, a time during which the Scottish tourism performance deteriorated dramatically, the identity of these individuals changed little over that time, and raises the question as to their inability to influence Scottish tourism policy decision-making, and the Scottish Executive's reluctance, despite numerous undertakings, to let the industry take the lead.

Network and Interest-group Approaches to Scottish Tourism Public Policy

Apart from being analogous to institutionalism, interest-group and network approaches generally explain policy stability better than policy change while being synonymous with pluralist and corporatist theories (John 1999), both of which were discussed in relation to Scottish tourism in Chapter 2. Patterns of interest-group interaction and experience of first the Scottish Office and then the Scottish Executive explain how Scottish issues were processed by political systems, particularly the way in which they negotiated the operation of formal institutional structures. For example, for groups such as the STF and others, the policies and structures set in place by the Conservative government and which remained unchanged after it lost power obfuscated matters in the lead up to the 1999 Scottish parliamentary elections. Groups, networks and elites had little idea who they should be dealing with in terms of priorities, both at certain levels and in certain circumstances, particularly as invariably one participant may be less enthusiastic than the others on both the inputs (sometimes financial) and the outcomes (sometimes to their disadvantage), meaning there was not always a cohesive approach. This was compounded by the fact that not only, as is evidenced in *the Scottish Tourist Board Management Review, Report and Recommendations* (2000) that the STB was confused as to who was their customer, and that their Chairman was unable publicly to defend this position (Gordon, personal communication 2000), but also that tourism and economic development policies and structures were the remnants of the previous administration. This meant that until a fundamental change was made the department responsible for them or the parliament felt no real ownership of them. This makes it clearer, from the way in which networks operate, how change manifests. For example, the manner in which the then Enterprise and Lifelong Learning Minister, Henry McLeish MSP was influenced to initiate a tourism strategy a few months after the opening of the new parliament in 1999 is one example of network effectiveness. An example of network ineffectiveness is that although the STCG was disbanded after devolution, with the promise that a new Strategy Implementation Group chaired by the tourism minister would be set up in its place to oversee the implementation of the new tourism strategy (2000), there was little evidence that such a group met formally or as a result communicated its deliberations. In fact, it was not until October 2002 that such a group, the tourism Steering Group, was established, almost two and a half years since it was first proposed.

   In contrast to institutions, group and network approaches are also effective in drawing attention to the differences in policy-making across sectors. Furthermore, studies of policy networks often assume that the character of a policy network determines the practice of policy-making (Marsh & Rhodes 1992). Moreover, networks are an essential ingredient of governance as they link together fragmented political institutions, and provide coordination in otherwise complex decision making environments. For example, the Local Economic Forums (LEFs) established by Henry McLeish in 2001, and in which tourism participated, created an environment in many areas where for the first time, the ATBs, the Local Authorities of which there were sometimes more than one in such areas, the Chambers of Commerce, the Federations of Small Business, the LECs etc., began to work much more cohesively than before to a common purpose. The initiative spearheaded by the new minister Iain Gray MSP in 2002 that the LEFs should work towards an economic development strategy for their areas based on *Smart Successful Scotland* (2001) was further proof that fragmentation and parochiality could be overcome.

For Scottish tourism, though, nothing is straightforward. Compare the influence on or importance in which they are held by government of the Road Haulage Association (RHA), the British Medical Association (BMA), or the National Farmers' Union (NFU), to tourism interest groups, for example, or most recently the Fire Brigade Union (FBU). Or, within the tourism sector, the British Hospitality Association's (BHA) influence to less strategically-orientated groups. For example, the Bed and Breakfast sector's influence in sheer numbers on the local ATB network, and the impact this has on policy decision-making. When it is dictated by lifestyle businesses as opposed to more strategically-orientated businesses it is little wonder that the Scottish tourism ATB network was under pressure in 2002.

An Advocacy Coalition Framework Approach to Scottish Tourism Public Policy

In this model, policy-making depends on change and stability in the wider political system, in society and in the economy. One extremely interesting example of this model is that of the ideologically opposites' Scottish tourism policy being one and the same thing during 1997–1999, and with very little policy variance thereafter, evidence that for the opposition parties that although they can become quite emotive about it in terms of challenging the Scottish Executive's policy, tourism is not a vote winner. As a model it is an amalgam of ideas and networks in public policy that focus on the interaction of advocacy coalitions. For example, the policy subsystems are driven and sometimes fractured by large socio-economic or external events, while the advocacy coalition consists of constituents who share a set of policy beliefs e.g. BHA members who although their overall policy for Scottish tourism will be a roughly consistent one, it will differ wildly from the Association of Scottish Bed And Breakfast Operators (ASBBO), and Association of Scottish Visitor Attractions (ASVA) sectors. As with *the Multiple-Streams Framework* (Kingdon 1984) and *the Punctuated-Equilibrium Framework* (Baumgartner & Jones 1993), *the Advocacy Coalition Framework* (Sabatier *et al.* 1991) is contemporary because it places ideas firmly at the centre of its analysis. It also regards policy-making as a continual service with no strict beginning and end, and from which participants learn over time.

From a Scottish tourism perspective, it makes the case for more strategically-orientated bodies that hold the same ideals for the purpose of arguing against their less strategically-orientated opponents. Yet, it also encompasses the fact that all of them have a role to play in the dissemination of ideas (John 1999). As a consequence, it ensues a dominance of such ideas over competing policy advocacy coalitions that can produce only short term and vested interests (Hann 1995: 19–26; Hoshino 1997), and as such is a vital contributory factor to a heterogeneous approach to Scottish tourism policy-making decisions.

A Multiple Streams Framework Approach to Scottish Tourism

This framework throws up some interesting political foresights. For example, policy outcomes arise from a continual interplay of participants which, based on what has already been discussed in regard to the Scottish tourism coterie and elite, is limited to those invited to participate, and in consequence excludes others. In fact, it could be claimed that the model encourages this form of clique. It is therefore a less than all embracing model, almost elitist, and justifies the claims of those that already feel excluded from policy decision-making in relation to tourism in Scotland.

Another aspect of the model is that it has no starting-point. Policy solutions instead appear unexpectedly and disappear as rapidly. As such, this is reminiscent of Scottish tourism. Ideas are manifest, but many in the main are unworkable, reflecting perhaps a limited area of interest, a small geographical area or a combination of both. This leads to parochiality, fragmentation, or people being ill-informed, or feeling excluded. For example, the common myth is that everyone in Scotland is an expert on tourism, the result being as we discover in subsequent chapters that there is no consensus of opinion in Scottish tourism on what should be done about it. Yet, such ideas, when they do materialise, are not uniquely associated with one person or organisation, instead materialising from shared agendas between decision-makers (John 1999).

It is, however, an interesting concept in that it introduces a set of processes consisting of problems, policies and politics, all echoes of the above scenarios. It argues that each of these processes acts as an impetus or a constraint on public policy by putting a proposal on or off the agenda. Applying this to tourism in Scotland, for example, and to current problems experienced by tourism operators and tourists alike, among others, the model would be a compelling one with which to analyse the various nuances and sensitivities associated with what may be assumed as highly contentious issues, and again is a vital contributory factor to a heterogeneous approach to Scottish tourism policy-making decisions.

A Governance Approach to Scottish Tourism Public Policy

Until the seventies most West European countries were governed by governments powerful enough to intervene in the economy to pursue goals of redistribution and social justice. Today, many of these countries pursue a much more modest agenda, instead governing by coordinating and facilitating other powerful participants in society. For example, governance quite simply covers the whole range of institutions and relationships involved in the process of governing, as opposed to the narrower term government (Pierre & Peters 2000). During this time government has been transformed from a system of local government into a system of local governance involving complex sets of organisations drawn from the public and private sectors (Rhodes 1999: 51), including tourism interest groups, ATBs, and forums. This use sees governance in broader terms than government. For example, the new LEFs initially set up to resolve duplication and overlap of business services, and on which tourism is represented; the growing importance with which the Scottish Executive holds the STF, or the establishment of the new *Tourism Framework for Action* 2002; 2005 (2002) Steering Group.

Policy networks are one of the most familiar forms of contemporary governance. Such networks comprise a wide variety of participants — state institutions, organised interests and so on, in a given policy sector. These networks vary considerably with regard to their degree of cohesion, ranging from coherent policy communities to single issue, or issue specific coalitions (Rhodes 1997). Policy networks facilitate coordination of public and private interests and resources, and in that respect, enhance efficiency in the implementation of public policy (Pierre & Peters 2000). For example, a group of individuals in the late nineties comprising the BHA Scottish Committee who, as a group working within a wider network, found themselves in a unique opportunistic position, particularly in relation to influencing policy, in an unparalleled period in Scottish tourism history. They were operating in an environment in which there had been a long period of stability, and it was not until 1999 that a long period of tourism public policy inaction ended, which was due to tourism policy being transferred to the Scottish parliament. That the BHA failed to influence the new agenda is not the point. What the BHA did do was to create an environment in which STF could emerge as the voice of the industry, recognised by government as being so.

An Elite Approach to Scottish Tourism

According to Hoppe (1992) the premise of elite theory is that the great majority of human actions are structured and directed as opposed to being random, and that the structure and direction is provided by people's identification and their role(s). The outcome of sharing identification and role(s) is that a group emerges either formally or informally consisting of those who are actively involved, the most influential becoming leaders, and the least influential followers accepting the kudos and benefits of membership without responsibility. However, this also means that such people can easily be influenced, won over and become useful later. In most instances there is a natural correlation between those who are actively involved and those who are most influential. Furthermore, a high degree of activity and participation in such a group inevitably leads to a person usurping power in the group, and depending on the nature of the group or its aims and objectives the leader and/or the most influential members of the group may either form an elite or become part of a larger elite external to that group and whom we will term the power elite e.g. those with BHA affiliations who progressed to membership of the STF and to the tourism Steering Group.

This prompts questions of the role of power elites/coteries within Scottish tourism, and within its institutions and policy networks. For example, their individual relationships with one another, and the relationships brought to bear by their organizational affiliations, their positions within such organizations and the status of their business or position within the hierarchy of that business or organisation. Such relationships between key participants or organizations in a policy sector shape the policy-making process through their associations, and their shared perceptions and understandings about the manner in which public affairs are conducted (De Grazia 2000). Furthermore, the transient nature of tourism employment or businesses, and the total concentration for many on the summer season to the exclusion of all else may mean an individual's fleeting or sporadic association with a group, during which time their role could bring disruption, instability and inconsistency to the group or indeed involve it in rapid and inconclusive change. On the other hand, sustainability of jobs and businesses often leads to some group members overstaying their welcome, resistant to change, a stasis, unconsciously cultivating inertia, as was evident of the BHA pre the nineties (see Kerr 2001 for a fuller description of the BHA and STF's evolution, and their roles in the period 1997–1999). Nevertheless, although elites may have different affiliations, which may mean a differing of opinion on other matters the homogeneity of their interests invariably means that they agree on the basic purpose (Di Zerega 1991), which in terms of the Scottish tourism elite is firstly to influence Scottish tourism policy, and secondly to do it in such a fashion as to be a means to their own ends i.e. improving the lot of their own business/organisation, or furthering their own advancement.

Power elites play essential roles in maintaining the Scottish tourism system's overall well-being, even if as is evident they often also try and undermine it e.g. the uncompromising stance taken by the Greater Glasgow and Clyde Valley (GGCVTB) and the Western Isles (WITB) ATBs against the establishment of eTourism Ltd a situation already discussed in Chapter 7, and which had a negative impact on the future of the ATB network at a time when it was under review (Department of Tourism Culture and Sport 2002). Furthermore, although elites are dependent upon a formal equality in terms of ATB membership and quality assurance, because of their subservience in the main to the rules and norms of institutionalism they have no alternative but to be participants in the institutions of Scottish tourism e.g. the quality assurance system dictates that to be classified and graded or to receive a grant from its LEC a business needs to participate in the VisitScotland classification and grading scheme, which means a business also has to be a member of its ATB, or in the Highlands and Islands to be an Investor in People (IIP), or at least be working towards the standard before receiving a grant. Subservience to the rules and norms of tourism institutionalism is not exclusive to Scotland. In England the new ETC Stepping Stones (English Tourism Council 2002) initiative means the introduction of an inspected only policy for resort establishments which wish to be included in local advertising, resort guide, conference guide, website or TIC (Satchell 2000). Without such accreditation they will no longer feature in local guides or other forms of promotion, a long-standing arrangement tourism businesses previously took for granted. Another scheme, Fit for Purpose, is intended to give Local Authorities responsibility to ensure hotels, restaurants, and guest houses adhere to all the regulations currently in place (Paton & Golding 2002). Furthermore, in December 2002 the Scottish tourism minister informed the industry that Hotels and Bed and Breakfast establishments would have to improve their standards or face being closed down (Stamp 2002). The combination of the above could be the first steps towards a national registration scheme. However, replicating the industry's stance of 1969 when *the Development of Tourism Act* came into force and provided for a system of compulsory registration of tourist accommodation, Bob Cotton, Chief Executive of the BHA, continues to call for the continuance of the voluntary system of classification and grading inspection of tourism establishments. In consequence, it would appear for the foreseeable future that despite the above initiatives inspection of tourism establishments will remain voluntary, not compulsory.

In Scottish tourism's private sector the power elite is composed of people whose positions enable them to transcend the industry and, in certain instances, the wider business community, and wider policies. The influence this accords them enables them to participate at various levels in decision-making that has major consequences for tourism policy. For example, in the private sector people such as Peter Lederer (VisitScotland); Michael Cantlay (VisitScotland, formerly SEn); Peter Taylor (BHA, STF), Paul-Murray-Smith (STF, BHA); Laurence Young (BHA, STF, the Steering Group); Denise Drummond (Tourism People); Ivan Broussine (STF) and others. Such individuals aspire to a hierarchy that occupies a pivotal position not only in the psyche of the tourism industry, but also in that of the wider public. In essence, they are the only visible and viable link between the industry and the major tourism institutions e.g. VisitScotland, SEn/HIE, the Local Authorities and so on, and yet are wholly unrepresentative of a large swathe of the industry. As Hoppe (1992) claims, such hierarchies constitute the means of power and influence to the exclusion of others which, in turn, clarifies for us an understanding of how a power elite influences the decisions that are made and implemented in Scottish tourism.

In addition to them are civil servants in tourism e.g. John Brown (Scottish Executive Tourism Unit), and other Scottish Executive departments, or those who take the public sector strategic high ground in Scottish tourism such as the senior executive of VisitScotland, SE and HIE. For example, Philip Riddle (VisitScotland); Willie Macleod (VisitScotland); Hugh Hall (VisitScotland); Malcolm Roughead (VisitScotland); Eddie Brogan (SE); Bob Kass (HIE); and certain members of their Boards, all of whom may be considered part of the power elite Scottish tourist continuum, as must be those with ministerial or Committee powers.

How effective they and their predecessors have been may in the author's view, be measured by Scottish tourism's dismal performance; its inability to realize its commercial potential; its failure to compete effectively with competitor destinations; its reluctance to transform the industry and so on. For, with influence come power and responsibility, and vice-versa. However, as has often been the case in Scottish tourism such powers and influences have been wasted by a succession of politicians. For example, failure to act or to influence, or to make the decisions necessary to the long-term sustainability of Scottish tourism is in itself an act that has often been of greater consequence than the decisions that have been made such as the interminable reviews and initiatives that fail to address the fundamental and long-standing problems in Scottish tourism: skills; access; professionalism; the transport infrastructure; fragmentation; parochiality; statutory funding of ATBs; re-organisation of the ATB and TIC network; compulsory (statutory) registration of tourism businesses; the insistence on professional qualifications before someone may open a tourism business and so on.

This situation is compounded by the fact that all participants, public and private, in the Scottish policy network seem to be engaged in a continuing battle, not only for specific power concerning their own survival or advancement, but in a general struggle for determination of tourism public policy as a whole. Furthermore, contests for power occur as one institution seeks to expand its responsibilities beyond the stated aims and objectives e.g. SE's attempt in the early nineties to absorb STB, and alternatively VisitScotland's attempt early in the new millennium to subsume SE and HIE's tourism responsibilities. Nevertheless, although those named above influence greatly the decisions that are vital and pertinent to the sustainability of the industry, ultimately it would be naïve to claim that it is anyone other than the politicians and their civil servants who draft policy for them that formulate policy. Furthermore, that Scottish tourism policy by dint of reserved powers or the fact that the same party is in power on either side of the border is not influenced by the wider U.K. tourism and economic policies. In any case, and on the basis that this situation will remain this may indeed be less important than the fact that the power elite (public and private sector), despite their best efforts are sadly failing to influence the dramatic change that is needed for Scottish tourism to realise its commercial potential.

Summary

The locus for a policy network approach to this chapter and a heterogeneous approach to this book was taken in order to provide us with the ability to understand and explain the processes behind the dominant issues and controversies in Scottish tourism in both the lead up to and for the length of the first parliament, enabling us also to make sense of the complex environment in which the Scottish tourism industry operated at that time.

This approach has aligned the most appropriate characteristics of contemporary theories that comprise John's *Evolutionary Theory* (1999), synchronizing them with the environment in which Scottish tourism is operating while bringing to the research an ability to deal with a number of issues pertinent to Scottish tourism during an era of rapid and uncharted change. In particular, the tourism networks; the individuals involved in them in their pursuit of specific agenda (the power elite); and the interaction between the various private and public sector Scottish tourism organizations such as Scotland's prime public sector tourism organization, STB/VisitScotland; and economic development agencies Scottish Enterprise (SE) and Highlands and Islands Enterprise (HIE). Furthermore, adapting a heterogeneous approach enabled us to understand better the processes that contributed to making such a convoluted environment and also the mechanisms by which tourism public policy-making in Scotland was derived.

For example, in Scottish tourism even beyond the policy networks, institutions and elites there is a continual debate and struggle for the success of ideas and their attendant interests across the multiple sectors that comprise tourism, all hoping to influence the policy process. It is what causes policy variations and change and the way in which certain initiatives, ideas and strategies are selected, how they are selected, and by whom they are put forward and selected that is of interest here, and these are among the things that we have discussed in this chapter, and which build upon previous chapters.

Chapter 9

Initiatives, Consultations, Reviews, and Strategies that Evolved During the First Scottish Parliament (1999–2003)

Introduction

This chapter addresses the Scottish parliament's influence on public policy in tourism in Scotland during the parliament's first four year term (1999–2003). Accordingly, it provides a comprehensive analysis of the numerous high profile national tourism and economic development initiatives, consultations, reviews and strategies that evolved during this time. For example, from a period of relative tourism public policy inactivity leading up to devolution in 1999, the tourism industry in Scotland as is evidenced in the Appendix (Tables 1 and 4), has been under constant review, the most recent being the Scottish Parliament's *Enterprise and Lifelong Learning Committee (E&LLC) Inquiry into Tourism* (May 2002), and the Scottish Executive's Tourism, Culture and Sport Minister's *Consultation on the future of the ATB network* (2002–2003). The latter, the second since 1999, (www.Scotland.gov.uk/consultations/tourism/areatourist.pdf May–September 2002), the first (Scottish Executive News Release SE4374/2001 19 November 2001) being inconclusive due to departmental responsibility for tourism moving to the Scottish Executive Education Department (SEED) (see the Appendix (Tables 1 and 4), and also later in this chapter for a fuller explanation of this change) from the Enterprise and Lifelong Learning Department (ELLD) (see Chapter 5). The sum total of these initiatives was designed primarily to have a far-reaching impact not only on tourism in Scotland, but also in terms of job and business creation.

Although these have had significant impact on tourism public policy and on the tourism industry, this continual navel gazing fails to confront the real and underlying problems of Scottish tourism (for these see Chapters 7, 8 and 10). For example, the number of interventions in Scottish tourism public policy between 1999 and 2003, in comparison to interventions in the decade leading up to the formation of the new parliament, although exemplary, may instead as Friel claims (2001) be one of the contributory factors holding it back from challenging competitor destinations and an impediment to its realising its full commercial potential.

To set this in context this chapter also provides a comprehensive overview of the economic environment in which Scottish tourism operated from the time of the 1999 Scottish parliamentary elections to the period leading up to the elections to the second parliament held in May 2003, particularly the environment in which economic development policy and hence tourism policy evolved.

The Scottish Economy 1999–2003

Although Friedli (2002 from information supplied by National Statistics www.statistics. gov.uk/pdfdir/rgv1102.pdf) claims that Scotland's economy grew faster in the 1990s than previously thought with an annual growth rate of 2.1% as opposed to official figures stating it at 1.9%, regardless of either figure, Scotland's past economic performance contextualized the task that faced the new parliament. For example, by the summer of 2002 following six months of negative growth, and although this situation lasted for only a few months, for the first time in twenty years, recession in Scotland became a reality. This was due to the collapse of the electronics industry, a dramatic fall in inward investment and the decline of the nation's manufacturing base during the post-devolution era, and was in contrast to the overall economic performance of Britain, and signs in the latter half of 2002 of a recovery in the tourism industry. Furthermore, gross domestic product (GDP) in Scotland continued to fall, whereas across the U.K. GDP rose by 0.2%. The fall in GDP was accompanied by a dramatic decline in inward investment as multinationals continued to invest in or move operations to East European countries. For example, the value of investment by foreign companies in Scotland in 2002 was £271 million compared with £1.7 billion the previous year, an 84% decrease (Peterkin 8 August 2002), while in the U.K. investment by foreign companies fell from £35 billion in 2001 to £8 billion in 2002, a 77% decrease. This in part was explained by the change in foreign investment in the EU since the launch of the Euro. For example, while Germany and France attracted 18 and 19% of foreign investment coming into the EU respectively, the U.K. saw its share fall from a pre-Euro figure of 16% to a post-Euro figure of 5.1% and this, to a certain extent, explains Scotland's disappointing performance (Ritchie, The Herald 29 October 2002).

This was mirrored by Scotland's overall productive performance which had a productivity gap of around 35% with the USA and 15–25% with Germany and France. Even the engineering sector which the previous year (2001) had accounted for more than 70% of Scotland's manufactured exports experienced a drop to less than 66% in 2002, or -£3 billion (Kemp 2002). Despite this and although unemployment remained at an historically low level and below the average for the European Union (apart from growth of 6% in the Highlands and Islands), there has been little variance in the approximate total 2 million employee jobs in Scotland in twenty years. Furthermore, variations in prosperity and unemployment between different parts of the country (e.g. from 136% of the U.K. GDP average in Grampian to 78% in the Highlands and Islands), and also within each area remains unaltered. For example, while in Lowland Scotland deprivation is still associated with areas where structural change from heavy manufacturing has had the most pronounced effect; in other parts of the country barriers to prosperity include population sparsity, remoteness, transport costs, low incomes, and skills gaps (Scottish Executive, Scottish Economic Report (SE/2000/4) 2000).

In essence, the Scottish economy was mirroring the world economy in undergoing massive and accelerating change of a kind not witnessed since the industrial revolution. This gave credence to the Scottish Office's and latterly the Scottish Executive's always somewhat vague and slim hope that tourism, together with other service sector industries, would take up the employment losses created by the decline of traditional manufacturing industries. This decline in itself was accelerated during the 1980s, for better or worse, by government policy, which affected Scotland greatly. Where it differed with England was that if tourism was not to be the nation's salvation, then at least, promotion of the Scottish tourism industry became integral to public sector philosophies and policies to deal with both urban and rural regeneration. During this period, the benefits of tourism were, in policy terms, advocated most forcefully in the hope they would stimulate conditions for employment creation. Thus, public sector organisations promoted policies and strategies to intervene in what was a largely private sector industry (Kerr & Wood 1999: 17). For example, in the nineties government economic and employment policy developed in combination with organisations such as LECs (via grant aid, which until 1992 had been the province of STB) and ATBs (via their promotional function), which provided an interwoven network of financial, social and organisational subsidies. This included everything from supporting small business or fast-growth start-ups, to vocational qualifications, to financial aid to industry and, of course, marketing of Scotland at home and abroad. The majority of such support was attributed to the largest section of the tourism industry, the hotel and catering (hospitality) sector, making it arguably as Wood (1996: 583–592) claims the U.K.'s last featherbedded industry.

Government job initiatives were also introduced, which assisted the industry in taking on new recruits at low cost. Recent programmes include SkillSeekers (which in October 2002 the ELLC recommended be abolished in favour of expanding Modern Apprenticeships), Modern Apprenticeships and New Deal. But despite an increase in the number of actual jobs in tourism during the past twenty years, the total proportion of national employment accounted for by such jobs remained fixed at around 8%. Furthermore, the hospitality industry accounts for between two-thirds and three-quarters of such jobs, some 5–6% of all Scottish employment (Scottish Tourist Board 1994), a situation that has remained unaltered. Perhaps the greatest irony is that espoused by Bull & Church (1994: 248–269). They claim that any growth in employment in the hotels and catering sector is almost certainly attributable not to huge influxes of tourists spending quantities of sterling, but to the role of hotels and catering as a producer service (meeting demand from other industries), and the demands of the indigenous population. Furthermore, only 42% of hotel and catering employment in the U.K. is attributable to tourism expenditure. Of course the total might be higher in Scotland (Kerr & Wood 1999: 16–23).

Also, as a result of the decline of the tourism industry in recent years; the industry's marginal potential for employment creation; and Scotland's location, climate and cultural position within the consciousness of the travel industry, limits tourism's capacity to act as a source of economic salvation. In this and other respects a tourism policy based on promotion within a wider industrial strategy means that tourism as a benefit of travel, of doing business in Scotland, has certain positive attractions (Kerr & Wood 1999: 23). Nonetheless, in 2001 when the Scottish tourism function transferred from Enterprise and Lifelong Learning Ministerial responsibility to Tourism, Culture and Sport this strategy changed, and tourism's ability (particularly as it was now absorbed by the Education Department — see later) to integrate itself with other ministries was sorely tested. In effect it was at odds with the conclusions of the ELLC's (which still retained parliamentary responsibility for overseeing tourism) review of local economic development (ELLC 2001) and with the Scottish Executive's 2001 *Framework for Economic Development in Scotland* (FEDS) in which the then Enterprise and Lifelong Learning Minister (Henry McLeish) advocated tourism being mainstream of economic development policy.

Ultimate Responsibility for Scottish Tourism 1999–2003

Pre-devolution the Scottish Tourism Unit was part of the Scottish Industry Department. However, from the new parliament's inception in May 1999 until November 2001, answerability for Scotland's tourism policy in the new parliament lay with the ELLD, which oversaw economic development policy, and within which the Tourism Unit became integrated. However, due to the second First Minister Henry McLeish's resignation over difficulties with his office expenses, Jack McConnell became the third First Minister in just over two years, and tourism was integrated with Culture and Sport under a new minister, Mike Watson.

Clearly, there were tremendous expectations from the Scottish tourism industry of the party or parties (the Scottish Executive 1999–2003 consisted of a coalition of the Labour and Scottish Liberal Democrats) that came to power after the May 1999 Scottish elections. However, the needs of the tourism industry were understandably among its least concerns: nor high in its priorities (see Chapter 5). However, when in November 2001 McConnell appointed Watson as Tourism, Culture and Sports Minister in recognition of tourism's growing importance to the Scottish economy, it was realistically also one less responsibility for Alexander, allegedly the minister for everything, whose ministry subsumed Transport at the expense of the Tourism industry.

There had also been an inevitability about such an appointment. Although during his term as Enterprise and Lifelong Learning Minister (1999–2000) McLeish had acknowledged accountability for the performance of Scottish economic development and that the performance of Scottish tourism lay not only within one government department but across various departments; the industry's continuing decline, the manner of the STB CEO Tom Buncle's demise, Alexander's embarrassing handling of the appointment of Rod Lynch to the short-lived position of CEO of the STB, foot-and-mouth, the events of 11 September, and lobbying from Peter Lederer among others appeared to have convinced him, had he remained in power, of the need for a dedicated Tourism Ministry (Caterer & Hotelkeeper 22 November 2001). How he would have reconciled this with his view that tourism should be mainstream of economic activity remains intriguingly unanswered.

McConnell, anxious to recognise the importance of tourism to the Scottish economy, but also wary of establishing too many ministries, instead of dedicating a ministry solely to tourism aligned it with culture and sport. However, not only did he neglect to transfer over the budget for tourism-related activities allocated to the Scottish Enterprise network (SEn) and Highlands and Islands Enterprise (HIE), therefore obfuscating further the relationship between the enterprise and tourism networks, which *A New Strategy for Scottish Tourism* (2000) had endeavoured unsuccessfully to address, at Parliamentary Committee level he also left tourism within the ELLC remit. Also, rather than create another department, Tourism as is revealed in Figure 9.1, was subsumed by the Culture and Sport Group which

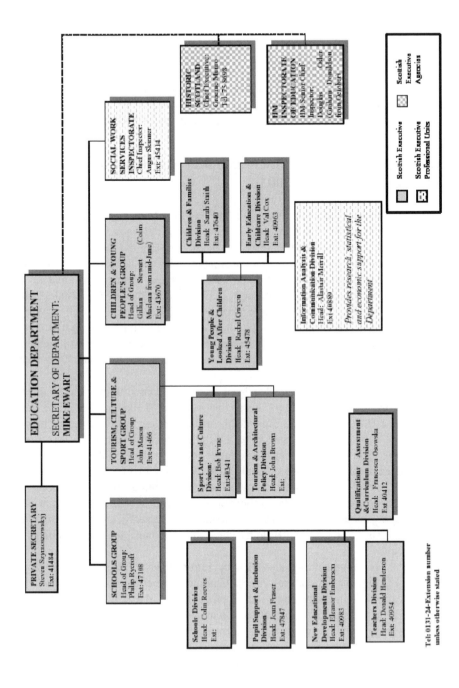

Figure 9.1: Education department organisation chart.

along with four other groups — the Children and Young People's Group, Social Work Services Inspectorate, Schools Group, and the Information, Analysis and Communication Division — formed the Education Department. Furthermore, in May 2002 the Major Events Team which was already part of the Culture and Sport Department was merged with the Tourism Team. From that point on the Tourism, Culture and Sport Group functioned as Watson's department; it had its own budget and its own Minister, and Deputy Minister, Dr Elaine Murray. But for management purposes it was part of the Education Department (Brown personal communication 2002), and worked alongside VisitScotland, SEn and HIE in developing the initiatives, consultations, reviews, and strategies discussed in this chapter.

The Economic Development Environment in which the New Parliament Operated (1999–2003)

In June 2000, a few months before he succeeded Dewar as First Minister McLeish published the Scottish Executive's *The Way Forward — Framework for Economic Development in Scotland* (FEDS). It recognised that in some instances, not only did the Executive's departmental responsibilities interact with specific competencies and designated institutional roles they also encompassed the roles of other parliaments. For example, regional aid to industry, where there were roles for the Scottish Executive, the U.K. Government and for the EU, and in trade policy, where there were substantial U.K., EU as well as World Trade Organisation (WTO) interest. In this context, although limited to what it could do, the Scottish parliament was able to legislate on a wide range of domestic matters, many of which influenced economic development. Among these was tourism. Others were discussed in Chapter 6 (Table 6.1).

The Scottish parliament, however, as has been already discussed in previous chapters, is not able to legislate on other matters designated as reserved matters (see Table 6.2), which rest with the U.K. government. This means, as has already been argued in Chapter 7, macroeconomic policies such as issues in regard to the overall stance of U.K. taxes and expenditure, or the level of interest rates, and the policy on exchange rates remain at the U.K. level. As does, it may be argued, a certain level of promotion of Scottish tourism via previously the BTA, a cross-border authority, which was a contentious subject to some, and a situation that has been convoluted further by both the establishment of Tourism U.K., which appears to be playing an insidious role in U.K. tourism (see Chapter 5), and the reformation of the BTA as of April 2003 as VisitBritain, which also encompasses responsibility for tourism in England.

Major economic development roles also lay at the European level. These spanned a range of sectoral (e.g. Common Agricultural Policy, Common Fisheries Policies, or research and technological development policies), developmental (e.g. the Structural Funds), and competition (e.g. anti-competitive behaviour, state aids, procurement) areas. Scottish tourism, as has been already discussed, was also to a certain extent reliant on European funds for specific projects, and Scottish industry had no choice but to comply with European employment and other wide-ranging laws. Furthermore, the power and responsibility in many vital policy areas rested outwith the Scottish Executive, and while it was evident that the Executive aimed to influence external policy-making by seeking to secure a broader economic environment that was supportive and contributed to its own vision, it was clear that due to the limitations of the devolved settlement it had little direct influence and that many important influences on the economic objectives of Holyrood still rested with Westminster. This means the Scottish Executive has only a limited set of powers, responsibilities and resources to direct economic development, including tourism. On the other hand, due to external forces such as the EU and the broader world economy, there are limits to the power of Westminster in relation to shaping the U.K. economy. Thus, Scottish tourism within the wider Scottish, U.K. and European economies has to operate within a complicated set of external forces. In certain circumstances these can conspire against it and its ability to compete effectively globally, and in others manifest opportunities of which it could never before have dreamed, meaning that issues for the new parliament are not only the affect of reserved powers but also in relation to tourism and the indisputable affect of globalisation upon the industry. This is compounded by the fact that the ever-increasing interdependence of tourism economies on each other has seen the deterioration in the capacity of individual tourism destinations to direct their future in isolation from events of the broader world order i.e. September 11, foot-and-mouth, Bali, Kenya (FEDS 2000), and now SARS and war in Iraq.

What is indisputable is that the Scottish economy is becoming much more service sector orientated and less manufacturing sector led. The service sector, of which tourism is a part, now dominates the Scottish economy, accounting for around 75% of employment and 63% of GDP. With Scotland becoming increasingly integrated within the global economy, it is not inconceivable that the Scottish-based service sector might increase further its share of the future Scottish economy to the detriment of more traditional industries such as the aforementioned manufacturing sector. Certainly, the service products that can more easily be traded outwith Scotland such as tourism have a central role to play in the economic well-being of the nation. But, to do so tourism as an industry has to compete for a diminishing and more parliamentary scrutinised government resource that is also being contested by other service industries and by other sectors (FEDS 2000). Furthermore, by no longer being mainstream of economic development tourism may become marginalised. Indeed, under Watson's stewardship there was little evidence that this was otherwise be the case.

To substantiate its case to government, among other statistics Scottish tourism looks to is a combination of positive-sounding ones. Among the best known of these prior to the election were those provided by the Central Statistical Office in 1995 and ratified by the STB in June 1998 (STB Prior Options Study). Following the election, *a draft of A New Strategy for Scottish Tourism* (1999) disclosed a raft of statistics (see Kerr 2001) that pre-dated the 2000 methodology change (see Chapter 7). This draft claimed that Scottish tourism contributes 5% of the Scottish economy's gross domestic product (GDP) and 8% of the total Scottish workforce: 20% of which is in the Highlands and Islands alone; or one in five of the Highlands and Islands work force. Such figures have been the bedrock on which all Scottish tourism strategies designed to attract more visitors have been built. Yet, as has already been discussed above, growth in employment in the hotels and catering sector is almost certainly attributable to the demands made upon it by the indigenous population combined with the role of hotels and catering as a producer service, rather than the yield from inbound tourism, meaning that less than half hotel and catering employment in the U.K. is attributable to tourism expenditure *per se*.

Therefore, as much as the overall tourism statistics in terms of employment, GDP and income go some way to validate the importance of tourism to the Scottish economy as a whole, they might also be construed as insignificant in comparison to other sector statistics. For example, although manufacturing has declined in real terms, as an industry it still accounts for around 20% of GDP and in excess of 65% of Scottish exports (FEDS 2000; Kemp 2002). This for the present puts tourism's contribution to the Scottish economy and the resultant view of the Executive of it within the economic development framework into perspective. Nevertheless, despite the fact that it had almost been given its own exclusive ministry, that it has moved across departments, and that it has been marginalised from the mainstream of economic development, the inescapable fact is that the benefit of tourism to the Scottish economy may, potentially, have more to contribute in the longer-term.

A Defining Moment — The House of Commons Scottish Affairs Committee Report (1999)

In public policy terms the initial defining moment for modern Scottish tourism came about not by devolution but by a report by the House of Commons Scottish Affairs Committee published in July 1999 (the House of Commons Scottish Affairs Committee Report on Tourism 1999). It contained damning condemnation of the management of Scottish tourism, as well as of the Scottish tourism product. The report also threw into relief several other pressing problems facing Scottish tourism including declining numbers of visitors, particularly outside of the urban centres of Edinburgh and Glasgow; poor quality accommodation in many areas; unwelcoming hosts; uncompetitive and inaccurate prices; poor standard of visitor attractions; and lack of accessibility. Sadly, if such a report were commissioned in 2003, and despite the initiatives, strategies and policies that have evolved since 1999, it is likely that similar problems could be identified: evidence of the failure of the Scottish tourism industry to address its underlying problems.

The report was a general document that offered a number of controversial recommendations for Scottish tourism. These included rejection of a bed tax as a way of funding public support for tourism, and support for the central funding of the ATBs by STB. At first, it was (for a very brief moment) uncertain as to what reaction the Committee's report would endure in Scotland. Although the Westminster parliament reserved certain responsibilities for Scotland to itself, tourism was devolved to the Scottish Executive. The research for the report had also begun before the creation of the Scottish Executive and the Scottish parliament, both of which could have treated its publication as purely advisory. In fact, the report received wide exposure in the Scottish media and the response from the Scottish Executive was swift (Kerr & Wood 2000). Within days, following a meeting with the Scottish Tourism Forum (STF) the Minister for Enterprise and Lifelong Learning, McLeish, announced that as a result of the report he would be taking action to improve tourism delivery. Less than two weeks after its publication, the Minister launched a consultation document for Scottish tourism, (Consultation, A New Strategy for Scottish Tourism 1999), inviting responses by the end of August 1999. The consultation process went some way to assuage the industry for overlooking it earlier particularly as it became clear that any changes might not be made in isolation.

The purpose of McLeish's consultation document was to support the development of a national strategy by the STB for the whole of the tourism industry, arguably the first occasion on which this had occurred. Furthermore, although certain industry factions were ambivalent over the integration of tourism with Enterprise and Lifelong Learning in a larger Ministry, the advantages to tourism by being integrated within the Enterprise and Lifelong Learning portfolio, together with other key industries such as oil and gas, and electronics, and the need for the industry to have access to all Enterprise and Higher and Further Education functions and funding intrigued McLeish, and until tourism was aligned with culture and sport in November 2001, influenced both his and his successor Alexander's strategic approach to tourism (STF 4 August 1999), and his 2000 tourism strategy — *A New Strategy for Scottish Tourism.*

Tourism Initiatives

A New Strategy for Scottish Tourism (2000)

By initiating a revised national strategic plan for tourism within a defined time-scale, and through the proposals listed in Table 9.1, *A New Strategy for Scottish Tourism* (2000) shifted the focus of attention drawn to it by *the House of Commons Scottish Affairs Committee Report* (1999) from the Scottish Executive to a para-statal organisation, the STB, an organisation that had a far from satisfactory record of success.

While the new strategy was flawed in that it failed to address areas of industry concern such as fundamental structures, funding, ATBs, access, and tourism delivery, or was ambiguous over the STB's relationships with SEn/HIE and other bodies, its apparent underlying purpose was to expose both the manner in which STB operated, and the failure of the administration of tourism in Scotland in the previous decade, and for which the new parliament could take no responsibility.

Furthermore, it resulted in the publication in October 2000 of *the Scottish Tourist Board Management Review, Report and Recommendations*, which was carried out principally by Mary Galbraith of PriceWaterhouseCoopers (PWC) and influenced heavily by Alexander.

The review of STB made ten recommendations (see Table 9.2), among them a change of name — visitscotland (later changed to VisitScotland); that there should be clarification of responsibility for tourism strategy and policy, contending that this should lie within the STB as opposed to SEn; and that candidates for the new senior posts would be assessed against a competency framework that specified the behaviours that would sustain the new organisation. This heralded wide-ranging management and structural changes to STB, the outcome of which meant the almost immediate resignation of the Chief Executive. This was followed a few months later by the resignation of the Chairman, and the demise of the senior management team.

Scottish Tourist Board Management Review, Report and Recommendations (2000)

In the context of the level of scrutiny and inquiry brought about by the new 2000 strategy, it was perhaps inevitable that the STB would be subjected to a management review; the

Table 9.1: Proposals from A New Strategy for Scottish Tourism (2000) measured against the Tourism Framework for Action (2002).

Timescale	Proposals	Progress/Outcome
2002 to 2005	The establishment of a direct e-commerce booking system with a target of 30% of all accommodation businesses to be trading by e-commerce by 2002 and 90% by 2005	E-booking was made available for serviced accommodation within visitscotland.com The industry e-commerce target is being addressed by the planned joint-venture project that suffered both massive delays and industry resistance (Greater Glasgow and Clyde Valley and Western Isles Tourist Boards refused to participate). Some operators have since set up their own site in opposition
	E-commerce expected to generate up to £360 million in revenue and create up to 2,600 jobs in the Scottish tourism industry	Although this is difficult to quantify the 2000–2001, and 2002 statistics for Scottish tourism bear out the fact that the industry fell well short of both targets and that it could be 2004 before they are reached
For the 2001 season	Tourism information and booking to be available through a single international telephone number	Although it was delayed due to the fact that this initiative was part of the joint venture project, it is now available
	A new multi-lingual call centre for tourist information and bookings	The Tourism Framework for Action (2002) neglected to mention this facility, and it is currently unavailable
	A new marketing campaign to increase the number of Scots holidaying in Scotland	The Scotland for the Scots campaign ran in the summer of 2000 and the spring of 2001 but according to the statistics it had little positive impact on Scottish tourism
	A new strategy to target niche markets focussing initially on golf, culture, genealogy and activity holidays	A £1.9 million joint public private golf tourism strategy was launched in 2000. A new £360k genealogy marketing campaign was launched in 2002
	Doubling the number of quality advisers to improve standards and encourage managers to take advantage of training opportunities	40 Quality Advisors had taken up their posts by February 2002 Food Quality Grading Scheme in place 2002
By the end of 2000	The creation of a National Transport Timetable to be incorporated in Scottish Tourist Board's website so that customers can plan visits using all modes of public transport	The Executive allocated £500,000 from the Public Transport Fund to Journey Plan Limited to assist with the development of the call centre which is now in place, but is not widely known about The web portal is in development
By April 2000	Set up, by April 2000, a major new industry-led Tourism Skills body to focus on meeting the needs of visitors through investing in people who provide the service.	Tourism People was established in April 2000

Source: A New Strategy for Scottish Tourism, 16.2.2000.

Table 9.2: Conclusions and outcomes of the Scottish Tourist Board Management Review, Report and Recommendations measured against the Tourism Framework for Action (2002).

Timescale	Conclusions	Progress/Outcomes
	The main conclusion to the report was that working with the industry and the Scottish Executive, the STB should identify long-term ambitions and aspirations to be encapsulated in the form of medium and long-term goals, and incorporated into the first review of the New Strategy for Scottish Tourism	The outcome of the review was such that because events superseded it, STB was not given time to pursue this goal. However, the Tourism Framework for Action (2002) eventually addressed many of these points
November 2000	STB had to adopt new business processes in the essential areas of governance (through the Management Statement), resource planning, performance indicators, and accounting procedures to reinforce the benefits generated by the new organisation structure	This occurred through the new organisational structure, the new Chairman and the new Chief Executive. However, compelled to work within parameters set for it by the Scottish Executive VisitScotland, as it is now named, still has progress to make to convince the industry that the changes that have taken place are effective. Furthermore, any change to the ATB network will impact significantly on VisitScotland
November 2000	STB had to take steps to secure broader representation from other associated bodies and partners on its Board, either by seeking appropriate appointments from Ministers, or co-opting individuals as necessary. This was to encompass ATBs, the industry via the STF and the local authorities via COSLA	As the minister still continued to influence such appointments, it was totally unrealistic to expect that the STB (VisitScotland) Board could influence such appointments. Evidence of this is the current dearth of appointees from organisations identified by the report
January 2001	The STB Board members had to assess candidates for the new senior posts using the competency framework that specifies the behaviours that will sustain the new organisation	The temporary appointment of Rod Lynch who was forced to step down due to strategic responsibility for an airline in which he was involved reveals this process as flawed
February 2001	STB was to pursue the visitscotland name change proposal, and develop the branding implications in consultation with the industry, Area Tourist Boards, and other interested parties	STB metamorphosised into VisitScotland, and is currently considering branding. However, although the ATBs had registered their websites as VisitAyrshire, VisitFife etc., there was further delay due to the ongoing consultation on ATBs
March 2001	STB was to adopt the proposed new organisational structure, which would equip it better to fulfil its purpose under demanding strategic circumstances	STB underwent a change in its senior management structure, replacing its team of seven with a team of four
March 2001	STB was to adopt a more sophisticated approach to its conduct of external relations built on the distinctive roles of the parties with whom relations were conducted. Along with the bodies with which it interacted, STB was to develop precise, unambiguous protocols that would guide and strengthen the relationships between the parties	Since Philip Riddle's appointment and with guidance from both Peter Lederer and Michael Cantlay VisitScotland has improved dramatically its external relations. However, there is still ambiguity in its relationship with SEn/HIE, and with BTA
April 2001	STB was to request that the Enterprise and Lifelong Learning Department clarify that responsibility for tourism strategy and policy lay with the STB, reallocating the existing costs incurred in SE/HIE to the STB	Not only did this not occur, when tourism became part of the culture and sport portfolio, the monies did not transfer across. Furthermore, tourism is now part of the Education Department.
May 2001	STB was to embark on a development process with ATBs to make more rational the basis of funding to ATBs, assess the feasibility of shared service centres, and develop the corporate affiliation package that could be made available	In 2000 ATBs were guaranteed three year budgets. However, the ongoing consultation on the ATB network has meant that shared services and other services have not been achieved
June 2001	STB was to request that the Enterprise and Lifelong Learning Department allocate challenge funding to STB that could be used to match private sector commitments for marketing initiatives	With tourism now subsumed by culture and sport this has not occurred. However, the Scottish Executive is investing more in VisitScotland than it or the Scottish Office was in the STB.

Scottish Tourist Board Management Review, Report and Recommendations (2000).

second in four years. However, while the 1998 *STB Policy and Management Finance Review* (PMFR) appears to have institutionally examined similar issues with little intention of change, the intention behind this review had been more precisely focused on the present circumstances and challenges, and the generation of wholesale change. In fact many of the recommendations were inter-dependent, and therefore to be able to achieve the timescales required action had to be taken almost immediately, particularly on the imminent decisions such as the Chief Executive, the name change, and the organisational structure. However, there was a certain ambiguity relating to the re-allocation of monies from SEn/HIE to STB, as was the spurious intent that responsibility for tourism strategy and policy lay with the STB, and failure to address the frailties of the ATB network.

The main conclusion to the report was that working with the industry and the Scottish Executive, the STB should identify long-term ambitions and aspirations which would be encapsulated in the form of medium and long-term goals. These, in turn, were to be in-corporated into the first review of the 2000 tourism strategy (the Tourism Framework for Action (2002)).

Tourism Framework for Action 2002: 2005 (2002)

The framework was a multi-partner initiative with the purpose of driving forward and developing the actions contained in the aforementioned tourism strategy (2000). It was designed to be a working blueprint and to reinvigorate the tourism industry, enable it to out-class competitors and make Scotland a must-visit destination. Its vision was that the industry, the support bodies, and Government direct their efforts to ensuring that in Scotland visitors' needs came first, that their expectations were not only met but exceeded, and that by out-classing its competitors, tourism made a vital contribution to economic growth.

The steps identified by the framework as necessary to achieve positive change for the industry were organised around three priorities as outlined in Table 9.3: market position; consumer focus; and the enhanced status of tourism. However, as a review of the strategy (2000) the framework failed to enthuse the industry. For example, it dealt more with rhetoric

Table 9.3: The steps necessary to achieve positive change for the industry.

Goal	Objective
Market position	Development of a better and stronger position with clearly defined brands and products to appeal to and meet customer needs
Consumer focus	To drive quality standards, develop new and enhanced products and services, improve customer research and skills in the industry
Enhanced status of tourism	To ensure the importance of tourism to the Scottish economy is recognized

The Tourism Framework for Action 2002: 2005 (2002).

than reality, and a number of areas addressed by the earlier strategy (see Table 9.1) had, by their absence, either been nonessential, inconsequential, or had still to be met. One of these was the future role of the ATBs which as far back as 1998 the PFMR had recognized as an issue, but claimed that it was not part of the review.

In March 2003, Watson reported on progress against the framework, publishing *Scottish Tourism, a Progress Report. First Progress Report on the Tourism Framework for Action.* In it he acknowledged in advance the difficulty the Scottish tourism industry would face in 2003, but was consumed by his conviction that over the longer term, there was no reason why his vision for Scottish tourism could not be achieved, stressing the need for the industry and the public sector that supported it to work in a much more integrated way (2003).

Area Tourist Board (ATB) Network Review (2001–2003)

In November 2001 in the wake of McLeish's demise and McConnell's forthcoming elevation to First Minister Alexander's last duty as Tourism Minister was to face a hostile audience at the EICC in Edinburgh for the successor to the Scottish Hospitality Industry Congress (SHIC 1999) (see Kerr 2001 for further information), Scotland United, where she announced a consultation concerned with improving the role of ATBs in transforming the industry both nationally and at a local level.

Alexander, who had little idea that within a week she would no longer be responsible for tourism, was concerned with the ATB's inability to fully support the industry in delivering their strategic objectives, the appropriateness of the present structure of the 14 Boards: the role the local authorities should play in ATBs; the relationship between the ATBs and VisitScotland; and the relationship between the ATBs and the LECs.

Although Alexander realized that the ATBs had long been key players through their marketing activities and the information and booking services, she also realized that customer and business needs were changing and to compete in an increasingly global market it was important that ATBs were equipped fully to respond to market changes to work effectively with partners at the local, national and international level. What was required was an ATB network that was modern, strong, adequately financed, and fully equipped to meet challenges that were constantly changing (Scottish Executive News Release SE4374/2001 19 November 2001), whereas the Minister oversaw one that was under resourced, disconnected, and lacked strategic direction to its marketing and promotional activities.

Organised by STF, BHA, VisitScotland, SEn/HIE, the conference attracted eight hundred delegates consisting of 65.5% from the private sector 19.5% from the public sector and 15% from education. Asked to vote electronically on two key issues they showed their frustration with the Executive by voting overwhelmingly for a dedicated minister for tourism in the cabinet (85.8% felt there should be; 8.5% strongly disagreed; and, 5.7% abstained) (Caterer & Hotelkeeper, 22 November 2001). In a further vote 60% felt they were not sufficiently consulted on the previous year's national tourism strategy (Business AM 20 November 2001).

However, due to tourism being aligned with culture and sport, a week later, Alexander's consultation was soon abandoned. Instead a further review of the ATB network was launched by Watson in May 2002 (five months after he took control) which focused on the delivery of the most effective service to tourists and tourism operators in Scotland, and which set out to ensure that the ATBs could deliver the key objectives in the Scottish Executive's *Tourism Framework for Action 2002: 2005* (March 2002). Furthermore, as with the production of the new national tourism strategy, the STB review and the framework, this meant that it could safely be expected to attract any hostility and opprobrium away from the government (Kerr & Wood 2000: 26–27).

Economic Development Initiatives (1999–2003)

A Programme for Government (1999)

In *A Programme for Government* (1999) Dewar set out the overall vision of the first Scottish Executive whose main aim was to improve the lives and opportunities of all the Scottish people. Dewar had recognised that one fundamental element in securing this goal would be the establishment of a vibrant and dynamic economy. Consequently, he undertook to create a knowledge-driven economy which would meet the challenges of a highly competitive global environment. The Executive's hope of the field of economic development was that it would not only generate higher incomes and better quality employment, but also would help the Executive to achieve its goals of social justice and sustainability.

Framework for Economic Development in Scotland (FEDS) (2000)

In June 2000 *the Framework for Economic Development in Scotland* (FEDS) was launched (the consultation document had been circulated in September 1999 and an Analysis and Background paper was published in November 2000), and was designed to be an economic development framework for all of Scotland, not just SEn/HIE, with the timetable (see Table 9.4) for implementation, which was more or less met, set for July 2000.

Through FEDS the Scottish Executive examined the full range of factors that affected economic development in Scotland, including tourism. In consequence, McLeish wanted the framework to bring a focus to a whole range of economic development activities out-with what had gone before. Also, to take a long-term view of Scotland's needs and to be flexible to changing events, priorities and economic development requirements, particularly in terms of globalisation. For example, one unmistakable implication of global integration was the decline in the capacity of individual economies to direct their future in isolation from events and policies in the broader world economy in which Scotland was no exception.

McLeish was also cognizant of the ELLC's claim that there was confusion and overlap in regard to the delivery of local economic development services. In consequence, he suggested this could be overcome by establishing the activities of the Local Economic Forums (LEFs) and tying them closely to the national strategy derived from FEDS to ensure that there was coherence in a developing system.

McLeish also looked to SEn/HIE to play a key role in stimulating the dynamic competitiveness of businesses particularly by promoting new markets; inward investment;

Table 9.4: The FEDS implementation process.

Immediate	September	October	November	December
Initiate the Strategy for Enterprise, with the involvement of Scottish Enterprise Networks, Scottish Tourist Board, and the Scottish Funding Council	Respond to the Enterprise and Lifelong Learning Committee's report on Local Economic Development	Host conference on economic development	Issue national guidelines on Local Economic Forums	Issue Strategy document
Initiate review of structures and relationships of the Scottish Tourist Board	Issue draft national guidelines on Local Economic Forums			
Implement preparation of National guidelines on Local Economic Forums				
Initiate review of red-tape in the Enterprise Networks				

Framework for Economic Development in Scotland (2000).

indigenous enterprises; and e-commerce; and by elevating innovation and the commercial-
ization of the Scottish science base to another level.

Given the range of the Executive's interests and the complexity of the economic development tasks set out in FEDS, it seemed clear that McLeish expected SEn/HIE to also assist
the Executive in breaking down the barriers to social and regional development and ensuring
the sustainability of such development. For instance, in the social justice area, there was
a key role for SEn/HIE focused around employability and employment, and developing,
advocating and implementing work-based solutions to social problems.

FEDS would also inform McLeish's successor Alexander's vision for a *Smart, Successful
Scotland* (2001). However, in parallel with the consultation on the framework, McLeish, as
would Alexander, needed to think about a series of more specific issues relating to SEn/HIE,
which necessitated their own review, and the framework was to provide among other things,
the broad context in which the activities of SEn/HIE would be set.

Smart Successful Scotland

Within weeks of succeeding McLeish, Alexander in January 2001, outlined her vision for
SEn/HIE, in which tourism was implicit to the strategy. Her vision was for a *Smart, Successful Scotland*, a Scotland where as is revealed in Table 9.5 in tourism terms, creating, learning
and connecting faster were the basis for sustained productivity growth, competitiveness, and
prosperity (2001).

The role of SEn/HIE was to be key partners in delivering her vision, and as has
already been discussed above, she outlined three key organising themes for their activities
replacing the four existing ones of Innovative and Far-Sighted Organisations (IFSOs);
Competitive Place; Inclusion; and Positive Attitudes to Learning and Enterprise, with
Growing Businesses; Global Connections; and Learning and Skills, also promising a
new global connections strategy for making Scotland the most networked small nation in
Europe (pages 196–198).

Smart, Successful Scotland claimed that other countries have shown that significantly
increased productivity is attainable, with higher skills sustaining both higher wages and
employment growth. It also claimed that while Scotland's strongest businesses were
on a par with the best in the world, there were too many under-performing companies.
Assistance was, therefore, needed for those companies with potential to match the best, to
improve their performance, create jobs, raise incomes and put Scotland on a new, higher
growth path. Alexander also wanted to ensure that Scotland was a better place to work
and a more productive place to do business. She also wanted to close the productivity gap
with other leading nations, which would raise the long term growth rate of the Scottish
economy above its trend rate of 2% (Scottish Executive Enterprise and Lifelong Learning
Department 2001).

Above all, Alexander wanted a high skill, high wage economy with a higher employment
rate across many parts of Scotland, and recognised that in an age where knowledge was a key
competitive weapon, skills and learning needed to be at the heart of the SEn/HIE activities.
She was also extremely concerned about Scotland's historical approach to globalisation in
that instead of being resistant to change, it should embrace it. Scottish global integration

Table 9.5: Smart, Successful Scotland's goals and objectives in a tourism-sense.

Goal

Objectives

Growing businesses: Scotland — a fast
learning, high
earning nation

Entrepreneurial Dynamism and Creativity: a central theme of the strategy and plan was promoting higher levels of innovation in individual tourism businesses and through collaboration geared to development of new tourism products and services

More e-business: as a fragmented industry in a world-wide consumer marketplace, the opportunities, and threats, for Scottish tourism from the Internet were massive. With around 20,000 businesses, it was planned that tourism would be a major factor in Scotland's overall adoption of e-business

Increased commercialisation of research and innovation: enhanced R&D within tourism businesses was a key objective. A specific effort was proposed to identify opportunities to commercialise university research in the tourism industry, including application of Proof of Concept funding in tourism

Global success in key clusters: the opportunity existed to re-establish Scotland's international competitiveness in tourism, to regain an estimated drop of £150m in overseas earnings, even before foot-and-mouth disease, and return to the previous pattern of sustained growth

Learning and skills: Every Scot ready for tomorrow's jobs

Improving the labour market: Tourism was a major employer but faced both general recruitment problems and specific skills shortages. These needed to be addressed so that the industry could continue to provide good employment opportunities, which were particularly important in rural areas

The best start for all our young people: tourism was a major employer for young people, often their first work experience and a potential opportunity to gain transferable core skills

Demand for in-work training. Tourism employed 193,000 people and provided the opportunity for a high proportion of the Scottish workforce to learn a wide range of modern skills

Global Connections: Scotland, a globally
connected
European nation

Involvement in global markets: whilst not a traditional export industry, overseas tourism sales accounted for approximately £800m annually. The Plan proposed action to build on previous initiatives to further develop overseas links for Scottish tourism businesses

Scotland to be a globally attractive location: developing Scotland's tourism product and infrastructure would enable it to attract substantial numbers of overseas visitors and associated economic benefit

Scotland's international reputation as a tourism destination would be a factor in its overall image and perceptions of quality of life

Tourism could also support infrastructure e.g. transport and digital connections that enhanced Scotland's attractiveness for business overall

More people choosing to live and work in Scotland: tourism supported a wide range of tourism and leisure opportunities for Scottish residents that enhanced its appeal as a place to live and work.

Source: Smart, Successful Scotland (2001).

was also underperforming, and she urged the nation to be globally connected, integrating the Scottish economy into the world economy.

Global Connections Strategy (2001)

In October 2001 Alexander, building on her predecessor's work, launched her new *Global Connections Strategy* (2001) which was designed to see Scotland recognised as the most globally connected small nation in Europe, and as evidenced in Table 9.6 identified four objectives which were to impact heavily on the Scottish tourism industry.

It recognised that if Scotland was to thrive rather than simply survive in the rapidly evolving, knowledge driven, global economy it needed to be more fully integrated within it; and to be well connected physically, digitally and intellectually with the rest of the world. Alexander and McLeish, who had started the process before becoming First Minister, wanted to improve the flow of products, technologies and ideas in and out of Scotland, measuring the success of the strategy by gauging how globally connected Scotland became as a people and as an economy.

In the weeks leading up to his demise McLeish (November 2001) claimed the new strategy, needed to be as visionary then as was the creation of Locate in Scotland (LiS) over two decades before; a strategy that would form a crucial element of Scotland's wider drive to maximise the benefits it obtained from its contacts with the rest of the world. McLeish and Alexander's vision was one of a fully integrated, world-wide organisation that brought together Scotland's economic development and international marketing activities, and the experience and expertise of LiS and Scottish Trade International (STI), which would become Scottish Development International (SDI). Within this single organisation there was to be three core specialisms. For example, attracting high value, economic activity to Scotland; the internationalisation of Scottish companies; and a new capability based on the exchange of skills, ideas, intellectual capital and the networking of people.

Change on this scale was ambitious. Its success demanded new capabilities. The policy direction of *Global Connections* defined a more strategic relationship between the Scottish Executive and SEn/HIE, and committed them to a process of joint strategy development setting out that strategy for Scotland. It recognised, in particular, the four specific challenges highlighted within *Smart, Successful Scotland* (2001) to ensure that Scotland was a globally connected nation. The strategic intent was to support the fullest possible Scottish participation in the global economy through helping Scottish organisations increase their involvement in global markets; contributing to making Scotland a globally attractive location; attracting the most appropriate higher-value activities from overseas and encouraging more people to choose to visit, live and work in Scotland.

In essence, this was an acknowledgement that it was time to move on from addressing the problems of the past — such as mass unemployment, transition from traditional heavy industries and an over-reliance on primary industries in rural areas, and time to meet the challenges of the future: a future where the productivity, knowledge and creativity of Scotland's people together with the flexibility and responsiveness of the public authorities, would together provide the sustainable competitive environment in which businesses would thrive (Smart, Successful Scotland 2001).

Table 9.6: Goals and objectives of Scotland's Global Connections Strategy.

Goal	Objective
Digital Connectivity	Scotland set out to be a leading digital nation and in so doing become one of the best places in the world from which to do business electronically. Collaboration between the Enterprise Networks, the Executive and the private sector was vital to achieve this and the Networks set out to promote on-line business models to ensure that all Scots would benefit from emerging digital technologies including the widest possible dissemination of digital technology, while responding to the challenges of connectivity for more remote rural or disadvantaged urban locations
Increased Involvement in Global Markets	Smart, Successful Scotland had recognised that many Scottish businesses urgently needed to become more global in their outlook and operations. The Networks set out to work closely with potential multi-national players to help them develop and implement globalisation strategies and to help instil greater ambition and confidence in the development of trading links, global alliances and strategic partnerships
Scotland to be a Globally Attractive Location	There was recognition that all capital — physical, financial and human — was increasingly mobile. As a result, Scotland needed to be a world class business location in order to retain and attract leading global companies and people as well as providing the environment for Scottish companies to grow and internationalise. Skills, a competitive infrastructure and public sector support were vital, and continuing partnership between the public and private sectors was required to improve Scotland's relative position
More people choosing to live and work in Scotland	An ageing population and the continuing migration of many talented people limited economic development ambitions. In consequence, Scotland needed to offer the jobs to encourage the young to stay and the more experienced to return. It also needed to tap into the network of Scots around the world to ensure that knowledge of Scotland and its opportunities was current and well understood. This was to be one part of a broader programme of action to portray a more contemporary view of modern Scotland

Scotland: A Global Connections Strategy (2001).

Alexander not only realised that her new vision for the economy in Scotland involved new relationships between SEn/HIE, their customers, stakeholders and the Executive, but also that both the Executive and SEn/HIE had to learn to better understand the competitive pressures facing Scottish-based companies. In return, SEn/HIE had to respond better to their customers while the Executive had to build relationships of trust that gave the specialist expertise and insight of SEn/HIE Board's and staff better leverage to enhance the prosperity of Scotland. She also recognised that HIE with its crucial social development remit, would continue to address the special difficulties of remote, sparsely populated areas through its strengthening communities' activities and that this remit supported community capacity building. SEn was also cautioned to be responsive to the integrated nature of rural development as business growth and high skills levels came from confident communities which recognised personal achievement and advancement (Smart, Successful Scotland 2001). For tourism, the relationship with VisitScotland/ATBs was a key partnership issue for SEn and HIE, which is as yet unresolved.

Scottish Enterprise/Highlands and Islands Enterprise

The Interim Conclusions of the Scottish Enterprise Network Review (2000) and Modernising the Enterprise Networks: The Interim Conclusions of the Enterprise Networks Review (2000)

The Interim Conclusions of the Scottish Enterprise Network Review, published on 6 July 2000 and *Modernising the Enterprise Networks: The Interim Conclusions of the Enterprise Networks Review* published on 6 November 2000 was a co-ordinated focus on the work of SEn and HIE. This included joint ventures between Scottish Executive and SEn/HIE such as LiS, and STI, both of which had just over twelve months existence left, and the structure of relationships with the LECs and other agencies.

SEn/HIE was in such a state of flux not only because it was the creation of another political party, but also because a decade after proposing the idea of SEn/HIE, their creator, Bill Hughes (see Chapter 5) had been among the first to call for their demise. Instead, he called for their overhaul to reflect the need for more enterprise initiatives and investment in order that the Scottish economy and the tourism industry could compete globally (The Herald 6 December 1999). Hughes wanted local organisations to remain but to be more orientated towards risk, through both government and private sector grants, with capital of upwards of £100m.

As what seemed to many commentators as a direct result of Hughes's stance and a growing momentum for an overhaul of SEn/HIE, McLeish, during various speeches on improving their efficiency, declared that any changes may even be part of a more strategic change to the whole economic delivery mechanism in Scotland. For example, he appeared to add credibility to Hughes stance, when he declared that there would be a full review of the workings of SEn/HIE. In effect, the ELLC commencing October 2000 was already reviewing local delivery mechanisms, through its *Local Economic Development Enquiry Remit* (1999) (The Herald 9th December 1999).

To add to the speculation over McLeish's ongoing tourism consultation (*A New Strategy for Scottish Tourism (Consultation Document) 1999*), Hughes added that perhaps after all the doubts there might after all be a radical shift to the delivery of tourism in Scotland (Scotland on Sunday 12 December 1999). There was even some suggestion that tourism might be subsumed by whatever it was that would replace SEn/HIE, whose future, as a creation of the Tory government, looked bleak at this point. This was despite the fact that the SE Board at one point in 2000 discussed a proposal that it should be responsible for tourism in its entirety which, if it had accepted it, in all likelihood would have seen it either aligned with STB or subsuming it. However, although the possibility of tourism being subsumed by SEn was discussed by the SE Board, Dr Robert Crawford, SE's Chief Executive was of the opinion that he had enough to do addressing SEn's problems without also becoming responsible for Scottish tourism (Personal Communication 1 November 2000).

Nevertheless, although a radically different organisation, SEn/HIE survived, particularly SEn which was under deeper threat than HIE, albeit without the same depth to its tourism function as previously. For example, its Business Transformation process, overseen by Crawford, has seen it reduce staffing by 25%, many of them previously with tourism-related responsibilities. It has also redefined its brand, and adopted *Smart, Successful Scotland's* (2001) three goals of Growing Businesses; Learning and Skills; and, Global Connections. It has also aligned itself with Careers Scotland a new National Careers Organisation a national all-age careers guidance service for Scotland, that reduced the number of career advisory organisations from a number circa 87 to a number coterminous with the LECs, and which will work alongside the LECs in improving opportunities, tackling unemployment and underachievement (SE, News Release: SE1029/200120 Apr 2001). Furthermore, and although Crawford is wary of them SEn is a key component of the Local Economic Forums (LEFs).

The Enterprise and Lifelong Learning Committee (1999–2003)

The Enterprise and Lifelong Learning Committee's Final Report of the Inquiry into the Delivery of Local Economic Development Services in Scotland (2000)

In May 2000 the ELLC's *Inquiry into the Delivery of Local Economic Development Services in Scotland* was published (Final Report of the Inquiry into the Delivery of Local Economic Development Services in Scotland). The report's 37 conclusions (see Appendix — Table 5) revealed that the Committee proposed some radical changes to the way in which local economic development services in Scotland should be delivered. These included rationalising the congestion, while eradicating confusion, overlap, duplication, and even active competition between the many agencies involved. Other important conclusions were the establishment of Local Economic Forums (LEFs), and a new economic development framework.

For tourism, it meant being integrated firmly into mainstream local economic development through ATBs becoming mandatory members of the LEFs. Each forum's strategy was supposed to include a tourism element, as is revealed in Table 9.7, which would set out the strategy and delivery mechanisms at local level. This would also be linked to the

Table 9.7: Tourism Conclusions of the Enterprise and Lifelong Learning Committee's Final Report of the Inquiry into the Delivery of Local Economic Development Services in Scotland (2000).

Situation and structures	Responsibility	Conclusion
	Final Conclusion 15	The development of tourism should be firmly integrated into mainstream local economic development
	Final Conclusion 16	Area tourist boards should be integrated into mainstream local economic development by becoming mandatory members of local economic forums
	Final Conclusion 17	Each forum's strategy should include a tourism element, which must set out the strategy and delivery mechanisms at local level. This must be linked to the national tourism strategy and identify each area's contribution to achieving the national strategy. The strategy should also indicate the resources dedicated by each partner, particularly by Local Authorities and LECs, to tourism development. The Committee will monitor the effectiveness of this method of operation and if it does not guarantee effective delivery of tourism support services or investment in the development of the tourism sector, the Committee will consider proposing further structural changes

Source: The Enterprise and Lifelong Learning Committee Review of Local Economic Development Services in Scotland (2000).

national tourism strategy, identifying what each area's contribution should be in relation to achieving the national strategy. This strategy would also indicate the resources dedicated by each partner, particularly by Local Authorities and LECs, to tourism development. The ELLC also undertook to monitor the effectiveness of this method of operation, warning that if this did not guarantee effective delivery of tourism support services or investment in the development of the tourism sector, it would consider proposing further structural changes (ELLC 2000). Although little of the above in relation to tourism transpired meant the ELLC returning to assess tourism in its 2002 inquiry into tourism, in 2002 the LEFs were obligated to produce economic development strategies for their areas, and for most this included a tourism element.

Enterprise and Lifelong Learning Committee Inquiry into Tourism (2002)

In July 2002, the Scottish Parliament's *ELLC* announced an inquiry into tourism. Despite the *Tourism Framework for Action 2002: 2006* (2002) the Committee wanted to examine the effectiveness of the Scottish Executive's tourism strategy, the structures and funding which supported it, and the levels of Government support for tourism.

In the course of its inquiry it questioned the effectiveness of the current tourism strategy; the effectiveness of VisitScotland post-reorganisation; the impact of, and the response to, foot-and-mouth and September 11th and what lessons can be learned from these experiences; the roles of VisitScotland/SEn/HIE/BTA; the sufficiency of the current budget and the appropriateness of the investment for tourism; and whether the focus of investment was appropriate, and the effectiveness of the ATB structure.

Support for Tourism: An International Comparison (2002)

In March 2002 the Research and Information Group of the Scottish Parliament and on behalf of the ELLC issued a brief for research on the topic of *Support for Tourism: An International Comparison* (Reference No. 030102EL). Prepared and researched by Stevens & Associates with The Scottish Tourism Research Group, the purpose of the research was to inform the Committee's *Inquiry on Scotland's tourism industry* (2002). The objectives of this research were, in essence, to compare the tourist industry in Scotland with other countries' tourism industry, and to make recommendations based on the findings.

The messages emerging from this research were clear. No single destination in the review was perfect in every way. However, several were clearly producing an environment of support for tourism that allowed the industry to grow and respond quickly to changing market conditions. The four most impressive destinations examined were Ireland, Catalonia (Spain), Veneto (Italy), and Ontario (Canada), from which the key lessons learned were to create a clear and focused national tourism strategy that involved leading private sector representatives; encourage different types of products and service; and, to encourage product innovation based upon clear evidence of market demand but incorporate a degree of risk. Furthermore, it recommended that VisitScotland should promote Scotland aggressively, at the expense of regions within Scotland, to grow international tourism and avoid duplication and overlap (Stevens *et al.* 2002), which in view of the ongoing ATB consultation was highly contentious. The most informative of all recent reports it remains to be seen if any heed is taken of it by the Scottish Executive.

Final Report on Lifelong Learning (2002)

Believing that it was a neglected area of policy, the ELLC launched its inquiry into lifelong learning (higher education, further education, vocational training and community/voluntary education) in July 2001. It had recognised that the future of advanced economies lay increasingly in their ability to supply a highly skilled workforce, and that workforce's capacity to drive productivity, innovation and to adapt. It also recognised that in Scotland 80% of the workforce of 2020 was already in work, and that over this time there will be a 25% decline in young workers. This, it claimed, will lead to an increased emphasis on training the existing workforce, and developing their motivation and ability to learn lifelong (ELLC Report 2002).

The report also investigated the equality of learning. For example, while 80% of university entrants in Scotland came from professional backgrounds only 14% came from an unskilled one. It was the Committee's intention, therefore, to create an environment whereby lifelong learning would provide a route towards equality by opening up opportunities for those engaged in it. In addition, the declining size of the Scottish workforce, and the demographic shift towards people living longer, meant that many more of those currently economically inactive would be required to be drawn into the workforce if Scotland is to prosper and promote itself up the OECD lifelong learning league table to improve its competitiveness (ELLC Report 2002).

The ELLC *Final Report on Lifelong Learning* (2002) set out a framework for making lifelong learning a reality by calling for every citizen to have access to a range of learning opportunities throughout their life, reaffirming the philosophy of entitlement first proposed in the Committee's interim report, and reinforced the need for a Scottish Executive lifelong learning strategy.

In response the Scottish Executive in *Enterprise and Lifelong Learning Committee: Final Report on Lifelong Learning Response From The Executive* (2003) suggested that there was a lack of coherence between the various sectors of lifelong learning — Higher Education, Further Education, vocational education and training, community and voluntary provision — and called for more cohesion and a more responsive system, characterised by ease of movement and equality of treatment (2003).

Building Better Cities — Cities Review

Following two year's work, the Cities Review was launched in January 2003. Apart from being designed ostensibly to redress Scotland's six cities non-domestic rates deficit, it was also Scotland's first urban framework. In consequence the city regions were requested by the First Minister to assemble a 10 year vision for which in return, over three years, they will receive £90 million as a growth fund and a further £20 million to reclaim derelict land, and which will impact on tourism development in their areas.

Summary

Since the inception of the new parliament in 1999 there has been an almost indecent haste to review every aspect of Scottish life for which the new parliament was responsible, reserved powers apart. This chapter as is revealed in the Appendix (Tables 1 and 4) demonstrates that this applies equally to tourism and economic development. For example, in relation to tourism, the Scottish Executive's Enterprise and Lifelong Learning Department, and the Scottish Parliament's Enterprise and Lifelong Learning Committee set out almost immediately to review every aspect of tourism in Scotland in the main within a framework of economic development; and, to devise strategies to enable those organisations empowered by the Scottish Executive to deliver tourism and economic development policy more effectively and efficiently.

Their aim was to develop a modern tourist industry which was in touch with its customers; a skilled and enterprising industry which embraced the culture of lifelong learning; and an industry which provided the quality of service visitors demanded.

In doing so, it was as though the parliament was making up for lost time, i.e. the three hundred years in which it lay dormant, decisions being made for it during that time four hundred miles away in London: decisions that were invariably attuned to the wider economy than Scotland.

In tourism terms it meant eventually being valued in a manner previously alien to it, i.e. cabinet recognition. Although it could be argued that tourism had more influence in being part of the Enterprise and Lifelong Learning Ministry (1999–2001) than Tourism, Culture and Sport (2001–), where it was no longer mainstream of economic development, instead sitting rather incongruously within the Education Department. Regardless, and despite its ministerial and departmental homes, for tourism devolution meant more accountability, expectations that issues that previous administrations had ignored such as those identified by the 1999 *House of Commons Scottish Affairs Committee Report* would be addressed, and that the industry would be involved fully.

However, despite a new strategy (A New Stratgey for Scottish Tourism 2000), a review (Scottish Tourist Board Management Review, Report and Recommendations (2000), a framework (Tourism Framework for Action 2002: 2005 (2002)), and an inquiry (Scottish Parliament Enterprise and Lifelong Learning Committee Inquiry into Tourism 2002), issues that concerned the House of Commons Scottish Affairs Committee in 1999 are still manifest in 2003, and Scottish tourism income according to the new methodology has still not reached the levels of 1997, further evidence of the strategic failure of Scottish tourism to realise its commercial potential.

Chapter 10

Scottish Tourism: Where to Now?

Introduction

This book evolved from a desire to explore tourism public policy, and to understand and explain more fully the dominant public policy issues and controversies in Scottish tourism in both the lead up to devolution, and for the significant post-devolution period which encapsulated the first four year term of the new Scottish parliament. To do so it had to demonstrate an implicit understanding and explicit explanation of the relationships of tourism public policy formulation; tourism policy-making; and tourism policy-making decisions; plus the constraints and fast moving environment within which tourism operated. Furthermore, it had to elucidate not only an understanding, in a much wider context, of the external influences on tourism, but also of the internal influences. Hence, while the initial chapters of this book deal with tourism and public policy approaches and theories and how these are applied in both macro and micro environments; the remaining chapters reflect the evolution of one relatively small tourism destination's tourism public policy, and its strategic management of failure to realize its commercial potential and challenge competitor destinations.

This book's particular significance lies in the fact that the research embodied therein has been conducted during conceivably the most fascinating (politically) and volatile (globally) period for the world's tourism industry. For example, in global terms it deals with the policy outcomes of the aftermath of September 11 where countries and destinations highly dependent on U.S. outbound travel; those that are a long distance from their main generating markets; and, those of the Moslem world were subject to a severe downturn in visitors (WTO 2002), and with foot-and-mouth and recession in local terms. Among others, it also deals with the policies of those countries where hard-line Arab socialist policies and antipathy to the west militated against any kind of tourism development; or conversely with Saudi Arabia where because of its economy's over-reliance on oil it has little alternative but to develop tourism as part of a larger plan to diversify its economy; Southeast Asia where some of the richest and poorest countries in the world joined together to stimulate economic growth; and, India where tourism is seen as a means of eradicating poverty; all demonstrating diverse and on occasion innovative approaches to the manner in which they pursue tourism public policy.

In specific terms, in latter chapters, this book proffered an informed analysis of the state of Scottish tourism in a global context during the first four year term of the new parliament; reviewed the arrangements of Scottish tourism both post and pre-devolution; commented on how recent policy initiatives have evolved and been perceived; and evaluated their impact. It also reviewed the development of Scottish tourism to this point in terms of the evolution of institutions, organizations, elites and coteries involved in Scottish tourism administration, and placed the recent economic performance of the Scottish tourism industry in a wider international context where ultimately its failure is much compared with the success of rival destinations such as the Republic of Ireland.

In addition, it explores Scottish tourism from a political policy perspective, and contains, as far as it is possible to ascertain, the first analysis of contemporary policy issues on Scottish tourism. Lastly, and perhaps most importantly, its originality is substantiated by the fact that no such integrated contemporary account of tourism and tourism public policy in Scotland during the first term of the new parliament existed until now.

The Research

During the research for and writing of this book the tourism industry has undergone significant and unanticipated change in the main through events outwith its control. This has meant that this manuscript has been in a constant state of flux as one event superseded another, creating different government and industry reactions from those previously documented, and altering earlier outcomes considerably from whence the initial draft was first written, evidence of a dynamic and fast-moving industry. However, the fact that the first term of the Scottish parliament terminated in May 2003 gave the book a natural conclusion in both terms of time and content to which to work.

The book has also been written during a time in which tourism destinations were faced with increasing competition, economic, and environmental issues combined with the continued threat of terrorism, and this necessitated governments' assessing and redefining their tourism public policies, and this is reflected in the earlier chapters. For example, foot-and-mouth and September 11 have meant a dramatic reduction in patterns of North American demand to Europe; the difficulties faced by the Japanese economy has had a significant impact on the Asian Pacific travel trade; the advent of the Euro has changed forever mainland European travel and trading; and, events in Bali in Indonesia and in Mombassa, Kenya have demonstrated further the vulnerability of tourism destinations at the hands of terrorists. SARS and the war in Iraq will further test tourism's resolve.

Although the industry reacted positively and swiftly to overcome such events, there is still the ongoing threat of terrorist activity worldwide a situation that has cast a dark shadow over travel and related activities, and future tourism development, and would appear to be now a fact of life for any tourist. Never again will any destination be as safe as it was in the twentieth century. This combined with the fragility of the world wide economy, as was demonstrated in earlier chapters, necessitated tourism destinations increasing security arrangements, cutting costs, addressing skills and quality issues, introducing more creative advertising campaigns and innovative promotions, while seeking new market opportunities. Furthermore, the Chancellor of the Exchequer's budget statement of November 2002, and which was confirmed in April 2003, when he downgraded his growth forecasts means that the British economy in particular was beginning to reveal frailties that would impact on consumer spending in 2003, and would eventually mean a raise in taxes. All of this is compounded by the war in Iraq and SARS.

Research for the latter part of the book focused on Scotland whose tourism public policy issues in the late nineties were focused, concentrated, and mutated by globalization, political devolution, and the restoration of the Scottish Parliament in 1999. During the lifetime of the first parliament in almost three hundred years, Scottish tourism was confronted by significant challenges which when added to those listed above appeared almost insurmountable. This chapter, therefore, will not only bring to a conclusion this investigation into the evolution of tourism public policy towards the end of the 20th and the beginning of the 21st centuries, it will also suggest a way forward for Scottish tourism public policy.

The Environment in Which Scottish Tourism Operated

Consumers' desire to experience products and services in a highly personalised way means that the changing nature of the customer supplier relationship has shifted the basis of power away from traditional providers towards the customer. These customers, in turn, are taking advantage of the fact that traditional competitive advantages in tourism have eroded. For example, restructuring and rationalisation combined with the proliferation of e-business has made it easier for developing countries to enter mature tourism markets and apply cost pressure to traditional leaders. This is compounded by the fact that despite September 11, Bali, and Mombassa, SARS, and the war in Iraq, growth in long haul international travel market will continue, as will more frequent holidays of shorter duration. In tandem with this, changing demographic profiles of tourists will produce new market opportunities, and these among the fundamental global challenges facing the Scottish tourism industry in the 21st century (Douglas & SE 2000).

This is why from the outset it was clear that the research had to be synchronous with the complex environment in which global tourism operated, and in particular with Scottish tourism. For example, one important initial outcome of the research, which remained constant throughout, was the industry's lack of confidence in firstly the Scottish Office, then ultimately the Scottish Executive's ability to demonstrate a strategic public policy focus for Scottish tourism. This was despite the various post devolution government initiatives (see Appendix — Tables 1 and 4). Although they aspired to confront the very real challenges that Scottish tourism faced, the outcomes of the underlying evidence of tourism in Scotland demonstrated that they failed miserably so to do. To compound matters further, following the May 1999 Scottish parliamentary elections, consultation with the industry, and the subsequent publication of *A New Strategy for Scottish Tourism* (STB/PriceWaterhouseCoopers 2000), and despite undertakings that tourism would be mainstream of economic development, the Scottish Executive's Enterprise and Lifelong Learning Department compelled Scottish tourism to continue to operate within the framework of a policy little altered from that laid down by its predecessors e.g. Conservative Scottish Office post-1997, and a Labour Scottish Office 1997–1999, but within a global environment that had changed dramatically.

This was convoluted further by the nature of this policy and its relationship to the wider Scottish economic development policy, and to other complementary policies, some derived from Edinburgh (devolved), others from Westminster (reserved). This was complicated further in that no one Scottish public body dealt in its entirety with Scottish tourism.

Instead, component parts were the responsibility of various public sector institutions e.g. STB/VisitScotland; BTA; SE/HIE; ATBs; LECs; Local Authorities; Scottish Natural Heritage (SNH); Forest Enterprise (FE); Historic Scotland (HS); Scottish Arts Council (SAC); Scottish Museums Council (SMC); and sportscotland. Furthermore, in 2001 when Tourism became part of the Culture and Sports Ministry, and the specific function of tourism was transferred from the Enterprise and Lifelong Learning Department to the Education Department it only served to complicate matters further, and to dislocate tourism from the mainstream of economic development.

Paradoxically, and contrary to speculation that the tourism industry in Scotland was treated indifferently by its politicians during this time, the book's progress was invigorated ironically by the activity that took place in the tourism and economic development spheres post-devolution. For example, the Scottish Enterprise and Lifelong Learning Department produced almost 150 reviews, inquiries, frameworks and strategies between July 1999 and April 2003, a number of which are included in the Appendix (Tables 1 and 4). Although this activity failed to materialize in a new tourism public policy, the fact there was much more focus on tourism than would have otherwise been the case pre-devolution, and that politicians were more accessible to the industry, raised expectations of the Scottish Executive that it was never able politically to meet. That such expectations did not eventually materialize in terms of changes in policy, funding or structure led to further industry disillusionment at the Scottish Executive's inability to confront the real issues tourism faced. This was exacerbated by the negative impacts upon the Scottish tourism industry that occurred throughout the length of the research e.g. neglecting to appoint a tourism minister immediately post devolution or a dedicated ministry; the Scottish Executive's handling of foot-and-mouth; the debacle over the appointment of the new STB/VisitScotland Chief Executive; the length of time it took to consult on the future of the ATBs; accepting the on-going subservient relationship with BTA; lack of consultation with VisitScotland on the massive structural and organizational change to BTA (VisitBritain), and, of course, the terrorist bombings in New York and Washington, and then Bali and Kenya, followed by war in Iraq and SARS.

The Approach

The relationships across the many organizations involved in Scottish tourism, as has been demonstrated throughout this book, were highly complex, and, in consequence, during the book's research Scottish tourism policy and Scottish tourism policy decision-making could not be separated from the milieu in which it evolved (Hall 1999: 191). In consequence a heterogeneous approach was required to make sense of this complexity: an approach that aligned the most appropriate characteristics of contemporary theories and synchronized them with the environment in which Scottish tourism operated. In consequence, the component parts such as the institutions, processes and people within this approach related in every respect to the methodology.

In adopting a heterogeneous approach, this book also correlated with and encapsulated social and economic processes that were rapidly changing and evolving over time. Furthermore, the industry's performance in relation to Scottish tourism public policy during this time was being measured more than ever against a background of global societal change, and also areas over which it had no control e.g. foot-and-mouth, international terrorism, war, the tension over powers reserved to Westminster and so on. In consequence, to survive and prosper, Scottish tourism businesses had to take into account the important transformational forces in the world such as the manner in which the quality of the visitor's experience in terms of value for money was becoming more dominant, and the resultant likely implications of this for a business's future.

The locus for a heterogeneous approach to this book is that Scottish tourism policy either in its own context or in tandem with other extraneous factors interacts with socio-economic processes which are slowly changing and evolving over time, at different rates of acceleration, reflecting tourism as being in a world of constant turmoil. It also draws on the aforementioned theories, seeking to incorporate their dynamic interplay, factors for change and adaption, and constraints on such actions (John 1999: 182). For example, in Scottish tourism there is a continual debate and struggle for the success of ideas and their attendant interests across the multiple sectors that comprise tourism, all hoping to influence the policy process. It is what causes policy variations and change and the way in which certain ideas are selected, and how they are selected that is of interest here, and these are among the things that I have endeavoured to identify, and to explain.

The Politics of Tourism

As international tourist arrivals continue to grow, there is little doubt that the political aspects of tourism development will increase in significance, in both the developed and developing nations of the world. In Spain, for example, it is often suggested that the Spanish government encouraged tourism development to broaden the political acceptance of Franco's regime, similarly Marcos in the Philippines, and now Korea and Taiwan (Youell 1998: 8–9). Although the Scottish Executive has no apparent substantial vote-winning need to broaden its acceptance through tourism development, there is growing recognition by it and by its rival political parties of the importance of tourism to the Scottish economy, and of the interest it can generate in the media particularly when it gets it wrong e.g. the premature appointment of the short-lived VisitScotland CEO Rod Lynch. However, although we are aware of negative approaches to tourism such as neglecting to recognize tourism e.g. failing to name a tourism minister following devolution, what we are not sure of is how tourism is really perceived by the political parties, and what elements go into their policy pronouncements.

What we are sure of is that although tourism became much more visible due to devolution, the recognition the industry desired in terms of policy, funding and decision-making, was to the industry to remain insignificant in comparison to that of other industries e.g. farming, fishing, and manufacturing. This was compounded by politicians' reaction to foot-and-mouth where concern was expressed that its impact on tourism appeared not to be taken as seriously as its impact on farming.

Paradoxically, the more politicians had to be seen to be doing something about the crisis the more harm their visibility did to the tourism industry. In particular overseas, where images of fraught politicians, pyres burning in the background, endeavouring to restore public confidence, led television news bulletins night after night and left the tourism industry frustrated and in no doubt as to where it featured in the political agenda of the time. Examples, such as this, where tourism was marginalized in favour of other disciplines, demonstrate that despite devolution the specifics of decisions in regard to Scottish tourism policy-making, from agenda setting to policy implementation are still multifarious, and that reserved powers will always take precedence over devolved powers.

Privileged Oligarchies

This book also addressed Marsh & Rhodes (1992a: 265) position that by creating privileged oligarchies (see Chapter 8), and being conservative in their impact, the rules of the game and access favoured established interests, an important point. Furthermore, these points and issues can be explained in terms of their relation to the heterogeneous and policy networks approaches (the latter approach taken in Chapter 8); and, to the forces of institutions, processes and people. For example, how these correlated with one another combined with their implications for Scottish tourism, and for complementary public policies. In effect, this also addressed Crozier's (1964: 107) position, that the behaviour and attitudes of people and groups within an organization cannot be explained without reference to the power relationships existing among them.

Such relationships were evident in Scottish tourism and brought tensions in terms of the individual's complementary roles. In addition, the institutions, power elites and the various associated Scottish tourism and economic development bodies were influenced heavily by the constraints of devolution and external influences e.g. Westminster's reserved powers, European legislation, and globalization. Furthermore, power elites associated with the institutions and interest groups vied to influence decision-making, in the process themselves becoming institutionalized, inadvertently impeding change.

Pre-devolution

In Scotland, in the 1990s, fragmentation, parochiality, and lack of vision did not greatly facilitate collaboration between tourism and economic development agencies, other organizations involved in tourism, the tourism industry, and government both north and south of the border. Nor did this situation engender the trust, flexibility and the ability needed to engage in strategic partnerships, or for them to work effectively, a situation which not only fostered a discordant labyrinth of dysfunctional policy networks and institutionalized silos, but also gave succor to those operators whose instincts were nonconformist, a situation that still remains. Furthermore, the fragmentation of the industry; the conflicting and contradictory views expressed at all levels of the industry; and, the disparagement with which the industry was held by government for most of the latter part of the twentieth century contributed to an almost irredeemable situation from which tourism in Scotland has barely recovered (Stevens *et al.* 2002). For example, the public and private sectors' involved in tourism demonstrated behaviours that reflected their own agendas, objectives and priorities, and by behaving in an insular fashion, they dissipated the potential of the industry, and the optimal use of scarce public financial resources (Reid 2001). Meanwhile, while devolution was the catalyst for change, and for government to bring tourism mainstream of economic development, the irrefutable fact is that despite numerous initiatives and strategies tourism in Scotland is still failing to address its underlying problems, and in consequence is failing to challenge competitor destinations and realize its commercial potential.

To suggest that there has been no tourism progression during this time would, however, be both fatuous and gratuitous. Even before the 1969 *Development of Tourism Act* the Highlands and Islands Development Board (HIDB) was deeply involved in tourism and certain destinations were beginning to market themselves at home and abroad. In 1979 Taste of Scotland had been established; since 1984 Scotland was allowed to market itself abroad; and, in that same year the ATB network was established. Furthermore, in 1987 the Scottish Tourism Co-ordinating Group (STCG) was established publishing in 1992 *Tourism and the Scottish Environment — A sustainable partnership* (STCG, Edinburgh 1992). By then Scottish Enterprise (SE), Highlands and Islands Enterprise (HIE) and the Local Enterprise Companies (LECs) had been established, replacing the Scottish Development Agency (SDA) and HIDB, subsuming the Scottish Tourist Board's (STB) responsibility for the administration of tourism grants, and offering skills opportunities previously mainly in the domain of other industries. Meanwhile, STB, in return became responsible for the Highlands and Islands tourism network. By 1994 *the Strategic Plan for Scottish Tourism* was published and the Scottish Tourism Forum (STF) established, and by 1996 the *Scottish Enterprise Network (SEn) Action Plan*, and the HIE *Tourism Action Framework* were launched, as was Welcome Host. The following year Scotland's Best was launched, and the *Scottish Tourism Strategic Plan, Progress Report* published. By 1998 STB had undergone a *Policy and Financial Management Review, Prior Options Study*, and in conjunction with SEn/HIE launched the Green Tourism Business Scheme, and by 1999 in the months leading up to devolution *the Scottish Tourism Strategic Plan Interim Review* was launched as was *the House of Commons Affairs Committee Report on Tourism* (1999), which was a defining moment for Scottish tourism launching a flurry of activity from which the tourism industry has barely recovered. So, it would be disingenuous to claim there was a lack of activity pre-devolution. However, it was clear that the inability of successive governments pre-devolution to deal with the underlying problems relating to Scottish tourism was one of the main contributory factors to Scottish tourism's failure to realise its commercial potential.

Recurring Themes

Throughout the research it had been important that the book's methodology illuminated its research questions. In consequence, a number of recurring themes emerged which, from the point-of-view of the approach adopted, were most relevant to the research. These were: deep dissatisfaction with the arrangements for the administration of tourism in Scotland; incompatible views at operator, institutional and policy-making level on the applicability of Scottish tourism's institutions and structures to the 21st century; and, disagreement on both tourism's contribution and importance to the Scottish economy.

To understand the intensity and depth of feeling behind these, there was a need to clarify to what factors such feelings could be attributed, and if such deep dissatisfaction, incompatible views and disagreements could be resolved. For example, in Chapter 8 we asked how deeply embedded institutionalism was in Scottish tourism policy-making. In response, the outcomes were quite clear. Institutionalism was intrinsic to the Scottish tourism infrastructure and along with structure and fragmentation were contributory factors that rendered Scottish tourism too slow to change and adapt to the demands placed upon it by globalisation. Furthermore, the power elite that grew around the institutions, who since the inception of devolution had some, albeit limited, influence over the tourism agenda, compounded this. However, although opposed to radical change, there is no evidence that this small but powerful coterie, although analogous in itself to an institution, was suppressing change. Indeed they were the instigators of many initiatives designed to change things. However, by having become part of the establishment, by colluding with MSPs, MPs and others they were still effectively and inadvertently impeding the fundamental change that the industry desired, much of which was due to their, and the industry's, innate conservatism, and the procrastination of a succession of Scottish Executive tourism ministers.

The Main Issues

In the course of the first parliament, the industry's frustration with the Scottish Executive's inability to demonstrate a strategic public policy focus for tourism in Scotland combined with widespread disillusionment at its disinclination to initiate major structural change, led to an inexhaustible preoccupation with the continued existence and futures of STB/VisitScotland, and the ATBs, and interrelated processes such as funding, membership, ATB network structure, and TICs. Concern was also evident at BTA's relationship with Scottish tourism e.g. as tourism was devolved why was a cross border authority still partly responsible for marketing Scotland overseas? Furthermore, the integration of the BTA with the English Tourism Council (DCMS ETC) in 2003, and the supposed autonomous role for Scotland within its framework gave further cause for concern particularly as the Scottish Executive appeared ambivalent to what these changes would mean, and also about the need to address Scottish tourism structures. For example, without addressing its own structures how could Scotland participate successfully in this new structure (McCaig, personal communication 4 November 2002)?

Further concern was expressed at the direction of SEn/HIE. SEn, in particular, during the lifetime of the first parliament, underwent a massive business transformation. This combined with tourism relocating from the department that oversaw SEn appeared to marginalize to some extent SEn's responsibility towards tourism.

There was also much discussion about the future of SEn in earlier chapters, and it would appear certain that based on the life cycle of its predecessor (16 years) that the organization will not survive this decade with its present structure, the likelihood being that it will either be replaced or that its network of LECs will be reduced in size, and perhaps in capability, and which will not only have implications for the Local Economic Forums (LEFs), but also the ATBs. Typically, as an ATB review will have taken place before then, this will be done in isolation, meaning that tourism and economic development will remain fragmented when in actual fact, marketing apart, it is one and the same thing, and that it would seem sensible to carry out a wider review of the economic development/tourism function, including the economic development responsibilities that Local Authorities currently possess.

Regardless, there is strong industry feeling that the Scottish Executive is ambivalent about the Scottish tourism industry. Such feeling is evidenced by the fact that following the 1999 parliamentary elections not only did it not appoint immediately someone to the tourism post; it also chose not to dedicate a ministry to tourism. Although McConnell has addressed the latter point, the dedicated tourism ministry with its own department did not materialize in the manner expected by the industry, and there is still widespread concern that tourism is no longer mainstream of economic development, instead incongruously subordinated with Culture and Sport in the Education Department alongside disciplines such as the Children and Young People's Group, Social Work Services Inspectorate, Schools Group, and the Information, Analysis and Communication Division.

There was also concern over the role of the various interest groups, many of which, including the British Hospitality Association (BHA), came together under the umbrella of the Scottish Tourism Forum (STF): a vehicle established to give a coherent voice to the industry. For example, initially representing the industry on the STCG, and ultimately on the organisations that superseded the STCG, the Strategy Implementation Group and the Steering Group, STF's role is undermined by the Scottish Executive who on the one hand appearing to embrace it, while on the other disregarding much of the advice STF gives it. In fact, the extent of the general problem of obtaining a mutual coherent voice from the industry and the Scottish Executive remained constant throughout the book. The fragmentation of this relationship was intensified further in that following a consultation that raised expectations of change (Consultation: A New Strategy for Scottish Tourism 1999); the industry was compelled to operate within an environment that had been created for it by a policy with which in terms of structure, funding and strategy it had little empathy. The end result was a strategy that was, largely an aspirational document that fell short of tackling issues such as funding, structures or the prioritisation of change (Reid 2001). Furthermore, rather than simplifying things, devolution has meant Scottish tourism policy and decision-making processes, and the context and environment in which the tourism industry in Scotland operates have become more complex. In consequence, in the context of endeavouring to understand Scottish tourism public policy (how institutional and networking approaches could be seen in Scottish tourism and its correlation with governance), issues such as those described above appear more complex than ever post-devolution, therefore necessitating the application of a heterogeneous approach to them.

The Implications for Scottish Tourism

In adopting a heterogeneous approach the ability to understand and explain the processes behind the dominant issues and controversies in Scottish tourism in both the lead up to and for the length of the first parliament enabled us to make sense of the complex environment in which the Scottish tourism industry operated at that time. It also brought an ability to the research to deal with a number of issues pertinent to Scottish tourism during an era of rapid and uncharted change, particularly the networks, the individuals involved in them in their pursuit of specific agenda, and the interaction between the various private and public sector Scottish tourism organizations such as Scotland's prime public sector tourism organization, STB/VisitScotland, to which along with others, we now turn.

STB/VisitScotland

Tensions exist in Scottish tourism between businesses that create economic wealth and employment, and those that are family or life style businesses, yet which in their own disparate ways are equally significant to the fabric of Scottish tourism and to every day Scottish life e.g. the disproportionate influence of the smaller operators on the ATB network. Such tensions are compounded further by the divergence of quality, products, and service across these sectors, and although it has little control over many of these aspects VisitScotland, as opposed to the Scottish Executive, is irrevocably held responsible for their failings by politicians, visitors, and the general public and the industry. For example, McLeish when minister responsible for tourism wanted a modern, focused, skilled and enterprising industry dedicated to providing the high quality of service visitors demanded. An industry that was confident, aspirational and ambitious. Nevertheless, he appeared reluctant to initiate the changes many in the industry expected of him, and which might have regenerated the then STB. What is more, as has already been mentioned, some of the contents of the review outcomes left a need for clarification e.g. who really is VisitScotland's customer: the industry or the tourist; what is VisitScotland/SEn/HIE's strategic relationship; how are the ATBs to be funded in future; how is VisitScotland addressing the inclusion of businesses that choose not to be classified and graded, and so on.

That these and other pertinent questions remained unanswered following the review, the framework and subsequent consultations, was compounded by the fact that the industry had thought that through its responses to his 1999 consultation it had made clear to McLeish that a policy status quo was unsustainable, advice that he ultimately rejected, further evidence of a top-down approach. As a result, the industry's confidence in McLeish was diminished, and later on, when he became First Minister and Alexander succeeded him, her inability to demonstrate a strategic tourism public policy focus for Scottish tourism paralleled his and conveyed to the industry an implacable Scottish Executive indifference to it, the sole recompense being that tourism was eventually given a seat at the cabinet table, albeit not in a dedicated ministry or department, or with a minister who inspired confidence that things would change for the better. For VisitScotland this means that the jury is still out, particularly for as long as the tourism figures it is held accountable for continue to fail to realize expectations, and the ATB network for which it is again held responsible continues to massively underperform.

ATBs

Due to its idiosyncrasies the ATB network is one with which many operators within the tourism industry are preoccupied e.g. those whose continued reason for membership is reliant upon their Tourism Information Centre (TIC) directly filling their bed spaces or, alternatively, those who were frustrated at the imbalance of influence on their ATBs of certain tourism sectors whose impact in terms of employment and the economy was to them negligible; or those who had lost confidence in their ATB's ability to market their immediate area.

That ATBs should exist at all is another issue. Although there appears to be support for a complete re-structuring, nobody is advocating the demise of the ATBs, nor is there one consensus as to how they should be re-structured. Their total demise would most probably see a proliferation of unstructured and unaccountable local tourism bodies formed throughout Scotland, some more competent than others, accountable to no-one, worsening an already deteriorating situation.

That the existence of ATBs was in jeopardy was a symptom of the process of inherent long-term funding problems. This was compounded by the fact that the proportion of ATB public sector funding was almost twice that of the private sector. The fact that public expenditure funding was diminishing and that there was no prospect of this being supplanted by the private sector was a matter of growing concern for many local tourist boards, and perhaps the real challenge for the industry in the future is whether *it* instead of the public sector should create, manage and fund local tourism organizations.

Setting aside the public sector/private sector funding anomaly, the reality for many ATBs was that despite the change in funding suggested by *A New Strategy for Scottish Tourism* (Scottish Executive 2000), and *Scottish Tourist Board Management Review, Report and Recommendations* (STB/PriceWaterhouseCoopers 2000) ATB funding remained wholly inadequate. This is despite the fact the strategy recommended that local authorities gave budget guidelines to the ATBs on a three year-rolling programme. This was combined with the implicit threat that failure to do so would mean that funding would be centralised with the local authorities' grants being reduced accordingly to compensate. However, there was no precedent to the calculation criteria that would relate to this funding, and as it also failed to guarantee ATBs adequate levels of funding; ATBs throughout Scotland were still in crisis. This meant that when councils prioritised expenditure preserving local authority jobs and services was placed before awarding funds to tourism.

There was also, of course, the resource time taken in securing such funding. For example, the ATB network spent as much time in negotiating for a diminishing resource with the funding agencies as it did on its primary function of attracting tourists. This was compounded by ATB membership of the new LEFs. For example, some Chief Executives and their Chair attended two or more such meetings, and were engaged in the many task forces that evolved from the LEFs. Again, time consuming, costly, and a catalyst for duplication, a predicament LEFs were designed to eradicate.

There has also been little evidence of ATB performance being measured, and it is suggested that in a reduced ATB network or one coterminous with the LECs, a funding model similar to the LECs where they draw down funds from the centre, fulfilling quotas, meeting targets and being benchmarked against performance should be considered. In addition, operators buying into advertising and promotional campaigns, as opposed to membership fees, would enhance the monies available to ATBs.

Resource implications apart, this leads us to perhaps one of the most fundamental issues which will remain as long as the ATBs are membership organizations reliant upon the subscriptions of a large majority of their members whose continued reason for membership is dependent upon their ATB TIC directly filling their bed spaces. For example, if public sector monies invested in tourism by SEn/HIE were granted mostly to businesses, who saw quality, skills development, training, and ICT as important to their businesses, and whose reliance on their ATBs for directly filling their bed spaces was minimal in comparison to their own marketing strategy, why did such businesses have so little influence on their ATBs, and consequently on VisitScotland, and in a wider sense, Scottish tourism? To invest large resource in terms of SEn/HIE support and other public sector initiatives, yet to allow the ATBs to be driven by the influence of businesses that thought diametrically to those that embraced modern business principles, and contributed little to the creation of economic wealth or employment (e.g. not paying business rates or VAT), was to sections of the industry anomalous, and caused polarization and fostered resentment.

The most efficient and effective ATB model would depend on many inter-related variables such as the source of funding, the geographical area, market segment, product streams, the definition of responsibility and so on. Consideration might also be given to city tourist boards, reflecting the growing popularity of cities as prime tourism destinations. Nevertheless, either there were too many or too few ATBs, or alternatively they could have been structured coterminously, aligned with the LECs on the basis that the LEC structure was right, that is, and that it itself will not be subject to change.

It is also worth considering the point that if at some future date the Scottish Executive decided to introduce a Tourism Tax, a number of the present less densely populated ATBs could not generate sufficient income from such a tax to sustain their area's individual needs. As suggested by Friel, among others, there might be a need if such a tax was introduced to reduce the number of ATBs to single figures (Friel 1995; Wilson 1998).

The success or otherwise of their ATB TIC was another fundamental issue. For many ATBs they were one, if not the main roots of their funding problems and, as has already been alluded to, sectors of the industry's expectations that they should fill their every bed space were wholly unrealistic and problematical. The reality for many ATBs was that the TIC network was not only too costly to maintain, it was also restrictive and its services and products could have been delivered by other means e.g. via existing tourism businesses such as hotels, visitor attractions, shops etc., which could register to become TICs, or even Post Offices. Their staff would be trained to handle enquiries locally, and through an 0800 number or the web, reserve accommodation for guests nationally, receiving commissions for doing so. The advantage to the customer would be that through time almost every tourism-related business would be able to furnish visitors with up-to-date information and make forward reservations. Through time this could also mean travel and entertainment. The advantage to the business is a much more knowledgeable staff, and the ability not only to make commissions, but also to attract business through being a source of local and national information. While the savings to ATBs could be significant the customer would experience a much more effective and efficient service.

SEn/HIE/LECs

VisitScotland and the ATB network's relationship with SEn/HIE and the LECs is an evolving one, determined on the one hand by their political masters and on the other the extent of the industry's use of them. Because of their different objectives, and the industry's differing and at times unrealistic expectations of them, their relationship will always be hard to reconcile, particularly as they are subject to constant review of one form or other. Furthermore, their relationships are under constant threat due to the tensions brought by duplication and overlap, and the industry finding it confusing at times as to where one's responsibility ends and the other's begins.

The establishment of the Tourism, Culture and Sports Ministry in 2001 further confused the issue. For example, McLeish's vision for the tourism industry was one that was to be deep in the framework of an enhanced SEn/HIE. Yet, when Alexander became responsible for tourism in 2000, she condoned the STB review that appeared to take a contrary view to McLeish, in that she wanted that STB should request that the Enterprise and Lifelong Learning Department clarify that responsibility for tourism strategy and policy lay with the STB, and the existing costs incurred in SEn/HIE be reallocated to the STB. Since then, tourism having moved departments, is no longer mainstream of economic development, and the aforementioned monies have remained within SEn/HIE, so neither aspiration was met. In effect, even prior to that, there was no integration with SEn/HIE, nor was there, as the industry appeared to want an undertaking for STB/VisitScotland (or one sole organization) to be responsible in its entirety for tourism.

VisitBritain (formerly BTA)

Due to devolution and the fact that BTA purported to be a cross-border authority there was a case for arguing that this situation no longer had any political relevance to Scottish tourism. The need for a reappraisal of the relationship due to the supposed London bias of BTA e.g. its remit is to attract tourists to Britain and then apply re-distributive marketing using London as the gateway city, a remit that left Scotland at London's behest, was addressed in October 2002, but remains unsatisfactory.

Long-term speculation of a BTA London bias apart, according to the *STB Policy Management Financial Review*: *Prior Options Study* (final report 1998: 18) in the late nineties Scotland ranked 8th in the world for tourism receipts per head of population derived from overseas income, yet this income was less than a third of Singapore and a quarter of Austria. Significantly, however, with the exception of Spain and Italy who were also listed in the top ten, none of the countries featured were large countries. It could, therefore, be construed from this survey that the income derived from tourism was of greater significance to small economies than large ones. For example, Scotland's tourism receipts per capita, based on the above criteria, were $539, compared to England's $358, 51% more. The simple conclusion that can be drawn from this is that in comparison to their relative positions on exporting, so the Scottish economy is more dependent on tourism than the English economy, an extremely important point in terms of the influence wielded from Westminster on the BTA, on the manner in which BTA marketed Britain and consequently Scotland, on reserved powers and policies, and on tourism policy in the U.K. in general.

A Ministry of Tourism

For many countries, the greater the importance of tourism to their economy, the greater the involvement of the public sector institutions and the stimulus governments are prepared to give to attract inward investment, to the point of there being a government ministry with sole responsibility for tourism. In such countries it is often the case that planning powers with respect to tourism are devolved to local government, while the executive arm of government is transferred to a quasi-public body in the form of the National Tourist Office (NTO) (Wanhill 1998). In Scotland, as in the U.K. as a whole, while planning powers are devolved to local authorities and there is a public body responsible for tourism, tourism is part of a much wider ministry. This situation creates an environment in which there are irreconcilable views regarding the seriousness with which successive governments take the industry.

The industry view in Scotland both pre-and post devolution was that somewhat reluctantly; government encouraged reasonably high public investment in tourism, yet refused to recognize it by setting up its own dedicated government ministry. Instead subjugating it within an economic development ministry, for example, as the Scottish Office did in consigning it to the Industry Ministry, or the Scottish Executive in assigning it to the Enterprise and Lifelong Learning Ministry. Until tourism was aligned with culture and sport in November 2001, the lack of a ministry devoted solely to the industry was construed by many Scottish tourism operators as evidence that the Executive did not value it highly enough. Furthermore, concern was also expressed that fishing, a much smaller industry in terms of employment and its contribution to the economy had more dedicated resource, and agriculture vastly more civil servants. The Executive's view prior to the change was that evidence of the seriousness with which it was taking the industry was that the promotion of tourism took place as part of general economic development not only within FEDS but also deep in the framework of an enhanced SEn/HIE network. Also, that such integration offered tourism the ability to take advantage of a wide range of economic development activities and initiatives from which it would otherwise be distanced. That tourism is now aligned with culture and sport refutes the above claim, and although the industry greeted the change positively evidence to date is that tourism, if it were not to be given a dedicated ministry and department, would have been better left mainstream of economic development in the Enterprise and Lifelong Learning Ministry, and department. Nevertheless, such diverse and irreconcilable opinion is further evidence that despite the McLeish tourism strategy, the review of STB, the publication of FEDS, or the 2002 framework, there is still fragmentation of the public bodies responsible for Scottish tourism. To a majority of the industry, this could be resolved by establishing a dedicated Tourism Ministry, a Minister of Cabinet status, a dedicated tourism department, and the formation of one organization responsible in its entirety for tourism, a policy change that would put Scottish tourism at the heart of the Scottish Executive's economic strategy. Furthermore, persevering with a system that is a major contributory factor to the industry's poor performance, to the poor perception of tourism as an industry in Scotland, and consequently to Scotland as a tourism destination is, to many operators, incomprehensible.

Tourism Tax

That the Scottish Executive should treat the tourism industry more significantly than in the past is substantiated by the fact that tourism is designated to be one of the major economic drivers of the 21st century (Boskin 1996: 3–11). It generates revenue of $4.4

trillion, world-wide, which represents 10% of global GDP, and provides 8% of total world employment (some 200 million jobs) (Douglas 2000). Despite September 11, Bali and Mombassa, this figure is forecast to continue to expand at 2–3% per annum until 2010 when it will reach $10.0 trillion, generating a further 100 million jobs worldwide. The significance of this to Scotland is quite clear. Tourism *is* an important part of the Scottish economy, with a potential in the next decade of generating £6 billion in output (10% of Scottish GDP) (using the new 2000 methodology). However, this is unattainable without significant investment, particularly in marketing, product development and skills development, which, on evidence of current tourism public policy, will not be financed from the public purse to the sustainable levels needed.

Although the answer may be a Tourism Tax, there is little support for it although suggestions that it might be hypothecated may prove more acceptable. Instead, there are expectations that the new parliament continues to provide the resource required for marketing and supporting the tourism infrastructure, a situation, as we have already described due to other more emotive demands, that may be untenable, and therefore why a tourism tax in the longer-term, may become its only viable funding alternative for the industry.

For example, even in the crudest calculations such a tax could at a 2.5% levy be more than £100 million. This sum equates extremely favourably with the existing £3.5 million invested in the ATB network by VisitScotland, the £40 million grant aid from government to VisitScotland, the £7.5 million contributed by Local Authorities and the unspecified monies that the LECs invest in tourism. Not only that, this could be a net saving to the Executive of at least £50 million which could be contributed towards health, transport, education etc.

Compulsory (Statutory) Registration

Due to tourism's growing international economic and social importance, and despite the new parliament's albeit limited powers to question and influence many aspects of the Scottish economy, it was a sign of the times that during the lifetime of the first parliament a significant section of the tourism industry in Scotland had a desire to be measured and valued not only against their own sector's performance (Quality Assurance) but also against other industrial sectors in terms of viability, sustainability and long-term growth (Benchmarking). On the other hand a significant number were opposed to any measures that would mean their standard of performance being compared even when this was in comparison to businesses in their own sector i.e. the VisitScotland Classification and Grading scheme, Taste of Scotland's Food Grading Company scheme.

This polarity was widespread and was typical of the vein of opinion that runs through Scottish tourism. For example, politicians who could legislate for such change were equally divided, particularly those that feared that the introduction of statutory registration of all tourism businesses would impact negatively on businesses in their own constituencies. Nevertheless, those that embraced measures that would improve quality, skills and performance believed that these combined with other measures were factors that would improve dramatically the Scottish tourism experience for visitors and those who earned their living by it. It would also have aligned the tourism industry much more with the visions intended for it in *A New Strategy for Scottish Tourism (2000)*, *A Smart, Successful Scotland* (2001), and *the Tourism Framework for Action 2002: 2005* (2002).

What is clear is that the industry has a fundamental problem in influencing those businesses whose service levels and quality thresholds are more evocative of the 19th than the 21st century. The recent poor performance of Scottish tourism demonstrated how much ground the majority of Scottish tourism businesses have to make up to compete in global terms. This is why many operators involved in wide-ranging improvement initiatives, and who reaped the benefits, are frustrated by the poor perception of Scottish tourism; much of this derived from poorly managed businesses, and as a result are supportive of the Scottish Executive taking a firm form of action. Among the suggestions to overcome the problems is some form of compulsory (statutory) registration, be it through a more widespread classification and grading of businesses or professional licensing of operators (see below) or a combination of both.

Although compulsory registration is contentious and in itself will not resolve the problem in the short-term, it would mean through time that to open or maintain a business, as in certain other industries, service level agreements, skills levels and quality thresholds would need to be sustained. Aligned to Classification and Grading, it is also a statement of the minimum standards and facilities the customer should expect.

Of course there are a number of difficulties with such a scheme. For example, some of Scotland's finest establishments e.g. Altnaharra, Ceilidh Place, The Cape Wrath, and Skibo Castle refuse to be Classified and Graded (Mercer, personal communication 2001). If compulsory registration were introduced would they be forced out of business if they refused to comply? Also, any large national or multi-national employer refusing to participate, if threatened with closure, would jeopardize numerous jobs. MSPs/MPs might also be compelled to oppose compulsory registration if it meant their local businesses being closed or jobs being lost in their constituencies, in particular rural ones. Nevertheless, at the Scotland United 2002 conference in Crieff (2nd December 2002), the Minister for Tourism, Mike Watson, during a speech, quoting statistics from VisitScotland, claimed that 80% of complaints about the quality of their accommodation came from visitors who stayed in the 20% of the accommodation not within the ambit of the quality assurance scheme, and that Scotland's worst hotels and bed and breakfasts will be shut unless they improve standards (Stamp 2002).

Scottish Tourism Professional Qualification

Riewoldt (1998) claims that the virtualization of work and leisure is increasing mobility and fragmenting living conditions. As a result of changing preoccupations, settings, jobs and attractions the temporary dominates everyday life. The consequence of this is that the 21st century guest is even more discerning and sophisticated than his or her 20th century counterpart. Above all, what counts most to guests is the atmosphere, the hotel, restaurant, guesthouse, visitor attraction's ambience being its chief attraction and its defining quality in an increasingly competitive market place, with the key concepts individualism and diversification. So much of this ambience is derived not from aesthetics but from the manner in which those involved in the tourism industry deliver their service quality and is the maxim by which they and the environment in which they work are judged. However, there is still a fundamental problem in influencing many proprietors and managers of the need to address skills development, staff conditions and remuneration.

The poor performance, lack of vision and dereliction of strategic thought of many such businesses demonstrates how far Scotland had as a destination to go to compete in global terms. Many Scottish tourism businesses, for example, choose to treat staff conditions and skills development as a low priority. This also exposes the failure to date of all the agencies involved to do something about this. Such businesses are the least likely to take up the initiatives they need most, yet which would benefit both their businesses and staff enormously, and ultimately their customers. This is why many others involved in wide-ranging improvement initiatives, and who have reaped the benefits, are supportive of some form of compulsory qualification becoming an industry norm. This would dispense with tourism businesses being purchased by those who have little or no previous experience, which contributes to a high turnover of businesses and over-capacity in some areas. Although controversial, it will mean training and developing staff properly, rewarding them accordingly, providing good conditions in which to work, offering them career progression and above all valuing them. Even being prepared to lose them when a better opportunity comes along: an opportunity that would not have otherwise materialized but for the skills they had developed in their current situation.

In essence, as tourism is one of Scotland's largest industries, the Scottish Executive needs to afford it a higher priority. For example, by 2002 its employment had increased to 193,000 (8% of the workforce and 20% of the Highlands & Islands workforce), paying the wages of more people than the oil, gas and whisky industries combined and employing over four times more than agriculture/fishing. Furthermore, for every £1 VisitScotland spends on promotion £12 is generated in return on behalf of Scotland's tourism industry (www.scotexchange.net, August 2001). But, where does Scottish tourism go from here? For example, will the tourism consultations and the Enterprise and Lifelong Learning Committee's (ELLC) inquiry into Scottish tourism outcomes reflect the industry's desire for fundamental change as evidenced by this research, or will Watson or whoever succeeds him after the May elections, replicate their predecessor's position that there is no overall consensus as to what to do with the Scottish tourism industry, therefore making change only incremental?

The Way Forward for Scottish Tourism

In the previous section of this chapter, various suggestions were put forward as to how the Scottish tourism industry might address issues that were holding it back from realizing its commercial potential. Although important to the future of Scottish tourism, to claim that these were the catalyst for the more fundamental improvement that needs to be made to Scottish tourism in the longer-term, would be to replicate the ambivalence shown towards the industry by a succession of ministers whose procrastination has undermined it, when what was needed was a change of seismic proportions.

Such change not only needs to be structural, it also needs to be attitudinal and cultural. For example, in a quest to understand the exigencies of tourism policy, and in order to suggest a more appropriate tourism public policy for Scotland, for all the activity described throughout, tourism public policies, no matter from which country they are derived, will be unsuccessful in isolation. If Scotland is to aspire to a truly world class tourism destination, not only will the Scottish tourism industry have to face up to its underlying problems, the Scottish Executive through complementary public policies will also have to improve transportation, communication, connectivity and access. Furthermore, Scotland, as a nation, will also have to address cultural, societal, educational and attitudinal behaviours, and the Scottish tourism industry will have to desist from compromising its skills, quality and products. For example, there is an increased emphasis on special interest tourism, whereby Scotland as a tourism destination, could capitalise on its very unique culture, history and art. Educational, genealogical and professional development travel, too, may strengthen greatly and enrich the meaning of the travel experience for many people attracted to and visiting Scotland, as will outdoor and environmental aspirations. As it is a not inexpensive destination, there is also more importantly an opportunity for Scotland to distinguish itself by becoming more widely valued as a cultural destination. This means over time (say within this decade), its art, film, music, literature, dance, and theatre could enhance Scotland's image. This unique cultural fusion of history and heritage combined with a vast improvement in its hospitality skills could ultimately differentiate Scotland from its competitors. The significance of this will not only affect its appeal as a tourism destination; it will also have wider societal influence.

Scotland, as a destination, will also have to become much more accessible than at present, both by sea and air, and the present apparent reluctance by the Scottish Executive to support new routes overcome. For example, the failure of Scottish tourism to take advantage of cabotage and air liberalisation, particularly low cost airlines which are targeting a range of non-traditional city destinations, and providing new opportunities is shameful, particularly since it would appear that Scotland has yet to fully grasp the fact that low-cost air travel has led to a new geography, changing the map of tourism in central and Western Europe. New inexpensive air services could be the catalyst for the acceleration of growth in tourism as well as stimulating short break tourism to cities such as Glasgow, Edinburgh, Dundee, Aberdeen and Inverness. In essence, providing city breaks and short holidays that are accessible and inexpensive to international travellers (Stevens *et al.* 2002).

Furthermore, unlike its predecessor, the Scottish Office, the Scottish Executive needs to desist from making change in isolation. If there is to be a wholesale structural review of Scottish tourism within this decade then it must be done in conjunction with the changes that will undoubtedly take place in both the economic development environment and in the Local Authority structure. But, above all, its politicians need with some urgency to demonstrate a strategic tourism public policy focus for Scottish tourism. To do otherwise will further accentuate the fragmentation and parochiality of the industry contributing further to its inability to compete with competitor destinations and realize its full commercial potential.

Summary

This chapter draws to a conclusion the research for this book. In doing so, it acknowledges the Scottish tourism industry during the period of the research was dependent upon numerous inter-related factors that were dynamic, complex and variable, many of which were outwith its control. It was also fragmented in terms of its infrastructure, institutionalized and unintentionally disadvantaged by the small but powerful elite that had grown around the institutions and, as a consequence was slow to adjust to the challenges of globalization and devolution This was compounded by the fact that there were also irreconcilable views at operator level in terms of the aspirations of the various sectors, and incompatibility of the aims and objectives of rural, urban and city destinations. The fact that Scotland was on the periphery of Europe meant it was also difficult and expensive to access. Above all it was disadvantaged by its politicians' inability to demonstrate a strategic tourism public policy focus for Scottish tourism and disinclination to initiate major structural and cultural change.

Adapting a heterogeneous approach enabled us to understand better the processes that contributed to making such a convoluted environment and also the mechanisms by which tourism public policy-making in Scotland was derived. However, it was also important to substantiate how relevant this approach was to our understanding of the way in which tourism policy decisions were implemented in Scotland. Such an approach, therefore, encapsulated the intricacies, tensions and opportunities of devolution, and was the most appropriate means by which this book could explain the nuances, complexities and vagaries of Scottish tourism policy.

Equally applicable is the policy network approach applied to Chapter 8 in terms of its focus on the links between people, institutions and networks, the processes by which these complex relationships were dealt with and the changes they were undergoing. Furthermore, as change defined the nature of modern tourism policy either in its own context or in tandem with other extraneous factors, capturing the transformation that was taking place globally and the impact this was having on Scottish tourism was one of the real challenges of the research. It was also clear that that the Scottish Executive had to learn to live with policy networks (Rhodes 1999: 59). The challenge for governments was to understand these new networks and devise ways of steering them and holding them to account (Rhodes 1999: 110).

Ultimately, the research posits that Scottish tourism cannot prosper within the existing policy, environment and structure, and has hypothesized the means by which many of Scottish tourism's deficiencies may be resolved. It also assumes widespread improvement if the perception of the industry as a low paid, low skills industry could be cured; consistent product, skills and service quality achieved; transportation, communication, connectivity and access improved; and cultural, societal, educational and attitudinal behaviours addressed. These factors, combined with the Scottish Executive taking a strategic public policy focus for tourism in Scotland, wrestling some (or all) reserved economic powers from Westminster, and initiating major structural and cultural change, could set Scotland on the way to aspiring to a truly world class destination, challenging competitor destinations, and realising its full commercial potential.

Note

That the Scottish electorate voted so differently on 1st May 2003 from 1999 is indicative of their dissatisfaction with the previous parliament, and their desire for change. With many more parties now involved in the parliament it is going to be extremely interesting to observe how the tourism agenda is influenced, and it could be that by the 2007 elections those organisations involved in tourism in Scotland will look very different. However, following the May 2003 elections the appointment of Frank McAveety MSP as Tourism, Culture & Sport Minister, but on a Deputy's salary, with no deputy, and no department has once more conveyed to the industry the lesser value put on it by the Scottish Executive.

References

AA, the (2000). Where to Stay, www.theaa.co.uk/hotels/Ratings.html. December.

ABC News.com/Magellan Geographix/Reuters/al-Eqtisadiah (2000). Saudis to increase tourism: Plans to Expand Travel Privileges Beyond Pilgrims' Sites, 4th April, www.i.abcnews.com/media/Travel/images/apr_saudi_arabia000404_a.jpg

ABC News.com (2000). News.com/Reuters/al-Eqtisadiah

Ady, J. (1997). Nature-Oriented Tourism in Saudi Arabia. Landscape Issues 3 (online), www.chelt.ac.uk/cwis/pubs/landiss/vol13/pages3.htm

Ady, J., & Wallwer, E. (1989). Urban and Rural Profiles in Saudi Arabia. In: K. Al-Ankary, & El-S. El-Bushra (Eds), *A contribution to the debate on internal tourism in Saudi Arabia, Gebr Borntraeger Verlagsbuchhandlung*. Stuttgart: Science Publishers. ISBN 3-443-37010-1.

Ain-Al-Yaqeen, Weekly Arab Political Magazine (1998). Asir Province Develops Tourism as a Major Source of Revenue. Prince Khalid Al-Faisal Emir of Asir Province: We hope to receive one and a half million visitors in our province this year, 26 August, www.ain-al-yaqueen.com/issues/19980826/feat4en.html

Ain-Al-Yaqeen (2000). Saudi Arabia Establishes A Supreme Commission for Tourism Chaired by Prince Sultan Ibn Abdul Aziz. The Commission is a New Turn in the Tourism Sector and a Contribution in the Local Production, 12 May, www.ain-al-yaqeen.com/issues/20000512/feat3en.htm

Aitken, K. (1992). The Economy. In: M. Linklater, & R. Dennison (Eds), *Anatomy of Scotland*. Edinburgh: Chambers.

Al Khoury, R. (1999). Saudi Arabia climbs on the tourism bandwagon, The Daily Star on line, March 26, www.dailystar.com.lb

Anderson, J. (1975). *Public policy making*. New York: Praeger.

Andresen, J. P. (2000). Concerning the Development of Corporatism on the EU Level, seminar, Bruxelles, AKP-arkivet, March, www.akp.no/arkiv/eu/corporatism-ipa.htm

Archer, B., & Cooper, C. (1994). The positive and negative aspects of tourism. In: W. Theobald (Ed.), *Global tourism: The next decade* (1998). Oxford: Butterworth-Heinemann.

Asean Tourism (2002). Asia's Perfect 10 Paradise, www.asean-tourism.com

Asia Times (2001). Southeast Asia Asean nations enjoy fruits of booming global tourism, March 16, www.atimes.com

Association of Southeast Asian Nations (2002). www.aseansec.org

Association of Southeast Asian Nations (2002). International Visitors and Arrival in ASEAN 1991–2000, www.Asean-Tourism.com

Association of Southeast Asian Nations (2002). Origins of International Visitor Arrivals in ASEAN 1991, www.Asean-Tourism.com

Association of Southeast Asian Nations (2002). Origins of International Visitor Arrivals in ASEAN 2000, www.Asean-Tourism.com

Australian Forecasting Council (2002). Projected International Visitors (000s). 1989–2012.

Australian Tourism Commission (ATC) (2002). Research and Statistics, www.australia.com/ProcessSplashResults.aust?C=GB&L=en

Bacon, B. (2001). Personal Communication, British Hospitality Association, London, 24 May.

Baumgartner, F., & Jones, B. (1993). Agendas and Instability in American Politics, University of Chicago Press, Chicago.

Belize Tourism (2002). Strategic vision for Belize tourism in the new millennium. Belize's Official Tourism Industry Information Website, www.belizetourism.org/policy.html

Belize Tourism (2002). Tourism Statistics. Belize's Official Tourism Industry Information Website, www.belizetourism.org/arrival.html

Belize Tourism (2002). Tourism Statistics, International Arrivals by mode of arrival. Immigration Department, Belize's Official Tourism Industry Information Website, www.belizetourism.org/arrival.html

Belize Tourism (2002). Tourism Statistics, International Arrivals by mode of arrival 1995–1999, Immigration Department, Belize's Official Tourism Industry Information Website, www.belizetourism.org/arrival.html

Belize Tourism (2002). Tourism Statistics, International Arrivals by nationality, Immigration Department, Belize's Official Tourism Industry Information Website, www.belizetourism.org/arrival.html

BHA (1999). *Hospitality and government in Scotland: A briefing document.* Edinburgh: BHA.

Bord Failte (2000). *The Failte Business 2000: The role of tourism in economic growth* (millennium issue).

Bord Fáilte Business (2000). www.bftrade.travel.ie/downloads/FailteBusiness.doc 2000

Bord Failte Business (2002). www.bftrade.travel.ie/downloads/FailteBusiness.doc 2002

Bord Failte (2002). Welcome to Bord Failte: History, www.bftrade.travel.ie/downloads/FailteBusiness.doc.Bord Fáilte Business.

Boskin, M. (1996). National Satellite Accounting for travel and tourism: A cold review of the WTTC/WEFA group research. *Tourism Economics, 2* (1), 3–11.

Boyle, S. (2002). The Scottish Labour Market 2002, Futureskills Scotland, Scottish Enterprise, Glasgow.

Bramwell, B. (1998). Sustainable tourism. *Annals of Tourism Research, 26* (1), December.

Brent Ritchie, J. R. (1984). Assessing the impact of hallmark events: conceptual and research issues. *Journal of Travel Research, 23* (1), 2–11.

Brent Ritchie, J. R., & Goeldner, C. R. (1994). *Travel, tourism & hospitality research* (2nd ed., pp. xiii & 3). New York: Wiley.

Brewer, G. D., & deLeon, P. (1983). *The foundations of policy analysis.* Monterey/CA: Brooks Cole.

Briggs, B. (2002). Scotland hits rock bottom in tourist table. *The Herald,* Saturday August 31.

British Tourist Authority (2000). VisitBritain, Your official travel guide to Britain, November, www.visitbritain.com

British Tourist Authority (2001). VisitBritain, Your official travel guide to Britain, July, www.visitbritain.com

Brittania.com (2003). The Referendum of 1997, A brief history of Wales, www.britannia.com/wales/whist30a.html

Brown, A., McCrone, D., & Paterson, L. (1996). *Politics and society in Scotland.* Basingstoke: Macmillan.

Brown, A., McCrone, D., Paterson, L., & Surridge, P. (1999). *The Scottish electorate.* Macmillan: Basingstoke.

Brown, J. A. (2002). Personal Communication, Tourism and Architectural Policy Division, Education Department, Scottish Executive, 24 October.

Bull, P., & Church, A. (1994). The hotel and catering industry of Great Britain during the 1980s: sub-regional employment change, specialisation and dominance. In: C. Cooper, & A. Lockwood (Eds), *Progress in tourism, recreation and hospitality management* (Vol. 5). Chichester: Wiley.

Bulleid, H. A. V. (1963). *Master builders of steam.* London: Ian Allan.

Burkart, A. J., & Medlik, S. (1975). *The management of tourism*. London: Pitman Publishers.

Burkart, A. J., & Medlik, S. (1981). *Tourism, past, present and future* (2nd ed.). London: Pitman Publishers.

Burns, P. M., & Holden, A. (1995). *Tourism: a new perspective* (ch. 3). London: Prentice-Hall.

Business AM (2001). 20 November.

Butler, R., & Jones, P. (2001). Conclusions — problems, challenges and solutions. In: A. Lockwood, & S. Medlik (Eds), *Tourism and hospitality in the 21st century*. Oxford: Butterworth-Heinemann.

Bwrdd Croeso Cymru/Wales Tourist Board (2002). Welcome/Croeso, www.wales-tourist-board.gov.uk

Bwrdd Croeso Cymru/Wales Tourist Board (2002). Welcome/Croeso www.wtbonline.gov.uk

Cabinet Office (2002). www.cabinet-office.gov.uk

Carter, E. F. (1952). *Britain's railway liveries 1825–1948*. London: Harold Starke Ltd.

Caterer and Hotelkeeper (1999). *Tomorrow's tourism*. London, 6 May.

Caterer and Hotelkeeper (2001). 22 November.

CERT (1997). *Tourism and travel in Ireland* (2nd ed.). Dublin: Gill and Macmillan.

Chamberlain, K. (2002). *Asia Pacific, from tourism and hospitality in the 21st century*. In: A. Lockwood, & S. Medlik (Eds). Oxford: Butterworth-Heinemann.

Child, G., & Grainger, J. (1990). *A system plan for protected areas for wildlife conservation and sustainable rural development in Saudi Arabia*. Riyadh: NCWCD.

Cochrane, P. (1997). *Tips for time travellers*. London: Orion Publishers.

Cohen, M. D., March, J. G., & Olsen, J. P. (1972). A garbage can model of organisational choice. *Administrative Science Quarterly, 17*, 1–25.

Coleman, S., & Fraser, D. (2002). Soiling the perfect pitch. *Sunday Herald*, 15 September, 14.

Commission of the European Communities (CEC) (1995). *Community Action Plan to assist tourism*. Brussels: DGXXIII.

Commission of the European Communities (CEC) (1995). *Community measures affecting tourism*. Brussels: EC.

Commission of the European Communities (CEC) (1995). EC Project Document 95/C/35/OC and COM (94). 582: Proposal for a Community Directive on the Collection of Statistical Information in the field of tourism, Brussels.

Commission of the European Communities (CEC) (1995). The role of the Union in the field of tourism, Green Paper COM (95), 97.

Commission of the European Communities (CEC) (1995). *Tourism and the environment in Europe*. Brussels: DGXXIII.

Commonwealth Department of Industry, Science and Tourism (1996). *Tourism facts, tourism industry trends*. Canberra, August.

Commonwealth Department of Industry, Science and Tourism (1998). *National action plan for tourism, tourism — a ticket to the 21st century*. Canberra, www.industry.gov.au/sport_tourism/publications/ticket/index.html

Commonwealth Department of Industry, Tourism and Resources (2002). Overseas Arrivals and Departures Data, Cat No 3401.0. www.industry.gov.au/content/policy.cfm 2002 ABS

Commonwealth Department of Industry, Tourism and Resources (2002). The 10 year plan for tourism: a discussion paper. www.industry.gov/.../Tourism10plandiscussionpaper.pdf www.industry.gov.au/content/policy.cfm

Commonwealth Department of Tourism (1991). *Directions for tourism*. Canberra.

Commonwealth Department of Tourism (1992). *Tourism: Australia's passport to growth, a national tourism strategy*. Canberra: Australian Government Publishing Service.

Commonwealth Department of Tourism, Sport and Recreation (1996). *National tourism plan*. Canberra.

Commonwealth of Independent States (2002). Commonwealth of Independent States, www.cisstat. com/eng/cis.htm

Connolly, E. (1999). Enterprise Ayrshire's Response to Enterprise and Lifelong Learning Committee Enquiry, November, Enterprise Ayrshire, Kilmarnock.

Cotton, R. (2001). Personal Communication, Dalmahoy Hotel, 3 September.

Crawford, R. (2000). Personal Communication, Scottish Enterprise, Glasgow, 1 November.

Crichton, T. (1992). 'The Highlands'. In: M. Linklater, & R. Denniston (Eds), *Anatomy of Scotland* (pp. 218–226). Edinburgh: Chambers.

Croeso I Gymru, Welcome to Wales (2002). www.croeso.com

Crozier, M. (1964). *The bureaucratic phenomenon*. Chicago: University of Chicago Press.

Cusick, J. (2002). Wish you weren't here. *Global tourism, Sunday Herald*, 20 October, 16.

Cynulliad Cenedlaethol Cymru, Welcome to the National Assembly for Wales (2002). The National Assembly for Wales, www.cymru.gov.uk

Dahl, R. (1997). In: S. Mayhew (Ed.), *A dictionary of geography*. Oxford: Oxford University Press.

Daneshkhu, S. (1998). Financial Times, London 18 June.

Davis, G., Wanna, J., Warhurst, J., & Weller, P. (1993). *Public policy in Australia* (2nd ed.). Sydney: Allen & Unwin.

Deaton, A., & Muellbauer, J. (1989). *Economics and consumer behaviour*. Cambridge: Cambridge University Press.

De Grazia, A. (2000). Discovering National Elites: A Manual of Methods for Discovering the Leadership of a Society and its Vulnerabilities to Propaganda (with the collaboration of Paul Deutschmann and Floyd Hunter), The Institute for Journalistic Studies Stanford University September 30 1954 First Public Edition, www.Grazian-Archive.com

Deloitte Touche Study (1998). *Hospitality and government in Scotland: A briefing document*. Edinburgh: BHA (1999).

Deloitte Touche Study (1998). *European hotel accommodation VAT rates*. London.

Department of Arts, Sport and Tourism (2002). Bill published to set up Fáilte Ireland, the new National Tourism Development Authority, Press Release, 25 November.

Department of Arts, Sport and Tourism (2002). O'Donoghue announces major review of tourism policy. *News Release*, www.gov.ie/arts-sport-tourism/pressroom/ressrel_2002/ pr_min_06112002, November.

Department of Arts, Sport and Tourism (2002). *Tourism*, www.gov.ie/arts-sport-tourism/ whatwedo/tourism/wwd_t_til.htm

Department of Arts, Sport and Tourism (2002). Tourism Promotion — Tourism Ireland Ltd, News Release, www.gov.ie/arts-sport-tourism/pressroom/ressrel_2002/pr_min_25112002, November.

Department of Culture, Media and Sport (1998). Tourism — towards sustainability, tourism consultation. London.

Department of Culture Media and Sport (1999). Tomorrow's tourism, English tourism council. London: The Stationery Office.

Department of Culture Media and Sport (1999). Tomorrow's tourism, English tourism council structure, English tourism council. London: The Stationery Office.

Department of Culture Media and Sport (1999). Tomorrow's tourism, how the main players in the support of England's tourism relate to the ETC, English tourism council. London: The Stationery Office.

Department of Culture, Media and Sport (DCMS). (1999). Tourism: Towards Sustainability (Consultation Paper), E. Christian & Co, www.culture.gov.uk

Department of Culture, Media and Sport (2001). Fourth report, Tourism — the hidden giant — and foot and mouth, 3rd May, www.publications.parliament.uk/pa/cm200001/cmselect/cmcumeds/ 430/43002.htm

www.parliament.uk/commons/selcom/cmshone.htm

Department of Culture Media and Sport (2002). Tessa Jowell, Secretary of State for Media, Culture and Sport, BTA Announcement by the Secretary of State for Culture Media & Sport on reform of U.K. tourism, 31 October.

Department of Economic Development (1989). *Tourism in Northern Ireland — A view to the future.* Belfast: HMSO.

Department of Environmental Affairs and Tourism (1995). A discussion document: Green Paper, Towards a New Tourism Policy of South Africa, Prepared by: The Interim Tourism Task Team, Pretoria, September.

Department of Environmental Affairs and Tourism (1996). White Paper, The Development and Promotion of Tourism in South Africa, Government of South Africa, May.

Department of Environmental Affairs and Tourism (1997). *Tourism in gear.* Government of South Africa.

Department of Environmental Affairs and Tourism (1999). *Tourism action plan.* Government of South Africa. September.

Department of Tourism, Culture and Sport (2002). Area Tourist Board Consultation www.Scotland.gov.uk/consultations/tourism/areatourist.pdf, May–September.

Department of Tourism and Sport (2000). *Strategy for tourism 2002–2006.* Government of Ireland.

Department of Tourism, Sport and Recreation (2002). Report of the Implementation Group on the Establishment of a New Tourism Development Authority, Dublin.

Department of Tourism, Sport and Recreation (2002). Tourism Promotion — Tourism Ireland Ltd, News Release.

Department of Tourism and Transport (1985). *White paper, Tourism policy.* Dublin: Government of Ireland.

Department of Tourism and Transport (1987). *Programme for national recovery.* Dublin: Government of Ireland, Stationery Office.

Department of Tourism and Transport (1987). *Improving the performance of Irish tourism.* Dublin: Government of Ireland.

Department of Tourism and Transport (1989). *National development plan.* Dublin: Government of Ireland, Stationery Office.

Department of Tourism and Transport (1989). *Operational programme for tourism 1989–1994.* Dublin: Stationery Office.

Department of Tourism and Transport (1994). *Operational programme for tourism 1994–1999* (2nd ed.). Dublin: Stationery Office.

Devine, T. M. (1999). *The Scottish nation, 1700–2000.* Allen Lane, London: The Penguin Press.

Dhlodlo, R. (2002). Sharing the Benefits: A Missed Opportunity for the Tourism Industry in Zimbabwe, www.zero.org.zw/community/whatsnew.htm www.zero.org.zw/community/EDITED%20Tourism%20Brief.doc

DiZerega, G. (1991). G. Elites and democratic theory: Insights from the self-organizing model. *Review of Politics*, June, 340–372, www.dizeraga.com/elites.htm

Doggett, L. R. (2000). Tourism's role in a changing economy, iota office of travel and tourism studies. Office of Travel and Tourism Industries, www.tinet.ita.doc.gov/about/

Douglas, L., & Scottish Enterprise (2000). *New tourism, the Scottish experience.* Glasgow: Scottish Enterprise Tourism Department.

Duff, L., Forsyth, F., & Kidner, C. (1998). Scottish Devolution Referendum 1997 — Referendum results, how Scotland voted, Engender, www.engender.org.uk/scotparl/elections/referendum97/

Duff, L., Forsyth, F., & Kidner, C. (1998). Scottish Referendum Results and turnout by District, Engender, www.engender.org.uk/scotparl/elections/referendum97/

Duff, L., Forsyth, F., & Kidner, C. (1998). Welsh Assembly — Referendum in Wales 1997, Referendum results, how Wales voted, Engender, www.engender.org.uk/scotparl/elections/referendum97/wales.html

Dye, T. R. (1992). *Understanding public policy*. Englewood Cliffs: Prentice-Hall.

Dyson, K. (1980). *State traditions in western Europe*. Oxford: Polity Press.

Edgell, D. L., Sr. (1990). *International tourism policy*. New York: Van Nostrand Reinhold, 1990.

Edgell, D. L., Sr. (1999). *Tourism policy: The next millennium*. Champaign, Illinois: Sagamore Publishing.

Elliott, J. (1997). *Tourism, politics and public sector management*. London: Routledge.

English Tourism Council (1999). *A framework for action*. Reference: FPFFAC0801, ISBN 0-7095-7156-9.

English Tourism Council (1999). *Focus on the English tourism council*. Reference: SFPCIECIO7993, ISBN 0-7095-7157-7.

English Tourism Council (1999). *Introducing the English tourism council*. Reference: SFP-CIEC07991, ETC Publications.

English Tourism Council (2000). Stepping Stones: A practical stepped approach to achieving the National Quality Assurance Standards (for local hotels), August.

English Tourist Board (ETB) (1998). Agenda 2000, ETB publications.

Enterprise Estonia (2002). ettevotiuse arendamise sihtasutus, www.ease.ee

Enterprise and Lifelong Learning Committee, the Scottish Parliament, 1st Report (1999). Local Economic Development Enquiry Remit — Inquiry into the Delivery of Local Economic Development Services in Scotland, Edinburgh, October.

Enterprise and Lifelong Learning Committee (2000). Conclusions of The Enterprise and Lifelong Learning Committee's Final Report of the Inquiry into the Delivery of Local Economic Development Services in Scotland, Edinburgh.

Enterprise and Lifelong Learning Committee (2000). Final Report of the Inquiry into the Delivery of Local Economic Development Services in Scotland, the Scottish Parliament, Edinburgh.

Enterprise and Lifelong Learning Committee, the Scottish Parliament, 1st Report (2000). Inquiry into the Delivery of Local Economic Development Services in Scotland, SP Paper 109, Edinburgh.

Enterprise and Lifelong Learning Committee (2002). Inquiry into Tourism, the Scottish Parliament, Edinburgh, 5 July.

Enterprise and Lifelong Learning Committee (2002). Support for Tourism: An International Comparison Researched and prepared by Stevens & Associates with The Scottish Tourism Research Group Commissioned by The Scottish Parliament Research and Information Group, Edinburgh.

Enterprise and Lifelong Learning Committee (2002). 9th Report, Final Report on Lifelong Learning, Scottish Parliament, Edinburgh, 28 October.

Equations: Tourism Policy (2002). Tourism Policy of India: An Exploratory Study, Equations, www.equitabletourism.org/tourpolicy.htm

Eshanova, Z. (2002). Central Asia: Freedom of Movement a Case Study in Lack of Cooperation, Eurasian Insight, A EurasiaNet Partner Post from RFE/RL Posted August 10 2002 © Eurasianet, December 17, www.eurasianet.org
www.eurasianet.org/departments/insight/articles/eav081002a.shtml

Estonia (2002). Estonian Tourist Board, Welcome to Estonia, www.visitesonia.com

EU (1998). Human Rights Act 1998, ISBN 0 10 544298 4, the Stationery Office.

EU Ireland (2002). Ireland — Catching Up, The European Commission Representation in Ireland, www.euireland.ie/ireland/ireland/

Europa Eurlex EEC (1988). Council Decision on an Action Programme for European Tourism Year 1990, 89/46/EEC of 21 December, OJ No L 17, 21.1.1989, p. 53, www.europa.eu.int/comm/enterprise/services/tourism/policy-areas/legislation.htm

Europa Eurlex EEC (1992). Council Decision on a Community action plan to assist tourism 92/421/EEC of 31 July, www.europa.eu.int/abc/doc/off/bull/en/9604/p103048.htm

Europa Eurlex EEC (1994). EEC: Council Decision establishing a consultation and cooperation procedure in the field of tourism 86/664/EEC, OJ No L 384, 22 December 1986: 52, www.europa. eu.int/smartapi/cgi/sga_doc?smartapi!celexapi!prod!CELEXnumdoc&lg=EN&numdoc= 31986D0664&model=guicheti

Europarl (1997–2000). Amended Proposal for a Council Decision on a First Multiannual Programme to Assist European Tourism "PHILOXENIA" (EN), www.europarl.eu.int/factsheets/4_15_0_en.htm

Europarl (2000). European Parliament fact Sheets, 4.15.0, Tourism, www.europarl.eu.int/ factsheets/4_15_0_en.htm#note1

Europarl (2002). The accession states, www.eu/accesssion

European Commission (1986). Consultation procedure: CSA0278, Council Recommendation on fire safety in hotels, Brussels, 22 December.

European Commission (1990). *Resolution on measures under European Year of Tourism.* Brussels, 13 July.

European Commission (1990). *Resolution on improving safety, consumers' rights and trading standards in the tourism sector.* Brussels.

European Commission (1991). *Resolution on a community tourism policy: A charter of the rights and obligations of tourists.* Brussels, 11 June.

European Commission (1994). *Background report — tourism policy in the EU.* Brussels: EC.

European Commission (1994). *Resolution on tourism in the approach to the year 2000.* Brussels, 18 January.

European Commission (1994). *Resolution on increased protection for tourists' interests, greater civil liability of travel agencies and stricter criteria for granting operating licences.* Brussels, 15 December.

European Commission (1994). *Resolutions on the commission report on community measures affecting tourism.* Brussels, 15 December.

European Commission (1994). *Resolution on the creation of a European tourism agency.* Brussels, 15 December.

European Commission (1995). *Directive 95/57: Consultation procedure: to harmonise national methods, COS0257.* Brussels, 23 November.

European Commission (1995/96). *Green paper on the role of the union in the field of tourism.* Brussels, 13 February.

European Commission (1996). *Resolution on the proposal for a council decision on an initial multiannual programme for european tourism.* 25 October.

European Commission (2001). *Communication on working together for the future of European tourism.* Brussels.

European Union (1991). *Maastricht Treaty.* Brussels.

Evans, G. (2002). Personal Communication, Information Resources Manager, English Tourism Council/British Tourist Authority Library.

Franklin, A., & Crang, M. (2001). The trouble with tourism and travel theory? *Tourist Studies, 1* (1), 5–22.

Fraser of Allander Institute (1991). *Quarterly economic commentary.* Glasgow: University of Strathclyde.

Friedli, D. (2001). VisitScotland's change to activity-based strategy will cut tourist boards' role: Themes rather than regions will be used to attract visitors, Business AM, 2 November: 3.

Friedli, D. (2002). Scottish growth gets a retrospective boost, Economy fared better than thought in 1990s; National Statistics revises data calculation, Business AM, 26 November: 4.

Friel, E. (1995). *Tourism in the ACE age.* Glasgow: University of Strathclyde.

Friel, E. (2001). *Personal communication.* Glasgow, March.

Friel, E. (2001). *The Journal.* Glasgow Chamber of Commerce, November.

Gallie, W. B. (1955–1956). Essentially contested concepts. *Proceedings of the Aristotelian Society* (Vol. 56).

Gardiner, J., & Wenborn, N. (1995). *The history today companion to British history*. London: Collins and Brown.

Garvey, A. (2002). Double blow for Irish tourism. *Caterer and Hotelkeeper*, 12 December, 6.

Goodall, B. (1987). Tourism policy and jobs in the United Kingdom. *Built Environment*, *13* (2), 109–123.

Gordon, J. (2000). Personal communication. Caledonian Hotel, Edinburgh, defending the STB review: 30 November.

Guiney, D. (2002). *The tourism and travel industry in Ireland*. Dublin: Gill and Macmillan.

Gunn, C. A. (1988). *Tourism planning* (2nd ed.). New York: Taylor and Francis.

Hall, C. M. (1999). *Tourism and politics, policy, power and place*. Chichester: Wiley and Sons.

Hall, C. M. (2000). *Tourism planning, policies, processes and relationships*. Harlow, Middlesex: Prentice-Hall.

Hall, C. M. (2001). Tourism and political relationships in southeast Asia. In: P. Teo, T. C. Chang, & K. C. Ho (Eds), *Interconnected worlds tourism in southeast Asia*. Oxford: Pergamon.

Hall, C. M., & Jenkins, J. M. (1995). *Tourism and public policy*. London: Routledge.

Hall, C. M., & Page, S. (2000). Introduction: Tourism in south and southeast Asia — region and context. In: C. M. Hall, & S. Page (Eds), *Tourism in south and southeast Asia, issues and cases*. Oxford: Butterworth-Heinemann.

Hamilton Ellis, C. (1953). *The Midland Railway*. London: Ian Allan Ltd.

Hann, A. (1995). Sharpening up Sabatier: belief systems and public policy. *Politics*, *15*, 19–26.

Hassan, G. (2002). *Anatomy of the new Scotland, power, influence, and change*. Edinburgh: Mainstream Publishing.

Hawkins, D. E., & Ritchie, J. R. B. (Eds) (1991). *World travel and tourism review: Indicators, trends and forecasts* (Vol. 1). Wallingford: CAB International.

Hazell, R. (2000). The unfinished business of devolution. In: G. Hassan, & C. Warhurst (Eds), *The new Scottish politics, the first year of the Scottish parliament and beyond*. Norwich: The Stationery Office.

Heath, E. (1968). Declaration of Perth, Conservative Party.

Heeley, J.(1989). Role of national tourist organisations in the United Kingdom. In: S. F. Witt, & L. Moutinho (Eds), *Tourism marketing and management handbook*. Hemel Hempstead: Prentice-Hall.

Held, D. (1989). *Political theory and the modern state*. Oxford: Polity Press.

Herald, the (1999). *Glasgow*. 6 December, 1.

Herald, the (1999). *Glasgow*. 9 December.

Heusten, J. (1997). *Kilkee — The origins and development of a west coast resort from Tourism in Ireland*, O'Connor, B., & Cronun, M., Tower Books, Dublin.

Highlands and Islands Enterprise (1996). *Network tourism action framework*. Inverness: HIE.

HMSO (1985). *Pleasure, leisure and jobs: The business of tourism*. London: HMSO.

HMSO (1993). *Scotland in the union: A partnership for good*. CM. 2225, HMSO, March.

Hogwood, B., & Gunn, L. (1984). *Policy analysis for the real world*. Oxford: Oxford University Press.

Holloway, J. C. (1998). *The business of tourism*. New York: Longman.

Honderich, T. (1995). *The Oxford companion to philosophy*. Oxford (Arthur Bentley, The Process of Government, Chicago 1908).

Hoppe, H.-H. (1992). Natural Elites, Intellectuals, and the State by Hans-Hermann Hoppe, Auburn, Alabama: Mises Institute, www.mises.org/intellectuals.asp

Hoshino, S. (1997). The Role of Think Tanks in a Civil Society, Speech text prepared for Middle East Think Tank Conference How to Market Ideas: From Education to Advocacy, held in Cairo, Egypt on 3 November, National Institute for Research Advancement (NIRA), Japan, www.nira.go.jp/newse/paper/txt03.html

Huang, M. (2000). Estonia: Beyond alcohol tourism. *Central Europe Review*, 2 (14), 10 April.

Hughes, H. L. (1994). Tourism and government: A subset of leisure policy. In: A. V. Seaton *et al.* (Eds), *Tourism. The state of the art*. Chichester: Wiley.

Hull, D. L. (1988c). A mechanism and its metaphysics: An evolutionary account of the social and conceptual development of science. *Biology and Philosophy*, *3*, 123–155.

Huntington, S. P. (1993). The clash of civilizations? *Foreign Affairs*, 72 (73), Summer, 22–49. A product of the Olin Institute's project on The Changing Security Environment and American National Interests.

Hussey, J., & Hussey, R. (1997). *Business research*. New York: Macmillan.

Ioannides, D., & Debbage, K. G. (Eds) (1998). *The economic geography of the tourist industry*. London: Routledge,.

Isaacs, A., Martin, E., Law, J., Blair, P., Clark, J., Isaacs, A., Allaby, M., & Chilvers, I. (Eds) (1998). *Oxford Paperback Encyclopaedia*. Market House Books, Oxford University Press.

ITA Office of Travel and Tourism Industries (2002). National Tourism Strategy, the White House Conference on Travel and Tourism, www.tinet.ita.doc.gov/

ITA Office of Travel and Tourism Industries (2002). The U.S. Trade Development Department, www.tinet.ita.doc.gov/tradedevelopment

ITA Office of Travel and Tourism Industries (2002). Welcoming of New Deputy Assistant Secretary and New Office Name, 2nd April, www.tinet.ita.doc.gov/about/index.html#TPC

Jackson A. A., & Campbell, J. (1993). The Fife Hotels and Catering Sector, St., Andrews, St., Andrews Economic Consultants 1993.

Jaensch, D. (1992). *The politics of Australian government*. South Melbourne: Macmillan.

Jenkins, W. I. (1978). *Policy analysis: apolitical and organisational perspective*. New York: St. Martin's Press.

John, P. (1999). *Analysing public policy*. London: Pinter.

John, P. (1999). Evolutionary theory, from *analysing public policy*. London: Pinter.

John, P., & Cole A. (2002). When do institutions, policy sectors and cities matter? Comparing networks of local policy-makers in Britain and France, www.website.lineone.net/~peter.john/PJPUB1.htm

Jones, C. (1970/1974/1984). *An introduction to the study of public policy*. Belmont, CA: Wadsworth.

Kee, R. (1980). *Ireland, a history*. London: Weidenfeld and Nicolson.

Kemp, A. (1993). *The hollow drum*. Edinburgh: Mainstream Publishing.

Kemp, K. (2002). Neil slams £750m R&D black hole. *The Sunday Herald*, Business Section, 17 November: 1.

Kerr, W. R., & Wood, R. C. (1999). Tourism in Ayrshire, from Scottish Tourism after Devolution, The Hospitality Review, Vol. 1, Issue 2, April, pp. 16–23.

Kerr, W. R., & Wood, R. C. (1999). Tourism policy challenges in a devolved state: The case of Scotland. *Anatolia International Journal of Tourism and Hospitality Research*, *10* (1), Summer, 15–28.

Kerr, W. R., & Wood, R. C. (2000). Political values of tourism and hospitality industry professionals: A Scottish case study. *Tourism Management*, *21* (4), 323–330, August.

Kerr, W. R., & Wood, R. C. (2000). *Tourism policy and politics in a devolved Scotland*. Glasgow: University of Strathclyde. Manuscript unpublished.

Kerr, W. R., & Wood, R. C. (2000). *Tourism policy challenges in a small state: The case of Scotland*. Glasgow: University of Strathclyde. Manuscript unpublished.

Kerr, W. R. (2001). A study of the attitudes of tourism industry professionals towards the future of Scottish tourism. PhD thesis. University of Strathclyde.

Keynes, J. M. (1921). *A treaty of probability* (ch. 9).

Kilbrandon, L. (1973). (Kilbrandon). Report, Royal Commission on the Constitution, Cmnd. 5460, HMSO.

Kingdon, J. (1984). *Agendas, alternatives and public policies*. Boston: Little Brown.

Knight, D. (1999). *Balancing the costs and benefits of tourism*. Indian Express Newspapers (Bombay) Ltd.

Koul (2002). Tourism Policy Thrusts On Private Participation and Domestic Tourism: Jha, Express Travel and Tourism, New Delhi, 16th–31st May, www.expresstravelandtourism.com/20020531/cover2.shtml

Lavery, P. (1996). *Travel and tourism* (3rd ed.). Huntington: Elm Publications.

Levy (1995). from McConnell, A. (2000). Issues of Governance in Scotland, Wales and Northern Ireland. In: R. Pyper, & L. Robins (Eds), *United Kingdom Governance*. Hampshire: Macmillan Press.

Lickorish, L. J. (1988). U.K. tourism development. A 10 year review. *Tourism Management, 9* (4), 270–278.

Lickorish, L. J., & Jenkins, C. L. (1997). An introduction to tourism. Oxford: Butterworth-Heinemann.

Linklater, M., & Denniston, R. (Eds) (1992). *Anatomy of Scotland*. Edinburgh: Chambers.

Lockwood, A., & Medlik, S. (Eds) (2002). *Tourism and hospitality in the 21st century*. Oxford: Butterworth-Heinemann.

Lynch, P. (2001). *Scottish government and politics: An introduction*. Edinburgh: Edinburgh University Press.

MacAnnaidh, S. (2001). *Irish history*. London: Star Fire.

MacLellan, R., & Smith, R. (Eds) (1998). *Tourism in Scotland*. London: International Thomson Business Press.

Macwhirter, I. (2002). Absence of body, presence and mind. *The Sunday Herald*, 11 August.

McCaig, I. (2002). Personal Communication, 4 November, Ayr.

McConnell, A. (2000). Issues of Governance in Scotland, Wales and Northern Ireland. In: R. Pyper, & L. Robins (Eds), *United Kingdom Governance*. Hampshire: Macmillan Press.

McCrone, D. (1996). *Understanding Scotland. The sociology of a stateless nation*. London: Routledge.

McDaid, J. (2002). New tourism body to be operational for 2003 — minister for tourism, sport and recreation. Republic of Ireland Government, 24 April.

McFadden, J., & Lazarowicz, M. (1999). *The Scottish Parliament, an introduction*. Edinburgh: T and T Clark.

McIntosh, R. W., Goeldner, C. R., & Ritchie, J. R. B. (1995). *Tourism, principles, practices, philosophies* (7th ed.). New York: John Wiley and Sons.

McKenna, R. (1999). The Environment, Northern Ireland's Greatest Tourism Asset: How Do We Preserve It? Submitted in partial fulfilment of the requirements for the degree of BA (Hons.) in Hospitality Management, the University of Ulster, May, www.busmgt.ulst.ac.uk/leisure/greenissues/ mckenna.html

McKillop, J. (2003). Heath floated plan of oil cash for Scotland. *The Herald*, Glasgow, 1st January, 6.

McLeish, H. (2000). Personal communication. Scottish Enterprise. Lanarkshire, Bothwell, 5 July.

Maggs, C. G. (1999). *Steam, tales from the footplate*. Stroud: Budding Books.

Marsh, D. (1996). Problems in network policy analysis. Birmingham: Department of Politics and International Studies, University of Birmingham.

Marsh, D., & Rhodes, R. A. W. (Eds) (1992a). *Policy networks in British government*. Oxford: Clarendon Press.

Martin, S. T. (2002). Tourism a tough sell, but the Prince is trying. *St Petersburg Times*, 21 July, www.sptimes.com/2002/webspecials02/saudiarabia/day1/story2.shtml

Mathews, H. G. (1975). Annals of tourism research. *International Tourism and Political Science Research*, 195–203.

Mathews, H. G. (1983). Editor's page on: tourism and political science. *Annals of Tourism Research, 10* (4), 303.

Maxwell, H. (Ed.) (1958). *The Railway Magazine, Miscellany*. London: Allen and Unwin.

Maythew, S. (Ed.) (1997). A dictionary of geography. Oxford: Oxford University Press.

Mercer, T. (2001). Personal communication. Inverness, 25 September.

Middleton, V. T. C., & Hawkins, R. (1998). *Sustainable tourism: A marketing perspective*. Oxford: Butterworth-Heinemann.

Mike's Railway History (2002). The way it was in 1935, www.mikes.railhistory.railfan.net

Mill, R. C., & Morrison, A. M. (1985). *The tourism system: an introductory text*. Englewood Cliffs: Prentice-Hall International.

Mills, S. (2002). *EU member states urged to adopt critical reform on tourism*. World Travel and Tourism Council.

Millett, M. (2002). Alarm bells as tourism falls into black hole, 3 September, www.smh.com.au/articles/2002/09/03/1030953437450.html

Ministry of Tourism (1982). *A national policy on tourism*. Calcutta: Government of India.

Ministry of Tourism (2001). A draft national tourism development policy. Government of India, aseansec.org Calcutta, www.fhrai.com/LatestIndustryNews/Tourism_policy_draft.htm

Ministry of Tourism and Culture (1992). National action plan for tourism. Calcutta: Government of India.

Ministry of Tourism and Culture (2002). National tourism policy 2002. Department of Tourism, Government of India, www.fhrai.com/LatestIndustryNews/Tour_Policy.htm

Mitchell, J. (1995). Unionism, assimilation and the conservatives, British territorial politics. *Contemporary Policy Studies*, 3, 1376–1383. University of Strathclyde.

Mitchell, J. (1996). New labour and devolution: From unitary state to union state: Labour's changing view of the United Kingdom and its implications. *Contemporary Policy Studies*, 564–572. University of Strathclyde.

Moore, C., & Boothe, S. (1989). Managing competition: Meso-corporatism, pluralism, and the negotiated order in Scotland. Oxford: Oxford University Press.

Morgan, K., Rees, G., & Garmise, S. (1999). Networking for Local Economic Development, The New Management of British Local Governance (Editor Stoker G), Macmillan, London 181–196 ISBN 0 333 72816 5.

Mullins, L. J. (1996). *Management and organisational behaviour* (4th ed.). London: Pitman Publishing.

Muqbil, I. (2001). The future of tourism. *Travel Impact Newswire*, Bangkok, www.asiatraveltips.com

Nakamura, R. (1987). The textbook policy process and implementation research. *Policy Studies Review*, 7 (2), Autumn, 142–154.

National Assembly for Wales (2000). *Achieving our potential*. Cardiff: TSO.

National Assembly for Wales (2002). *Achieving our potential — A tourism strategy for Wales*. Cardiff: TSO.

National Assembly for Wales (2002). *National action plan*. Cardiff.

National Committee on Tourism (1988). *Seventh plan 1899–1992*. Calcutta: Government of India.

National Committee on Tourism (1992). *Eighth plan 1992–1997*. Calcutta: Government of India.

National Statistics (2002). www.statistics.gov.uk/pdfdir/rgv1102.pdf.

Naysmith, S. (2002). Tourist chiefs should be sacked, says Ryanair boss after low-cost deal fails. *Sunday Herald*, 22 September, 4.

Nicolson, S. (2002). Spain leads way in Europe's mish-mash of devolved power. *Business AM*.

Northern Ireland Tourist Board (1993). *A sustainable approach*.

Northern Ireland Tourist Board (1995). *A development strategy 1995 to 2000*.

Northern Ireland Tourist Board (2002). *NITB draft corporate plan 2002–2005*. Belfast.

OECD (1997). Tourism Policy and International Tourism in OECD Member Countries, Science, Technology and Industry, Industry Issues, www.oecd.org/pdf/M000014000/M00014901.pdf

OECD (2002). Performance of OECD tourism policies, Science, Technology and Industry, Industry Issues,www.oecd.org/EN/document/0,,EN-document-53-1-no-21-16433-53,00.html

Office of Travel and Tourism Industries (2001). *Forecast of International Travel to the United States, estimates in thousands*. The U.S. Trade and Development Department.

O'Maolin, C. (2000). *North-South co-operation on tourism. A mapping study*. The Centre for Cross Border Studies, 14 June, http://www.crossborder.ie/maptour.html

Pant, R. D. (2002). *The sick budget*. The Kathmandu Post, Kantipur Publications, Kathmandu, 21 January, Magh 08 2058, www.nepalnews.com.np/contents/englishdaily/ktmpost/2002/jan/jan21/features1.htm

Pantin, D. (1995). A Policy Framework and Action Plan for Sustainable Economic Development in Small Caribbean Islands, Department of Economics, UWI, St. Augustine, Trinidad and Tobago, Draft paper for ECLAC meeting 17–19 May, on Implementation of the SIDS Programme of Action. www.tidco.co.tt/local/seduweb/research/dennisp/eclacsid.htm

Paterson, L., Brown, A., Curtice, J., Hinds, K., McCrone, D., Park, A., & Surridge, P. (2001). *New Scotland, new politics?* Edinburgh: Edinburgh University Press.

Paton, N., & Golding, C. (2002). Government bid to stamp out poor standards. *Caterer and Hotelkeeper*, 28 November, 4.

Pearce, D. G. (1988). Tourism and regional development in the European Community. *Tourism Management*, *9* (1), 13–22.

Peterkin, T. (2002). Scottish economy in recession for the first time in 20 years. *The Daily Telegraph*, 8 August 2002.

Peters, T. J., & Waterman, R. H. (1988). *In search of excellence*. New York: Warner Books, ISBN: 0446385077.

Peterson, J. (1995). Policy networks and European Union policy making: a reply to Kassin. *Western European Politics*, *18*, 389–407. In: P. John (Ed.), *Analysing public policy* (1999). London: Pinter.

Phelps, E. (2000). Financial Times, Europe's stony ground for the seeds of growth: Continental nations must cast off corporatism if they are to emulate thriving economies, 9 August, www.nejtillemu.com/phelps.htm

Philip's (1998). *Illustrated atlas of the world*. London: Guild Publishing.

Phillips, D., & Thomas, C. (2001). The Effects of Tourism on the Welsh Language in North-East Wales, Canolfan Uwchefrydiau Cymreig a Cheltaidd Prifysgol Cymru, University of Wales, Centre for Advanced Welsh and Celtic Studies.

Picard, M., & Wood, R. E. (Eds) (1997). *Tourism, ethnicity and the state in Asian and Pacific societies*. Honolulu: University of Hawaii Press.

Pierre, J., & Peters, B. G. (2000). *Governance, politics and the state*. Basingstoke, Hants: Macmillan.

Pizam, A., & Mansfield, Y. (Eds) (1996). *Tourism, crime and international security issues*. Chichester: Wiley.

Press Information Bureau (2002). New Tourism Policy, Milestones, October, www.pib.nic.in/archieve/ppinti/milestones2002/milestones_02_tourism_culture.html

Preston, P. W. (1996). *Development theory: An introduction*. Oxford: Blackwell.

Public Opinion (2000). sfu.edu/amerpol/lectures5.htm

Pyper, R., & Robins, L. (Eds) (2000). *United Kingdom governance*. Basingstoke, Hants: Macmillan.

Rafferty, N., & McSherry M. (2002). They're off. *The Sunday Times, Focus*, 29 December, 13.

Reid, D. (2001). *The current state of Scottish tourism considered*. University of Abertay, Dundee, 28 June.

Republic of Ireland Government (1987). *National development plan 1988–1993*. Dublin.

Republic of Ireland Government (1993). *Community support framework 1999*. Dublin.

Republic of Ireland Government (1993). *National development plan 1994–1999*. Dublin.

Republic of Ireland Government (1999). *National development Plan 2000–2006*. Dublin.

Republic of Ireland Government (2002). Failte Ireland Bill, the new National Tourism Development Authority, Dublin 19th November.

Rhodes, R. A. W. (1997). Shackling the leader? Coherence, capacity and the hollow crown. In: P. Weller, H. Bakvis, & R. A. W. Rhodes (Eds), *The hollow crown, countervailing trends in core executives*. London: Macmillan.

Rhodes, R. A. W. (1999). Understanding governance, policy networks, governance, reflexivity and accountability. Buckingham: Open University Press.

Riewoldt, O. (1998). *Hotel design*. London: Laurence King Publishing.

Ritchie, M. (2002). Foreign investment in U.K. drops 77%. £27bn shortfall prompts call for adoption of single currency. *The Herald*, 29 October, 6.

Roethlisberger, F. J., & Dickson, W. J. (1996). Management and the worker, Harvard University Press. In: L. J. Mullins (Ed.), *Management and organisational behaviour* (4th ed.). Pitman Publishing, London.

Sabatier, P. (1987). Knowledge, policy-orientated learning, and policy change: an advocacy coalition framework. *Knowledge: Creation, Diffusion, Utilization*, 1.

Sabatier, P. A. (Ed.) (1999). Theories of the policy process, theoretical lenses on public policy. Boulder, Colorado: Westview Press.

Sabatier, P., & Jenkins-Smith, H. C. (Eds) (1993). Policy change and learning, an advocacy coalition approach. Boulder, Colorado: Westview Press.

Satchell, A. (2002). Resorts act to raise accommodation quality — Key resorts promote inspected only accommodation schemes, Quality Matters, British Hospitality Association, Issue 31, October, pp. 10–12.

Satour (1999). Launch of Tourism Action Plan, Tourism SA Media releases, September, www.tourism.org.za/media/releases/newsmessages/16.html

Satour (1999). Projected South African Tourism Growth 1997–2002, from the Tourism Action Plan, September.

Saudi Embassy.net (2000). Commission for Tourism Established 17 April, www.saudiembassy.net/press_release/00_spa/04-17-econ.html

Schattschneider, E. E. (1960). The semi-sovereign people. New York: Holt, Rinehart & Winston.

Schmitter, P. (1979). Still the century of corporatism. In: P. Schmitter, & G. Lembruch (Eds), *Trends Towards Corporatist Intermediation*. London: Sage Publications.

Scotland on Sunday (1999). 12 December.

Scotexchange (1999). *Average spends*. December, www.scotexchange.net

Scotexchange (2001). August, www.scotexchange.net

Scotsman, the (1999). Edinburgh 19 May.

Scott, J. (2001). The Impact of Scottish devolution on the U.K. Business Community, ACCA, The Association of Chartered Certified Accountants, www.acca.co.uk/publications/corpsecrev/29/24626.

Scottish Affairs Committee (1999). Commons Report, the Stationery Office, London.

Scottish Crofting Foundation (1987). Edgeland, www.Scu.co.uk

Scottish Enterprise Network (1996). *Tourism action plan*. Glasgow: SEN.

Scottish Executive (1999). Making it work together: A programme for government, www.scotland.gov.uk/library2/doc03/miwt-00.htm

Scottish Executive (2000). Scottish Economic Report, Edinburgh, SE/00/4/2000.

Scottish Executive (2003). Building Better Cities, 8 January.

Scottish Executive (2003). Enterprise and Lifelong Learning Committee: Final Report on Lifelong Learning Response from The Executive laid before the Scottish Parliament by Scottish Ministers on 12 February 2003, SE No SE/2003/64.

Scottish Executive Education Department (2002). Organisation Chart, www.scotland.gov.uk/library5/education/edorg.pdf

Scottish Executive Education Department (Tourism) (2002). The steps necessary to achieve positive change for the industry: Tourism Framework for Action 2002:2005, Department of Tourism, Culture and Sport, The Stationery Office, Edinburgh.

Scottish Executive Education Department (Tourism) (2002). *Tourism framework for action 2002:2005.* Edinburgh: Department of Tourism, Culture and Sport, The Stationery Office.

Scottish Executive Enterprise and Lifelong Learning Department (1999). A new strategy for Scottish tourism [a consultation document dated July 1999, responses by 31 August 1999], www.scotland.gov.uk/library2/doc02/stbcd-00.htm

Scottish Executive Enterprise and Lifelong Learning Department (1999). Consultation: The Way Forward — Framework for Economic Development in Scotland, Glasgow, September.

Scottish Executive Enterprise and Lifelong Learning Department (1999). Analysis and background: The way forward — Framework for economic development in Scotland. Glasgow, November.

Scottish Executive Enterprise and Lifelong Learning Department (1999). *Draft — A new strategy for Scottish tourism.* Edinburgh, November.

Scottish Executive Enterprise and Lifelong Learning Department, the Scottish Executive (1999). *Objectives for Scottish tourism. Draft — A new strategy for Scottish tourism.* Edinburgh, November.

Scottish Executive Enterprise and Lifelong Learning Department (2000). *A new strategy for Scottish tourism.* The Stationery Office, Edinburgh, February, ISBN 0 7480 9328 1.

Scottish Executive Enterprise and Lifelong Learning Department (2000). *Highlights from a new strategy for Scottish tourism. A new strategy for Scottish tourism.* The Stationery Office, Edinburgh, February, ISBN 0 7480 9328 1.

Scottish Executive Enterprise and Lifelong Learning Department (2000). Modernising the enterprise networks, the interim conclusions of the enterprise networks review. Edinburgh.

Scottish Executive Enterprise and Lifelong Learning Department (2000). The FEDS Implementation Process, The Way Forward — Framework for Economic Development in Scotland, SE/2000/58, the Stationery Office, Edinburgh.

Scottish Executive Enterprise and Lifelong Learning Department (2000). The Way Forward — Framework for Economic Development in Scotland, SE/2000/58, the Stationery Office, Edinburgh.

Scottish Executive Enterprise and Lifelong Learning Department (2001). *A smart, successful Scotland. Ambitions for the enterprise networks.* Edinburgh.

Scottish Executive Enterprise and Lifelong Learning Department (2001). *Goals and objectives, a smart, successful Scotland. Ambitions for the enterprise networks.* Edinburgh.

Scottish Executive Enterprise and Lifelong Learning Department (2002). *Global connections strategy.* Edinburgh: The Scottish Executive.

Scottish Executive Enterprise and Lifelong Learning Department (2002). *Goals and objectives, global connections strategy.* Edinburgh: The Scottish Executive.

Scottish Executive, Enterprise and Lifelong Learning Department (2003). Measuring progress towards a smart, successful Scotland 2003, 26 March.

Scottish Executive News Release (2000). Henry McLeish launches Strategy for 21st century tourism industry, SE0362/2000, 16th February.

Scottish Executive News Release (2001). Wendy Alexander welcomes VisitScotland new Chief Executive, SE1021/2001, 19th April.

Scottish Executive News Release (2001). SE1029/2001, 20th April.

Scottish Executive News Release (2001). Scotland United in tourism goals, SE4374/2001, 19th November.

Scottish Executive Tourism Team, Scottish Tourism (2003). A Progress Report. First Progress Report on the Tourism Framework for Action, March.

Scottish Office (1982). *The Local Government (Scotland) Act.* Edinburgh: HMSO.

Scottish Office (1984). *Tourism (Overseas Promotion) (Scotland) Act.* Edinburg: HMSO.

Scottish Office (1988). Scottish Enterprise: A New Approach to Training and Enterprise Creation, white paper, the Secretary of State for Scotland, Edinburgh.

Scottish Office (1989). Scottish Enterprise: A New Approach to Training and Enterprise Creation, the Secretary of State for Scotland, Edinburgh.

Scottish Office (1990). *The 1990 Enterprise and New Towns Act (1990).* Edinburg: The Stationery Office.

Scottish Office News Release (1998). Devolution, Dewar issues guidance on concordats between Scottish Executive and U.K. departments, 27 February.

Scottish Parliament Public Information Service (2001). *Business influencing devolved powers, the path to devolution* (2nd ed.), March.

Scottish Parliament Public Information Service (2001). *Devolved powers, the path to devolution* (2nd ed.), March.

Scottish Parliament Public Information Service (2001). *Reserved powers, the path to devolution* (2nd ed.), March.

Scottish Parliament Public Information Service (2001). *Reserved tourism powers, the path to devolution* (2nd ed.), March.

Scottish Parliament Public Information Service (2001). *The path to devolution* (2nd ed.), March.

Scottish Tourism Co-ordinating Group (1992). *Tourism and the Scottish environment.* Edinburgh: STCG.

Scottish Tourism Co-ordinating Group (1994). *Scottish tourism strategic plan.* Edinburgh: STCG.

Scottish Tourism Co-ordinating Group (1997). *Scottish tourism strategic plan, progress report.* Edinburgh: STCG.

Scottish Tourism Forum (1999). Council Meeting, Agenda Item 5, Debriefing report, 4 August, Edinburgh.

Scottish Tourism Forum (1999). Extract from Strategy Document, Edinburgh.

Scottish Tourist Board (1998). Policy and Financial Management Review, Prior Options Study (PFMR POS), Final Report, Edinburgh.

Scottish Tourist Board (2000). Signpost, Summer, Issue 21, Edinburgh.

Scottish Tourist Board (2000). Scottish Tourist Board Management Review, Report and Recommendations, PriceWaterhouseCoopers, Edinburgh, October.

Sectur (2002). Argentina Tourismo, Department of Tourism and Sports, www.sectur.gov.ar

Sessa, A. (1984). Comments on Peter Gray's the contributions of economics to tourism. *Annals of Tourism Research, 11,* 283–286.

Settle, M. (2002). Tourism chiefs kept in the dark: Scotland could lose out under new plans to promote the U.K. *The Herald,* 27 November: 2.

Shenoy, T. V. R. (1997). *The Kerala model is an abject failure.* November, www.ask.co.uk/metasearch.

Simon, J. (2002). Glowing prospects for Saudi tourism: Saudi Arabia's profile as a tourist destination is growing as government and private sector efforts begin to pay off. *Saudi Arabia Review, 19* (8), August, www.ttnworldwide.com/bkArticlesF.asp?Article=1752&Section=228&IssueID=213

Simmons A. M. (2002). South African bargains drawing world of tourists. Published in the Milwaukee Journal Sentinel, 3 April 2002 Los Angeles Times.

Sivitier, R. (1984). *The Settle to Carlisle: A tribute.* London: Bloomsbury Books.

Skapinker, M. (1998). Air travel. *Financial Times,* 18 June, London.

Smith, R. (1998). Public policy for tourism in Scotland. In: R. MacLellan, & R. Smith (Eds), *Tourism in Scotland* (pp. 42–69). London: International Thomson Business Press.

Smith, S. (1997). Ministerial membership of Scottish Office 1970–1997, Keele University, 25 May, www.psr.keele.ac.uk/table/york/Scottish.html

Stamp, G. (2002). Watson's ultimatum to hotels and B&Bs: Get up to standard or faced being closed down, warns minister. *Business AM,* 3 December: 3.

Star U.K. (1999). Tourism facts and figures, December, www.staruk.org.uk

Star U.K. (2000). Tourism facts and figures, December, www.staruk.org.uk

Stationery Office, the (1931). The Tourism Traffic (Development). Act Irish government publication, Dublin.

Stationery Office, the (1939). *Holiday with Pay Act (1939)*. London.

Stationery Office, the (1948). *Development of Tourism Traffic Act (N Ireland)*. Dublin: Irish government publication.

Stationery Office, the (1958). *Programme for economic expansion*. Dublin: Irish government publication.

Stationery Office, the (1969). *Development of Tourism Act (1969)*. London.

Stationery Office, the (1972). *Tourist Traffic (Northern Ireland)*. Dublin: Order Irish government publication.

Stationery Office, the (1982). *The Local Government (Scotland). Act*. Edinburgh: The Scottish Office.

Stationery Office, the (1992). The Tourism (Northern Ireland). Order, Statutory Instrument 1992 No. 235 (N.I. 3), Belfast, www.hmso.gov.uk/si/si1992/Uksi_19920235_en_1.htm

Stationery Office, the (1994). *Operational programme for tourism 1994–1999*. Dublin: Irish government publication.

Stationery Office, the (1998). *The Government of Wales Act 1998*. Cardiff: The Stationery Office.

Stationery Office, the (1998). *The Scotland Act*. Edinburgh: The Scottish Office, HMSO.

Stationery Office, the (1998). *The Northern Ireland Act*. Dublin: Irish government publication, ISBN 0 10 544798 6.

Stationery Office, the (1999). Objective 1 Single Programming Document for the Period: 2000–2006 for Wales, Cardiff, www.archive.official-documents.co.uk/cgi-bin/htm_hl?DB=off-

STCG/SE/HIE/STB (1999). *Scottish tourism strategic plan interim review*. Edinburgh: The Stationery Office.

Stevens, T., & Scottish Tourism Research Unit, University of Strathclyde (2002). Support for Tourism: An International Comparison (Reference No. 030102EL), Stevens and Associates, on behalf of the Enterprise and Lifelong Learning Committee, Scottish Parliament, Edinburgh.

Stillman, P. G. (1974). Ecological problems, political theory, and public policy. In: S. Nagel (Ed.), *Environmental politics* (pp. 49–60). New York: Praeger Publishers.

Structures and Features of the Political System (2000). www.sfu.edu/amerpol/lectures5.htm

Sunday Herald, the (2002). Glasgow, 16 June.

TAB (1997). Summary of TAB working report No. 52, Tourism — trends and impacts, Office of Technology Assessment at the German Parliament, www.tab.fzk.de/en/projekt/zusammenfassung/ Textab52.htm

Teo, P., Chang, T. C., & Ho, K. C. (2001). *Interconnected worlds, tourism in southeast Asia*. Oxford: Pergamon.

Thatcher, M. (1995). *The path to power*. London: Harper Collins.

Theobald, W. F. (Ed.) (1998). *The meaning, scope and measurement of travel and tourism, in global tourism* (2nd ed). Oxford: Butterworth-Heinemann.

Theodoulou, S. Z., & Cahn, M. A. (Eds) (1995). *Public policy: The essential readings*. New York: Prentice-Hall.

Thurso, Viscount. (1999). Viewpoint. *Caterer and Hotelkeeper*, London, 11 March.

Tinbergen, J. (1995). *The Oxford Companion to Philosophy* (edited by T. Honderisch). Oxford: Oxford University Press.

Tourism Industry Professionals Site (TIPS) (2002). Market Intelligence BTA, Key Tourism Facts www.ips.bta.org.uk/viewpage

Tourism Society, the (1989). *Implications of the 1989 tourism review. A memorandum to the Department of Employment*. London: The Tourism Society.

Tourism Training Scotland (1998). *Straight to business*. Edinburgh: TTS.

Tuplin, W. A. (1963). *North Western steam*. London: George Allen and Unwin Ltd.

UK Government, Republic of Ireland (1998). *Good Friday Agreement*, 10 April, www.nio.gov.uk/issues/agreement.htm

UK Law Line (2002). www.uklawline.co.uk

UKTS, IPS. (1999). Enterprise and Lifelong Learning Department, the Scottish Executive. Draft — A New Strategy for Scottish Tourism. Edinburgh.

United Kingdom Parliament (197/72). House of Commons, col. 1454, from Elliott: Tourism, politics and public sector management. London: Routledge.

United Kingdom Parliament, the (2002). *The Finance Bill*, 23 April.

Universal Dictionary (1994). *Reader's Digest*. London.

United States Council of State Governments (1979). Tourism: State structure, organisations and support. Lexington, KY: The Council.

USA Congress (1977). *Senate committee on commerce, service and transportation, ascertainment phase: National tourism policy study*. Washington, DC: U.S. Government Printing Office.

USA Congress (1978). Senate committee on commerce, service and transportation, final report: National tourism policy study. Washington, DC: U.S. Government Printing Office.

USA Government (1974). *International Travel Act*. Washington, DC: U.S. Government Printing Office.

USA Government (1981). *National Tourism Policy Act*.Washington, DC: U.S. Government Printing Office.

USA Government (1984). *National study on trade and services*. Washington, DC: U.S. Government Printing Office.

U.S.–USSR Trade and Economic Council Journal of the U.S.-USSR Trade and Economic Council (1986). Vol. 2, No. 4.

Vigdorchik, M. (1998). Financial Crisis Changes Structure of Travel and Tourism Business in Russia, Business Information Service for the Newly Independent States (BISNIS), Moscow.

VisitScotland (2000). The official web site of VisitScotland, www.visitscotland.co.uk (2000). August.

VisitScotland (2002). *Report and accounts 2001–2002*, Edinburgh.

VisitScotland (2002). Scottish Tourism Revenue 1997–2001 under both the old and new UKTS system, Tourism in Scotland 2001, Research Department, VisitScotland.

VisitScotland (2002). *Signpost, New voice for tourism, 33*, November/December: 3.

VisitScotland (2002). *Tourism in Scotland 2001*. Research Department, VisitScotland.

VisitScotland (2002). *Volume and value of tourism in Scotland 1997–2001*. Tourism in Scotland 2001, Research Department, VisitScotland.

Wales Tourist Board (1993). Tourism: Draft Strategy for Wales, Cardiff.

Wales Tourist Board (1998). A consultative paper. Communication in the Tourism Industry in Wales — The Regional Challenge, July.

Walker B. (2002). Tourist bodies to merge next year. *Caterer and Hotelkeeper, 7*, November, 5.

Wanhill, S. R. C. (1987). U.K.-politics and tourism. *Tourism Management, 8* (1). 54–58.

Wanhill, S. (1998). 'The Role of Government Incentives'. In: W. F. Theobald (Ed.), *Global tourism* (2nd ed., pp. 339–360). Oxford: Butterworth-Heinemann.

Webb, H. (1972). Maniffesto Cymdeithas yr Iaith Gymraeg Aberystwyth, p. 40. Cymdeithas yr Iaith. the Manifesto, Planet, 26/27 (1974.5), 136.

Weiler, B. (2002). Tourism Research and Theories: A review: 82–93. In: A. Lockwood, & S. Medlik (Eds), *Tourism and hospitality in the 21st century* (2002). Oxford: Butterworth-Heinemann.

Weir, D. G. J. (1999). Devolution for Scotland, The Scottish Budget and the Barnett Formula, abel.co.uk/~febl/Barnett.html

Welsh Office, the (1988). Framework Development Strategy (1988).

Welsh Office, the (1994). *Tourism 2000, a strategy for Wales*. Cardiff: TSO.

Welsh Office, the (1998). *Pathway to prosperity*. Cardiff: TSO.

Welsh Office, the (1998). *The Government of Wales Act 1998*. Cardiff: TSO.

Williams A. M., & Shaw G. (Eds) (1988b). *Tourism and economic development: Western European experiences*. London: Belhaven Press.

Williams, A. M., & Shaw, G. (1988c). Tourism and development introduction. In: A. M. Williams, & G. Shaw (Eds), *Tourism and economic development: Western european experiences* (1988c, pp. 1–11). London: Bellhaven Press.

Wilson, D. (1997). Tourism, public policy and the image of Northern Ireland since the troubles. In: B. O'Connor, & M. Cronin (Eds), *Tourism in Ireland*. Dublin: Tower Books.

Wilson, I. (1998). The one unwelcome visitor. *The Herald*, Glasgow, 8 December, p. 10.

Wilson, I. (2001). *The Herald*, 21 November.

Wood, R. C. (1996). The last featherbedded industry? Government, politics and the hospitality industry during and after the 1992 General Election. *Tourism Management, 17* (8).

Woods, C., Roberts, D., & Sim, H. (2000). Taking a Cluster Approach to Tourism, Scottish Enterprise Board Paper, SE (00). 88, Scottish Enterprise Knowledge Management Team, Glasgow.

World Information (2002). The World at your fingertips www.worldinformation.com

World Tourism Organisation (WTO) (1995). Madrid: Agenda 21 for the Travel and Tourism Industry: Towards environmentally Sustainable Development, available from Agency Section. London: The Stationery Office, June.

World Tourism Organisation (1997). World Tourism Organisation. *Yearbook of Tourism Statistics*. Madrid: WTO.

World Tourism Organisation (1998). World Tourism Organisation. *Yearbook of Tourism Statistics*. Madrid: WTO.

World Tourism Organisation (1999). World Tourism Organisation. *Yearbook of Tourism Statistics*. Madrid: WTO.

World Tourism Organisation (2000). Tourism 2020 Vision, Madrid; World Tourism Organisation. Madrid: WTO.

World Tourism Organisation (2001). www.world-tourism.org/

World Tourism Organisation (2002). *International Arrivals % Change. January to August, September to December*. Madrid.

World Tourism Organisation (2002). *International Arrivals % Change*. Madrid.

World Tourism Organisation (2002). *International Tourism Arrivals*. Madrid:WTO.

World Tourism Organisation (2002). *International Tourism Receipts by Sub Region*. Madrid, June.

World Tourism Organisation (2002). *International Tourism Receipts, Market Share by Region 2001*. Madrid.

World Tourism Organisation (2002). *International Tourist Arrivals 2001 — Regional Trends*. Madrid.

World Tourism Organisation (2002). *The World's Top Five Destinations*. Madrid, January.

World Tourism Organisation (2002). *World International Tourist Arrivals (% change)*. Madrid.

World Tourism Organisation (2002). *World International Tourist Arrivals (volume)*. Madrid.

World Tourism Organisation (2002). *World's Top 15 Tourism Destinations*. Madrid, June.

World Tourism Organisation (2002). *World's Top 15 Tourism Earners*. Madrid, June.

World Tourism Organisation (2002). WTO Tourism 2020 Vision. WTO Forecasts 2000. Forecast Change in the Share of International Tourism Arrivals between Developed and Developing Regions, Madrid.

World Tourism Organisation (2002). www.world-tourism.org/

World Travel Guide (2002). www.worldtravelguide.net

World Travel and Tourism Council (1998). Research and Statistical Data, Projections for Economic and Employment Growth, www.wttc.com

World Travel and Tourism Council (1999). Research and Statistical Data, www.wttc.com

World Travel and Tourism Council (2002). Research and Statistical Data, www.wttc.com

World Travel and Tourism Council (2002). The World: The Impact of Travel and Tourism on Jobs and the Economy — 2002 plus Special Report on September 11th Impacts, www.wttc.org/impact/specialreport_World.pdf

World Travel Tourism Council (2002). Tourism Satellite Account (TSA). Estimates and Forecasts.

World Travel and Tourism Council (2002). Travel Business Roundtable 19 March, www.tbr.org/indx0102.htm

Youell, R. (1998). *Tourism, an introduction*. Essex: Longman.

Young, A. (2002). Autonomy remains a taxing problem for our politicians. *The Herald*, 22 November: 20.

Further Reading

Amin, A., & Thrift, N. (1994). Living in the Global. In: A. Amin, & N. Thrift (Eds), *Globalisation, institutions and regional development in Europe* (pp. 1–22). Oxford: Oxford University Press.

Anderson, P. (1976). *Considerations on western Marxism*. London: New Left Review Books.

Argentine Republic Tourism Hotels Association (2002). *What is AHT?* www.aht.com.ar/2001/eng/institucional/queeslaaht.htm

Bailey, K. D. (1978). *Methods of social research*. New York: Free Press.

Bannock, G., Baxter, R. E., & Davis, E. (1998). The Penguin Dictionary of Economics. London.

Barron, G., Kerr, W. R., & Wood, R. (2001). *Arguing for and against tourism taxation: Insights from the Scottish context*. Glasgow: The University of Strathclyde. Manuscript unpublished.

Baybeck, B., & Huckfeldt, R. (2000). Urban Networks, Urban Contexts, and the Diffusion of Political Information, Brady Baybeck, Harvard University, Robert Huckfeldt, Indiana University, Paper prepared for presentation at New Methodologies for the Social Sciences: The Development and Application of Spatial Analysis for Political Methodology, Boulder, Colorado, March 10–12.

Becker, G. (1976). *The economic approach to human behaviour*. Chicago: University of Chicago Press.

Bennington, J., & Harvey, J. (1994). Spheres or Tiers? The significance of transnational local authority networks. Conference paper, PSA Annual Conference, University of Swansea, March, pp. 29–31.

Benson, J. K. (1982). A framework for policy analysis. In: D. Rogers, & D. Whiten & Associates (Eds), *Interorganisation co-ordination, Ames*. Iowa: Iowa State University Press.

Bentley, A. (1908). *The process of government*. Chicago: University of Chicago Press.

BHA (1997). *Annual Report*. London: British Hospitality Association.

BHA (1998). *Members' Yearbook*. London: British Hospitality Association.

BHA (1999). *Members' Yearbook 1999*. London: British Hospitality Association.

BHA (2001). *Response to Strategy Review*. Edinburgh: British Hospitality Association, Scotland Committee, 14 September.

Bhaskar, R. (1975). A Realist Theory of Science, Leeds Books, London (2nd edition published by Verso (London), 1997), ISBN 1-85984-103-1.

Black, J. A., & Champion, D. J. (1976). *Methods and issues in social research*. New York: John Wiley and Sons.

Black, L., & Kerr, W. R. (1999). *Tourism in Ayrshire, from Scottish affairs committee, inquiry into tourism in Scotland*. London: The Stationery Office.

Blaug, M. (1992), *The methodology of economics, and how economists explain* (2nd ed.). Cambridge: Cambridge University Press.

Brown, L. B. (1973). *Ideology*. Harmondsworth: Penguin.

Bryman, A. (1988). *Quantity and quality in social research*. London: Unwin Hyman.

Buchanan, D., Boddy, D., & McCalman, J. (1988). Getting in, Getting on, Getting out and Getting back. In: A. Bryman (Ed.), *Doing research in organisations*. London: Routledge.

Catan, T. (2002). Patagonia tourism reaps benefits of peso devaluation. FT.Com Financial Times, March 26. www.news.ft.com/ft/gx.cgi/ftc?

Clandinin, D. J., & Connelly, F. M. (1994). In: N. K. Denzin, & Y. S. Lincoln (Eds), *Handbook of qualitative research* (pp. 418–424). California: Sage.

Crandall, L. (1994). The social impact of tourism on developing regions and its measurement. In: J. R. Brent Ritchie, & C. R. Goeldner (Eds), *Travel tourism and hospitality research. A handbook for managers and researchers*. New York: John Wiley and Sons.

Cunningham, F. (2000). Overview of Tourism Infrastructure Industry, International Marketing Insight. www.tradeport.org/ts/countries/ireland/mrr/ma

Darling, R. (1998). Tourism Industry Support: An Evaluation of Tourism Fora in Lowland Scotland, Dissertation for SAC Auchincruive/University of Glasgow.

Davidson, T. L. (1998). What are Travel and Tourism: Are they really an industry? In: W. Theobald (Ed.), *Global tourism* (2nd ed., pp. 22–28). Butterworth-Heinemann. Oxford.

Deaton, A., & Muellbauer, J. (1989). *Economics and consumer behaviour*. Cambridge: Cambridge University Press.

Department of Employment (1991). *Tourism and the environment: Maintaining the balance*. London.

Department of the Environment (DOE) (1991). Government Task Force, Tourism and the Environment: Monitoring the Balance 1991.

Department of the Environment (DOE) (1992). Planning Policy Guidance Note no. 21, Planning and Tourism, HMSO 1992.

Department of the Environment (DOE) (1992). Tourism Task Force, Tourism in the U.K.: Realising the Potential, HMSO 1992.

Department of Environmental Affairs and Tourism (2000). Annual Review 2001–02, www.environment.gov.za/AR2001–02/visionmission_contents.htm

Department of National Heritage (1995). *Tourism: Competing with the best*. London.

Department of National Heritage (DNH) (1997). *Success through partnership: A strategy for tourism*. London.

Dey, I. (1993). *Qualitative data analysis*. London: Routledge.

Dorsey, K. (1999). *The Herald*, Glasgow 19 August: 21.

Dowding, K. (1995). Model or metaphor? A critical review of the policy network approach. *Political Studies*, *XLIII*, 136–158.

Easton, D. (1971). *The political system. An inquiry into the state of political science* (2nd ed., ch. 6). New York: Alfred. A. Knopf.

Edgell, D. L. (1983). United States International Tourism Policy. *Annals of Tourism Research*, *10* (3), 427–434.

Edgell, D. L. (1984). U.S. government policy on international tourism. *Tourism Management*, *5* (1), 67–70.

Edgell, D. L., Sr (1990). *Charting a course for international tourism in the nineties*. Washington, DC: U.S. Department of Commerce,.

English Tourism Council (2001). *Perspectives on English tourism*. January.

English Tourism Council (2001). *Time for action (strategy for sustainable tourism)*. April.

English Tourism Council (2002). *The work of the English tourism council and an executive summary of framework for action*. London.

English Tourist Board (1991). *Planning for success: A tourism strategy for England 1991–1996*. London.

Enterprise and Lifelong Learning Committee (2002). Scottish Parliament's Enterprise Committee Calls For Every Citizen To Have Standard Basic Entitlement To Learning, Cent 014/2002, 28 October, Committee News Release, Edinburgh.

European Commission (1990). Directive 90/314 on package travel; creating a Community legal framework for safety in tourist accommodation, and protection from overbooking in hotels.

European Commission (1994). Directive 94/47 on timeshare properties (Co decision procedure: COD0419), Brussels, 26 October.

European Commission (1996). Commission communication, COM(96)0547, European tourists' behaviour in developing countries, Brussels.

European Commission (1997). Resolution on the Commission communication on combating child sex tourism action against travel agencies, airlines and hotel chains that encourage child sex tourism, Brussels, 6 November.

Fisher, D. (1998). *Caterer and Hotelkeeper*. London, 1 October.

Frewin, A. (1999). *Caterer and Hotelkeeper*. London, 1 October.

Gabriel, Y., & Lang, T. (1995). *The unmanageable consumer. Contemporary consumption and its fragmentations*. London: Sage Publications.

Goldsmith, J. (1994). The New Utopia: Gatt and Global Free Trade, Federal Document Clearing House, Congressional Testimony Senate Commerce Gatt Implementation, 5th October.

Goymour, D. (1999). Refreshing changes, millennium hospitality. *Caterer and Hotelkeeper*, London, 23 December.

Grassie, J. (1983). Highland experiment: The story of the highlands and islands development board. Aberdeen: Aberdeen University Press.

Guerrier, Y. (1998). *Caterer and Hotelkeeper*, London, 1 October.

Gunn, C. A. (1988). *Tourism planning* (2nd ed.). New York: Taylor and Francis.

Hall, C. M., & Page, S. J. (1996). *Tourism in the Pacific: Issues and cases*. U.K.: International Thomson Business Press.

Heclo, H. (1974). *Modern social politics in Britain and Sweden*. New Haven: Yale University Press.

Henley Centre (1998). *Tourism futures: An update*. Glasgow: Scottish Enterprise.

Herald, the (1999). Glasgow 19 August: 21.

Herald, the (1999). Glasgow 19 December.

Herald, the (1999). Glasgow 20 December: 6.

Herald, the (2000). Glasgow, 2 May.

Herald, the (2001). Glasgow, 29 August.

Horsburgh, F. (1999). Cinderella joins the revolution. *The Herald*, 20 December, p. 6.

Hudson, R. (Ed.) (1993). *The Grand Tour*. London: The Folio Society.

Inglis, A. S. (2000). Implications of devolution for participatory forestry in Scotland, www.fao.org/docrep/x3030E/x3030e0b.htm

Internet Encyclopaedia of Philosophy, the (2002). http://www.utm.edu/research/iep/

Isaac, S., & Michael, W. B. (1971). *Handbook in research and evaluation*. San Diego, CA: Edits Publishers.

Jones, M., & Mcleod, G. (1999). Towards a regional renaissance? Reconfiguring and rescaling England's economic governance. *Transaction of the Institute of British Geographers*, 24 (3), 295–313.

Korsch, K. (1923). *Marxism and philosophy*. London, 1970.

Labour Party (1996). *Breaking new ground: Labour's strategy for the tourism and hospitality industry*. London.

Langlois, R. N. (Ed.) (1986). *Economics as a process. Essays in the new institutional economics*. Cambridge: Cambridge University Press.

Lasche, C. (1995). *The revolt of the elites and the betrayal of democracy*. New York: W. W. Norton & Company.

Leicester, G., & Peat, J. A. (2000). Scottish Council Foundation Economic Policy Network, Towards an economic policy for Scotland, The first report of the Scottish Council Foundation Economic Policy Network, Edinburgh.

Levy, (1995). In: A. McConnell (Ed.), *Issues of governance in Scotland, Wales and Northern Ireland* (2000). In: R. Pyper, & L. Robins (Eds), *United Kingdom governance*. Hampshire: Macmillan Press.

Library Association (2001). LA Policy Advisory Group Devolution and Regionalism in the U.K. Report of the La Policy Advisory Group, www.la-hq.org.uk/directory/prof_issues/reg0.html

Lijphart, A. (1977). *Democracy in plural societies*. Conneticut: New Haven.

Logie, J. (1998). *Caterer and Hotelkeeper*. London, 1 October.

Macaulay, I. R., & Wood, R. C. (1992). *Hard cheese: A study of hotel and catering employment in Scotland*. Glasgow: Scottish Low Pay Unit.

McLeod, M. (2001). *Scotland on Sunday*. 22 April: 1.

Maher, D. J. (1986). *The tortuous path: the course of Ireland's entry into the EEC 1948–73*. Dublin: Institute of Public Administration.

Manson, K., & Adams, I. (2001). *Sunday Times*. 22 April: 5.

Martin, L. L. (2001). Governance Patterns in Tourism: The Leverage of Economic Theories Department of Government, Harvard University, March.

Mepham, J., & Ruben, D. H. (Eds) (1979). *Issues in Marxist philosophy*. Brighton: Harvester.

Merrington, J. (1968). Theory and Practice in Gramsci's Marxism, in Western Marxism: A Critical Reader (Verso 1978), pp. 140–75.

Michels, J. (2000). New Links to Latin America Issue: August 14, 2000.

Ministry of Environment and Tourism (1999). Tourism Policy for Namibia, Draft Tourism Policy for Namibia, for Discussion, Windhoek, January.

Mitchell, B. (1979). *Geography and resource analysis*. London: Longman.

Muller, J. Z. (1993). *Adam Smith in his time and ours. Designing the decent society*. Princeton: Princeton University Press.

Munday, S. (2000). *Markets and market failure*. Oxford: Heinemann.

Murphy, P. (1985). *Tourism: A community approach*. New York and London: Methuen.

New Left Review (1977). *Western Marxism: A critical reader*. London.

Nicholls, D. (1977). The Pluralist State. The Political Ideas of J. N. Figgis and his Contemporaries, London, Basingstoke: Macmillan 1994, zweite Auflage 190 S.

Northern Ireland Tourist Board (1990). *Tourism in Northern Ireland: An indicative plan*. Belfast: NITB.

O'Connor, B., & Cronin, M. (Eds) (1997). *Tourism in Ireland*. Dublin: Tower Books.

OECD (2000). Measuring the Role of Tourism in OECD Economies, The OECD Manual of Tourism Satellite Accounts and Employment, Science, Technology and Industry, Industry Issues, 78 2000 02 1 P, ISBN 92-64-18500-3.

Page, S. (1999). *Transport and tourism*. Harlow, Essex: Addison Wesley Longman. ISBN 0-582-32025-9.

Page, S., Brunt, P., Busy, G., & Connell, J. (1999). *Tourism: A modern synthesis*. London WC1: Thomson Learning. ISBN 0-556-08222-5.

Page, S., & Goetz, D. (1998). The business of rural tourism. *Tourism Management, 19* (3).

Parkin, M. (1990). *Economics*. Reading: Addison-Wesley.

Philips, M. (1998). *Caterer and Hotelkeeper*. London, 1 October.

Pollit, C. (1984). *Manipulating the machine: Changing patterns of ministerial departments 1960–1983*. London: Allen and Unwin.

Randall, M. H. (1989). Perspectives on U.S.–Soviet joint ventures. *The CPA Journal Online*, July, www.nysscpa.org/cpajournal/1989/Features.

Rhodes, R. (1996). The new governance, Governing without government. *Political Studies, 44* (4), 652–657.

Rhodes, R. A. W. (1986a). *The national world of local government* (ch. 2). London: Allen and Unwin.

Rhodes, R. A. W. (1991a). *Local governance*. Swindon, ESRC.

Robson, C. (1993). *Real world research*. Oxford: Blackwell.

Robson McLean, W. S. (1999). The Scottish Parliament, an Overview, Articles and News. www.robson-mclean.co.ukscottish_devolution.htm, June.

Sabatier, P. A. (Ed.) (1999). *Theories of the policy process, theoretical lenses on public policy.* Boulder, Colorado: Westview Press.

School of Public Policy, Constitution Unit (2001). The Nations and Regions: The Dynamics of Devolution, The Leverhulme Trust, www.ucl.ac.uk/constitution-unit/leverh/index.htm

School of Public Policy, Constitution Unit (2002). The Nations and Regions: The Dynamics of Devolution, Second Annual Report, October 2000–September 2001, The Leverhulme Trust, F134/CH.

Scotsman (1999). Edinburgh, 9 February: 25.

Scottish Executive (1999). Concordat between Department for Culture, Media and Sport and the Scottish Executive, www.scotland.gov.uk/concordats/dcms-00.asp

Scottish Executive News Release (2001). SE4374/2001, 19 November.

Scottish Executive News Release (2002). Tourism blueprint points way ahead, SE5490/2002, 11 March.

Scottish Executive News Release (2002). Tourism review of visitor satisfaction, SEtc019/2002, 27 May.

Scottish Executive News Release (2002). Scottish Economic Report, SEet071/2002, 26 June.

Scottish Executive News Release (2002). Enterprise Committee Calls For Tourism Industry Views for New Parliamentary Inquiry, Cent 007/2002, 5 July.

Scottish Executive News Release (2002). BTA promises stronger Scots push overseas, 31 October.

Scottish Liberal Democrats (1999). *Scotland's tourist future — A policy paper for the new parliament.* Edinburgh.

Scottish National Party (1999). Saltire paper No. 5, Edinburgh.

Scottish Tourism Forum (1999). *Annual report.* Edinburgh.

Scottish Tourist Board Information Unit (1999). STB Board Composition (telephone enquiry), May, Edinburgh.

Scottish Tourist Board (2000). *Report & accounts 1999–2000.* Edinburgh.

Scottish Tourist Board (2000). *Signpost*, Summer, Issue 21. Edinburgh.

Seaton, A. (1998). The history of tourism in Scotland: Approaches, sources and issues. In: R. MacLellan, & R. Smith (Eds), *Tourism in Scotland* (pp. 1–41). Oxford: International Thomson Business Press.

Sessa, A. (1976). The tourism policy. *Annals of Tourism Research, 3* (5), 234–247.

Sky News (2001). Councils Veto Tourism Offensive, 8 April, www.sky.com/skynews/article/0,,15410-1010804,00.html

Sky News (2001). Blair Virus Spin Damaged Tourism, 8 August, www.sky.com/skynews/article/0,,15410-1062471,00.html

Smith, R. (1992). Tourism Administration in Scotland. *Quarterly Economic Commentary, 18* (2), 67. Fraser of Allander Institute.

Stationery Office, the (1972). *The accession of Ireland to the European Communities, Irish government publication.* Dublin: Stationery Office.

Stationery Office, the (1997). *Referendums (Scotland and Wales) Act.* London: HM Government.

Stationery Office, the (1998). *Government of Wales Act.* Cardiff: Welsh Office.

Stationery Office, the Northern Ireland (1998). *(Elections) Act.* Belfast: Northern Ireland Office.

Stationery Office, the (1998). *Northern Ireland Act.* Belfast: Northern Ireland Office.

Stationery Office, the (1998). *Regional Development Agencies Act.* London: HM Government.

Stationery Office, the (1998). *The Scotland Bill.* Edinburgh: The Scottish Office.

Steel, T. (1984). *Scotland's story.* London: Collins.

Sunday Times, the (1999). Glasgow, 8 August: 5.

TIANZ (2002). Key Facts and Figures about the New Zealand Tourism Industry Tourism Industry Association of New Zealand, www.tianz.org.nz/industry-facts/key-facts–Figures.asp

TIANZ (2002). Policies for a Sustainable Tourism Industry: Overview, Issues and policies for a sustainable Tourism Industry, Tourism Industry Association of New Zealand, www.tianz.org.nz/Policy/General-Policy-Principles.asp

Tourism Futures International (2002). Australian Bureau of Statistics/New Zealand Statistics www.tourismfuturesintl.com/tourismanalystnologin/2002/january/contentpage.html

Tourism SA Media Releases (1999). Launch of the Tourism Action Plan, September, www.tourism.org.za/media/releases/newsmessages/16.html

Tourism Society, the (2001). Action plan for the U.K. tourist industry. London: Tourism Society. August.

Travel Industry Association of America (1999). Launch of the tourism action plan, 16 September, Washington.

U.K. Government (2001). Tourism - the hidden giant - and foot and mouth: Government response to the fourth report from the Culture, Media and Sport Select Committee, Commons session 2000–2001, Cm 5279, TSO, October, ISBN: 0-10-152792-6.

United Kingdom Election Results (2002). www.election.demon.co.uk/ge1997.html

United Kingdom Tourism Survey 2001 (2002) www.statistics.gov.uk/cci/nscl.asp?ID=8257.

U.S. Commerce Department News Release (2002). Forecast: international travellers returning to the U.S. Travel and tourism industry continues to show steady improvement well into 2005, Victoria Park, 27 May.

Wales Tourist Board (1993). *The Wales Tourist Board 1988–1993*. Cardiff: WTB.

Washington Times, the (2002). Argentina. Administration focuses on creating Marca Argentina, a defining moment in Argentina's tourism market. A Special International Report prepared by the Washington Times Advertising Department, 13 June. www.internationalspecialreports.com/theamericas/00/argentina/11.html

Webster, J. (1989). *Tis better to travel*. Edinburgh: Mainstream Publishing.

Which Online (1998). Holiday Reports, www.which.net/holiday/reports/may, May.

Williams, A., & Shaw, G. (1991). *Tourism and economic development — Western European experiences*. London: Belhaven Press.

Wood, P. (1999). Key Sectors of the Scottish Economy. In: J. Peat, & S. Boyle (Eds), *An illustrated guide to the Scottish economy* (ch. 8). London: Gerald Duckworth and Company Ltd.

World Tourism Organization (2002). Tourism Recovery Already Underway, 16 March, www.world-tourism.org/

World Travel and Tourism Council (2000). Guide to Tax Policy Literature, June, www.wttc.traveltax.msu.edu

World Travel & Tourism Council (2002). The World: The Impact of Travel & Tourism on Jobs and the Economy — 2002 plus Special Report on September 11th Impacts.

Wright Mills, C. (1956). *The power elite*. Oxford: Oxford University Press.

Yin, R. K. (1994). *Case study research: Design and methods* (2nd ed.). Beverley Hills, California: Sage Publications.

Appendix

Table 1: The development of tourism in Scotland from 1965 to 2003.

Date	Political	Institutional	Tourism
1965		Formation of Highlands and Islands Development Board (HIDB).	Lowland Scotland tourism is operated mainly by eight regional councils and a voluntary association in Dumfries and Galloway.
			15 Local Tourist Associations established formally in the Highlands.
1966	Labour Government re-elected increased majority.		
1969	Development of Tourism Act.	STB established.	
		BTA established.	
1970	Conservatives come to power.		
1971	Decimal currency introduced.		
1972	UK signed the EEC Treaty.		The British Hotels Restaurants and Caterers Association (BHRCA) formed, replacing the British Hotels and Restaurants Association (BHRA).
1973	UK enters European Economic Community.		
	Local Government (Scotland) Act.		
1974	Labour comes to power in March, then goes to the polls again in October, and wins with a tiny majority.	Two-tiered local (53) and regional (9) councils were established including the massive Strathclyde Regional Council (SRC).	
		In tandem, the three island groupings of Orkney, Shetland, and the Western Isles, became single-tier, multi-purpose authorities.	
1975	Margaret Thatcher becomes Tory leader.	Scottish Development Agency (SDA) established.	
	Positive outcome for referendum on continued membership of European Common Market.	Voluntary system of Classification and Grading introduced.	
1979	Conservatives win election,		Taste of Scotland established.
	Thatcher becomes first woman Prime Minster.		
1982	Local Government (Scotland) Act gives lower tier District Councils a discretionary tourism function, leading to Lowland Scotland setting up ATBs in conjunction with STB.		32 Area Tourist Boards (ATBs) established.
1983	Conservatives re-elected.		
1984	Amendment to 1969 Tourism Act means STB can market Scotland abroad.		
1985	BTA becomes responsible to the Department of Employment (It had previously been responsible to the Department of Trade & Industry).	Seven regional SDA offices opened, and the inward investment function passed to a joint SDA-Scottish Office bureau, Locate in Scotland (LiS).	

Table 1: Continued.

Date	Political	Institutional	Tourism
1987	Tories elected for a third term.	STB (seen by some as the driving force behind the initiative), ETB and WTB agreed to a common classification and grading scheme which graded hotels into six categories using a criteria of one to five crowns, or a listed category for the most basic of establishments.	Scottish Tourism Co-ordinating Group (STCG) set up.
1988		Scottish Enterprise: a New Approach to Training and Enterprise Creation (1988) published.	
1989		The three Tourist Boards improved the Classification and Grading scheme further by awarding symbols from Approved, through Commended, and Highly Commended to Deluxe.	
1990	Mrs Thatcher resigns. John Major comes to power. Enterprise and New Towns (Scotland) Act outlines plans for Scottish Enterprise Network.		
1991		Scottish Enterprise (SE), Highlands and Islands Enterprise (HIE), Local Enterprise Companies (LECs) set up. HIDB, SDA and Training Agency disbanded.	
1992	Conservatives retain power.	BTA becomes the responsibility of the Department of Natural Heritage. Investors in People introduced. Also SVQs. Tourism Training Scotland (TTS) set up.	Scottish Tourism Coordinating Group publishes "Tourism and the Scottish Environment." British Hospitality Association (BHA) formed, replacing the BHRCA. STCG strengthened to ensure a more cohesive approach to the direction of policy.
1993	Scottish Secretary of State, Ian Lang, orders review of STB.	SE/HIE assume responsibility for tourism development funds from STB. STB becomes responsible for the Highlands and Islands Tourism network.	Tourism Training Scotland (TTS) established.
1994	Local Government (Scotland) Act empowers the Secretary of State to set up new independent ATBs.	Review of Scotland's place in the Union ('taking stock') transfers training from the Employment Department to the Scottish Office thus reinforcing the distinctiveness of Scottish policy.	Strategic Plan for Scottish Tourism published. Scottish Tourism Forum (STF) established.
1996		Single-tier authorities re-established. Area Tourist Board (ATB) network reduced from 32 to 14. Tourism Training Associates (TTAs) established.	Scottish Enterprise Network (SEn) Tourism Action Plan, and HIE Tourism Action Framework launched. Welcome Host launched.
1997	Labour takes power from the Conservatives. Brian Wilson becomes responsible for Scottish tourism. Devolution, a manifesto promise, begins to gain momentum. Positive outcome on referendum for Scottish devolution.	BTA becomes the responsibility of the Department of Culture, Media and Sport (DCMS).	Scotland's Best launched. Scottish Tourism Strategic Plan, Progress Report published. Project Ossian planned.

Table 1: Continued.

Date	Political	Institutional	Tourism
1998	Lord Macdonald becomes responsible for Scottish tourism	STB Classification & Grading Scheme changed in order that no organisation can become a member of their ATB unless Classified and Graded. New Deal launched.	STB Policy and Financial Management Review, Prior Options Study (PFMR, POS). Green Tourism Business Scheme launched.
1999	Labour/Liberal Democrat coalition comes to power in the new Scottish parliament.	Henry McLeish launches a review of SEn/HIE. Scotland launches its own quality-based Classification and Grading Scheme. The first time since 1975 that the British NTOs utilised different schemes. Tourism Training Associates initiative ends.	Scottish Tourism Strategic Plan Interim Review launched. Scottish Affairs Committee Report. Enterprise and Lifelong Learning Industry Minister, Henry McLeish launches a new consultation document — A New Strategy for Scottish Tourism. Draft — A New Strategy for Scottish Tourism launched.
2000	New Enterprise and Lifelong Learning Minister and new Tourism Minister, Wendy Alexander, appointed, due to Donald Dewar's death, and the fact that Henry McLeish becomes First Minister.	Launch of the Framework for Economic Development Scotland (FEDS). ELL Committee Review of Local Economic Development Delivery Mechanisms. McLeish reviews the Scottish Enterprise Network. A review of STB undertaken by Lord Gordon/Price Waterhouse Coopers, Mary Galbraith (Scottish Tourist Board Management Review, Report and Recommendations). Outcome of review is 10 recommendations. STB CEO resigns. Peter McKinlay, former Scottish Prisons and Scottish Homes CEO takes over temporarily from Tom Buncle. Chairman, Lord Gordon signals intention to step down in March 2001. All senior STB directors have to apply for own positions. Peter Lederer becomes STB Vice- Chairman.	A New Strategy for Scottish Tourism. Skills Group set up, chaired by Peter Lederer. STCG disbanded. Strategy Implementation Group set up to replace STCG. ATBs to become members of the Local Economic Forums.
2001	Foot and mouth blights the industry. Terrorist assaults on America lead to calls for an all out war against the perpetrators, which meant a 'fortress' America environment, and thousands of cancellations of trips across the Atlantic in Autumn 2001 and a collapse in forward reservations for 2002. Henry McLeish resigns and is succeeded by Jack McConnell. Tourism becomes a cabinet level post in the Ministry of Tourism, Culture and Sport. The Minister is Mike Watson.	A Smart, Successful, Scotland, Ambitions for the Enterprise Network launched. Peter Lederer becomes Chair of VisitScotland, formerly STB. Michael Cantlay, Chairman of Scottish Enterprise Forth Valley, becomes his deputy. Rod Lynch appointed STB/VisitScotland CEO, then offer withdrawn a few days later when it was discovered that he held another post. Six senior STB Directors step down. Three new Directors recruited. Philip Riddle, an ex-Shell Senior Executive becomes the new VisitScotland CEO.	Wendy Alexander launches a new consultation 'Time to look again at the new strategy for tourism in Scotland 2001'. Scotland's bid for the 2010 Ryder Cup fails. It had been put back one year from 2009 due to the cancellation of the 2001 tournament as a result of the terrorist bombs in the USA which had a dramatic impact on air travel, stopping the USA team from flying. As a consolation prize it was awarded to Gleneagles for 2014. The airline industry lays off tens of thousands of staff and cancels masses of schedules. Wendy Alexander announces an ATB review.

Table 1: Continued.

Date	Political	Institutional	Tourism
2002	Wendy Alexander resigns as Minister for Enterprise, Transport and Lifelong Learning, and is succeeded by Iain Gray.	Enterprise and Lifelong Learning Committee (2002) launches an inquiry into Tourism	Mike Watson launches Tourism Framework for Action 2002:2005.
		Enterprise and Lifelong Learning Committee (2002) report Support for Tourism: An International Comparison Researched and prepared by Stevens & Associates with The Scottish Tourism Research Group Commissioned by The Scottish Parliament Research and Information Group, Edinburgh.	Mike Watson announces the replacement of the Strategy Implementation Group (which replaced the STCG), with a Steering Group to oversee the Framework for Action. Mike Watson announces a review of the ATB network.
		At Scotland United (November) the industry's annual conference the Minister threatens compulsory registration.	Plans made to change the role of the BTA. Scotland fails to secure the 2008 European Cup of Football
2003	May elections return Labour/Lib Dem coalitions. Frank McAveety becomes Tourism Minister but as a Deputy status and salary.	Building Better Cities launched — the Cities Review. Scotland's first urban framework. Funding comprised of a £90 million growth fund and a further £20 million to reclaim derelict land to be invested by the Scottish Executive in Scotland's six city regions	Outcome of ATB consultation delayed due to Scottish elections

Table 2: Scottish tourism organisations and what they do or did.

Who does what	In Scottish tourism
Scottish Executive	Responsible for administering non-reserved (devolved) aspects of U.K. Government policy in Scotland including tourism. However, and despite proposed changes, the British Tourism Authority (BTA) is still responsible to the Westminster Government for substantial U.K. overseas marketing.
VisitScotland	Established subsequent to the Development of Tourism Act (1969), VisitScotland is the lead agency in Scotland for promoting tourism; overseas marketing functions are shared with the BTA. STB's development powers were transferred to the Enterprise Networks in 1993. From April 1st 2001, STB was re-named visitscotland, and in July 2001 VisitScotland. It also operates the Classification and Grading scheme.
Scottish Enterprise (SE)	Formed from a merger of the Training Agency and Scottish Development Agency in 1991, originally established in 1975, SE is charged with supporting economic development in Scotland outside of Highlands and Islands Enterprise (HIE), with whom it co-operates on a number of issues. Both SE and HIE are responsible for co-ordinating the activities of the Local Enterprise Companies (LECs), collectively known as SEn. In 2000, they underwent a radical review, and LECs became SE subsidiaries.

Table 2: Continued.

Who does what	In Scottish tourism
Highlands and Islands Enterprise (HIE)	Formed in 1991 from a merger of the Training Agency and with the predecessor organisation Highlands and Islands Development Board (HIDB) originally established in 1965. HIE supports economic development initiatives, including tourism, in the Highlands and Islands region of Scotland. The aforementioned review, apart from its LECs becoming subsidiaries, left HIE virtually untouched.
Area Tourist Boards (ATBs)	Regional organisations with strong trade membership, responsible for local marketing and visitor services. The ATB Network is part of STB/VisitScotland. Along with the LECs and the LAs and other bodies they participate in the new Local Economic Forums (LEFs). A fundamental problem, however, is funding. The 1969 Tourism Act neglected to fund them by statute, leaving this instead to the discretion of local authorities and membership fees.
Local Enterprise Companies (LECs)	Established at the same time as SE and HIE, these were, until April 2001, when they became subsidiaries of SE and HIE, private companies limited by guarantee. Frequently compared with the Training and Enterprise Councils (TECs) in England and Wales, which have been superseded by Regional Development Agencies (RDAs), LECs, however, have more emphasis on economic development and are contracted by SE and HIE to deliver local economic initiatives and support, government training programmes and so on.
Scottish Enterprise Network (SEn)	Name for Scottish Enterprise and the Local Enterprise Companies it co-ordinates (see Scottish Enterprise) as a network.
Local Authorities (LAs)	Single tier authorities since 1996 that support the ATBs through funding and other assistance in their areas in promoting tourism. Also have a significant accountability in that they are also responsible for many of the services that impact on tourism.
Scottish Tourism Co-ordinating Group (STCG)	Disbanded following McLeish's 2000/2001 tourism strategy, STCG was established in 1987 and strengthened in 1993. Chaired by the Scottish Executive's Tourism Minister (the Enterprise and Lifelong Learning Minister), STCG met two to three times a year and had representation from twelve organisations involved in tourism in Scotland. Its role was to devise, monitor and revise a national strategic plan for tourism for Scotland. A new body described below has superseded it.

Table 2: Continued.

Who does what	In Scottish tourism
Tourism Training Scotland (TTS)	Also now disbanded, TTS was launched in 1992. Its remit was to encourage improvements in service delivery in tourism organisations. In 1996 Tourism Training Associates (TTAs) were established in each LEC area, but within two years the funding for the TTAs evaporated and those that were left took one more general responsibilities. A new body described below has also superseded it.
Scottish Tourism Forum (STF)	Established in 1994, by mid-2000, STF had almost thirty member organisations representing all sectors of the industry, and by 2001 claimed 6000 members. It represents the private sector view on strategic issues to national policy makers and its Chair sat on the STCG, and also sits on the body that supersedes it, and along with its CEO is set to meet the Tourism Minister formally regularly.
Strategy Implementation Group, subsequently a Steering Group	It was intended that this group, comprising industry, STB, SE, HIE and the Chair of the new training group monitor the implementation of the new strategy (2000), and replace the STCG. It failed to communicate satisfactorily with the industry, and in 2002 was superseded by a Steering Group.
Skills Development Group (Tourism People)	Superseding TTS, this group brings together the industry and the organisations that have key supporting roles to play in this area — the Enterprise Networks, the NTOs and Springboard Scotland. Until tourism became the responsibility of Tourism, Culture and Sport, It reported directly to the Minister for Enterprise and Lifelong Learning.
New Scottish Tourism Research Liaison Group	Established to co-ordinate tourism research in Scotland. As with the Strategy Group there has been little communication of this group's progress.
Local Economic Forums (LEFs)	A recommendation by the document FEDS that all organisations interested in economic development work together for the common good — the first occasion that Area Tourist Boards have had a seat at the top table.
Careers Scotland	The distillation of over 80 careers guidance organisations to 22 organisations coterminous with the LECs. Incongruously part of SE at national level, but with separate Advisory Boards at local level, and charged with improving dramatically careers advice including tourism and hospitality.

Table 2: Continued.

Who does what	In Scottish tourism
Taste of Scotland	A scheme that endeavours to exemplify everything good about Scottish food and hospitality.
Food Grading Company	Launched in autumn 2001 it implemented VisitScotland's new Food Quality Assurance Scheme.

Table 3: Government initiatives and programmes relating to tourism.

Initiative	Objective
Scottish Vocational Qualifications (SVQs)	Devised to ensure ability was recognised in the workplace by assessing competence against prescribed indicators.
Investors in People (IIP)	In the late eighties government recognised that there was a skills gap between the U.K. and the remainder of the world, and in the early nineties launched IIP as a framework to enable organisations to meet their objectives through developing the skills of their workforce in line with company's objectives.
SkillSeekers	Grants were made available by government via LECs to enable 16–18 year olds to work towards a Level II SVQ.
Modern Apprenticeships	Launched in 1997, grants were made available through the LECs to enable 16–25 year olds to gain recognised apprenticeships combined with a level III SVQ. Different levels of grant were applied for the two age groups; 16–18 and 18–25, with the latter, in the majority of LECs receiving 50% of the funding available to 16–18 year olds. It is now being extended to over 25s.
New Deal	Introduced in 1998 to get people, particularly the young, back to work. Companies were encouraged to sign up to New Deal and for every new employee who had been on the dole for over six months, companies were paid £60 per week for a period of six months, plus £750 towards their training costs, which were usually tied in to a Level II SVQ. For over 25 year olds, the funding was £75 per week.
Welcome Host	Imported by STB from Alberta in Canada via the Wales Tourist Board (WTB), in 1996, a short one-day course designed to improve customer care in the tourism industry.

Table 3: Continued.

Initiative	Objective
Growing Businesses or IFSOs (Innovative and Far-Sighted Organisations)	A new model, based on an SE goal, to develop companies in line with 14 IFSO characteristics and 65 indicators.
Taste of Scotland	A scheme that endeavours to exemplify everything good about Scottish food and hospitality.
Burns Familiarisation Course	Launched in Ayrshire in 1996 to enable local business's staff to converse much more knowledgeably with the vast influx of visitors expected for the Bi-centenary of Robert Burns' death.
Conference Care	Launched in 1997 to enable Glasgow to deal efficiently with Rotary International.
Welcome Golfer	Launched in Carnoustie in 1999 to enable the local tourism operators to deal with the vast influx of visitors
Green Tourism Business Scheme	Launched in 1998 to encourage Scottish tourism businesses to go 'green', also to make cost efficiencies in energy, water etc.
USEIT	Launched by SEn in 1999 to encourage more tourism business staff to develop their IT skills.
Excellence through People	Launched by BHA in 1998 to encourage good employment practice.
Hospitality Assured	An HCIMA quality programme.
European Foundation Quality Management Model (Business Excellence Model)	The equivalent of the Baldridge model in the USA, the EFQM has been in existence in Europe since the mid-eighties. It is championed in Scotland by the Quality Scotland Foundation (SQF), which was founded in the early nineties, and is currently being launched in various areas as the Business Excellence Model. A number of tourism businesses are using it as a tool to benchmark against other industries and to improve performance.
Springboard	Springboard Scotland was founded in 1998, and is based on the model launched in London in the early nineties. Ostensibly, Springboard is designed to attract school leavers into the industry by promoting it as a first choice career. To this end it works in schools and in industry trying to raise the image and improve the perception of tourism as a worthwhile career.
Benchmarking	SEn launched a pilot in 1999 administered by Scher International. Forty Scottish Hotels were involved in an effort to expand to cover a large number of operators, enabling them to measure their performance against each other.

Table 3: Continued.

Initiative	Objective
International Professional Development Programme	Developed by the University of Strathclyde Hotel School, this programme develops strategic planning, innovation and creative leadership skills for hospitality managers.
Focus on Feedback	Deals with service recovery, handling complaints and other customer feedback in a positive manner.
European Computer Driving License	The ultimate opportunity for tourism and hospitality staff to obtain ICT qualifications that are valid Europe-wide.
Natural Cook	Launched by SEn/STB in 1997 in order to promote Scottish produce in Hotel and Restaurant kitchens.
Scotland's Best	A superior Welcome Host, that endeavoured to instil a sense of pride.
Individual Learning Accounts (ILAs)	Participants could access £175 towards upgrading their skills for a £25 investment. Now discontinued.
Welcome Sailor	Recognising that sailing is a growing market, this short course has been designed to inform businesses and their employees of sailor's needs of businesses.
Future Skills Scotland	Part of the SE infrastructure that looks at a more informed and active labour market policy, and a shared understanding between the education system and the wider economy of the needs of young people, and the skills, attitudes and expectations they will require to develop.
The Food Grading Company	A VisitScotland initiative established in 2002, and operated by Taste of Scotland along similar lines to the AA's Rosette system awarded on a one to five basis for an organisation's quality of food, awarding medallions instead of rosettes.

Table 4: The various initiatives that came about after the election.

Date	Initiative	Responsibility	Objective	Eventual outcome
3 Aug 1999	A New Strategy for Scottish Tourism (Consultation Document)	Scottish Executive Enterprise and Lifelong Learning Department, STB/SEn/HIE	To identify the opportunities and constraints that faced the industry, and also what needed to be done, how it was going to be done and who was going to do it	A New Strategy for Scottish Tourism (2000)
6 Sep 1999	Making it Work Together — A Programme for Government	Scottish Executive	To realise the overall vision of the first Scottish Executive	All of the initiatives that followed
15 Sept 1999	Consultation on the Framework for Economic Development in Scotland (FEDS)	Scottish Executive Enterprise and Lifelong Learning Department	To lead a team to develop Scotland's knowledge economy	Framework for Economic Development in Scotland (FEDS) (2000)

Table 4: Continued.

Date	Initiative	Responsibility	Objective	Eventual outcome
7 Oct 1999	Inquiry into the Delivery of Local Economic Development Services in Scotland	Scottish Parliament Enterprise and Lifelong Learning Committee	A focus on the work of the Scottish Enterprise network (SEn) and Highlands and Islands Enterprise (HIE)	The pursuance of a national strategy that would encompass the whole economic future of Scotland as a nation that could compete globally
15 Dec 1999	Inquiry into the Delivery of Local Economic Development Services in Scotland: Interim Conclusions 1	Scottish Parliament Enterprise and Lifelong Learning Committee	Consensus on the way ahead for Local Economic Development Services	Means by which congestion within the field of local economic development and confusion, overlap, duplication and even active competition between the many agencies involved could be dealt with
10 Feb 2000	Enterprise Networks Review — Issues Paper	Scottish Executive Enterprise and Lifelong Learning Department	To examine the responsiveness, effectiveness and appropriateness of SEn/HIE for the challenges the Scottish Economy will face in the 21st Century	Enterprise Network review which brought about massive change to SEn, while leaving HIE virtually untouched
16 Feb 2000	A New Strategy for Scottish Tourism	Scottish Executive Enterprise and Lifelong Learning Department, STB/SEn/HIE	To develop a modern tourist industry which is in touch with its customers; a skilled and enterprising industry which has embraced the culture of lifelong learning; and an industry which provides the quality of service visitors demand	Exclusive of structural changes, and as with the previous review — Financial Management Review, Prior Options Study (1998) (see Chapter Five) it appeared reluctant to tackle the very real and underlying Scottish tourism problems
12 May 2000	Inquiry into the Delivery of Local Economic Development Services in Scotland: Final Report Volumes 1 & 2	Scottish Parliament Enterprise and Lifelong Learning Committee	To address duplication and inconsistency of services, and suggest means by which individuals could be signposted to the most appropriate means of support	The mess that was economic delivery in Scotland was to a certain extent sorted out.
29 Jun 2000	The Way Forward: Framework for Economic Development in Scotland (FEDS)	Scottish Executive Enterprise and Lifelong Learning Department	To raise the quality of life of the Scottish people through increasing economic opportunities for all on a socially and environmentally sustainable basis	It provided an integrated and coherent framework within which the promotion of economic development could be taken forward
6 Jul 2000	Interim Conclusions of the Enterprise Network Review	Scottish Executive Enterprise and Lifelong Learning Department	The Scottish economy needed to react to a world that was changing at a faster pace than ever before. These changes meant a comprehensive review of SEn/HIE	FEDS had provided the foundation for economic development policies. A detailed review of the role of SEn/HIE flowed directly from it
Oct 2000	Scottish Tourist Board Management Review, Report and Recommendations	Scottish Executive Enterprise and Lifelong Learning Department	A wide-ranging review of STB, its structure, management functions, personnel and relationships with partners	It recognised that STB was not meeting the needs or aspirations of the industry and recommended ten areas that the Executive might wish to implement, bringing with it widespread change to STB, including a complete management and name change

Table 4: Continued.

Date	Initiative	Responsibility	Objective	Eventual outcome
6 Nov 2000	FEDS — Analysis and Background	Scottish Executive Enterprise and Lifelong Learning Department	To supplement the Framework by setting out some of the technical questions and arguments that lay behind economic thinking on growth and development; and illustrating, where possible, some of the statistical trends which were important in thinking about where Scotland was in terms of economic development and what the challenges were that it faced	It provided information on some of the economic and statistical background to FEDS. It enabled a few broad conclusions to be made about the performance of the Scottish economy, and it highlighted some of the information needs to improve the understanding of the economy
6 Nov 2000	Modernising the Enterprise Networks: The Interim Conclusions of the Enterprise Networks Review	Scottish Executive Enterprise and Lifelong Learning Department	To modernise and position the SE/HIE Networks to play the leading role in local economic development, as part of a wider partnership of interests	A range of actions required to take forward modernisation of SE/HIE in Scotland. This was to be done through a strategy for Enterprise — Smart, Successful Scotland
6 Dec 2000	Scottish Executive Response to the Final Report of the Enterprise and Lifelong Learning Committee Inquiry into the Delivery of Local Economic Development Services in Scotland	Scottish Executive Enterprise and Lifelong Learning Department	To build upon the work done by the Committee and to adopt and adapt where necessary recommendations made by the Committee	It informed the work of the LEFs, and of Smart, Successful Scotland (2001)
6 Dec 2000	Consultation on draft guidelines for Local Economic Forums	Scottish Executive Enterprise and Lifelong Learning Department	The main emphasis was on reducing or removing replicate functions locally	LEFs were in place by April 2001, their first task in 2001/2002 sorting out overlap and duplication of business services, their second in 2002/2003 to develop an economic strategy for their area
30 Jan 2001	A Smart, Successful Scotland: Ambitions for the Enterprise Networks	Scottish Executive Enterprise and Lifelong Learning Department	SEn/HIE to respond better to their customers in order to better leverage and enhance the prosperity of Scotland	A vision of a smart, successful Scotland which identified three priorities — growing businesses, learning and skills and global connections
7 Mar 2001	Local Economic Forums: National Guidelines	Scottish Executive Enterprise and Lifelong Learning Department	The setting up and servicing of the Forums based on LEC boundaries	To collectively tackle overlap and duplication of business services
9 July 2002	Inquiry into Lifelong Learning	Scottish Parliament Enterprise and Lifelong Learning Committee	To inquire into the need for a long-term, comprehensive strategy for continuing post-compulsory education and training in Scotland	Lifelong Learning Report published October 2002
1 Sep 2001	6th Report 2001, Report on the Inquiry into the Impact of the New Economy — Scottish Executive Response	Scottish Executive Enterprise and Lifelong Learning Department	To build upon the work done by the Committee and to adopt and adapt where necessary recommendations made by the Committee	It helped to inform future strategies
4 Oct 2001	A Smart, Successful Scotland Launch	Scottish Executive Enterprise and Lifelong Learning Department	The first comprehensive policy statement of what the Scottish Executive expects from SEn/HIE	A clear sense of direction and identifiable priorities for SEn/HIE

Table 4: Continued.

Date	Initiative	Responsibility	Objective	Eventual outcome
4 Oct 2001	Scotland: A global connections strategy	Scottish Executive Enterprise and Lifelong Learning Department	It had been long recognised that there was a need to alter the way Scotland was connected globally and that inward investment, as it had been known, e.g. the creation of large numbers of lowly paid jobs, had changed dramatically	Harnessing of the experience, skills and energy of the Scottish business community overseas for the advancement of the Scottish economy
Nov 2001	ATB Network Consultation	Scottish Executive Enterprise and Lifelong Learning Department	Improving the role of ATBs in transforming the industry both nationally and at a local level	It ground to a halt when tourism became part of the culture and sport ministry
11 Mar 2002	Tourism Framework For Action 2002:2005	Scottish Executive Tourism, Culture and Sport	A working blueprint designed to reinvigorate the tourism industry, to out-class competitors and make Scotland a 'must-visit' destination	A review of the original strategy (2002) setting out new objectives and challenges for the industry which identified further actions that needed to be taken
18 Mar 2002	Measuring Scotland's progress towards a Smart, Successful Scotland	Scottish Executive Enterprise and Lifelong Learning Department	How the Scottish Executive intended to measure Scotland's progress towards a smart, successful Scotland, and what it was doing to achieve its ambitions	Overall measures of progress and the more detailed operating targets
March 2002	Support for Tourism: An International Comparison	Scottish Parliament Enterprise and Lifelong Learning Committee	To inform the Committee's Inquiry on Scotland's tourism industry. By comparing the tourist industry in Scotland with other countries' territories, and to make recommendations based on the findings.	Although the research carried out by Stevens Associates and the Scottish Hotel School's Research Unit revealed that no one country's tourism approach is exemplary, it also revealed that Scotland paled in comparison to those destinations with which it was compared
March/April 2002	Interim Report and Lifelong Learning Convention	Scottish Parliament Enterprise and Lifelong Learning Committee	To report on outcomes of the consultation, and of the convention that was held	The beginnings of a document that would identify the lifelong learning needs and aspirations of individuals and society as a whole
May 2002	ATB Network Review	Scottish Executive Tourism, Culture and Sport	Scottish tourism was competing in an increasingly global market. The minister wanted to ensure that the ATBs were fully equipped to respond to market changes and that they were able to work effectively with partners at the local, national and international level.	For the second time in a year the industry was consulted on the future of the ATBs, the first consultation superseded by the second one because of Tourism being moved to the Culture and Sports Ministry
July 2002	Inquiry into the Scottish Tourism Industry	Research and Information Group of the Scottish Parliament /Scottish Parliament Enterprise and Lifelong Learning Committee	The Committee wanted to examine the effectiveness of the Scottish Executive's tourism strategy taking evidence from industry representatives at all levels on the way forward.	The Stevens Report (2002) and a review of the ATBs (2002)

Table 4: Continued.

Date	Initiative	Responsibility	Objective	Eventual outcome
Oct 2002	Report on Lifelong Learning	Scottish Parliament Enterprise and Lifelong Learning Committee	To inform the Minister's thinking on the need for a long-term, comprehensive strategy for continuing post-compulsory education and training in Scotland which meets the needs and aspirations of individuals and society as a whole in respect of quality, relevance, efficiency, effectiveness, accessibility, accountability, funding levels and structures and delivery mechanisms	It was discovered that lifelong learning did not operate as a single system in Scotland and that vocational training, higher and further education and community and voluntary education were treated as separate sectors. This meant that there needed to be more cohesion between the sectors to create a more responsive lifelong learning system
Jan 2003	Building Better Cities	Scottish Executive	Scotland's first urban framework. It was designed to redress the non-domestic rates issues the cities had with the Scottish Executive and to regenerate the cities with funding of up to £110 million; £20 million of which was old money.	Strategies were submitted in Spring 2003, and monies awarded accordingly
Feb 2003	Enterprise and Lifelong Learning Committee: Final Report on Lifelong Learning Response from the Executive laid before the Scottish Parliament by Scottish Ministers on 12 February 2003 SE No SE/2003/64	Scottish Executive	Response from the Executive laid before the Scottish Parliament by Scottish Ministers on 12 February 2003 SE No SE/2003/64	The Committee suggested that there is a lack of coherence between the various sectors of lifelong learning — Higher Education, Further Education, vocational education and training, community and voluntary provision — and calls for more cohesion and "a more responsive system, characterised by ease of movement and equality of treatment
Mar 2003	Scottish Tourism a progress report for 2003/04	Scottish Executive Tourism Team	First progress report on the Tourism Framework for Action	The report sets out what has been achieved since it was published, describes the issues facing tourism in Scotland today and sets out what the Executive believe needs to be done in the years ahead to get Scottish tourism growing again
Mar 2003	Measuring Scotland's Progress Towards a Smart, Successful Scotland	Scottish Executive	A further progress report	This weighty report revealed how Scotland was progressing for McLeish and Alexander's vision for a Smart, Successful Scotland. While the latest data continue to show that Scotland's comparative economic performance is mixed there is little evidence, from the indicators studied, to suggest any relative deterioration since the first report. Indeed, given that there has been some improvement in comparative productivity performance it would appear that some progress is being made in securing a smart, successful Scotland.

Table 5: Conclusions of the Enterprise and Lifelong Learning Committee Review of local economic development services in Scotland and what this meant to the Scottish tourism industry.

Situation and structures	Responsibility	No.	Conclusion
Current Situation		Final Conclusion 1	There is congestion within the field of local economic development in Scotland. There is confusion, overlap, duplication and even active competition between the many agencies involved
		Final Conclusion 2	There has been significant progress in co-operation and partnership working between local economic development providers over the past three years. Examples of good practice exist at the local level, which have been examined and can be recommended as models to influence developments elsewhere in Scotland
		Final Conclusion 3	However, intensified partnership working alone is unlikely to deliver a level of rationalisation of services, cost-effectiveness, and consumer focus that is desirable. Local economic development services should be re-structured to achieve this
New Local Economic Development Structure		Final Conclusion 4	A new structure should be introduced for local economic development in Scotland. The structure should have a number of components
	Scottish Executive	Final Conclusion 5	The Executive should take the lead in guaranteeing that a simpler, more cohesive structure exists in Scotland for the delivery of local economic development services. The Executive should initiate a process of eliminating duplication in service provision at local level and be prepared to penalise publicly-funded bodies who do not co-operate in this process
		Final Conclusion 6	The Executive should withdraw from operational programmes and concentrate on strategic guidance, setting targets and measurable outcomes, ensuring value for money in service provision, promoting good practice, reporting and evaluation

Table 5: Continued.

Situation and structures	Responsibility	No.	Conclusion
		Final Conclusion 7	A key tool in assisting the Executive in this process should be a fully developed Economic Framework for Scotland. The framework should specify outcomes that reflect the need for Scotland to be globally competitive. It should also set out the Executive's aims for the Scottish economy and what contribution is expected toward these aims from local organisations operating in the field of economic development
	Scottish Enterprise and Highlands and Islands Enterprise	Final Conclusion 8	Scottish Enterprise and Highlands and Islands Enterprise should concentrate on managing the Enterprise Network and setting strategic targets, as well as introducing core standards and operational targets for LEC activities
	Local Economic Forums	Final Conclusion 9	An economic forum should be introduced for each LEC area, comprising the following minimum membership: the local authorities; the LEC; the chamber of commerce (if any); the area tourist board(s); and representatives of the local higher and further education institutions
		Final Conclusion 10	Each economic forum should create an economic strategy for its area that is capable of achieving the contribution expected of the area to the Economic Framework for Scotland, including the achievement of the measurable outcomes established for it by the Executive. The strategy must include the definition of lead agencies and the unambiguous delineation of their areas of responsibility. It must also identify the process of eradicating duplication in the provision of services. The strategy should comprise the economic element of the Community Plan for the area. As a minimum, the strategy should set out clearly the forum's goals for the next three years in the areas of: new business starts; support for existing small businesses; key local industries; skills training etc. The strategy should also set out clearly the division of labour proposed by the forum, which should

Table 5: Continued.

Situation and structures	Responsibility	No.	Conclusion
			aim to ensure value for money and transparency. The Committee does not wish to stifle local discretion by setting a prescriptive national model. The Committee does wish to stress that a process of eradicating duplication in service provision is a crucial first step in improving the effectiveness of services provided to the consumer, and that the Executive must be prepared to penalise publicly-funded organisations that do not participate effectively in this process
		Final Conclusion 11	The progress of economic forums in achieving the measurable outcomes set for them by the Scottish Executive and in eliminating duplication in service provision should be assessed by a joint study by the Auditor-General for Scotland and the Accounts Commission via Audit Scotland in 2002
A Common Small Business Support Service		Final Conclusion 12	A new business support service should be introduced in Scotland that merges the services of existing providers and markets them clearly to consumers through a nationally branded service. The Executive should initiate the process of introduction of this service, which at local level should be delivered within the strategy agreed by the economic forum. The service must be inclusive, merging the business support services currently run by LECs, local authorities, enterprise trusts and other publicly-funded organisations. As part of this process, enterprise trusts should be merged into the LECs.
Local Enterprise Companies		Final Conclusion 13	Local Enterprise Companies (LECs) should significantly change their character. They should: change their status from private companies to public bodies; open up their boards to other non-business members; increase the level of transparency in their activities; and consider the introduction of membership systems. The moves already made by Scottish Enterprise in this direction are welcomed

Table 5: Continued.

Situation and structures	Responsibility	No.	Conclusion
		Final Conclusion 14	An enterprise ombudsman should be appointed to provide an independent channel for the investigation of complaints directed at the enterprise network
Tourism		Final Conclusion 15	The development of tourism should be firmly integrated into mainstream local economic development
		Final Conclusion 16	Area tourist boards should be integrated into mainstream local economic development by becoming mandatory members of local economic forums
		Final Conclusion 17	Each forum's strategy should include a tourism element, which must set out the strategy and delivery mechanisms at local level. This must be linked to the national tourism strategy and identify each area's contribution to achieving the national strategy. The strategy should also indicate the resources dedicated by each partner, particularly by Local Authorities and LECs, to tourism development. The Committee will monitor the effectiveness of this method of operation and if it does not guarantee effective delivery of tourism support services or investment in the development of the tourism sector, the Committee will consider proposing further structural changes
An Economic Framework for Scotland		Final Conclusion 18	Since the publication of the Interim Report, the Executive has announced the construction of an Economic Framework for Scotland, which is currently underway. The evidence that the Inquiry has received very much supports the need for such a framework, and its creation is very much welcomed
		Final Conclusion 19	The Framework should incorporate: a vision of the future for the Scottish economy; coverage of both conventional economic development and lifelong learning; an anchorage for the significant number of initiatives that have been announced by the Executive; a framework for organisations operating in the field of economic development

Table 5: Continued.

Situation and structures	Responsibility	No.	Conclusion
Business Support Services		Final Conclusion 20	The account manager system of working with companies should be applied across Scotland and integrated between providers. It should be promoted as a long-term relationship, and the Executive should make it mandatory for public agencies to share information, subject to issues of commercial confidentiality, to promote account management
		Final Conclusion 21	There is scope for providing a greater level of general advisory support to start-up companies, and to more of them. Support provided to start-up companies should also be longer term, and based more on enhancing the company's own development capacity (e.g. exporting, e-commerce and product development)
		Final Conclusion 22	It is reasonable to expect public resources to be targeted on particular sectors or types of business, especially those with growth potential. Nevertheless the criteria and basis for the allocation of resources should be made more transparent by the organisations concerned
		Final Conclusion 23	There is a need for the development of a new model of support, and new breed of business adviser/mentor to accommodate the different needs of new technology companies, such as those in the e-commerce or bio-technology fields.
		Final Conclusion 24	There is an urgent need for better professional training of business advisers, and the development of a formal accreditation system. This system should be tiered according to the level of advice to be offered
		Final Conclusion 25	The Executive should take a lead in bringing together the professional associations and education bodies to develop a common system of accreditation
Lifelong Learning		Final Conclusion 26	The field of lifelong learning is as congested as economic development generally. More co-ordination and less competition is required as well as more leadership. The Committee is minded to

Table 5: Continued.

Situation and structures	Responsibility	No.	Conclusion
			undertake further investigation of this point at a later stage in the term of the Parliament
		Final Conclusion 27	In general LEC-managed training programmes are currently constrained by frameworks that are too rigid, 'volume driven' and focused on easily measurable outputs. An example of these problems is provided by the implementation of the SkillSeekers programme at local level, where Scottish Vocational Qualifications are the only option offered
		Final Conclusion 28	There is scope for more flexibility in locally delivered training, including that managed by the LECs, based on local labour market circumstances and information
		Final Conclusion 29	There has been considerable progress in developing the portability of qualifications, but there is scope for further progress
	Workplace Learning	Final Conclusion 30	Initial pilot work that has been undertaken by enlightened employers in developing workplace learning has demonstrated the benefits of this activity to both employees and employers
		Final Conclusion 31	The Executive should take the lead in promoting the further dissemination of workplace learning which could help in the implementation of its lifelong learning strategy. Each local economic forum should address this issue
		Final Conclusion 32	The Executive should develop a strategy for ensuring that the benefits of workplace learning can be extended to employees and employers of smaller businesses
Information	Performance Measurement	Final Conclusion 33	The Executive should set a framework for the measurement of local economic development activity, to be consistently applied across different agencies, and across Scotland. The framework should be based on the work currently being undertaken by the professional associations and the enterprise network, and should be benchmarked globally

Table 5: Continued.

Situation and structures	Responsibility	No.	Conclusion
		Final Conclusion 34	The Executive should ensure independent monitoring of all agencies' performance, as measured against the outcomes that have been specified. This should be linked to the Community Planning process. It should also make provision for the independent periodic review of the effectiveness and efficiency of economic development in Scotland
	Economic Data	Final Conclusion 35	The work being undertaken by the Executive to improve economic data at the national level is welcomed
		Final Conclusion 36	The Executive should extend this work to ensure that a consistent framework of relevant economic data is available at the local level. This is particularly important, and achievable, in the area of local labour market information
		Final Conclusion 37	The Executive should ensure that economic information held by public bodies is shared, except where commercial confidentiality would dictate otherwise

Source: The Enterprise and Lifelong Learning Committee Review of Local Economic Development Services in Scotland (2000).

Table 6: Ministerial membership of Scottish Office 1970–99.

Date of appointment	Secretary of State	Ministers of State	Parliamentary under Secretary of State
19.6.70	Gordon Campbell	Baroness Tweedsmuir	Alick Buchanan-Smith (64) Edward Taylor (64) George Younger
28.7.71.	Gordon Campbell	Baroness Tweedsmuir	Alick Buchanan-Smith (64) Hector Monro (64) George Younger (64)
24.3.72	Gordon Campbell	Lord Polwarth	Alick Buchanan-Smith (64) Hector Monro (64) George Younger (64)
8.1.74	Gordon Campbell	Lord Polwarth	Alick Buchanan-Smith (64) Hector Monro (64) Edward Taylor (64)
4.3.74	William Ross (46*)	Bruce Milan (59) Lord Hughes	Robert Hughes (70)
27.6.74	William Ross (46*)	Bruce Milan (59) Lord Hughes	Robert Hughes (70) Hugh Brown (64)
18.10.74	William Ross (46*)	Bruce Milan (59) Lord Hughes	Robert Hughes (70) Hugh Brown (64) Harry Ewing (71*)
22.7.75	William Ross (46*)	Bruce Milan (59) Lord Hughes	Frank McElhone (69*) Hugh Brown (64) Harry Ewing (71*)
8.8.75	William Ross (46*)	Bruce Milan (59) Lord Kirkhill	Frank McElhone (69*) Hugh Brown (64) Harry Ewing (71*)
5.4.76	Bruce Milan (59)	Gregor Mackenzie (64) Lord Kirkhill	Frank McElhone (69*) Hugh Brown (64) Harry Ewing (71*)
15.12.78	Bruce Milan (59)	Gregor Mackenzie (64)	Frank McElhone (69*) Hugh Brown (64) Harry Ewing (71*)
4.5.79	George Younger (64)	Earl of Mansfield	Alexander Fletcher (73*) Russell Fairgrieve (74) Malcolm Rifkind (74)
14.9.81	George Younger (64)	Earl of Mansfield	Alexander Fletcher (73*) Malcolm Rifkind (74) Allan Stewart (79)
6.4.82	George Younger (64)	Earl of Mansfield	Alexander Fletcher (73*) Allan Stewart (79) John Mackay (79)
9.6.83	George Younger (64)	Lord Gray	John McKay (79) Michael Ancram (74*) Allan Stewart (79)
9.1.86	Malcolm Rifkind (74)	Lord Gray	John McKay (79) Michael Ancram (74*) Allan Stewart (79)
10.9.86	Malcolm Rifkind (74)	Lord Glenarthur	John McKay (79) Michael Ancram (74*) Ian Lang (79)
11.6.87	Malcolm Rifkind (74)	Lord Sanderson Ian Lang (79)	L-J Douglas Hamilton (74) Michael Forsyth (83)
28.11.90	Ian Lang (79)	Michael Forsyth	L-J Douglas Hamilton (74) Lord Strathclyde Allan Stewart (79)
9.4.92	Ian Lang (79)	Lord Fraser	L J Douglas-Hamilton (74) Allan Stewart (79) Hector Monro (64)
7.2.95	Ian Lang (79)	Lord Fraser	L J Douglas-Hamilton (74) George Kynoch (92) Hector Monro (64)
5.7.95	Michael Forsyth (83)	L J Douglas-Hamilton (74)	Earl of Lindsay George Kynoch (92) Ray Robertson (92)
2.5.97	Donald Dewar (66*)	Brian Wilson (87) Henry McLeish (87)	Lord Sewel Sam Galbraith (87) Malcolm Chisholm (92)
1998–1999	Donald Dewar (66*)	Henry McLeish (87) Helen Liddell (94)*	Lord Sewel Sam Galbraith (87) Lord Macdonald * Calum MacDonald (87)

Table 6: Continued.

Source: Smith, S. (1997).

NB: The date in brackets after each Minister's name is the year that they entered parliament. An * after this date indicates either that a By-election was won to enter parliament, or that the Minister has been out of the House of Commons for a time. Figures in brackets are years elected.

* William Ross was elected MP for Kilmarnock at a By-election on 5.12.46.

* Harry Ewing was elected MP for Stirling and Falkirk at a By-election on 16.9.71.

* Frank McElhone was elected MP for Glasgow Gorbals at a By-election on 30.10.69.

* Alexander Fletcher was elected MP for Edinburgh N at a By-election on 8.11.73.

* Donald Dewar was MP for Aberdeen S 1966–70 and was elected MP for Glasgow Garscadden at a By-election on 13.4.78.

* Michael Ancram was MP for Berwickshire and East Lothian Fed–Oct 1974 and for Edinburgh South 1979–87.

* Helen Liddell became an MP in 1994 inheriting the Airdrie and Shotts seat in a By-election following the death of the Labour leader John Smith.

* Gus Macdonald was Chair of the Scottish Media Group (SMG) prior to being elevated to the House of Lords as Lord Macdonald of Tradeston.

Table 7: Scottish Devolution Referendum 1997 — Referendum results, how Scotland voted.

Parliament has decided to consult people in Scotland on the Government's proposals for a Scottish Parliament:		Parliament has decided to consult people in Scotland on the Government's proposals for a Scottish Parliament to have tax-varying powers:	
I AGREE THAT THERE SHOULD BE A SCOTTISH PARLIAMENT		I AGREE THAT A SCOTTISH PARLIAMENT SHOULD HAVE TAX-VARYING POWERS	
1,775,045	74.3%	1,512,889	63.5%
I DO NOT AGREE THAT THERE SHOULD BE A SCOTTISH PARLIAMENT		I DO NOT AGREE THAT A SCOTTISH PARLIAMENT SHOULD HAVE TAX-VARYING POWERS	
614,400	25.7%	870,263	36.5%

In 1997 in the United Kingdom, the Labour Party honoured its manifesto commitments to offer the people of Scotland and Wales the chance to vote on devolution.

A referendum was held in Scotland on Thursday 11th September 1997 to decide whether there should be a Scottish Parliament and whether it should have tax-varying powers.

Duff, L., Forsyth, F., and Kidner, C. (1998) www.engender.org.uk/scotparl/elections/referendum97/

Table 8: Scottish Referendum Results and turnout by District.

District	Turnout (%)	Parliament for	%	Parliament against	%	Tax for	%	Tax against	%
City of Aberdeen	53.0	65,035	71.8	25,580	28.2	54,320	60.3	35,709	39.7
Aberdeenshire	57.0	61,621	63.9	34,878	36.1	50,295	52.3	45,929	47.7
Angus	60.2	33,571	64.7	18,350	35.3	27,641	53.4	24,089	46.6
Argyle and Bute	65.0	30,452	67.3	14,796	32.7	25,746	57.0	19,429	43.0
East Ayrshire	64.8	49,131	81.1	11,426	18.9	42,559	70.5	17,824	29.5
North Ayrshire	63.4	51,304	76.3	15,931	23.7	43,990	65.7	22,991	34.3
South Ayrshire	66.7	40,161	66.9	19,909	33.1	33,679	56.2	26,217	43.8
Borders	64.8	33,855	62.8	20,060	37.2	27,284	50.7	26,497	49.3
Clackmannan	66.1	18,790	80.0	4,706	20.0	16,112	68.7	7,355	31.3
Dumfries and Galloway	63.4	44,619	60.7	28,863	39.3	35,737	48.8	37,499	51.2
East Dunbartonshire	62.7	40,917	69.8	17,725	30.2	34,576	59.1	23,914	40.9
West Dunbartonshire	63.7	39,051	84.7	7,058	15.3	34,408	74.7	11,628	25.3
City of Dundee	55.7	49,252	76.0	15,553	24.0	42,304	65.5	22,280	34.5
City of Edinburgh	60.1	155,900	71.9	60,832	28.1	133,843	62.0	82,188	38.0
Falkirk	63.7	55,642	80.0	13,953	20.0	48,064	69.2	21,403	30.8
Fife	60.7	125,668	76.1	39,517	23.9	108,021	64.7	58,987	35.3
City of Glasgow	51.6	204,269	83.6	40,106	16.4	182,589	75.0	60,842	25.0
Highland	60.3	72,551	72.6	27,431	27.4	61,359	62.1	37,525	37.9
Inverclyde	60.4	31,680	78.0	8,945	22.0	27,194	67.2	13,277	32.8
North Lanarkshire	60.8	123,063	82.6	26,010	17.4	107,288	72.2	41,372	27.8
South Lanarkshire	63.1	114,908	77.8	32,762	22.2	99,587	67.6	47,708	32.4
East Lothian	65.0	33,525	74.2	11,665	25.8	28,152	62.7	16,765	37.3
West Lothian	62.6	56,923	79.6	14,614	20.4	47,990	67.3	23,354	32.7
Midlothian	65.1	31,681	79.9	7,979	20.1	26,776	67.7	12,762	32.3
Moray	57.8	24,822	67.2	12,122	32.8	19,326	52.7	17,344	47.3
Orkney	53.4	4,749	57.3	3,541	42.7	3,917	47.4	4,344	52.6
Perthshire and Kinross	63.1	40,344	61.7	24,998	38.3	33,398	51.3	31,709	48.7
East Renfrewshire	68.2	28,253	61.7	17,573	38.3	23,580	51.6	22,153	48.4
Renfrewshire	62.8	68,711	79.0	18,213	21.0	55,075	63.6	31,537	36.4
Shetland Islands	51.5	5,430	62.4	3,275	37.6	4,478	51.6	4,198	48.4
Stirling	65.8	29,190	68.5	13,440	31.5	25,044	58.9	17,487	41.1
Western Isles	55.8	9,977	79.4	2,589	20.6	8,557	68.4	3,947	31.6

Duff, L., Forsyth, F., and Kidner, C. (1998) www.engender.org.uk/scotparl/elections/referendum97/

Table 9: Abbreviations/Acronyms.

AA	AUTOMOBILE ASSOCIATION
ADRLT	ASSOCIATION OF DIRECTORS OF RECREATION, LEISURE AND TOURISM
ASBBO	ASSOCIATION OF SCOTTISH BED AND BREAKFAST OPERATORS
ASEAN	ASSOCIATION OF SOUTH EAST ASIAN NATIONS
ASSC	ASSOCIATION OF SCOTLAND'S SELF CATERERS
ASVA	ASSOCIATION OF SCOTTISH VISITOR ATTRACTIONS
ATB	AREA TOURIST BOARD
ATC	AUSTRALIAN TOURISM COMMISSION
ATCO	ASSOCIATION OF TRANSPORT COORDINATING OFFICERS
ATF	ASEAN TOURISM FORUM
AU	AFRICAN UNION
BA	BRITISH AIRWAYS
BHA	BRITISH HOSPITALITY ASSOCIATION
BHHPA	BRITISH HOLIDAY AND HOME PARKS ASSOCIATIONS
BHRA	BRITISH HOTELS AND RESTAURANTS ASSOCIATION
BITOA	BRITISH INWARD TOURISM OPERATORS ASSOCIATION
BMA	BRITISH MEDICAL ASSOCIATION
BTA	BRITISH TOURIST AUTHORITY
BUAC	BRITISH UNIVERSITIES ACCOMMODATION CONSORTIUM
CBI	CONFEDERATION OF BRITISH INDUSTRY
CIS	COMMONWEALTH OF INDEPENDENT STATES
CPTS	CONFEDERATION OF PASSENGER TRANSPORT, SCOTLAND
CSF	COMMUNITY SUPPORT FRAMEWORK
DCMS	DEPARTMENT OF CULTURE MEDIA AND SPORT
EAGGF	EUROPEAN AGRICULTURE GUIDANCE AND GUARANTEE FUND
EC	EUROPEAN COMMISSION
EC	EUROPEAN COUNCIL
EEC	EUROPEAN ECONOMIC COMMUNITY
EETB	EAST OF ENGLAND TOURIST BOARD
EIB	EUROPEAN INVESTMENT BANK
ELLC	ENTERPRISE AND LIFELONG LEARNING COMMITTEE
ELLD	ENTERPRISE AND LIFELONG LEARNING DEPARTMENT
ERDF	EUROPEAN REGIONAL DEVELOPMENT FUND
ETB	ENGLISH TOURIST BOARD
ETC	ENGLISH TOURISM COUNCIL
ETC	ESTONIAN TOURIST BOARD
ETC	EUROPEAN TRAVEL COMMISSION
EU	EUROPEAN UNION
FBU	FIRE BRIGADE UNION
FC	FORESTRY COMMISSION

Table 9: Continued.

FE	FOREST ENTERPRISE
FEDS	FRAMEWORK FOR ECONOMIC DEVELOPMENT SCOTLAND
FSB	FEDERATION OF SMALL BUSINESS
FPTP	FIRST PAST THE POST
GDA	GLASGOW DEVELOPMENT AGENCY
GGCVTB	GREATER GLASGOW AND CLYDE VALLEY TOURIST BOARD
GLA	GREATER LONDON ASSEMBLY
GMS	GREATER MEKONG SUB-REGION
HIAL	HIGHLANDS AND ISLANDS AIRPORTS LIMITED
HIDB	HIGHLANDS AND ISLAND DEVELOPMENT BOARD
HIE	HIGHLANDS AND ISLANDS ENTERPRISE
HS	HISTORIC SCOTLAND
IFSO	INNOVATIVE AND FAR-SIGHTED ORGANISATION
ITA	INTERNATIONAL TRADE ADMINISTRATION
ITA	IRISH TOURIST ASSOCIATION
ITIC	IRISH TOURISM INDUSTRY CONFEDERATION
ITTT	INTERIM TOURISM TASK TEAM
JMC	JOINT MINISTERIAL COMMITTEE
LDA	LANARKSHIRE DEVELOPMENT AGENCY
LDO	LOCAL DELIVERY ORGANISATION
LEC	LOCAL ENTERPRISE COMPANY
LEEL	LOTHIAN AND EDINBURGH ENTERPRISE LTD
LEF	LOCAL ECONOMIC FORUM
LiS	LOCATE IN SCOTLAND
MAs	MODERN APPRENTICESHIPS
MEP	MEMBER OF THE EUROPEAN PARLIAMENT
MP	MEMBER OF PARLIAMENT
MPC	MONETARY POLICY COMMITTEE
MSP	MEMBER OF THE SCOTTISH PARLIAMENT
NAC	NORTH AYRSHIRE COUNCIL
NAW	NATIONAL ASSEMBLY FOR WALES
NCC	NATIONAL CARAVAN COUNCIL
NFU	NATIONAL FARMERS UNION
NITB	NORTHERN IRELAND TOURIST BOARD
NTO	NATIONAL TOURISM ORGANISATION
NTP	NATIONAL TOURISM POLICY
NWTB	NORTH WEST TOURIST BOARD
OAU	ORGANISATION OF AFRICAN UNITY
OECD	ORGANISATION FOR ECONOMIC COOPERATION AND DEVELOPMENT
OEEC	ORGANISATION FOR EUROPEAN ECONOMIC COOPERATION
OTTI	OFFICE OF TRAVEL AND TOURISM INDUSTRIES
PMFR	POLICY AND MANAGEMENT FINANCE REVIEW

Table 9: Continued.

RDB	REGIONAL DEVELOPMENT AGENCY
RHA	ROAD HAULAGE ASSOCIATION
RLM	REGIONAL LIST MEMBER
RTA	REGIONAL TOURISM AUTHORITY
RTB	REGIONAL TOURIST BOARD
RTC	REGIONAL TOURISM COMPANY
RTC	REGIONAL TOURISM COUNCIL
RTO	REGIONAL TOURISM ORGANISATION
RTP	REGIONAL TOURISM PARTNERSHIP
PHILOXENIA	PROPOSAL FOR A COUNCIL DECISION ON A FIRST MULTIANNUAL PROGRAMME TO ASSIST EUROPEAN TOURISM
PWC	PRICE WATERHOUSE COOPER
SA	SCOTTISH AIRPORTS
SAC	SCOTTISH ARTS COUNCIL
SBG	SMALL BUSINESS GATEWAY
SCA	SCOTTISH CONFERENCE ASSOCIATION
SCC	SCOTTISH CHAMBERS OF COMMERCE
SCC	SCOTTISH CONSTITUTIONAL CONVENTION
SCDI	SCOTTISH COUNCIL DEVELOPMENT INDUSTRY
SCOT	SCOTTISH CONFEDERATION OF TOURISM
SCOTRAIL	SCOTTISH RAIL AUTHORITY
SCT	SUPREME COMMISSION FOR TOURISM
SDA	SCOTTISH DEVELOPMENT AGENCY
SDI	SCOTTISH DEVELOPMENT INTERNATIONAL
SDMA	SCOTTISH DESTINATION MANAGEMENT ASSOCIATION
SE	SCOTTISH ENTERPRISE
SE	SCOTTISH EXECUTIVE
SEED	SCOTTISH EXECUTIVE EDUCATION DEPARTMENT
SEEL	SCOTTISH ENTERPRISE EDINBURGH AND THE LOTHIANS
SEG	SCOTTISH ENTERPRISE GLASGOW
SEL	SCOTTISH ENTERPRISE LANARKSHIRE
SEn	SCOTTISH ENTERPRISE NETWORK
SFSB	SCOTTISH FEDERATION OF SMALL BUSINESSES
SHH	SCOTTISH HIGHLAND HOTELS
SHIC	SCOTTISH HOSPITALITY INDUSTRY CONGRESS
SHRA	SCOTTISH HOME RULE ASSOCIATION
SLTA	SCOTTISH LICENSED TRADE ASSOCIATION
SMC	SCOTTISH MUSEUMS COUNCIL
SNH	SCOTTISH NATIONAL HERITAGE
SNP	SCOTTISH NATIONAL PARTY
SRC	STRATHCLYDE REGIONAL COUNCIL
STB	SCOTTISH TOURIST BOARD

Table 9: Continued.

STCG	SCOTTISH TOURISM COORDINATING GROUP
STDA	SCOTTISH TOURIST DEVELOPMENT ASSOCIATION
STF	SCOTTISH TOURISM FORUM
STI	SCOTTISH TRADE INTERNATIONAL
SYHA	SCOTTISH YOUTH HOSTEL ASSOCIATION
TA	TRAINING AGENCY
TAC	TOURISM ADVISORY COMMITTEE
TDG	TOURISM DEVELOPMENT GROUP
TIC	TOURIST INFORMATION CENTRE
TPC	TOURISM POLICY COUNCIL
TPCG	TOURISM POLICY COORDINATING GROUP
TSA	TOURISM SATELLITE ACCOUNTS
TTA	TOURISM TRAINING ASSOCIATE
TTS	TOURISM TRAINING SCOTLAND
UKTS	UNITED KINGDOM TOURISM SURVEY
UN	UNITED NATIONS
USNTO	US NATIONAL TOURISM ORGANISATION
USTS	UNITED STATES TRAVEL SERVICE
USTTA	UNITED STATES TRAVEL AND TOURISM ASSOCIATION
WDA	WELSH DEVELOPMENT AGENCY
WITB	WESTERN ISLES TOURIST BOARD
WTB	WALES TOURIST BOARD
WTO	WORLD TOURISM ORGANISATION
WTO	WORLD TRADE ORGANISATION
WTTC	WORLD TRAVEL AND TOURISM COUNCIL

Author Index

Note: this index contains only personal name. Corporate organisations and institutions are included in the subject index.

Subject Index